D1554461

THEORY OF THE SUBJECT

Also available from Continuum:

Being and Event, Alain Badiou
Conditions, Alain Badiou
Infinite Thought, Alain Badiou
Logics of Worlds, Alain Badiou
Theory of the Subject, Alain Badiou
Seeing the Invisible, Michel Serres
After Finitude, Quentin Meillassoux
Dissensus, Jacques Rancière
The Politics of Aesthetics, Jacques Rancière
The Five Senses, Michel Serres
Art and Fear, Paul Virilio
Negative Horizon, Paul Virilio
Desert Screen, Paul Virilio

THEORY OF THE SUBJECT

Alain Badiou

Translated, and with an introduction, by Bruno
Bosteels

continuum

Continuum International Publishing Group
The Tower Building
11 York Road
London
SE1 7NX
www.continuumbooks.com

80 Maiden Lane
Suite 704
New York
NY 10038

Originally published in French as *Théorie du sujet* © Editions du Seuil, 1982

This translation © Continuum 2009

British Library Cataloguing-in-Publication Data
A catalogue record for this book is available from the British Library.

ISBN: HB: 978-0-8264-9673-7

Published with the assistance of the French Ministry of Culture – National Book Center.

Liberté • Égalité • Fraternité
RÉPUBLIQUE FRANÇAISE

This book is supported by the French Ministry of Foreign Affairs as part of the Burgess programme run by the Cultural Department of the French Embassy in London. (www.frenchbooknews.com)

Library of Congress Cataloguing-in-Publication Data
A catalog record for this book is available from the Library of Congress.

Typeset by Servis Filmsetting Ltd, Stockport, Cheshire
Printed and bound by MPG Books Group, UK

Contents

Translator's Introduction   vii
Preface   xxxviii
References and Abbreviations   xliii

Part I. The Place of the Subjective   1
Everything that belongs to a whole constitutes an obstacle to
    this whole insofar as it is included in it   3
Action, manor of the subject   13
The real is the impasse of formalization; formalization is the
    place of the forced pass of the real   22
Hegel: 'The activity of force is essentially activity reacting against
    itself'   29
Subjective and objective   37

Part II. The Subject under the Signifiers of the Exception   51
Of force as disappearance, whose effect is the Whole from which
    it has disappeared   53
Deduction of the splitting   65
'A la nue accablante tu'   74
Any subject is a forced exception, which comes in second place   84
Jewellery for the sacred of any subtraction of existence   98

Part III. Lack and Destruction   111
The new *one* forbids the *new* one, and presupposes it   113
On the side of the true   116

CONTENTS

There are no such things as class relations 125
Every subject crosses a lack of being and a destruction 132
The subject's antecedence to itself 140
Torsion 148
Theory of the subject according to Sophocles, theory of the
    subject according to Aeschylus 158
Of the strands of the knot, to know only the colour 169

Part IV. A Materialist Reversal of Materialism 177
The black sheep of materialism 179
The indissoluble salt of truth 190
Answering—to the Sphinx—demands from the subject not to
    have to answer—for the Sphinx 201
Algebra and topology 208
Neighbourhoods 215
Consistency, second name of the real after the cause 224
So little ontology 234

Part V. Subjectivization and Subjective Process 241
The topological opposite of the knot is not the cut-dispersion
    but the destruction-recomposition 243
Subjectivizing anticipation, retroaction of the subjective process 248
'Hurry! Hurry! Word of the Living!' 254
The inexistent 259
Logic of the excess 265

Part VI. Topics of Ethics 275
Where? 277
The subjective twist: ψ and α 285
Diagonals of the imaginary 297
Schema 304
Ethics as the dissipation of the paradoxes of partisanship 309
Classical detour 317
Love what you will never believe twice 324

Translator's Endnotes and References 333
Thematic Repertoire 359
Index of Proper Names 365

Translator's Introduction

1

Théorie du sujet, which hereby at last becomes available in English translation, is Alain Badiou's most passionate and experimental book. In terms of sheer personal engagement, it is perhaps comparable only to his early novels, *Almagestes* (1964) and *Portulans* (1967), or to his writings for the theatre such as the opera-novel *L'Écharpe rouge*, which dates from the same period (1979), or *Ahmed le subtil*, a hilarious farce composed in 1984 during a brief period of isolation and calm shortly after the present book was first published in French. In my eyes, *Théorie du sujet* is also Badiou's most daring, hermetic, and bewildering work of philosophy, and the time that has passed since its original appearance only seems to have added to the effect of bewilderment. Some introductory remarks may therefore be in order so as to situate the book in its wider context.

Presented in the form of a seminar between January 1975 and June 1979, which is to say during the closure of the so-called 'red years' (1966–76) and in a time that would witness the deplorable rise to fame of the 'new philosophers' (1976) as well as the false hopes surrounding the creation of the 'common programme' (signed in 1972) uniting Communists, Socialists, and radical Leftists in France; written in the midst of what can only be called an active campaign of ostracism against its author because of his undying Maoism, with some going so far as to call him a 'Maoist pit-bull'; and published in 1982 in the aftermath of the widely celebrated electoral victory in 1981 of François Mitterrand to the Presidency, the book makes no concessions to the dominant wisdom and post-political euphoria of its time. To the contrary, solitude only seems to have had an emboldening effect. In this sense, we could apply Badiou's own words, taken from *Saint Paul: The Foundation of Universalism*, to the author of the present book: 'Everything indicates that he refused any compromise when it came to fidelity to principles.' Or again: 'His discourse is one of pure fidelity to the possibility opened by the event.'[1] The pivotal event in this case being not so much the outburst of May '68, whose remarkable intensity and short-lived experience—the two usually going hand in hand within the tradition of ultra-leftism—the book otherwise also seeks to diagnose, so much as the patient action needed to work out the consequences of this uprising, during the first half of the 1970s, in the guise of French Maoism.

The upshot of this principled, not to say stubborn, approach is a work whose legendary difficulty until recently turned away many more readers than it attracted lasting admirers, even from among Badiou's most ardent followers. As Peter Hallward admits: '*Théorie du sujet* is by any criteria the most difficult to approach of Badiou's works.'[2] Rumour has it that for a long time, in student circles around the University of Paris-VIII at Vincennes, where Badiou taught for thirty years before occupying the post of his former teacher Louis Althusser as head of the Philosophy Department at the École Normale Supérieure in rue d'Ulm, to point a finger at someone and whisper that he or she was in the process of reading *Théorie du sujet* was tantamount to declaring this person either insane or fanatical, if not both at once. This rumour goes a long way toward explaining the belated arrival of the book's translation in any language and, even more so, the relative scarcity of sustained critical engagements with its central theses.[3]

Today, however, there can be no doubt that *Theory of the Subject* stands as an indispensable building block in the overarching system of Badiou's philosophy, on a par with his two other 'big' books, *Being and Event* and its recent follow-up, *Logics of Worlds*. To illustrate this centrality perhaps I may be allowed to invoke my personal experience as someone who, after reading Badiou's *Manifesto for Philosophy* out of a shared interest in a notion of the 'generic' that would be compatible with Platonism, for political reasons turned to the Maoist pamphlets from the mid-1970s, *Theory of Contradiction* and *Of Ideology*, and then decided to tackle *Theory of the Subject*: I distinctly remember having sat down almost non-stop—this was before the birth of my two sons—for an incredibly long weekend, frantically making my way through the entire book as though it were a novel of intrigue, frequently bursting out in laughter—it is also an extremely funny book—and, in general, sensing as though the whole field of contemporary theory and philosophy opened up freshly before my eyes along the sharpest lines of demarcation to have been traced in the sand since Althusser's *For Marx*. All of this happened long before I mustered the courage and dared to take on *Being and Event*, intimidated as I was—never mind that for Badiou this is a cultural prejudice that is as vacuous as it is stubborn—by the formalization of its extensive mathematical apparatus. Reading *Theory of the Subject* before *Being and Event*, though, is not merely a matter of personal preference or anecdotal happenstance. After years of actively following the worldwide reception of Badiou's thought, in fact, I have come to the conclusion that this order of reading, which somewhat conventionally corresponds to the chronological order of the books' publication and thus to their author's trajectory as a philosopher and militant, even though it runs counter to the more common practice among English-speaking readers who tend to start with one or other of the books published and translated after *Being and Event*, makes all the difference in the world in terms of the image of thought that can be attributed to Badiou's philosophy as a whole. Above all, there where a privileged focus on *Being and Event* frequently leads to the conclusion that this thinker's trajectory involves a clean and irreversible break away from the tradition of the dialectic, *Theory of the Subject* allows the reader both to nuance, if not exactly refute, this conclusion as far as the idea of the break itself is concerned and to uncover subtle dialectical threads even in the overall metaontological argumentation which, grounded in a solid command of set theory, is supposed to come after this break.

2

For sure, in hindsight it is not difficult to enumerate the possible limitations and shortcomings of *Theory of the Subject*. In *Being and Event*, first of all, Badiou himself indicates that the earlier book remains limited insofar as it presupposes from the start that there is such a thing as subjectivity, without giving this presupposition much ontological support in mathematics. Perhaps this self-criticism is unnecessarily harsh since *Theory of the Subject*, even though this is often forgotten, already introduces the whole question of Cantorian set theory, all the way to the point of locating the emergence or 'pass' of the subject in the immeasurable excess of inclusion over belonging, or of parts over elements—an excess which will constitute the central 'impasse' in the conceptual arrangement of *Being and Event*. Even so, it is true that only the later work will systematically elaborate the underpinnings of this thesis from a metaontological, that is to say metamathematical, point of view. As Badiou writes in the Preface: 'The (philosophical) statement that mathematics *is* ontology—the science of being *qua* being—is the stroke of light that illuminates the speculative scene which I had restricted, in my *Theory of the Subject*, by presupposing purely and simply that 'there was some' subjectivization.'[4] The new task in *Being and Event* then consists in articulating, by way of the impasse of being, a coherent ontology together with an interventionist theory of the subject—a task which dialectical materialism in the old days would have accomplished by means of an homology between the dialectics of nature and the dialectics of spirit, and which today requires a careful reformulation of both poles of nature and spirit, or of substance and subject—this time, in *Being and Event*, above all in an oblique polemic with Heidegger and not only or not primarily with Lacan, as is the case in *Theory of the Subject*.

Philosophy itself, secondly, still appears to be sutured onto the sole condition of politics. The other three truth procedures of art (poetry and tragedy), science (mathematics), and love (psychoanalysis)—as well as the eternal shadow condition of religion (Christianity)—certainly are all already present, but not only are they implicit and mixed, they also do not seem to operate quite yet as conditions of philosophy in the strict sense, since the subject of truth is defined exclusively in terms of politics: 'Every subject is political. Which is why there are few subjects and rarely any politics.'[5] Later, in *Conditions*, a collection of essays which builds on the new foundations of *Being and Event*, Badiou would correct this statement from *Theory of the Subject*: 'Today, I would no longer say "every subject is political", which is still a maxim of suturing. I would rather say: "Every subject is induced by a generic procedure, and thus depends on an event. Which is why the subject is rare."'[6] Similarly, in *Manifesto for Philosophy*, Badiou states the principle that the four domains of truth, once they are unsutured and separated out, are all equally capable of bringing into existence a subject: 'Every subject is artistic, scientific, political, or amorous. Besides, this is something everyone knows from experience, for out of these registers, there is only existence, or individuality, but no subject.'[7] What will remain unchanged, in any case, is the conviction that subject and truth necessarily co-implicate one another so that a theory of the subject, at the farthest remove from any purely experiential or moral account, is always the theory of the formal conditions for the emergence of a universalizable truth.

Thirdly, within the condition of politics, the book still considers the party the only effective organizational structure, albeit with an eye toward a 'party of a new type', that is, a form of post-Leninism whose task is here openly ascribed to Maoism.[8] Going one step further than merely acknowledging the uncertainties of this task given the undeniable crisis of Marxism, Badiou has since then abandoned this strict identification of the political subject with the party, which in all its incarnations over the past century—whether as a single party or as part of the parliamentary-electoral multi-party system—has remained overly bound to the form of the State: 'The balance sheet of the nineteenth century is the withering away of the category of class as the sole bearer of politics, and the balance sheet of the twentieth century is the withering away of the party-form, which knows only the form of the party-State.'[9] Philosophically, more-over, this search for a new figure of militantism without a party is pre-cisely what will bring Badiou back to an old acquaintance, in *Saint Paul*, as though almost thirty years had to pass before he could finally come to terms with his personal road to Damascus that was May '68 or, rather, its Maoist aftermath: 'For me, Paul is a poet-thinker of the event, as well as one who practises and states the invariant traits of what can be called the militant figure.'[10] Even the self-criticism implied in this move from party-politics to a form of militantism without a party, however, should not let us forget that another crucial point that has remained intact is the idea that any emancipatory politics must take an organized form: 'Must we argue that organization alone can make an event into an origin? Yes, insofar as a political subject requires the historical underpinning of an apparatus and insofar as there is no origin except for a determinate politics.'[11] Eventually, this emphasis on the need for any truth, whether political or otherwise, to become incorporated in some organized form or apparatus will lead to a new theory of the body—a new physics to buttress the metaphysics of the subject—in *Logics of Worlds*.

Another point of self-criticism, finally, concerns the violent language of destruction with which Badiou in *Theory of the Subject* seeks to counter what he calls the structural dialectic of lack in Mallarmé or Lacan. Toward the end of *Being and Event*, the author admits: 'I went a bit astray, I must say, in *Theory of the Subject* concerning the theme of destruction. I still maintained, back then, the idea of an essential link between destruction and novelty.'[12] The idea was that every new truth would necessarily involve a destruction of the old order. From a strict ontological view, however, the part of loss in novelty must be rephrased in terms not of destruction but of subtraction and disqualification. A new truth cannot suppress any existence, but by extending a given situation from the point of its supplementation that is an event, an engaged enquiry into the truthfulness or veridicality of this event can disqualify, or subtract, certain terms or multiples—namely, those inegalitarian ones that are incompatible with the generic and universal nature of all truth. Destruction, then, would be only a reactive name for the fate of that part of knowledge that no longer will have qualified as truthful or veridical in the extended situation in which an event has taken place.

However, this last self-criticism too may have to be tempered in the extent that the distinction between the two paths of destruction and subtraction remains a key topic of the author's ongoing enquiries. Much of Badiou's *Ethics*, for instance, deals with the specific restraints that must apply to any truth procedure in order to avoid the 'disaster' of forcing an entire situation in the name of truth, to the point of completely destroying the old order of things, while the opposite operation of subtraction, which proceeds by way of a principle of 'minimal difference', is the topic of several of Badiou's lectures in *The Century*.[13] What is more, whereas *Being and Event* seems to point to the notion of destruction as the principal misgiving in Badiou's own earlier thought, which is still very much sutured onto politics under the influence of Maoism, in *Logics of Worlds* a new balance is struck between destruction and subtraction. A truth, then, involves *both* a disqualification or subtraction (of being) *and* a destruction or loss (of appearing): 'The opening of a space of creation requires destruction.'[14] In fact, this is just one of many regards in which the second volume of *Being and Event* is once more closer to *Theory of the Subject*. The point is certainly not to move in a self-righteous and linear fashion from the ravaging blindness of destruction, associated with the dialectical work, to the cool insights of subtraction, afforded by the turn to mathematics.

Indeed, though this remains somewhat of a bone of contention among critics and commentators, Badiou's subsequent trajectory suggests that there are certainly as many intriguing lines of continuity and resurrection between the earlier and the later writings as there have been points of acute self-criticism and discontinuity. This becomes nowhere more evident than in the Preface to *Logics of Worlds* where Badiou gladly adopts the name 'materialist dialectic' to describe his lifelong endeavour, in sharp contrast to *Being and Event* where the orthodox tradition of 'dialectical materialism', as I mentioned above, is considered beyond salvage as the 'stillborn' attempt to render homologous the dialectic of nature and that of spirit. After nearly two decades of expressly anti-dialectical fervour, particularly in texts such as *Metapolitics* and *The Century*, Badiou's work in recent years thus seems, if not exactly to have come full circle, then at least to be spiralling back to some of its original premises, since already one of his earliest philosophical texts, a review of Althusser's canonical *For Marx* and *Reading Capital*, received the programmatic title 'The (Re) commencement of Dialectical Materialism'. But then to provide Marxism with a materialist and dialectical philosophy compatible with its strictly political definition is precisely the ambitious overall programme behind *Theory of the Subject*, a programme which Badiou now argues—against the canonical teachings of Althusser and with the unexpected help of Lacan—cannot be accomplished without the very concept of the subject that materialism previously had the purpose of debunking as sheer idealist humbug.

3

Lenin once famously described Marx's teaching as 'the legitimate successor to the best that humanity produced in the nineteenth century, as represented by German philosophy, English political economy and French socialism'.[15] In a similar vein, we could sum up the 'three sources' or 'component parts' of *Theory of the Subject* by saying that Badiou's teaching in this work draws its strength from a unique articulation of French poetry and psychoanalysis (Mallarmé and Lacan), German philosophy (Hegel and, to a lesser degree, Hölderlin), and Greek tragedy (Aeschylus and Sophocles). If the ultimate goal of this triangulation is a redefinition of Marxism, understood as a periodized mode of doing politics rather than as an established body of doctrines to be saved from crisis and kept pure against all odds, then we should add that the medium of this operation—or the general ideological atmosphere in which it is able to redraw the lines of demarcation between dialectical materialism and rivalling philosophies— is an original investigation into the contemporary role of Maoism, well beyond its specific site in China: 'That which we name 'Maoism' is less a final result than a task, a historical guideline. It is a question of thinking and practising post-Leninism.'[16]

In Part One, Badiou first of all redefines the Hegelian dialectic in terms of a logic of scission, instead of the typical textbook notions of alienation, negation, the negation of negation, and so on. To be more precise, he distinguishes two matrices of the dialectic in Hegel: an idealist one, defined by the externalization and return to self, and a properly materialist one, in which every term is split without unity either at the origin or in the end. Badiou examines this distinction in a remarkable reading of Hegel's *Science of Logic*, especially those parts on determination and limit which, as is often the case with early moments in Hegel's presentation, are not yet contaminated by the idealist pressures of the Absolute. Badiou's reliance on Hegel's *Logic*, moreover, provides a refreshing and much-needed contrast to the heavy influence of the *Phenomenology of Spirit* in the tradition of French Hegelianism from Alexandre Kojève to Georges Bataille, aside from obviously running counter to the general anti-Hegelianism of the Althusserian school.[17] A bold reading of Christianity in light of this dialectic of scission, furthermore, allows Badiou not only to circumscribe the twin 'heresies' or 'deviations' of 'left-wing' Gnosticism (for which, if we may simplify matters of doctrine to an extreme, Christ is purely divine or infinite) and 'right-wing' Arianism (for which Christ is purely human or finite), but also to specify the point where Hegel's dialectic remains after all idealist in terms of the historical periodization that it allows or, rather, disallows, insofar as it moves in circles and ultimately leads back to the split term that was always already present from the origin (God as Father/Son or infinity/finitude). 'Hegel, on this point, must be divided once again' so as to break out of the 'circle of circles' of the Absolute, Badiou concludes: 'To be brief, we will oppose (materialist) *periodization* to (idealist) *circularity*.'[18] The reading of Hegel thus lays the groundwork for a theory of what we might call 'historicity without History', which throughout the remainder of the book will continue to inform the periodization of Marxism.

Part Two, after a discussion of ancient atomism as a limited or failed attempt by way of pure chance or the clinamen to inject some measure of dialecticity into the stark contradiction of void and atoms, offers Badiou's longest and most detailed engagement with the writings of Mallarmé, considered to be one of the two great modern French dialecticians, together with Lacan. Like the atomism of Democritus or Lucretius, Mallarmé's dialectic is unpacked into a limited number of formal operations, three to be exact: vanishing, annulment, and foreclosure. Of these operations, the efficacy of a vanishing cause is without a doubt the most important, insofar as it also implies an unspoken critique of the whole Althusserian concept of structural causality, that is, of a cause that vanishes into the totality of its effects.[19] Badiou highlights the extraordinary power of this concept while at the same time revealing its weakness, namely, the place where the notion of a causality of lack, even or especially when it is raised to the level of a formal concept thanks to the anxiety-inducing operation of annulment whereby lack itself comes to lack, turns into a forbidding obstacle or stopping point, prohibiting the actual transformation of the totality put in place by the effects of the vanishing cause itself. Mallarmé's writing, though eminently dialectical, in this sense would remain idealist, presenting what Badiou calls a structural—though not structuralist—dialectic. 'All this forms a precious legacy,' Badiou concludes, even though there is a need to dialecticize the structural dialectic beyond itself: 'No, I find no fault with all this, except that I am not swayed by an order of things in which all thought is devoted to the inspection of that which subordinates it to the placement of an absence, and which brings salvation for the subject only in the already-thereness of a star.'[20]

In Part Three, the exploration of the promises and deadlocks of this structural dialectic is extended and taken into the field of Lacanian psychoanalysis. Of all Badiou's works, in fact, *Theory of the Subject* contains his most thoroughgoing discussion of Lacan's *Écrits* and the few seminars published at the time, especially Seminar XI: *The Four Fundamental Concepts of Psychoanalysis* and Seminar XX: *Encore*, together with scattered texts published in the Lacanian journals *Ornicar?* and *Scilicet*. Long before Slavoj Žižek would popularize such readings in a similarly political key, Badiou thus distinguishes between the earlier Lacan, for whom the dominant term is the symbolic that dissolves the imaginary, and the later Lacan, whose mathematical obsessions revolve around the real that absolutely resists symbolization. Or, rather, there would be two different conceptions of the real itself: the first, which Badiou calls 'algebraic', follows closely in Mallarmé's footsteps by defining the real as a vanishing cause, whereas the other, called 'topological', relies on notions such as the Borromean knot in order to give the real a minimum of consistency. 'There are, broadly speaking, two successive Lacans, the one of the lack of being and the one of the ontology of the hole, of the nodal *topos*, and, consequently, of the being of lack', Badiou writes: 'Beginning in the seventies, which one can mark by the primacy of the knot over the chain, or of consistency over causality, it is the historical aspect that gains the upper hand over the structural one.'[21] Ultimately, the goal of this delimitation of the structural dialectic is to find the formal means—for the most part absent or dissimulated in Hegel and Mallarmé yet obliquely hinted at by Lacan—by which to exceed the boundaries of the causality of lack so as to change the coordinates of the entire order put in place by its efficacy. Otherwise, there still would be no novelty, no event, and no historicity, but only the repetition of the totality of assigned places under the effects of the vanishing cause.

Destruction is the name for this process by which the structural dialectic of lack is exceeded and opened up to the historicity of change. Badiou is thus able to sum up the stakes of his polemic with psychoanalysis: 'Our entire dispute with Lacan lies in the division, which he restricts, of the process of lack from that of destruction.'[22] The real, then, no longer returns always to the same place. Or, put otherwise, that which will have taken place is not just the place itself. Instead, it becomes possible for a certain coefficient of force to interrupt and work back upon the place that determines it, just as history no longer automatically moves in circles but opens up the minimal gap necessary for conceiving of a spiralling and asymmetrical process of periodization. 'Destruction divides the effect of lack into its part of oblivion—of automatism—and its part of possible interruption—of excess over the place, of the overheating of the automatisms,' Badiou concludes: 'By this thin gap, another mastery can be said to come into being, together with an asymmetrical balancing of loss and gain.'[23]

Badiou then takes an enormous step back in time so as to illustrate and expand on the disjunction between lack and destruction through the example of Greek tragedy. In particular, he wonders not just why psychoanalysis, as George Steiner and Judith Butler also ask, has been so exclusively focused on the figure of Oedipus instead of taking into consideration Antigone but also, more generally, why it is Sophocles, and not Aeschylus, who has provided Freud and Lacan with their most illustrious tragic myths: 'The whole purpose of our critical delimitation with regard to the psychoanalytic contribution to the theory of the subject can be evaluated by asking the following question: why is its theory of the subject essentially based on Sophocles, that is, predicated on the Oedipus complex?'[24] Picking up on a brief suggestion from Lacan's very first seminar, Badiou proposes that if the Sophoclean model of tragedy and, by extension, of psychoanalysis can be concentrated in the twin subjective figures of anxiety (Antigone) and the superego (Creon), then the Aeschylean model supplements these with the great dialectical figures of courage (Orestes) and justice (Athena): 'Thus we see that there exist indeed two Greek tragic modes: the Aeschylean one, the direction of which is the contradictory advent of justice by the courage of the new; and the Sophoclean one, the anguished sense of which is the quest, through a reversal, for the super-egoic origin.'[25] Anxiety, superego, courage, and justice hereby come to name the four fundamental concepts in any theory of the subject. What is more, this return to ancient tragedy gives Badiou the occasion both to address Hölderlin's remarks on Sophocles and to elaborate his own unique theory of justice, of the force of law, and of its ferocious underside of violence and nonlaw, with which he may be said to have anticipated more recent debates from the likes of Jacques Derrida or Žižek.[26]

The original seminars for Part Four coincide with the media uproar caused by the various attacks coming from the hands of self-proclaimed 'new philosophers'—many of them, like André Glucksmann, ex-Maoist renegades—against the 'master discourse' of Marxism that with Stalinist necessity would have led from diamat to the Gulag. In response to this media event, Badiou tactically shifts the terrain so as to answer the charges of the anti-Marxist war machine with reference not to the much-maligned 'totalitarianism' of the dialectic but to a contemporary definition of the 'black sheep' of materialism. Here, too, a principle of periodization applies, based on the fact that any materialism is defined by its immanent scission from a rivalling idealism: 'There are three materialisms, for the excellent reason that there are three idealisms: religious idealism, humanist idealism, and then—the fruit of this historical cul-de-sac in which imperialism casts its last rays of languishing modernity—linguistic idealism.'[27] Insofar as there is no point in denying the constituent role of symbolic structures such as language, the idealism that results from the linguistic turn also cannot be overcome merely by reaffirming matter as some hard prelinguistic fact. Instead, materialism itself must be split in terms of a double determination: to the thesis of identity, according to which all being is matter, we thus must add the thesis of primacy, according to which there are two regions of being, matter and thought, with the first ruling over the second: 'We can say, in short, that the thesis of identity names the place (of being), and the thesis of primacy the process (of knowledge) under the rule of the place.'[28]

With regard to the theory of knowledge, this double determination of materialism can be summarized in the 'mirror' that functions as the metaphor for knowledge in the notorious reflection theory, and the 'asymptote', which metaphorizes knowledge from the point of view of the remainder left behind by all exact reflection. 'Let us say that for materialism reflection is the metaphor of the thesis of identity', Badiou concludes: 'The second metaphor mathematizes the thesis of primacy into an asymptote.'[29] Both of these theses must be maintained at the same time, lest the dialecticity of the dialectic that traverses materialism through and through is allowed to lapse back into a 'rightist' or 'leftist' exaggeration, which would reduce knowledge, respectively, to being a simple mirroring reduplication of the existing structure of things or to following an infinite line of flight caused by some indivisible leftover. Given the current theoretical panorama, which bathes in the obscure light projected by notions such as difference, the remainder, or the asymptotic approach of the real in the night of non-knowledge, there is thus something refreshingly counterintuitive in this return to materialism in the bright mirror of reflection theory.

Parts Five and Six, finally, move the argument with increasing speed and concision in the direction of an overview of the entire theory of the subject in order to elucidate a possible 'ethics of Marxism'. This is accomplished by mapping out the four fundamental concepts, on one hand, into two analytical temporalities respectively of 'subjectivization' (based on the hasty time of interruption, itself split into anxiety and courage) and of the 'subjective process' (based on the durable time of recomposition, itself in turn split into the superego and justice); and, on the other, into two synthetic modes or trajectories, one which Badiou dubs the mode ψ (from anxiety to the superego) and the other, the mode α (from courage to justice). The theory of the subject thus becomes a complex topological space or network, ordered around the four basic concepts and their articulations. In fact, in addition to the vertical and horizontal pairings, there are also diagonal correlations that mark the trajectories of ideology in the theory of the subject, that is, the great imaginary functions of dogmatism (along the courage-superego axis) and scepticism (along the justice-anxiety axis). Badiou furthermore includes a brief phenomenological account of the different figures and trajectories in this overview, in which he once again returns to Hegel and Hölderlin.[30]

Ethics comes into the picture in this context as the name for different subjective formations that constitute so-called discourses, rather than either concepts or trajectories. Badiou distinguishes two extreme cases: the discourse of praise, based on belief in an essential wisdom of the world, and the openly Promethean discourse of rebellious confidence. Between these two extremes of belief and confidence, there lie the discourses of what Badiou calls the ethics of the impasse, whether nihilist or dissident, insofar as they reject all linkages between the supposed wisdom of the existing world and the subject's evaluation of what is to be done. The book's final propositions, which argue in favour of an ethics that would refuse to give up on the subject's confidence, in this sense can be considered an early anticipation of Badiou's *Ethics* as well as a welcome counterpart to the latter's all too polemical overtones.

4

Implicit in the notion of an 'ethics *of* Marxism', as opposed to a 'Marxist ethics', is a strictly political understanding of Marxism. This matter of principle guides the selection of texts from the tradition: 'We can never repeat enough that the texts of Marxism are first and foremost those of militant politics.'[31] The reader thus will search in vain for Badiou's personal interpretation of Marx's *Capital* ('the elephant *Capital*', Badiou says) or even of the *Grundrisse* (which play such a central role, around the same time in the late 1970s, in Antonio Negri's recasting of Marxism). Instead, it is with reference to interventionist texts such as *The Communist Manifesto* or Lenin's 'The Crisis Has Matured' that the present work claims to be standing in the lineage of political Marxism. Likewise, Badiou repeatedly rejects any notion of a 'science of history' that would be embodied in Marx's own study and critique of the political economy of advanced capitalism, in favour of a militant definition of the reference to texts by Marx, Lenin, and Mao in concrete political experiments: 'Science of history? *Marxism is the discourse with which the proletariat sustains itself as subject.* We must never let go of this idea.'[32] If ethics has any role at all to play in this context, it is only in order to serve as a practical principle, or maxim, for sustaining the rational and partisan calculations of politics.

Scattered throughout *Theory of the Subject* the reader will thus be able to find Badiou's reflections on the role of masses, classes, and the State; on the party of a new type as the body of politics; and on communism, revolution, and the dictatorship of the proletariat. Anyone interested in probing the exact nature of Badiou's Marxism, in this sense, should pay close attention to the present book. Perhaps above all, the reader will come to appreciate a side of Badiou's work that usually is not as visible as it is in *Theory of the Subject* or, once again, in *Logics of Worlds*, that is, his flair for historical periodization. Not only does he present what I earlier called a materialist theory of historicity without History; but he also steps into the trenches in order to intervene in the actual historicization of Marxism, as the discourse of reference in at least three crucial sequences of events: the popular riots from the time of the *Communist Manifesto* all the way to the experiment of the Paris Commune; the victory of the October Revolution and the constitution of socialist States throughout the Soviet bloc; and the Cultural Revolution in Maoist China. The reasons for this otherwise fairly orthodox effort at periodization are consistent with the principle of a militant—as opposed to a scientific, not to mention purely academic—understanding of the discourse founded by Marx: 'For Marxism, seized from any point that is not its effective operation which is entirely of the order of politics within the masses, does not deserve one hour of our troubles.'[33]

This does not mean neglecting the crisis of Marxism: 'Yes, let us admit it without detours: Marxism is in crisis; Marxism is atomized.'[34] However, unlike what happens in the anti-Marxist war machine of the discourse against totalitarianism, this crisis must be understood immanently, from within the weakness or the exhaustion of the referential value of the Marxist discourse in actual political and militant processes: 'Past the impulse and creative scission of the 1960s, after the national liberation struggles and the cultural revolution, what we inherit in times of crisis and the imminent threat of war is a narrow and fragmentary assemblage of thought and action, caught in a labyrinth of ruins and survivals.'[35] If Marxism, in addition to its undeniable historical crisis, must also undergo an active conceptual destruction, then it is always with an eye on its possible recomposition as a political discourse. This is why, several years after *Theory of the Subject*, it can come to function as one of the two fundamental 'intervening doctrines of the subject', the other one being psychoanalysis, that from the outside condition the philosophy of the event, as Badiou will state explicitly in the Preface to *Being and Event*: 'A post-Cartesian doctrine of the subject is unfolding: its origin can be traced to non-philosophical practices (whether those practices be political, or relating to 'mental illness'); and its regime of interpretation, marked by the names of Marx and Lenin, Freud and Lacan, is intricately linked to clinical or militant operations which go beyond transmissible discourse.'[36] Besides, the double historical stamping of these doctrines of the subject, with Marx/Lenin—aside from recalling Jesus/Paul at the origin of Christianity—being strictly homologous to Freud/Lacan, leads Badiou in *Theory of the Subject* to raise an intriguing question: 'Where is, yet to come and making three, the Mao of psychoanalysis?'[37] This question is not rhetorical and to a large extent remains open to this day—with Lacan himself still having important lessons to teach, as Badiou shows, regarding a theory of the subject that would be compatible with the destruction and recomposition of Marxism.

In other words, while it is certainly true that in *Theory of the Subject* Badiou acknowledges to be speaking from defeat, as when he says: 'To defend Marxism today means to defend a weakness', we should not neglect the fact that this acknowledgement is immediately followed by a statement in which the weakness of the indefensible at once prescribes the task of a new duty: 'We must *practise* Marxism.'[38]

At least two major interrogations admittedly still remain open with regard to the Marxist inscription of *Theory of the Subject*. The first concerns the place of (the critique of) political economy. As Žižek frequently insists, this dimension appears to be completely absent from Badiou's work after *Being and Event*. Through the concept of the absent cause itself, though, there is certainly a good case to be made for the argument that *Theory of the Subject* both includes and problematizes the role of the economy in a strictly political understanding of Marxism. Between Althusser and Badiou, in fact, we might say that a decisive reversal of perspective takes place whereby the absent cause, instead of providing us with the master key to unlock the structural causality of overdetermination, becomes synonymous with the transformative potential of an event. The economical instance, which for Althusser serves as the principal example of a cause that vanishes into the totality of its effects, thus continues to be present as it were virtually in Badiou's doctrine of the event, except that the emphasis now shifts away from the structural dimension towards the rarity of a subjective intervention. There can be no doubt, however, that much more work needs to be done in order to follow the destiny of this concept of the economy *qua* absent cause in the wake of Althusserian Marxism. Jacques-Alain Miller's early writings from the time of his participation in *Cahiers pour l'analyse*, especially 'Matrix' and 'Action of the Structure', even more so than his widely known 'Suture (Elements of the Logic of the Signifier)', should prove particularly relevant in this context, and they already receive much attention in Badiou's *Theory of the Subject*.[39]

In the end, though, even a return to the concept of the absent cause along the path that leads from structural to post-structural forms of thought is unlikely to convince the die-hard Marxist who is in search of an account of political economy in this thinker's work. For in the eyes of Badiou, the fact of the matter remains that Marx's *Capital*, while essentially true in its diagnostic, and perhaps even truer today than a century and a half ago, nonetheless puts us on the wrong track if our aim is to define a political rather than an analytical Marxism. This is because the critique of political economy has been unable to perform its own critique, as Badiou will write in *Can Politics Be Thought?* In this sense, the economical instance marks the fixation, or the becoming-fiction, of Marxism:

> What was supposed to be a strategy of the event, a hypothesis regarding the hysterias of the social, an organ of interpretation-interruption, a courage of fortune, has finally been presented, by way of the economy, as giving a convenient measure to social relations. Thus, Marxism has been destroyed by its own history, which is that of the fixion, with an x, the history of its fixation by the philosopheme of the political.[40]

Marxism can be freed from this fixation only if the crises and hysterias, to which the critique of political economy was supposed to provide access, are seen neither as social facts nor as empirical illustrations of antagonism as the metaphysical essence of 'the political', *le politique*, but as the retroactive outcome of 'politics', *la politique*, or rather, of *une politique*, that is, of 'a (specific mode of doing) politics'. *Theory of the Subject* aims to come to grips precisely with the logic of such retroactive interventions, as described almost on the spot in the feverishly militant writings of Marx, Lenin, and Mao.

A second interrogation concerns the historical nature of the theory of the subject as such. For Badiou, this question never even poses itself insofar as his theory is purely formal or axiomatic. What is more, as he recently reiterates, over time not much has changed at all either in the configuration of being, truth, and subject, which constitutes the matrix for philosophy, or in the types and figures of truth to which a subject can be faithful: 'The fact is that today—and in this regard things haven't budged much since Plato—we know only four types of truth: science (mathematics and physics), love, politics, and the arts.'[41] From a Marxist perspective, though, we might want to ask whether there are not also important historical breaks that need to be taken into account within the formal conditions of existence that are constitutive of such processes of subjectivization, particularly in politics. Does not capitalism introduce a major cut into these processes? Or does the formal apparatus remain fundamentally unchanged, even if any given truth procedure, like any political intervention, must appear in a specific historical world?

Clearly, Badiou's insistence on the eternal, transhistorical, or transtemporal nature of all truths is meant in the first place to avoid the relativistic consequences of a thoroughly historicized account of the subject. This is precisely the gist of his outspoken attack in *Logics of Worlds* against the historicism that he associates with so-called 'democratic materialism', as opposed to the 'materialist dialectic'. The real issue, however, concerns the compatibility, or not, between a formal and a historical theory of the subject. In Marxist terms, this would bring us back to the familiar stumbling block of defining the relations between dialectical materialism and historical materialism. Along these lines, aside from a return to Étienne Balibar's discussion of periodization and other basic concepts of historical materialism in his contribution to *Reading Capital*, future investigations based on a thorough grasp of *Theory of the Subject* might want to revisit not only the role of capitalism but also, in a possible dialogue with Michel Foucault's contemporary work in *The History of Sexuality* or in his seminar on *The Hermeneutics of the Subject*, the role of religion and psychoanalysis in the changing faces of ancient, medieval, and modern subjectivity.[42]

5

At this point, we might actually turn around our initial question and ask whether, even from such a cursory overview of *Theory of the Subject* as the one I have just outlined, Badiou's other major books, *Being and Event* and *Logics of Worlds*, do not also appear in a different and perhaps even critical light. In any case, while I do not wish to suggest something that Badiou jokingly has come to attribute to my reading of *Theory of the Subject*, namely, that after this book it all goes steeply downhill, with only a brief flaring up of hope with *Logics of Worlds*, we are far removed from the common prejudice according to which the work of philosophers, in an ongoing series of self-criticisms and emendations, is supposed to follow a steady path of linear progression.

The very relation between *Being and Event* and *Logics of Worlds* (subtitled *Being and Event, 2*), to begin with, can best be understood in terms of the articulation of algebra and topology. But then it soon appears that this comparison with one of the pivotal conceptual divisions from *Theory of the Subject* at once implies an anticipatory critique of the work to come. From within the strictly metaontological parameters proper to *Being and Event*, indeed, the event can only emerge as a vanishing cause whose entire being lies in disappearing. Now from the older work, we know that such an 'algebraic' viewpoint, for which the salient feature of the event—a feature forbidden in axiomatic set theory—would be its self-referentiality or its self-belonging, must be supplemented with a 'topological' orientation, which, on the basis of category theory or the theory of *topoi*, investigates the event in terms of its consequences and the consistency of its implicative structure, as happens in the sequel to *Being and Event*. In this sense, we might conclude, an astute reader of *Theory of the Subject* could have predicted a long time ago that *Being and Event* was to remain one-sided— triggering the hackneyed objections against Badiou as a dogmatist if not a downright mystic of the punctual event—until its extension that would take almost twenty years to come to fruition in *Logics of Worlds*.

Theory of the Subject not only provides us with a key to understand the dialectic between *Being and Event* and *Logics of Worlds*—especially if 'by "dialectic", in a direct lineage from Hegel, we are to understand the idea that the essence of all difference lies in the third term that marks the gap between the two others'.[43] But the earlier book also is capable of reorienting our reading of each of the later two volumes taken on its own. As I suggested above, this constitutes one of Badiou's major virtues as a philosopher in general, namely, his capacity to draw up a sharp picture of the stakes involved in the most burning polemics of our time so as to confront the reader with the obligation of a decision in favour of one line of thought or the other. What needs to be added here is that this capacity for giving thought a decisive orientation obviously can be extended to include Badiou's own work as well.

Thus, when read in light of *Theory of the Subject*, the project of *Being and Event* no longer appears to fall so easily in the traps of a rigid, undialectical or even anti-dialectical dualism. Nor does the event appear only as a punctual instance of self-belonging, wholly delinked or cut off from the existing situation. Instead, or rather in addition, the emphasis also falls on the fact that the event is always an event *for* a specific situation, by virtue of the evental site that only a concrete analysis of the concrete situation can circumscribe. Furthermore, rather than a relapse into the inert binaries of being/event, knowledge/truth, and so on, commonly associated with Badiou's thought, what a careful understanding of *Theory of the Subject* brings out in *Being and Event* is not only the extent to which each founding concept is internally split (in other words, the bar separating two terms of a binary must be transposed onto each term, so that being itself is split into consistent and inconsistent being; consistent being into presentation and representation; the event into itself and its site; the subject into the mortal individual and the immortal participant of a truth process, and so on), but also the role of a whole series of intermediary or intercalated concepts and operations (such as the concept of the evental site, which symptomatically links the event to a given situation and for which, significantly, no mathematical formula is available since with this concept we enter the realm of thick historical analysis; or the operation of forcing, which in a backward torsion makes a truth operative so as to produce new forms of knowledge within the situation of departure). Finally, even though the next to last meditation of *Being and Event* is titled 'Theory of the Subject', this newer version actually appears to be rather one-dimensional in comparison to the earlier book of the same title, in the sense that the subject is defined exclusively in terms of fidelity or not to the event. Unlike what happens with the dialectical interplay among the four fundamental concepts of anxiety, courage, justice, and the superego, there thus seems to be little or no space for internal strife within the subject as such. This, too, will be corrected in the first 'book' of *Logics of Worlds*, titled 'Formal Theory of the Subject (Metaphysics)'.

I have already pointed out some of the other topics, such as the role of destruction, by means of which Badiou in this recent book seems to be hearkening back to *Theory of the Subject*. But there are many more points of recurrence. For instance, contrary to the narrow definition of the subject that we find in *Being and Event* in terms of fidelity or the lack thereof, *Logics of Worlds* once again opens up a complex subjective space, structured around two other figures, the reactive one (which denies that any event actually has taken place) and the obscure one (which further obfuscates the very need for an event to happen at all insofar as there would exist a 'full' body in the guise of a race, nation, or God). What is more, the book explicitly resumes the formalization of the space of subjectivity by returning to what are now called the four 'affects' of anxiety, courage, justice, and terror: 'Four affects signal the incorporation of a human animal into the subjective process of a truth', Badiou writes, all the while insisting on the equal importance of all four. 'They are not be hierarchically ordered. War can have as much value as peace, negotiation as much as struggle, violence as much as gentleness.'[44] Finally, given this for many perhaps unexpected line of continuity between *Theory of the Subject* and *Logics of Worlds*, it really should not come as a surprise anymore that Badiou also returns to some of his old favourites for references: Hegel, more specifically his *Science of Logic*, thus appears once again as a key interlocutor in *Logics of Worlds*, and the book opens and closes with examples drawn from the history of Maoism.

All this obviously is not to say that there are no ruptures or discontinuities in Badiou's work. To say so, moreover, would be highly paradoxical, given the centrality for this work of the category of the event as a radical cut or break, albeit an immanent one. Even such discontinuities, though, must be placed against the backdrop of a larger articulation whose complex and divided nature can be grasped with special clarity from the vantage point of Badiou's first and most experimental attempt at formulating a materialist dialectic, in *Theory of the Subject*. From this point of view, not only *Being and Event* but *Logics of Worlds*, too, appears to be traversed by a divided orientation, comparable to the split between the algebra of a vanishing cause and the topology of a newly consistent world. On one hand, that which in the new book is called a 'site', which is not to be confused with the older notion of an 'evental site', is marked precisely by the punctuality of what disappears no sooner than it appears, as if in a lightning flash. On the other hand, however, there is a truth of this disappearing only thanks to the elaboration of a series of consequences, that is, a new mode or regime of appearing: 'Self-belonging annuls itself as soon as it is forced, as soon as it happens. A site is a vanishing term: it appears only in order to disappear. The problem is to register its consequences in appearing.'[45] Both of these aspects, the site as vanishing term and the regime of its consequences, can be separated only at the level of conceptual exposition, whereas in actual fact one cannot exist without the other. Badiou highlights this dilemma, for instance, in his periodization of the Paris Commune, a talk reworked and included in *Logics of Worlds*: 'For what counts is not only the exceptional intensity of its surging up—the fact that we are dealing with a violent and creative episode in the realm of appearing—but what this upsurge, despite its vanishing, sets out in its duration in terms of glorious and uncertain consequences.'[46] To ignore one of these aspects to the detriment of the other will lead to a radically different image of the philosophy of the event, either as an absolute but empty discontinuity or as a lasting but predictable continuity. As Badiou insists over and over again in *Theory of the Subject*, however, the whole trick consists in combining these two orientations in an open-ended dialectic of beginnings and rebeginnings. In fact, a subject is precisely such an articulation, as is confirmed in *Logics of Worlds*: 'A subject is a sequence involving continuities *and* discontinuities, openings *and* points. The "and" incarnates itself as subject.'[47]

6

Stylistically, *Theory of the Subject* adopts the format of a seminar inspired by Lacan's example. Badiou's fidelity to this model is actually quite extensive, ranging from the use of idiosyncratic wordplay, syntactic ambiguities, funny asides, and bold provocations of the audience, all the way to the disposition of the written text with numbered sections and a list of subtitles at the start of each chapter, as in Jacques-Alain Miller's edition of Lacan's original seminars.

In fact, the style of Badiou's three 'major' books could not be more different. Thus, while the ludic and dense quality of *Theory of the Subject* could be attributed to an almost complete indifference to an actual readership, the seminar-format nonetheless allows Badiou to rely on a generous 'we' that is truly collective and acknowledges the participation of his audience. I therefore frequently render the French *nous* as 'we' instead of seeing it merely as a polite form of the 'I', as is customary in English translations. Besides, *Theory of the Subject* still shows confidence in the possibility of speaking in the name of 'we Marxists', whereas this collective 'we' is precisely part of the tradition that collapses together with Soviet-style Communism and the Berlin Wall: 'Communism named the effective history of "we"' now dead: 'There is no longer a "we", there hasn't been for a long time.'[48] *Being and Event*, on the other hand, is written with an almost classical or, some would say, neoclassic impersonality, whose calm serenity does not exclude a monumental ambition. *Logics of Worlds*, finally, is written from a self-confident position of international fame, with an 'I' who does not hesitate to refer to 'Badiou' in the third person, side by side with Plato and Kant. Each of these three works, furthermore, adopts a unique generic format, following three different models in the history of philosophy: *Theory of the Subject* is a Lacanian-inspired seminar; *Being and Event* is made up of 37 Cartesian or post-Cartesian meditations; and *Logics of Worlds* adopts a structure vaguely reminiscent of Spinoza's *Ethics*, ordered into seven 'books', including several 'scholia' and a list of 'propositions' at the end.

Aside from certain technical terms, which I will list and explain in the next section, two stylistic idiosyncrasies deserve a brief comment here, as they also necessarily require a decision on the part of the translator. The first concerns Badiou's reliance on the fluency and ambiguity of certain constructions in French which, while by no means being obscure or out of the ordinary, resist easy translation into English. These are instances of almost colloquial speech that in translation may turn out to be awkward or simply unidiomatic. Some of these instances, especially those borrowed from Lacan, receive an extensive commentary from Badiou himself. For others, I have tried to give a literal translation, all the while explaining the ambiguity in the translator's notes included at the end of this volume.

The second idiosyncrasy, which Badiou also seems to have adopted from Lacan even though a similar trend is typical of a certain French style of writing in general, consists in using single-sentence paragraphs whose bold and compact syntax gives them the feel of gnomic or oracular statements. While in English it would have made sense to produce a smoother rhythm by incorporating such sentences into the flow of longer paragraphs, I have opted instead for a faithful rendering, respectful of the graphic effect with which these one-liners punctuate, in a well-nigh clinical sense, the gradual process of analysis undertaken by Badiou in *Theory of the Subject*.

* * *

I would like to thank all the friends whose help and support allowed me to see this project through to the end. Many more could be named but I want to single out Peter Hallward, Adrian Johnston, Alberto Toscano, and Slavoj Žižek. Their advice during the final stages in particular turned out to be invaluable. I also benefited from being able to consult translations of shorter portions of this book by Ed Pluth, Alberto Toscano, and Marina de Carneri. Audrey Wasser and Ricardo Arribas helped me with bibliographical references when I was far away from the libraries of Cornell and on sabbatical in Mexico. Alessandro Russo and Fabio Lanza's expertise about the Cultural Revolution was indispensable for locating obscure quotations from Mao. Simone Pinet, as always, was my compass; without her presence in my life, none of this would have been possible.

A separate word of thanks and appreciation goes out to Alain Badiou himself, who never stopped listening to my queries ever since our friendship began, precisely in response to that first reading of *Theory of the Subject* that blew me away, now more than a decade ago. At Continuum, finally, I want to thank Tom Crick for his patience and his continued belief that one day he would actually receive a complete manuscript, with diagrams and all included; and Andrew Mikolajski and Tracey Smith for their hard work with the editing.

Notes on the translation

A number of recurrent technical terms used in *Theory of the Subject* merit a brief explanation. Especially when combined with the author's own 'Thematic Repertoire', included at the end of this volume, this list may simultaneously serve as a basic glossary. The four fundamental concepts of the theory of the subject—courage, anxiety, justice, and the superego—do not receive a separate entry in this glossary, since Badiou himself in the course of the book amply defines them. Certain grammatical ambiguities and occasional technicalities, on the other hand, will be annotated together with additional bibliographical references in the final section of 'Translator's Endnotes and References'.

Annulation (**'annulment'** or **'annulation'**): This is one of the three basic operations associated with Mallarmé's poetry in terms of the structural dialectic, together with the chain effect caused by a vanishing term and the null effect of foreclosure. By annulling a vanishing term, this operation so to speak carries out a lack of lack, which raises lack to the level of a concept all the while producing anxiety. Alternative translations would be 'rescission', 'nullification', 'cancellation', or 'revocation'.

Basculement (**'tipping over'** or **'toppling'**, occasionally **'changeover'** or **'turnabout'**): A term used in the present context to refer to the sudden transformation whereby a structural or algebraic orientation tips over and opens out onto a historical or evental orientation. From the very beginning of *Theory of the Subject*, there are clear hints of the Hegelian-Marxian dialectic, as in the 'passing-over', or *übergehen*, of quantity into quality, especially when the whole process of contradictory transformation takes on a more abrupt, leap-like aspect of a sudden overthrow or inversion, as in the German *Umschlag*. Jason Barker, in the English translation of Badiou's *Metapolitics*, renders this term as 'overbalancing', for example, of what exists into what *can* exist, or from the known towards the unknown, as the result of a political intervention.

Battement (**'oscillation'** or **'vacillation'**, occasionally **'batting'**): A term used to describe the movement around an empty place, as part of what Badiou defines as the structural dialectic. Alan Sheridan, in his translation of Lacan's Seminar XI, *The Four Fundamental Concepts of Psycho-analysis*, opts for 'pulsation', which is perhaps all-too-physical for the purely structural function that Badiou has in mind, even though Lacan's own explanation is wholly to the point for the term's use in *Theory of the Subject*. 'I have constantly stressed in my preceding statements', Lacan says, 'the *pulsative* function, as it were, of the unconscious, the need to disappear that seems to be in some sense inherent in it—everything that, for a moment, appears in its slit seems to be destined, by a sort of pre-emption, to close up again upon itself, as Freud himself used this metaphor, to vanish, to disappear' (S XI, 43). Still in the same seminar, Lacan also uses the term to refer to the 'fluttering' wings of Chuang Tzu when he imagines he is a butterfly, while Badiou in *Theory of the Subject* refers to a 'batting' of eyelashes to name the appearing-disappearing of Mallarmé's vanishing cause. The term also evokes the role of the 'signifying battery', *la batterie signifiante*, in Lacanian psychoanalysis, and, insofar as Badiou seeks to go beyond the idealism of this structural model, there is nothing wrong with hearing echoes of 'beating' in *battement*, including in the pejorative sense of 'beating around the bushes'.

Brin **('strand')**: This term refers to the sections, strands, or bits that are knotted or braided together in a subject, especially the strand-α (combining courage and justice) and the strand-ψ (combining anxiety and the superego). Badiou thus relies on the concept-image of a cord or a piece of textile weaving together multiple strands or filaments.

Coupure **('cut', occasionally 'break' or 'rupture')**: In *Theory of the Subject*, this term most often retains the meaning of 'cut' that Lacan invokes, for example, in his topological discussions regarding the tying, untying, and cutting of a knot. The other connotation, which via Althusser would refer us back to the concept of an epistemological 'break' or 'rupture', *coupure épistémologique*, in the work of Gaston Bachelard, Georges Canguilhem, and Michel Foucault, seems less meaningful in the context of *Theory of the Subject*.

Déviance and *déviation* **('deviation')**: A term used in *Theory of the Subject* to translate *clinamen*, i.e. the slight 'deviation', 'swerve', or 'inclination' of atoms falling in the void whereby a world is formed according to the ancient atomism of Lucretius. While *déviance* has the same sexual and/or criminal connotations in French as 'deviance' or 'deviancy' in English, I have opted for the more neutral 'deviation' instead. The term then openly begins to resonate with the religious and political debates regarding *déviations* or 'deviations' from orthodoxy or from the correct line, debates that Badiou constantly has in mind throughout *Theory of the Subject*. Another possible translation for *clinamen*, used in certain English versions of Marx's doctoral dissertation on Democritean and Epicurean atomism, is 'declination'.

Épuration **('purification', sometimes 'purging')**: A term used to describe the process by which force—and the subject more generally—works back upon the system of places that otherwise determines its identity as this or that force: this or that subject. The term could obviously be translated as 'purge' or 'purging', but the Stalinist overtones of this expression, while never wholly absent, should not be allowed to dominate the term's interpretation in *Theory of the Subject*. In *The Century*, Badiou will discuss the path of destruction and purification, including in its Stalinist excesses, in opposition to the path of subtraction and minimal difference. Even here, in any case, he insists that purification and purges, including the excommunication of traitors and the sectarian defence against deviations and heresies of all kinds, are common practices throughout the twentieth century in many artistic avant-garde groups, from surrealism under André Breton to the situationists under Guy Debord, as well as in psychoanalytic groups, from Freud to Lacan.

Esplace ('splace'): This is a neologism or portemanteau word based on a contraction of *espace de placement*, 'space of placement'. It can be understood as a near-synonym for 'structure' or even 'symbolic order', even though there is no strict parallelism with either Althusser or Lacan. That which Badiou calls 'state of a situation' in *Being and Event* and 'world' in *Logics of Worlds* also roughly corresponds to 'splace' in *Theory of the Subject*. The dialectical counterpart to the 'splace' is the 'outplace', just as 'place' in general functions in a dialectical opposition with 'force' starting as early as in Badiou's *Theory of Contradiction*.

Étatique and *étatisme* ('statist' and 'statism'): While in *Theory of the Subject* Badiou has not yet fully developed the notion of 'state of the situation', which will be pivotal in *Being and Event*, he does rely on a series of terms to describe the static, statist, or state-like nature of certain historico-political phenomena. In English, these terms cannot easily be separated from the ones that translate the French *statique*, which Badiou uses both as an adjective ('static') and a noun, *une statique* (a 'static', or 'statics', perhaps even a 'statistics' in the etymological sense of the term as a science of the state, *Statistik* in German) as opposed to *une dynamique* (a 'dynamic' or 'dynamics'). A related expression is *faire état*, 'to draw up an overview', 'to inventory', or, for the present context, 'to define a state of affairs', for example, regarding the being of the working class.

Evanouissement and *terme évanouissant* ('vanishing' and 'vanishing term'): The basic operation of the structural dialectic, whereby a totality or whole is constituted as the effect of an absent or vanishing cause. *S'évanouir* also means 'to faint', 'to fade (away or out)', 'to pass out' or 'to die away'. In this sense, the term is not without recalling the role of *aphanasis* or 'fading' in Lacanian psychoanalysis. The main implied reference, however, is to the Althusserian conceptualization of 'structural causality' in *For Marx* and *Reading Capital*— unless Jacques-Alain Miller is right, against Althusser, in claiming paternity for this concept under the name of 'metonymical causality'. A third genealogical line, finally, would take us from Spinoza's 'absent' or 'immanent cause' to Deleuze's 'quasi-cause' as discussed in *The Logic of Sense*, all the way to Žižek's recent return to the same structuring principle. What should become clear from this network of references surrounding the concept of the 'vanishing term' is the extent to which Badiou in *Theory of the Subject* is giving form to a unique type of 'post-structural' thinking that takes to task the entire tradition of the 'structural dialectic' without ignoring its fundamental insights.

Force ('force'): The counterpart of history to the structure of assigned places, force is a term first borrowed from Hegel's *Science of Logic* that in the course of the argument developed in *Theory of the Subject* will come to designate what Badiou will later systematically discuss in terms of 'event'. Already in *Theory of Contradiction*, force stands in opposition to place, while readers of Jacques Derrida's *Writing and Difference* may be more familiar with the opposition of force and form. Three other idiomatic expressions are related to this concept in *Theory of the Subject*: *coup de force* ('stroke of force', 'violent overthrow', 'strike', 'trick', or sudden 'blow'), *passer en force* ('forcing one's way through' or 'pushing through') and *forcément* ('by force', 'per force'). Wherever possible, I have tried to retain the conceptual link with 'force' in English, while in the case of *coup de force* I have most often left the expression in French. Finally, I have already mentioned that Badiou uses the expression *force de loi* ('force of law') long before Derrida would make this into a topic for deconstruction. Derrida, too, discusses how there is no *force de loi* without some intrinsic and violent *coup de force*. This is also by far the most significant connotation that the reader should keep in mind for *Theory of the Subject*.

Forclusion and *forclos* ('foreclosure' and 'foreclosed'): A term used to describe the effect of the *points d'arrêt* or 'halting points' in Mallarmé's poetry, that is, terms such as the meaningless 'ptyx', which put an abrupt stop to the infinitely sliding metonymical and metaphorical chains. In French, *forclusion* also serves as the official translation of Freud's *Verwerfung*, which together with *Verneinung* ('denial') and *Verleugnung* ('disavowal') constitutes one of the many forms of negation considered in the practice and theory of psychoanalysis. By rejecting the existence of 'halting points' (there are no unknowables), at least in *Theory of the Subject* and once again in *Logics of Worlds*, Badiou could thus be said to be negating foreclosure. Whether this negation, in turn, takes the form of a denial, a disavowal, or a foreclosure remains to be decided.

Horlieu ('outplace'): This is a neologism or portemanteau word based on a contraction of *hors-lieu*, 'out of place' or 'out of site', as when someone is *hors-jeu*, 'off-side', in soccer. An alternative translation might have been 'outsite', or 'offsite', which is the term preferred by Oliver Feltham in his introduction to Badiou, but in my eyes this creates unwarranted confusions with the use of '(evental) site' in *Being and Event* and *Logics of Worlds*. Badiou sometimes uses the full grammatical expressions *hors-lieu* and *hors du lieu*, which I have rendered accordingly as 'out-of-place' and 'out of place' in English. An interesting analogy could be established with the expression *hors-sexe*, 'outside (of) sex', in Book XX of *The Seminar of Jacques Lacan: Encore*, which Lacan relates to Guy de Maupassant's fantastic short story 'Le Horla', itself often read as a contraction of *le hors-là*, 'that which remains outside (of what is) there'. More generally, Badiou's *horlieu* echoes the logic of the 'nonplace' or *non-lieu* in its interplay with the *lieux* or 'places' of a given structure, which is pivotal in the transition from structuralism to poststructuralism for French thinkers as diverse as Roland Barthes, Michel Foucault, Jacques Derrida, Jacques Rancière and Michel de Certeau, before its depoliticization in the anthropological work of Marc Augé.

Idéalinguisterie ('**idealinguistery**'): A portemanteau word to the second degree, which Badiou creates by contracting *idéalisme*, 'idealism', and Lacan's own portemanteau word *linguisterie*, based on *linguistique*, 'linguistics', and the mostly pejorative suffix *-erie*, which suggests a 'fake' or 'false' version. François Raffoul and Bruce Fink respectively propose 'linguistrickery' and 'linguistricks' for Lacan's *linguisterie*. This would give us 'idealinguistrickery' or 'idealinguistricks' for Badiou's *idéalinguisterie*, to which I have preferred the less cumbersome 'idealinguistery'.

Lalangue ('**llanguage**' or '**lalangue**'): A term Badiou directly borrows from Lacan to refer to the unique, slippery, and playful dimension of language taken into account by psychoanalysis, as in the possibilities opened up in puns or homonyms. While Bruce Fink in his English edition of Book XX of *The Seminar of Jacques Lacan* proposes 'llanguage' as a translation, I have chosen to leave the term in French.

Lieu ('**place**', occasionally '**locus**'): The structural element determining the nature and identity of anything whatsoever, as defined by the general space of assigned places. To distinguish *lieu* from *place*, one could have relied on 'locus' or 'site' for the former and 'place' for the latter. In *Theory of the Subject*, however, I see no strong reasons to differentiate the two except in the context of the four mathemes of anxiety, courage, justice, and the superego, where *lieu* and *place* are kept separate. The use of 'site' to translate *lieu* not only would have caused misunderstandings in suggesting an early anticipation of the terms *site* ('site') and *site événementiel* ('eventual site') as used in *Being and Event* and *Logics of Worlds*, but the reader would also have missed out on the play in *Theory of the Subject* between *lieu* and *horlieu*, whose internal rhyme is best rendered as 'place' and 'outplace'. English-speaking readers of Michel Foucault and Jacques Lacan may be familiar with 'locus' as a common translation for *lieu*.

Manque and *manque à être* ('**lack**' and '**lack of being**'): This is without a doubt the most central concept of the structural dialectic, which Badiou attributes to both Mallarmé and Lacan. Other French terms, such as *défaut* ('defect', 'fault', 'lack') and *défaillance* ('shortcoming', 'failure', 'miss', 'faint'), are parts of the same conceptual constellation in *Theory of the Subject*. For this reason, I sometimes render them as 'lack' as well, even though this comes at the price of missing out on the terminological diversity. Lacan proposed 'want-to-be' as the official English translation for *manque-à-être*. Badiou, however, does not use the dashes that would make *le manque à être* into a more stable technical term, and, insofar as he also plays on the inverted expression *l'être du manque*, 'the being of lack', I consistently stick to 'lack of being' instead of 'want-to-be'.

Passe **('pass' or 'passing')**: Badiou frequently has recourse to this term both in its common sense and in its technical meaning in the Lacanian school of psychoanalysis. For Lacan, who instated the procedure in 1967 as part of his *École Freudienne de Paris*, the *passe* provides an institutional structure for the 'passage' from analysand to analyst, that is, the end of analysis testified by the *passant* to a committee of *passeurs* or 'passers', who in turn relay the account to a jury who decides whether or not to award the 'pass'. In *Theory of the Subject* Badiou refers to the heated debates provoked by this procedure up to ten years after its introduction by Lacan (who, upon listening in silence to the formal complaints raised at a meeting in 1978, went so far as to call it a 'complete failure'). Insofar as the procedure involves the possibility of transmitting knowledge (*savoir*) about the analytical practice, Badiou takes an interest in *la passe* similar to the role of the universal transmission of mathematics in the scientific community. Among the many common meanings, the noun *la passe* and the verb *passer* can refer to 'passage', 'pass', 'patch', 'passing (for, over, by)', 'crossing', 'going through', 'skipping', 'lending', and so on. Relevant expressions include *passer un examen*, 'to pass an exam', *faire une passe*, 'to make a pass', *passer en force*, 'push through', and *mot de passe*, 'password'. In addition, Badiou systematically plays on the dialectic between *passe* and *impasse* (sometimes spelt *im-passe*, with a dash, so as to highlight the pun), in a key argument that will reappear in *Being and Event*.

Place **('place')**: Throughout *Theory of the Subject*, Badiou exploits the tension between that which can be mapped topologically in terms of spaces, places, and splace, on one hand, and, on the other, that which is a-topological, that is, force or the event. I did not find a significant difference between *place* and *lieu* that would warrant a solid distinction between 'place' and 'locus' or 'site'. Badiou frequently insists on the deadening effect of that which remains *sur place*, 'in its place' or 'on the same spot', most often as the result of an overly structural emphasis in which place and splace take precedence over force and the outplace. *Faire du surplace* is also a colloquial expression that refers to the quasi-immobile gesture by which a cyclist at a stoplight or at the start of a race tries to remain still with both feet strapped on the pedals. Interestingly, in *The Logic of Sense*, Deleuze describes an ethics of willing the event in terms of 'a sort of leaping in place', *saut sur place*.

Point d'arrêt **('halting point' or 'stopping point')**: A term used in *Theory of the Subject* to refer to those signifiers that put an end to the sliding of metaphors and metonymies in Mallarmé's poetry. Badiou refers especially to the amphora, the master, and the ptyx in the famous 'Sonnet allegorical of itself', and proposes to read these three signifiers in terms of death, the poet, and the pure signifier of the signifier as such. Invoking a quotation from Chairman

Mao ('We will come to know everything we did not know before'), a quotation that will be reused in *Logics of Worlds* against the dogma of finitude, Badiou denies the existence of insuperable halting points and affirms the open-ended nature of the periodized dialectical process. *Point d'arrêt* in *Theory of the Subject* thus has a completely different meaning from the one it has in *Being and Event*, where the void or empty set is said to be the only 'halting point' of multiplicity, that is, multiplicity goes all the way down, *qua* multiple of multiples, until the void. In *Ethics*, finally, aside from its ontological meaning, *point d'arrêt* also refers to the 'unnameable' that must not be 'forced' in the name of truth, lest one falls into the evil of a disaster. This concept of the unnameable, with its connotation of an insuperable limit-point calling out for an ethics of respect, is purely and simply abandoned in *Logics of Worlds*, where Badiou once again—consistent with his return to the quotation from Mao—affirms that there are always consequences, and no unknowables. In this last sense, it is worth keeping in mind, for *Theory of the Subject* as well, that *point d'arrêt* can be understood not only as 'halting point' or 'stopping point' but also as 'no halting' or 'no stopping at all'. Derrida, in his reading of Maurice Blanchot's *Arrêt de mort* (*Death Sentence*), has exhaustively deconstructed the linguistic possibilities afforded by the signifier *arrêt*.

Processus subjectif (**'subjective process'**): A term directly and explicitly borrowed from Lacan's *Ecrits* to designate one of the two aspects or temporalities of the subject, namely, the durable, ongoing, and most often laborious time of recomposition that gives a subject consistency, either in the guise of a new form of justice or in the guise of the superego's terrorizing call to order. The other moment or time of the subject is called subjectivization.

Réel (**'real'**): Badiou tends to use this term in a way that is reminiscent of Lacan's use without ever fully coinciding with its technical meaning or meanings in the triad of the real, the symbolic, and the imaginary. I have chosen not to use a large capital when translating the term as '(the) real', in an effort both to leave intact the fluidity of Badiou's use of the term and to avoid associations with New Age terminology, as in English discussions of Badiou's work that render all his key concepts with large capitals: Being, Event, Truth, and so on. Badiou also plays on the French expressions *point du réel* ('point of the real' but also 'not real' or 'not of the real at all') and *point réel* ('real point' with *point* as a noun but also 'not at all real' with *point* as an adverb).

Retournement (**'reversal', occasionally 'return'**): This term, used in the title of Part IV in order to propose a 'materialist reversal of materialism', is reminiscent of, but also somewhat different from, the usual 'inversion' (*Umkehrung* in German, or *renversement*, in the typical French translations) by which Marx, for example, claims to put the Hegelian dialectic 'back on its feet'. The difference stems from the fact that *retournement*, aside from a 'turning (over, upside down, inside out)', also evokes a 'return' (*retour*) and a 'turning back' or 'sending back' (*retourner*). Finally, the French term also serves to translate Hölderlin's notion of a 'return' or 'reversal' (*Umkehr* in German) in his 'Remarks on "Antigone"', in a figure amply commented upon in Part III of Badiou's *Theory of the Subject*.

Subjectivation ('subjectivization'): A term directly and explicitly borrowed from Lacan to designate one of the two aspects or temporalities of the subject, namely the hasty, slightly hysterical, and most often short-lived time of interruption and destruction, which according to *Theory of the Subject* takes the form of either anxiety or courage. Bruce Fink, in his translation of Lacan's *Écrits*, and Oliver Feltham, in his translation of *Being and Event*, opt for the spelling 'subjectivization', which I have adopted as well, while Slavoj Žižek and Alberto Toscano usually prefer the more literal 'subjectivation'.

Topique ('topology', occasionally 'topic'): A term used in *Theory of the Subject*, first, to designate Marx and Freud's respective 'topologies' or 'topographies' of the subject of class and of the unconscious and, then, to map out the various discourses of 'ethics', in the book's final part, titled *Topiques de l'éthique*, which I have translated as 'Topics of Ethics' so as to maintain something of the worldplay that would be lost if I had chosen 'Topologies of Ethics' or 'Ethical Topologies'. Badiou also has in mind and openly discusses Lacan's topological investigations from his final seminars. There may even be a faint echo of Claude Lévi-Strauss' great work of structural anthropology, *Tristes Tropiques*.

Torsion and *torsade* ('torsion' and 'twist'): This is one of the pivotal and most obscure concepts of *Theory of the Subject*. In part conditioned by mathematics, whose algebraic 'torsion groups' Badiou discusses at some length in the book, the concept of 'torsion' at the same time functions in a much broader sense to refer to the way in which a subject works back upon the structure that determines it in the first place. In this sense, *torsion* is related to *forçage*, another concept borrowed from mathematics and discussed in *Theory of the Subject* that will become even more central in *Being and Event*. *Torsade*, like *tresse* ('interlacing'), designates the twisted unity of the subject itself, that is, the divided articulation of courage, anxiety, justice, and the superego into two basic trajectories: the so-called mode-α (from courage to justice) and mode-ψ (from anxiety to the superego); and according to two temporalities: the time of interruption or destruction (anxiety and courage) and the time of recomposition (justice and the superego). Interestingly, Jacques Rancière also defines politics in terms of a constitutive 'torsion' that treats a specific *tort* or 'wrong', in *Disagreement: Politics and Philosophy*.

(Le) Tout ('Whole', 'Totality', or 'the All'): Again, a term used with a combination of Hegelian and Lacanian connotations to designate both the effect of a vanishing cause, namely, the resulting Whole, and that which, like any splace, by force must include-exclude something, namely, the outplace, in order to

come into being *qua* totality, so that the Whole is also always not-Whole or not-All.

Tresse (**'interlacing'**): A term used, in the same topological vein as *brin*, *nœud*, and *torsade*, to designate the subject's divided articulation. Other translations could have been 'braid', 'plait', 'weave' or '(inter)weaving'.

Unité de contraires (**'unity of opposites' or 'unity of contraries'**): This basic concept of the dialectic, which is as old as philosophy, is usually translated as 'unity of opposites' in English. Whenever Badiou insists on the role of 'contraries' or 'contrariness' in relation to the principle of *unité de contraires*, I retain the more literal translation as 'unity of contraries'.

Versant (**'aspect', 'strand', 'side', 'tendency', or 'slope'**): A term most often used to designate the two 'sides' or 'aspects' of the dialectic according to *Theory of the Subject*—its structural side and its historical side, the side of place and the side of force, its algebraic side and its topological side, the idealist aspect and the materialist aspect.

Voie (**'path' or 'road'**): A common noun that Badiou further associates with the Marxist and more specifically Maoist discussions about the struggle between two 'paths' or two 'roads', the bourgeois and the proletarian, the revisionist and the socialist. More generally speaking, the term is part of the topological orientation behind *Theory of the Subject*.

Preface

'To introduce myself into *your* story':[1] my reader, this is really the aim of pre-faces, so aptly named in that they must furnish a profile of what they precede.

I have nothing to profile, if not the certainty that I have, and to which the whole labour of this book testifies, namely, that the modern philosopher is—as Auguste Comte said already so long ago—a systematic proletarian.[2]

1

Philosophy today is deserted.

Never expecting anything from the State, I hardly expect that the recent libations in honour of the rose (I'm writing this in July 1981[3]) will make our largely disaffected national province flourish.

The inevitable result of the lack of ambitious thoughts is a mediocre politics and a devalued ethics.

In actual fact, it is probably the other way around. From the practical renunciation of egalitarian universalism, the inevitable inference is that the few forms of specialized knowledge to which thought is relegated, at least beyond the walls of journalistic idiocy, assure only the returns of the 'functionariat'.

Is it presumptuous to claim to ward off the inconveniences of the void on one's own? I object that any enterprise of this type has its emblems, and that moreover I am the least alone of persons.

Of all those for whom I am testifying, and who know that I know it—militants, friends, students, difficult interlocutors, provisional or returning enemies—I wish to inscribe here the name of only one: Paul Sandevince.

Hundreds of meetings with him, on which depended a thousand thoughts put into practice against our surroundings, make it impossible for me to mark the limits of my indebtedness to him.

Even though, as a consequence of his purely political conception of the truth, Sandevince always makes the oral take precedence over the written, the directive over analysis, in what follows the reader will find the few public traces of what the *real* world, so rarely noticed, has found in him of unparalleled significance, without even knowing it.

2

The form. It is that of a seminar, a genre to which Lacan has given a definitive dignity.

Who will say whether the lessons that make up this work were really pronounced on the date that punctuates them?

This ideal seminar—a mixture of an effective succession, some retroactions, supposed interpolations, and written compositions—certainly did take place. The present book is its second occurrence.

The easiest method is no doubt to go from the opening, January 1975, to the final suspension, June 1979. While it is hardly ever admitted, I know that this is not the common practice in philosophy. Thus, it is legitimate to suppose, and to support, an acute wandering on behalf of the reader.

At the end can be found:

- A thematic index with seven headings: art and literature, historical circumstances, God, logic and mathematics, traditional philosophy, psychoanalysis stricto sensu, and political theory. Of course, none of these headings concerns the central theme of the book, which I hope cannot be placed under any heading, since it is omnipresent.
- An index of proper names, which is so useful for knowing, by bouncing off the Other, where I can be located: a tactic of the drawer of which I do not at all disapprove.

  I point out—and in so doing I already begin to put my cards on the table—that this index does not include those names whose usage is so permanent that listing them would be unwieldy. Namely:

a) The two great classical German dialecticians, Hegel and Hölderlin. The entire beginning of the book is devoted to the first. The second is treated at the end of Part III, and in Part VI. But both can be found elsewhere, too.

b) The two great modern French dialecticians: Mallarmé and Lacan. There is an exhaustive treatment of the first in Part II, and of the second principally in Parts III and V.

The two great classical French dialecticians, Pascal and Rousseau, for their part do end up in the list.

c) Four of the five great Marxists: Marx, Engels, Lenin, and Mao Zedong.

The fifth, Stalin, is on the index.[4]

3

It is no doubt more instructive to write with respect to what one does not want to be at any price than under the suspicious image of what one wishes to become.

I am strongly attached to my country, France, even more so today since here people are becoming multinational—an advantage of internal internationalism indirectly provoked by the imperialist pillaging of goods and peoples.

In a little less than a century this country has had only three claims to greatness, three moments of real existence, three figures of a possible universalism: the Paris Commune in 1871, the Resistance between 1941 and 1945, and the uprising of youths and workers in May–June 1968.

I know they are of unequal importance. It is not clear that my hierarchy is the one in which they should be given. The present book is also written to shed some light on this matter.

In the same period there has been no shortage of abject moments. They sometimes followed their explosive contraries—the triumph of Versailles after the Commune, the colonial wars after the Liberation, and, minuscule, the 'new philosophers' after the establishment of revolutionary intellectuals in the factory.

The two World Wars were disastrous. The people fought when they should not have (1914–18) and they did not fight when they should have (1939–40). The sinister signifier 'Pétain' covers both debasements.

I could say right away that I do not want to be a part of any of these abjections. Philosophy is not worth a single effort if it does not shed light on the commitment that, even if it is restricted, seeks to prohibit the return of the five catastrophes, or of whatever resembles them, by carrying the memory and lesson of the three moments of existence.

More profoundly, I know that the essence of what has happened to us, in forcefulness as in humiliation, bears the mark of a deficiency *in the long term*. It is for this reason that the irruption, while certainly thunderous, is also fragile, without making the moral disorientation, which is predictable from afar, any less inevitable.

This deficiency is essentially subjective. It touches on the manner in which the potential forces, at the heart of the people, are kept at a distance from their proper concept.

Those French intellectuals who have not stopped spitting on themselves, on 'ideologies', on Marxism, on the Masters, on their most incontestable experience, and who have given credibility to the formless and the multiple, to spontaneity and scattered memory, to rights and enjoyments, to works and days, have a painful responsibility in all of this—that of irresponsibility.

I write and I act, but it is hard to distinguish between the two, in order not to be, if possible, explicitly mixed up in these phenomena of failure and bitterness. The fact that it has taken fifty years does not matter to me, because all the rest will be a futile shipwreck in a world henceforth headed for war, if there is not at least the fixed will, collectively submitted to the high level of its stakes, to go against the current and imprint if only a gesture of *direction* to that which might get us out of the slump.

4

In Julien Gracq's *Lettrines* there is a terrible passage, a fascinating portrait of the French intellectual—lost and useless when he is asked, when *the workers* ask him, simply to be someone enlightened, a realist leader. It concerns once again this inexhaustible analyser, the Commune:

Bohemians of the pen, journalists paid by the line, greying tutors, over-aged students, half-licensed graduates in search of private lessons: it is indeed in part the small world from *Scenes of Bohemian Life* turned sour, which has made such a pretty burial for Victor Noir and which with such incapacity has governed the Commune among the casks, the glasses, the *Glorias*, the smoke and the gab sessions of the board room of a 'small newspaper'. Marx was forgiving of the officers in command of the Commune, whose insufficiency he otherwise was well aware of. The revolution also has its Trochus and its Gamelins. The frankness of Vallès is consternating and would horrify this self-proclaimed government, these wannabe revolutionaries who were spit upon by the insurgents on the barricades when they passed through Belleville during the Commune's final bloody week. There is no excuse for leading even a good fight when it is led so half-heartedly.

A type of atrocious nausea arises while following the ubuesque and pathetic chaos of the last pages, wherein the unfortunate delegate of the Commune, his sash—which he does not dare to show—hidden in a newspaper under his arm, a sort of neighbourhood irrepresentative, a fire-starting Charlot hopping among the exploding shells, wanders around like a lost dog from one barricade to the other, unable to do anything at all, bullied by the teeth-baring rebels, distributing in disorderly fashion vouchers for herrings, bullets, and fire, and imploring the spiteful crowd—which was hard on his heels because of the fix into which he had plunged them: 'Leave me alone, please. I need to think alone.'

In his exile as a courageous incompetent, he must have awoken sometimes at night, still hearing the—after all quite serious—voices of all those people who were to be massacred a few minutes later, and who cried so furiously at him from the barricade: 'Where are the orders? Where is the plan?'[5].

Of all the possible nightmares, that of being exposed one day to such a figure is for me the most unbearable. It is clear to me that to ward off this risk supposes a thorough reshuffling that certainly touches upon the intellectuals but also upon the workers, for what is at stake is the advent between them of an unheard of type of vicinity, of a previously unthinkable political topology.

I write here so that neither I nor my interlocutors—intellectuals or not—ever become the one who, all told, can only meet the great dates of history by distributing herring vouchers.

References and Abbreviations

As far as the major authors are concerned, the following abbreviations and editions have been used:

Karl Marx and Friedrich Engels, *Selected Works in Three Volumes* (Moscow: Progress Publishers, 1969). Hereafter SW followed by volume and page number.

Vladimir I. Lenin, *Selected Works in Three Volumes* (Moscow: Progress Publishers, 1970). Hereafter SW, followed by volume and page number.

Mao Zedong, *Selected Works* (Beijing: Foreign Languages Press, 1961–77). Hereafter SW, followed by volume and page number.

G. W. F. Hegel, *The Phenomenology of Spirit*, trans. A. V. Miller (Oxford: Oxford University Press, 1977). Hereafter Ph, followed by the page number.

—— *Science of Logic*, trans. A. V. Miller (Amherst, NY: Humanity Books, 1969). Hereafter L, followed by the page number.

Stéphane Mallarmé, *Collected Poems and Other Verse*, trans. E. H. and A. M. Blackmore (Oxford: Oxford University Press, 2006). Hereafter CP, followed by the page number. I will indicate in an endnote whenever I preferred to use *Collected Poems*, trans. Henry Weinfield (Berkeley: University of California Press, 1996).

—— *Divagations*, trans. Barbara Johnson (Cambridge: Harvard University Press, 2007). Hereafter D, followed by the page number.

Friedrich Hölderlin, *Essays and Letters on Theory*, ed. and trans. Thomas Pfau (Albany: State University of New York Press, 1988). Hereafter ELT, followed by the page number.

—— *Poems and Fragments*, trans. Michael Hamburger (London: Anvil Press Poetry, 1994). Hereafter PF, followed by the page number.

Jacques Lacan, *Ecrits. The First Complete Edition in English*, trans. Bruce Fink in collaboration with Héloïse Fink and Russell Grigg (New York: W. W. Norton, 2006). Hereafter E, followed by the page numbers referring to the English and

REFERENCES AND ABBREVIATIONS

the French editions, separated by an oblique.

—— *The Seminar of Jacques Lacan, Book I: Freud's Papers on Technique, 1953–1954*, ed. Jacques-Alain Miller, trans. John Forrester (New York: W.W. Norton, 1988). Hereafter S I, followed by page numbers to the English and the French editions, separated by an oblique.

—— *The Four Fundamental Concepts of Psycho-Analysis*, ed. Jacques-Alain Miller, trans. Alan Sheridan (New York: W.W. Norton, 1981). Hereafter S XI, followed by the page numbers of the English and French editions, separated by an oblique.

—— *The Seminar of Jacques Lacan, Book XX: Encore, 1972–1973*, trans. Bruce Fink (New York: W.W. Norton, 1988). Hereafter S XX, followed by the page number.

—— 'Conférences et entretiens dans des universités nord-américaines', *Scilicet* 6–7 (1975): 7–45. Hereafter 'Conférences' followed by the page number.

Handbook of Mathematical Logic (Amsterdam and New York: North-Holland Publishing Company, 1977). Hereafter HML, followed by the page number.

Texts of the Cultural Revolution, *Important Documents on the Great Proletarian Cultural Revolution in China* (Beijing: Foreign Languages Press, 1970). Hereafter GPCR, followed by the page number.

All other references will be quoted in the text, with bibliographical information provided in the Translator's Endnotes and References.

As for Paul Sandevince's writings, the reader may want to consult the following, all published by Potemkine editions:

– *Qu'est-ce qu'une politique marxiste?* (1978)
– *Un bilan de Mai 68* (1978)
– *Notes de travail sur le post-léninisme* (1980)

PART I

The Place of the Subjective

Everything that belongs to a whole constitutes an obstacle to this whole insofar as it is included in it

January 7, 1975

Old Hegel split in two—Scission, determination, limit—Splace and outplace—Deviations on the right and left

1

There are two dialectical matrices in Hegel. This is what turns the famous story of the shell and the kernel into such a dubious enigma. It is the kernel itself that is cracked, as in those peaches that are furthermore so irritating to eat whose hard internal object quickly cracks between one's teeth into two pivoting halves.

In the peach there is still a kernel of the kernel, the bitter almond-shaped nut of its reproduction as a tree. But out of Hegel's division, we will draw no secondary unity, not even one stamped with bitterness.

We must understand what Lenin repeated a bit all over the place: the retrospective good news that Hegel is a materialist! It is worthless merely to oppose an (acceptable) dialectical kernel to an (abominable) idealistic shell. The dialectic, inasmuch as it is the law of being, is necessarily materialist. If Hegel touched upon it, he must have been a materialist. His other side will be that of an idealist-dialectic, in a single word, which has nothing real about it, not even in the register of an inverted symbolic indication (standing on its head, as Marx said).

So at the heart of the Hegelian dialectic we must disentangle two processes, two concepts of movement, and not just one proper view of becoming that would have been corrupted by a subjective system of knowing. Thus:

a) A dialectical matrix covered by the term of alienation; the idea of a simple term which unfolds itself in its becoming-other, in order to come back to itself as an achieved concept.

b) A dialectical matrix whose operator is scission, and whose theme is that there is no unity that is not split. There is not the least bit of return into itself, nor any connection between the final and the inaugural. Not even 'integral communism' as the return, after the exteriorization into the State, to the concept of which 'primitive communism' would be the simple immediacy.

Yet things are far from being so simple.

2

Let us begin with an empty notion, at once limited and prodigiously general: the notion of the 'something', which is the first form of being-there in Hegel's *Logic*.

Hegel's objective, with his 'something', is nothing less than to give rise to the dialectic of the One and the many, of the infinite and the finite, that is, the principle of what we orthodox Marxists call quantitative accumulation, which, as everyone knows, is reputed to produce a qualitative leap.

The mystery, moreover, is that all of this in Hegel's *Logic* can be found under the heading of 'quality', which in the order of exposition precedes quantity.

However, it is Hegel who is right, as always, because nothing can be said of the One without engaging the qualitative and force. This is why one of the objectives of what we are saying here is to establish that the famous 'leap' from the quantitative to the qualitative, far from being the measure that makes all the thermometers explode, includes the effect of a subject.

Hegel in any case is at pains to engender the multiple, the denumerable, insofar as his idealist propensity pushes him always to obtain everything on the basis of a simple term. How can the multiple proceed from the One, and from the One alone? This is a question as old as philosophy, but it has always held more punch for someone who claims to historicize the Whole, instead of merely giving us the law of its fixed order. Already with the Church Fathers, those great founders of conceptual history, it was necessary to account for the fact that God, the absolute form of the One, was able to pulverize a universe of such lasting multiplicity. To prove God by the marvels of nature—from the frog to the unicorn (except that the unicorn rather proves the existence of the Devil)—is one thing; to prove the marvels of nature by God is much more complicated, since God is necessarily the marvel of marvels.

Hegel is the modern conjurer of this ecclesiastical question. Instead of saying that there is creation of the Whole by the One, Hegel will show that the Whole is the history of the One, so that the space of the multiple is the effect of the time required for the concept. For the *coup de force* of the miraculous Creator, he substitutes the work, the suffering, and the circular duration of a kind of self-exposure, through which the absolute arrives at the completely unfolded contemplation of itself. And it is this journey through the galleries of the One that is the whole of the world.

Of course, the initial *coup de force* that is thus glossed over shows up again in every subsequent paragraph. Just as it makes the heavy machinery of the global system advance, it is the very accumulation of these arbitrary local decrees that everywhere gives form to the acute and partial framework of Hegel's materialism.

3

From the start, Hegel does not posit the 'something' all on its own, but the difference between something and something other (*Etwas und Anderes*). What is thus recognized is that no dialectic is conceivable if it does not presuppose division. It is the Two that gives its concept to the One, and not the other way around.

Naturally, there are all sorts of contortions on Hegel's part that serve to mask this recognition. Everything happens—especially in the first edition from 1812, which is the most idealist because the old Hegel, contrary to what is sometimes said, always holds on to a reality principle—as if the 'something else' were the post-position of the 'something', its categorial becoming. But this is a smokescreen. In fact, Hegel is going to study the scission of the something in a movement that is prestructured by a first scission, which is in a way hidden *because it is essentially repetitive*: it is what repeats the something in the position of itself as other, as something-other. This is exactly the operation of the very beginning of the *Logic*, where being and nothing are the same thing posited twice. Here, too, one can 'track down' the becoming-split of a category only because one gives oneself, whether secretly or publicly, this minimal primary differential: two times One.

I say that it is 'the same thing' posited twice because alterity has here no qualitative support. We are, if you will, at the dawn of the qualitative, at its structural skeleton. *This* only differs from *that* by the statement of the difference, by the literal placement. One could name this infimous stasis of the contradiction the indexical stasis. There is A, and there is A_p (read: 'A as such' and 'A in another place', namely, the place p distributed by the space of placement, or P).

It is the same A twice named, twice placed.

This will more than suffice for them to corrupt one another.

For you can consider A either in its pure, closed identity, or in its indexical difference from its second occurrence. A is itself, but it is also its power of repetition, the legibility of itself at a distance from itself, the fact that at a place, p, the other place, it is still A itself that is read, albeit 'other' than there where it stands, even if it is nowhere, since it is seen there *too*.

Hegel names these two determinations the something-in-itself and the something-for-the-other. The 'something', as a pure category, is the unity of these two determinations, the movement of their duality.

This is proof that in order to think anything at all, something no matter what, it must be split in two.

What is the meaning of the something-in-itself and the something-for-the-other? Pure identity and placed identity; the letter and the space in which it is marked; theory and practice.

The givenness of minimal difference (something *and* something else) necessarily contracts into the fixed term of the difference, the 'thing', whether it be some- or else. A, we said (and A is the thing), is at the same time A and A_p, whereby A_p is the generic term for any placement of A. Indeed, this can be A_{p1}, A_{p2}, A_{p3} . . . with all the p_1, p_2 . . ., p_n . . . belonging, for example, to P. This is what we will see later on: there are an infinity of places. A_p is A in the general-singular of placement. Now, it is always in this way that A presents itself (it is always placed) and refuses itself (because, as placed, it is never only itself, A, but also its place, A_p). Furthermore, this is true of anything whatsoever—of something in general, of such-and-such a thing.

We must thus posit a constitutive scission: $A = (AA_p)$.

The index, p, refers back to the space of placement P, the site of any possible reduplication of A. Note that this does not have to be spatial or geometrical: a reduplication can be temporal, or even fictive.

What Hegel does not state clearly is that, fundamentally, the true initial contrary of the something, A, is not something else, not even the same A 'placed', A_p. No, the true but camouflaged contrary of A is the space of placement P: it is that which *delegates the index*. The givenness of A as being itself split into:

– its pure being, A
– its being-placed, A_p

(Heidegger would say: into its ontological being and its ontic being) is the effect on A of the contradiction between its pure identity and the structured space to which it belongs, between its being and the Whole. The dialectic divides A based upon the contradiction between A and P, between the existent and its place. It is this contradiction, whose latent theme is Mallarméan ('Nothing will have taken place except the place'), which, introjected into A, founds its effective being as scission.

All of this is too much of an anticipation, because the contradiction between A and P opposes a force to a system of places, and we have not reached that point yet.

Let me throw just a little flash of light, one that moreover is perfectly excessive.

The true contrary of the proletariat is not the bourgeoisie. It is the bourgeois world, imperialist society, of which the proletariat, let this be noted, is a notorious element, as the principal productive force and as the antagonistic political pole. The famous contradiction of bourgeoisie/ proletariat is a limited, structural scheme that loses track of the torsion of the Whole of which the proletariat *qua* subject traces the force. To say proletariat and bourgeoisie is to remain within the bounds of the Hegelian artifice: something and something else. Why? Because the project of the proletariat, its internal being, is not to contradict the bourgeoisie, or to cut its feet from under it. This project is communism, and nothing else. That is, the abolition of any place in which something like a proletariat can be installed. The political project of the proletariat is the disappearance of the space of the placement of classes. It is the loss, for the historical something, of every index of class.

You will say: and what about socialism? Socialism where, in fact, bourgeoisie and proletariat are more than ever at loggerheads, including in the guise of unprecedented revolutions, the cultural revolutions? Socialism does not exist. It is a name for an obscure arsenal of new conditions in which the capitalism/communism contradiction becomes somewhat clarified. Socialism designates a shifting mutation of the space of the place-ment of classes. Socialism is P' in the place of P. If there is a major point in Marxism, which this century confirms almost to the level of disgust, it is that we should certainly not inflate the question of 'socialism', of the 'con-struction of socialism'. The serious affair, the *precise* affair, is communism. This is why, all along, politics stands in a position of domination over the State, and cannot be reduced to it. And you will never reduce all of this to the binary poverty of the contradiction, term against term, of proletariat/ bourgeoisie. Marxism begins beyond this contradiction.

4

With Hegel we thus posit the scission $A = (AA_p)$, the effect of the com-pletely veiled conflictual relation between A and the distributor of places to which it is connected. Everything that exists is thus at the same time itself and itself-according-to-its-place.

Now Hegel says that what *determines* the split term, what gives it the singularity of its existence, is not of course A, the generic term closed in on itself, indifferent to any dialectic. It is rather A_p, A according to the effect of the whole into which it is inscribed.

Consider, for example, that if the working class is internally split, including during those heady times marked by mass movements, between the onset of its true political identity, on one hand, and, on the other, its latent corruption by bourgeois or imperialist ideas and practices, then it is surely owing to the effect of that which *still* disposes it in a Whole, whether national or global, governed by capital and empires. This is what holds together two otherwise so contrary paths in the practical unity of an uprising, and which makes of the pure emergence of itself a process of purification in the divisible contact with its opposite.

This is true even under socialism. In 1967, in China, armed factions resist in all the large factories. Mao declares: 'Nothing essential divides the working class.'[1] Does this amount to the factual observation of a fixed place? No. This is a directive for combat, meaning that the proletariat must take the lead of the revolution, and that such is the historical guiding thread it must hold onto for its unity, that is, *for its existence* (as political class).

All that is relates to itself at a distance from itself owing to the place where it is.[2]

If $A = (AA_p)$, this is determined by the indexical effect of P on A. We will thus write $A_p(AA_p)$ as the first notation of the determination of the scission, the first algorithm of the unity of opposites.

In other words, what Hegel calls *Bestimmung*.

Bestimmung is, in turn, divided by what it unifies. It is a major strength of the dialectic to grasp how the One of the unity of contraries supports contrariness in its very being.

Let us begin with our example: the practical (historical) working class is always the contradictory unity of itself as proletariat and of its specific bourgeois inversion (today, modern revisionism, the PCF, the trade unions, everything that organizes the rallying of the working class to imperialist society, or even to the idea of leading this class for the direct benefit of the working aristocracy, partially authorized by bureaucratic state capitalism). This unity of opposites is determined (in the sense of the Hegelian *Bestimmung*) by the general bourgeois space, which bears the possible unity of the politically active (Marxist) proletariat and of the working class as Place of the new state bureaucratic bourgeoisie (revisionism). Thus, A = the working class, P = contemporary imperialist society. This gives us A_p = modern revisionism, and the algorithm: $A \rightarrow A_p(AA_p)$, in which is indicated that what determines the dialectical actuality of the proletariat today is its internal purification from modern revisionism.

But what does 'determination' mean? Two things:

- On the one hand, that the combative Marxist core of the working class is determined by the new revisionist bourgeoisie. This is dialectical determination in the strong sense, which can be written $A_p(A)$.
- On the other hand, that revisionism, in the final analysis, and more and more so, is never anything but the specific and homogeneous form, adapted to the working class, of the general bourgeois and imperialist space, or P. In the struggle to purify itself of this, the proletariat *unmasks* (this is the authorized term) the part of itself that is engaged in revisionism, and posits it as an integral part of the external antagonistic term, which, as we saw, is not the bourgeoisie but imperialist society of which the PCF, the unions, and so on, are the modern, effective, and active standard-bearers. As such, determination only reconvokes—repeats—the space of placement, the general alterity P of which p is the index for A. We will write: $A_p(A_p) = P$. This is a sort of dead branch of the dialectical process, the reminder that the determination of the scission $A(AA_p)$ originates from the fact

that A only ex-sists in the site P. This is the inert, divisible part of the total determination—with the other part, marked $A_p(A)$, truly being the intimate core of the determination *for A*.

In general, we can say that the determination of any split ex-sistent is distributive:

$$A_p(AA_p) \begin{cases} \longrightarrow A_p(A) \quad \text{determination proper} \\ \\ \longrightarrow A_p(A_p) = P \quad \begin{array}{l}\text{relapse in to the general space} \\ \text{'Nothing will have taken place but the place'}\end{array} \end{cases}$$

Does Hegel really speak of these dead branches of the process? Absolutely. He calls them 'relapses' (*Rückfälle*). They are the shadow cast by the place in its pure, evocative dimension. Determination, on the other hand, is the new.

We thus obtain, at this stage, the following great dialectical concepts, endowed with an absolutely general ontological import:

a) *Difference* of itself from itself, A and A_p, commanded by the *contradiction* between force A and the space of placement P, of which A_p is the indexical instance for A. An important point to note is that it is the contradiction that commands difference, and not the other way around.
b) *Scission* as the only form of existence of the something in general: A = (AA_p).
c) *Determination* as unity of the scission, thinkable only from the indexed term (and not from the pure term): $A_p(AA_p)$.
d) The scission of the determination according to what it determines:
  – determination of the new, $A_p(A)$
  – relapse: $A_p(A_p) = P$.

The essence of the relapse is the space of placement, the place.

A remark on terminology: if one opposes force to place, as I shall continually do, it will always be more homogeneous to say 'space of placement' to designate the action of the structure. It would be even better to forge the term *splace*. If, on the contrary, one says 'place', which is more Mallarméan, we will need to say, in the Lacanian manner, 'place-holding' or 'lieutenancy' for 'place'. But 'force' is then heterogeneous to designate the a-structural topological side. It would be more appropriate to say: the *outplace*.

The dialectic, in the sawdust-filled arena of the categorial combat, is the outplace against the splace.

5

The relapse is the inert negative of strict determination only if $A_p(A)$ includes a specific resistance of the term A to allowing itself to be exhaustively determined by its indexical instance A_p. If not, $A_p(A)$ would be swallowed up in A_p. In other words, *there would only be relapses*. This is the principle of structuralism in all its forms.

But neither I nor Hegel are structuralists. I think, for example, that, in its antagonistic determination that is specific to the new revisionist bourgeoisie, the proletariat emerges as a positive newness. This happens, timidly, during May '68 in France, and, with great uproar, in January 1967 in China—for instance, in the guise of a thoroughly transformed Marxism (Maoism). The interiority proper to A thus comes to *determine the determination*. After all, in the Cultural Revolution, it is the people in revolt who designate the new bureaucratic bourgeoisie as the global determination of the revolutionary antagonism itself. Unless what is new in the dialectical process is annulled in the pure relapse into P, the place or space of placements, it is thus necessary to posit a determination of the determination, namely: $A(A_p(A))$.

This is a process of torsion, by which force reapplies itself to that from which it conflictually emerges.

The determination of the determination splits itself in a distributive manner just as much as the determination does. Indeed, it can be a simple reaffirmation of the pure identity of A: $A(A)$, that is, a pure emergence of itself, against (but outside of) determination, and this in a strict parallelism to the relapse into P. Thus, a revolt without a future that would pit the combative fraction of the working class against the new bourgeoisie of the PCF and the unions solely in the name of lost purity, hence against the treason of the PCF—without perceiving the internal newness of the new bourgeois phenomenon. This is largely what happened in May '68, leading many to dream either of a 'renewed' PCF or of a working class re-purified following the school example of its great ancestors of the nineteenth century. The intimate force of A is thus called upon again in the illusory repetition of its closure onto itself and in the inability actively to support the determination.

There is the deviation 'to the right', which leads back to the objective brutality of the place P in order to deny the possibility of the new inherent in the old. But there is also the ineluctable deviation 'to the left', which vindicates the original and intact purity of force while denying, so to speak, the old inherent in the new, that is, determination. The schemas for these two deviations are $A_p(A_p) = P$, and $A(A) = A$.

But if what is at stake is not this reconvocation of essential origins, it is the effective process of the limitation of determination, the work of force on place, the differential of A turning back upon its own indexation in order to reduce its necessary import. This is $A(A_p)$, the direct, limiting application of the efficacy of A onto the determination that it is.

Everything that is of a place comes back to that part of itself that is determined by it in order to displace the place, to determine the determination, and to cross the limit.[3]

Hegel gives the name of limit (*Grenze*) to this counter-process, which must be understood in the sense of the 'limitation of bourgeois right'— nothing less, for example, than the reduction of the gaps between intellectual and manual labour, city and countryside, agriculture and industry. Limit and limitation are the essence of the labour of the positive.

Everything that belongs to a whole is an obstacle to this whole insofar as it is included in it.[4]

This is why 'totalitarianism' does not exist. It is a pure, structural figuration without any historical reality. It is the idea that in this world only the necessary rightist relapse and the impotent suicidal leftism exist. It is $A_p(A_p)$ or $A(A)$ intermittently, that is, P and A in their inoperative exteriority.

The State and the plebs.

But the true terms of all historical life are rather $A_p(A)$, determination, and $A(A_p)$, the limit, terms by which the Whole affirms itself without closure, and the element includes itself therein without abolishing itself.

Action, manor of the subject

January 14, 1975

Structural synthesis of a dialectical sequence—The Father and the
Son, consubstantial—Gnostics and Arians, councils and congresses—
Circularity and periodization—Everything must be taken up again from
scratch

1

You can see below the schema of any dialectical fragment whatsoever,
such as we deduced it last time from the chapter on the 'something' in
Hegel's *Logic*.

We must clearly understand that the contradiction A/P is only given
as a structural horizon. It always opposes a term to its place. Any contradiction is fundamentally asymmetrical, in that one of the terms sustains
a relation of inclusion to the other. The including term, which is to say
the place, the space of placement, is named (particularly by Mao) the
dominant term, or the principal aspect of the contradiction. The one that
is included, for its part, is the subject of the contradiction. It is subjected
to the other, and it is the one that receives the mark, the stamp, the
index. It is A that is indexed in A_p according to P. The inverse makes
no sense.

Does Hegel say this? No. Hegel conceals the principle of dissymmetry.
Or, rather, he links it back to the idea of an integral whole that would
retrospectively index each sequence. We shall come back to this.

Rigorously speaking, contradiction does not exist. How could it exist,

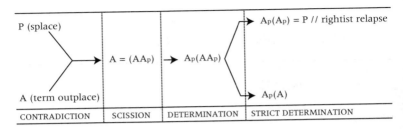

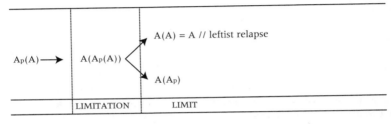

since to exist (to ex-sist) is precisely to be 'something', that is, to support the scission-effect of which contradiction is the cause? Contradiction is a pure, structural principle. It *insists* in the index p of A, it marks the repetition of A, but nowhere do you have a real, existing conflict between A and P as constituted and isolatable terms. P, the splace for all isolation and all repetition, cannot be isolated any more than it can be repeated. A, the outplace, is repeatable only as split by inclusion in the splace.

Contradiction has no other mode of existence but scission.

In concrete, militant philosophy, it is thus indispensable to announce that there is only one law of the dialectic: One divides into two. Such is the principle of observable facts and of action.

What does the opposition of imperialist society and the revolutionary people amount to in the order of facts? It is the political division of the people, because the two modes of politics, bourgeois and proletarian, possess reality only insofar as each one of them organizes the people on its own terms. A politics 'without people', not based in a structured mass, does not exist. Thus, the principal contradiction in a country like France, between the proletariat and imperialist society, between proletarian politics and bourgeois politics—a contradiction, it must be said, still completely embryonic in its form—has no effective content other than the historical movement of the division of the people.

This is why the strong and fully deployed existence of the political proletariat can never do without the revolutionary civil war. This is why it is always essential to pay attention not only to the state bourgeoisie, but also to the civil bourgeoisie and its tight popular ramifications.

We must repeat with force that the existence in action of the contradiction between splace and outplace, whatever they are, is the scission of the outplace. Scission is that by which the term is included in the place as out-of-place. There is no other content to the idea of contradiction.

2

Regarding my examples, some could voice the suspicion that all these dialectical algorithms and theorems stand in a relation of absolute dependence to the contents which they organize—the proletariat, imperialist society, revisionism, and so on—and that this is a syntax of little interest from the moment that the semantics of it is forced.

To this I will object:

– *primo*, that this is a matter of indifference to me. Because as a Marxist, I in fact posit that the contents drain the forms, and not the other way around. What is certain is that the dialectical formulations are rooted in an explicit political practice.
– *secondo*, that this is not true. The 'model' on which Hegel implicitly works is Christianity. And I will establish right away the appropriateness of this theological model.

Take P as the splace of the finite, and A, God as infinite, hence, as radical out-of-place.

As such, this contradictory duality has no dialectical meaning, and thus no meaning at all.

What gives it meaning is its historicization in scission, which makes the infinite ex-sist in the finite. Therein lies the necessary stroke of genius of Christianity. For this to happen, God (A) is indexed (A_p) as specific out-place of the splace of the finite: this is the principle of the Incarnation. God becomes man. God divides into himself (the Father) and himself-placed-in-the-finite (the Son). A is the Father, and A_p the Son, that historic son by whom God ex-sists. God thus occurs as scission of the outplace, A = AA_p, God = Father/Son, a scission that the Council of Nicea, the first of the great modern politico-ideological conferences in history, will designate as sole existence—as unity of opposites—in the well-known dialectical axiom: 'The Son is consubstantial with the Father.'

From this starting point, our dialectical fragment unfolds in its entirety:

- $A_p(A)$ designates the determination of the (infinite) identity of God by its marking in the splace of the finite. The radicality of this determination is the Passion: God *qua* Son dies. The infinite climbs up the Calvary.
- $A(A_p)$ designates the counter-determination (the limit of death) by the infinity of the Father: the Son is resurrected and rejoins (Ascension) the Father's bosom, which represents a figurative outplace.

The consubstantial duality Son/Father, that is, the Incarnation, the death of the infinite (the Passion), and its non-death (the Resurrection) are the immediate theological contents of scission, determination, and limit.

At the end of this redemptive adventure, you find in heaven a God who reconciles in himself, in his historical self-unfolding, the finite and the infinite. And on earth, what subsists is only the simple *empty trace* of the completed process: namely, the tomb of Christ about which Hegel—mysteriously symbolizing the effacement of the trace, the abolition of the abolished—will say that consciousness has 'learned from experience that *the grave* of its actual unchangeable being has *no actuality*' (Ph 132).

Except for this funereal, aleatory waste, to which Mallarmé will consecrate so many of his poems, the affair here comes *full circle*. The ascensional limit redistributes the splace and the outplace in the fusion of Glory. Seated to His own right side, God (the Son) is no more than the immutable intercessor for the tribunal of God (the Father). The revolution is dissolved into the State. The splace, for its part, declares this lure of being illuminated from within by force, as for those who fetishize the socialist State.

Such a stopping point and such a circle are only the advantages of the imaginary and of theology. To enjoy them to the fullest, the heretics must be burned. Which is, it must be admitted, quite real.

3

Indeed, our relapses 'to the right and left' have obviously marked the whole ideological history of Christianity.

$A_p(A_p) = P$ is the reconvocation of the purely finite identity of the Son, the rejection of any torsion in the splace of the world. These are the heresies that underline unilaterally the humanity of Christ, his exteriority to divine transcendence. In short, the heresies that give in to the objective heteronomy of the finite and the infinite, and break with the axiom of Nicea—that God is the split identity of Father and Son. For Arianism, in fact, the Son is only the first in the hierarchy of beings that the Father engenders.

Naturally, this rationalist deviation 'to the right' annuls the essence of the Christian dialectical proposition.

Symmetrically, those who posit the reconvocation $A(A) = A$ unilaterally unfold the divine infinity, and reduce the determination $A_p(A)$, that is, the death of God as the finitude of the infinite (the Passion of Christ), to being nothing but a semblance, an appearance. The first in history of a long list of Gnostic heresies, Docetism, posits that the Son is *absolutely* divine, which prohibits him from having a real body, from truly dying on the Cross, from having a sexed and precarious being. It is only in appearance, for the fable's revelatory virtue, that God took on the figure of the finite. Gnostic radicality maintains an ironclad divergence between the original purity of the divine Father and the blemishes of sex, the world, and death. If God comes to *haunt* the world in order to indicate the true way, he cannot establish himself therein in his essence.

Obsessed by the pure and the original and violently inclined toward Manichaeism, this ultra-leftist heresy blocks the dialectical fecundity of the message just as much as the rational and peaceful hierarchical ordering proposed by the Arians.

In this respect, Hegel helps us establish the rule of the orthodoxies against the objective recurrence of the splace (Arianism, right-wing opportunism) as well as against the fanaticism of the outplace (Gnosticism, left-wing opportunism).

Against Liu Shaoqi and economic objectivity; against Lin Biao and ideological fanaticism.

Gnostics and Arians have not finished obstructing—and nourishing—the path of the new. Every party congress, like every council, speaks out against them.

4

Let us take a close look at the dialectical fragment in its religious instance. The following schema is in fact circular since at the end of it all we obtain only the pure scission of the Father and the Son as integral concept of the

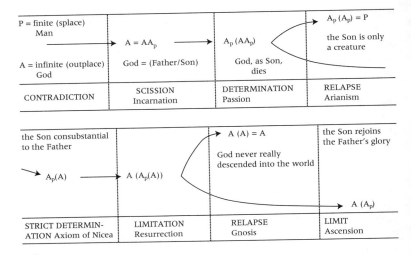

CONTRADICTION	SCISSION Incarnation	DETERMINATION Passion	RELAPSE Arianism

STRICT DETERMIN- ATION Axiom of Nicea	LIMITATION Resurrection	RELAPSE Gnosis	LIMIT Ascension

redemptive absolute. $A(A_p)$ ultimately does not exceed $A = (AA_p)$: it only leads back to it.

This is one of the great problems of our dialectical fragment. How does it continue? Where are we going? After all, the limit is not, and cannot be, only the result-concept of scission. The proletariat, subjectively constituted, is not the accomplishment of the internal concept of the bourgeoisie. Maoism cannot be reduced to the concept of revisionism.

We do not sit on the right side of the Father.

Hegel, on this point, must be divided once again. He must be divided in terms of the procedures he proposes for looping back the whole process.

To be brief, we will oppose (materialist) *periodization* to (idealist) *circularity*.

In order to put this opposition to work, let us place ourselves in the echo of three Hegelian statements:

a) 'The objective element, into which conscience exposes itself *qua* acting, is nothing other than the Self's pure knowledge of itself' (Ph 481–2, trans. modified).

b) 'The absolute Idea has shown itself to be the identity of the theoretical and the practical Idea' (L 824).

c) 'Action is the first inherent scission of the simple unity of the concept and the return out of this scission' (Ph 482, trans. modified).

Where do these three statements converge? They gesture toward the idea that action is what shows itself when one is in the vicinity of completion. The Hegelian absolute, which is the name of the procedure of looping back the dialectical process, turns out to be the fusion of the process as concept and the process as effectuation.

When in any active reality the reflection upon its own history comes to the surface, it is because this reality has run its course. There is nothing left but to absolve it: the absolute gives it its blessing.

This is the reason why Minerva's bird, the owl of patient knowledge, only takes flight at dusk, with its silent wing saluting the contrary light of the Truth.

If it does take flight, however, it is so as to go eat some mice. But where then is the mouse in the absolving benediction of the absolute?

This is where Hegel vacillates, namely, in the vicinity of this rock that we Marxists call the 'primacy of practice', and Lacan the real. A rock, let us specify this right away, which is neither clear nor obviously marked, and which is entirely similar to the one that Mallarmé talks about in *A Dice Throw*: 'some rock/ a false manor/ suddenly/ evaporated in mists/ which laid/ a limit on the infinite' (CP 175, trans. modified). Which gesture is evaporated in the mists, manor of the subject, if not the rare action about which nobody knows anything other than the real that it changes, the effect which unrepresents it, the infinite of the dream at last delimited?

At issue is the irreducibility of action. Hegel is standing on both edges of the knife—two dialectical matrices, as always. The general idea is that a dialectical sequence approaches its closure when the practical process carries its theory in its own wake, when it possesses in itself the active clarity of its temporal trace.

But this can be taken in two senses:

- Either in the sense of the theological circularity which, presupposing the absolute in the seeds of the beginning, leads back to this very beginning once all the stages of its effectuation, its alienation, its going-outside-itself, and so on, are unfolded. Thus, the dead Son reintegrated into the divisible immanence of the Father *completes* the world-concept of the Christian God, which is the holiness of the Spirit.
- Or in the sense of the pure passage from one sequence to the other, in an irreconcilable, unsuturable lag, where the truth of the first stage gives itself to begin with only as the condition of the second as *fact*, without leading back to anything other than the unfolding of this fact.

19

In the periodizing (or spiralled) view, we are allowed to say that the second sequence sets in when the conditions for the theoretical assessment of the first are accumulated. However, we must add that the very existence of this assessment is purely practical. All that is needed is for one of the terms of the new contradiction, the one whose outplace the splace was unable to *keep* hold of, to become the bearer of the intelligibility of the preceding sequence.

It is here, we shall see later on, that it comes about as subject.

But, of course, the emphasis then falls entirely on discontinuity, even on failure. Thus, Lenin's Bolshevik party is certainly the active bearer of an assessment of the failures of the Paris Commune. This is what Lenin seals by dancing in the snow when power is held in Moscow in 1917 for one day longer than had been the case in Paris in 1871. It is the rupture of October that periodizes the Paris Commune, turning a page in the history of the world. And what took place was the Party as subject. It is the least of things to say, with Hegel, that it 'exposes itself *qua* acting' or that it is the 'first scission'—from the Mensheviks, no doubt. To say that it is the unity 'of the practical and the theoretical Idea' is what will be repeated ad nauseam in the time of Stalin: the party is the fusion of Marxist theory and the real workers' movement.

But that still does not work out quite yet. It does not work out very well. Because in all this, we have produced *only one term* of the new sequence: the one that 'detains' the balance sheet of the preceding sequence. And, thus isolated, it is the Hegelian absolute, now no longer the outplace of a splace, but quite properly the space of places.

Indeed, circularity is nothing other than the fact of this annulment—the outplace finds a space in the place.

How to think of the gap between the periodization and the circle without producing a pure centre?

Throughout the world the Third International has sung the paean of the 'just and glorious' parties, simply because they were the party. At the stage where we are at—that of the Cultural Revolutions—we see better what a rat's nest the party of the Third International can also be, to the point where it becomes exemplarily unjust and without glory, in the form of the new bureaucratic state bourgeoisie.

The underlying philosophy for accepting such trajectories amounts to positing the splace as the general foundation of the dialectic, of which the outplace is the motor, but only fictively speaking. The place from which the outplace was excluded—the index from which it was purified—comes back to it at the end of the journey. Then the mystery of lack is retrospectively unveiled: within the splace there was the unaffected, *supernumerary* index, which the outplace turns to its advantage at the end. There was the right hand of the Father, as invisible place from which the outplace took its appearance of the excluded, whereas in its essence it is much rather the founder of all inclusion.

Now, nothing in the real corresponds to this machinery. Nobody has ever encountered such circles, without their failing and their inflating at the same time being the ironic stigmata of their scant reality.[5]

May this serve as an invitation, once this structural trajectory is completed and now that Hegel has been given the proper salute, for us to take things up again from zero. For we must think periodization through to the end. We must keep steadily out of place.[6]

This is not feasible without the redoubling of the place by that which is no longer of its order and which is no longer spatially figurable.

That is to say, force after place.

The real is the impasse of formalization; formalization is the place of the forced pass of the real

February 4, 1975

One, multiple, two—What is a contradiction?—Base and motor

1

Dialectics states that there is the Two, and intends to infer the One from it as a moving division. Metaphysics posits the One, and forever gets tangled up in deriving from it the Two.

There are others, like Deleuze, who posit the Multiple, which is never more than a semblance since positing the multiple amounts to presupposing the One as substance and excluding the Two from it. The ontology of the multiple is a veiled metaphysics. Its mainspring comes from Spinoza: first, affirmative substance, then the multiple that unfolds itself in the latter without ever becoming equal to it, and whose unifying nature one can pretend to have bracketed. This is only a feint. In the case of Spinoza, who is truly great, the spectre of the Two passes through the attributes, thought and extension. But in accordance with the beginning, this apparition must be rescinded: '[A]n absolutely infinite being is necessarily defined [. . .] as an entity which consists of infinite attributes.'[7] The fact that human beings have access to the true only by the adequate connection of the idea and the thing, ultimately of the soul and the body, and can think Substance only in the double attributive infinity of extension and thought, attests exclusively to their limitation: this Two is an impairment of the multiple. The presupposed One only has the effect of the integral, infinite multiplicity, the infinity of infinites. It is at this price that the

Cartesian problematic of the subject can be made to disappear—something for which Althusser so strongly credited Spinoza.

For me, this 'process without a subject' of the multiple is the pinnacle of the One.

We have deduced the 'there is the Two' from Hegel, all negation set aside, according to the term and its index of placement, according to the out-place and the splace. And we hit upon a circle: if the two depends only on the division between the thing and the placed thing, we certainly engender the precious process of scission, determination, and limit—but only to wind up occupying the impasse of the return to self, to discover that either we are stopped up, or we have to assume the inaugural presence of the result, the secret lack towards which everything moves: we are in a theodicy.

How is it that the real passes beyond? How is it that it periodizes, rather than running in circles? 'To encircle' is said of barrels, and before it was said of suitcases. The voyage of the real is sometimes without baggage, and, according to Saint Luke, the old cask does not exclude the new wine that must be poured into it.

If, as Lacan says, the real is the impasse of formalization, as we saw when we ran up against the limit as return, we must venture from this point that formalization is the im-passe of the real.

The algorithm scission-determination-limit, with its deviations to the right and to the left, is the truth of the structural dialectical sequence but only up to the point where this impeccable formalism is summed up in the 'do not trespass' that orders a return.

We need a theory of the pass of the real, in the breach opened up by formalization. Here, the real is no longer only what can be lacking from its place, but what *passes through by force*.[8]

And there is no other way of grasping this excess than to return to the Two.

2

What is a contradiction? We shall break the concept down into three parts, a work in which Mao will be our guide.

1. A contradiction is first of all some Two, that is, a *difference*. Difference will be strong or weak, depending on whether its terms are violently heterogeneous, or merely distinct.

The weakest difference is precisely that of places, the one that P distributes between A_{p1} and A_{p2}. Or, better yet, it lies in the gap of writing, between A and A, that is, the same named twice and, thus, other than itself.

The strongest difference does not exist. This is a case, familiar from Leibniz, in which there exists a minimum, but no maximum. Relative to the conflictual field, the major difference is that in which one of the terms affirms itself only by destroying the other, not only in its manifestation (in the way a true discourse destroys a false discourse), but in its support (in the way the proletariat destroys the bourgeoisie, all the while destroying itself, by the way, which is a point worth noting to which we will have occasion to return).

This is what Mao calls an antagonistic contradiction.

2. A contradiction does not concern a numerical, indifferent Two, but the Two connected in division, the Two linked in a process. Difference is implicated *qua correlation*. This is the principle of the unity of opposites, which does not register any fusion of the Two into a third, but posits the One of the movement of the Two, the One of their effective divergence.

The minimal correlation lies in observing the scission, the pure and simple position of the Two as a processual unity. That is: this is *one* contradiction, a unity of opposites; this two is the division-in-the-act of the One. Much stronger is the correlation contained in the theme of the *struggle* of opposites, which designates a process of destruction that engages the identity of each term in the dislocation from the one from which it splits off. Struggle means correlation as the ruin of the One.

The simple class contradiction is a permanent structural fact, which can be mapped economically (weak correlation); the class struggle is a process under particular conditions, entirely political in essence, which is not deducible from the simple weak correlation. To confuse the class contradiction with the class struggle, to practise the correlative indistinction of the contradiction, is the philosophical tendency of economism, of workerism, of somniferous Marxism for the lecture hall.

3. A contradiction is not the equilibrium of the Two, but on the contrary the law of its inequality. The principle of dissymmetry is essential. Mao concentrates this in the doctrine of the principal aspect of the contradiction.

THE PLACE OF THE SUBJECTIVE

Asymmetry itself can be merely an invariance of *position*: one term is dominant, another subjugated. One term fixes the game of assigned places; the other must subject itself to it.

However, the fully developed version of the theory of the principal aspect is the one that considers the transformations. The essence-in-becoming of the asymmetry is the inversion, not the invariance, of position. It is the advent, centred on the outplace, of a splace overthrown. It is the logic of reversal, not that of inclusion.

Thus, in its three components—difference, correlation, and position—the concept of contradiction is made divisible. We can legitimately inscribe in it a dialectical bipolarity, according to whether the contradiction is 'weak' (structural) or 'strong' (historical). This is recapitulated in the following table:

COMPONENTS OF THE CONCEPT	DIVISION OF THE CONCEPT	
	structural contradiction	*historical contradiction*
difference	weak (difference of place)	strong (qualitative heterogeneity)
correlation	weak (scission)	strong (struggle)
position	invariant asymmetry	reversible asymmetry

Every real dialectical process entangles a structural contradiction and a historical contradiction, *affecting the same terms*. The second is anchored in the first. This anchorage (purely metaphorical, at the point where we are now) is the nodal point of the question of the subject.

3

Take for instance the political subject. It will require several more months in order for us to find clarity in this. Let us build a portico in the style of the nineteenth century.

What characterizes a capitalist society as such? The question can be handled in terms of two universal contradictions—with universal here meaning nothing other than the historical course, today still

25

prehistorical, of humanity—under which some ordinary social body can be subsumed:

- the contradiction, called fundamental, between productive forces and social relations of production;
- the contradiction, called principal, between the antagonistic social classes.

The specification of the *fundamental* contradiction gives us a definition constructed in the following manner: capitalist is any social formation in which the private appropriation of the means of production tends to constitute a barrier to the necessary and growing socialization of the productive forces. Under capitalism, the competitive dispersion of property (the multiplicity of subjects-profits) enters into a restrictive collision with the process of the organic concentration of the means of production. There you have, the classics say in one voice, what constitutes the base of the social history of humanity. All the rest is superstructure.

The specification of the *principal* contradiction provides us with an entirely different definition of capitalism. Capitalist is any society in which the central class conflict, the one that organizes political life, opposes the bourgeoisie to the proletariat. Such is, the classics state unanimously, the motor of the social history of humanity. The rest is ideology.

Base and motor. Two contradictions, two definitions, a single object—capitalism—and a single doctrine—Marxism.

This would be an aporia, except that *the working class forms a knot*. The class plays an active part both in the first definition, where it is the principal productive force, and in the second, where, in the guise of its political unity and under the name thus conquered of the proletariat, it confronts the bourgeoisie.

Thus, *the definition of capitalism ultimately leads to the divided definition of the working class*. This confirms that any society whatsoever is indeed defined by the split identity that pertains to its real subject, which makes a knot therein.

We are only apparently confronted with the choice of saying that the working class is designated either as a place in the relations of production or as the concentration of all antagonism to the bourgeoisie. Taken in isolation, the first designation leads directly to the result that the class, which would exist only in the factory, confines its subjectivization to the gloomy protestations of trade unionism, or its variants. The second, antagonism, detached from all anchoring in the process of production, makes one believe that cutting open the belly of an empirical bourgeois with the tip of the terrorist pick weakens the dictatorship of Capital.

In truth, terrorism and trade unionism are the heads and tails of the dialectic abolished by no dice throw whatsoever. They are separate in identical ways.

Class, apprehended according to the dialectical division of its dialecticity, means partisan political action anchored in the productive historicity of the masses.

I repeat: it is fitting to think of class as antagonistic party and as productive mass in revolt.

The whole point is to know how all this works together, because it is this working-together that *is* class. This entails nothing less than to make the rectifiable singularity of politics rise up in the real movement of history.

Productive place and antagonistic politics, worker and proletarian, history and politics: here one will recognize the structural and historical sides of our table, in their subjective complicity.

This becomes clear if one refers back to the two inaugural contradictions.

The fundamental contradiction—relations of production/productive forces—only reveals to us the arrangements of places, quantities, and invariants (in itself, this contradiction, which is tendential, does not reverse anything). It is the structural side of things.

For its part, the principal contradiction—bourgeoisie/proletariat—has all the attributes of history:

- strong difference (the subjective project of the proletariat, that is, communism, cannot be represented by the bourgeoisie);
- class struggle, and not a simple binary distribution of the social;
- reversible asymmetry, within the problematic of the revolution.

The fully deployed thought of capitalist society organizes the subjective unity of the structural and the historical in the action of the proletariat, tying together the contradiction of contradictions—from productive force to class party—in which the dialectic is fulfilled.

Any subject whatsoever and first of all we ourselves, when it occurs to us to come into being as subjects—which, fortunately, is quite rare—require the stumbling encounter of the base and the motor.

As for knowing which one of the two is principal, the principal or the fundamental, the motor or the base, we can orient our thinking by meditating on this sentence from Lenin: 'Politics is the concentration of the economy.'[9]

Even, I would say, when it is a matter of libidinal economy, the economy of the drives.

Every subject is political. This is why there are few subjects and rarely any politics.

Hegel: 'The activity of force is essentially activity reacting against itself'

March 4, 1975

The enigma of correlation—Force: from active/reactive to qualitative expansion—The Whole, force, and the interior/exterior entanglement

1

We focus our efforts on the correlation, which is the enigma of contradiction. You can sense that correlation, insofar as it unites the opposites, introduces a contradiction within the contradiction.

Lenin says that the whole notion of the dialectic is summed up in the principle of the unity of opposites. This is true enough. Only, by limiting oneself to this formula, one places the whole dialectic precisely in a frame that denies it. After all, when taken too firmly in their unity, the contraries reveal only a secondary contrariness between them, a contraried contrariness.

Note that if we remain on this structural side of the enigma, the latter dissolves, which is quite agreeable. Correlation designates, then, nothing other than the Two as such. You have the One, insofar as you have only *this* Two.

That is, based on the simple inspection of the splace and of what it keeps outside of itself (out of place), you posit the unity of the process as exclusion. There is *this*, of which *that* is not.

The obvious objection is that on this account, the One of the contradiction is quite uniformly reabsorbed into the One of the splace. This is exactly like saying that the unity of the contradiction bourgeoisie/proletariat poses no problem, since it is the historical being of . . . bourgeois society, which is in fact governed by this contradiction. As outplace, the proletariat comes to be of a piece with the place. The one of its unity with the other is the other as Whole.

Put differently, the unity of the signifying chain where the Lacanian subject shows up, insofar as it enacts the unity of repetition and the drive, must be read as the compulsion to . . . repeat.

The structural is weak before the one of splace ('*Y a d'l'un*', Lacan said. 'There's such a thing as One'[10]). This is a dialectical materiality without leverage.

In 'Marxist' politics, especially in our context, there are those who hold on strongly to this weakness. They adore studying the 'laws' of bourgeois society and inferring from them what the proletariat is, and what it must 'do'. What eludes them is the fact that 'proletarian society', if one can risk such an unimaginable expression, or socialism, which they claim to wish for with all their might, is just as much governed by the contradiction bourgeoisie/proletariat as bourgeois society is—a fact of which the cultural revolutions provide the tumultuous proof.

This proves that the unity of opposites is not what one believes it to be.

Look also at those Yankee psychoanalysts of the *belle époque* who, in an entirely militaristic spirit, finding the ego of their patients too weak, proposed to 'strengthen its defence mechanisms'. Where the devil did they lodge the unity of the attacker—this deplorably asocial id—and the defender—the ego of affable normalities—if not in the normative path of this normality, that *way of life* that is not for nothing called *American*?

As for the Russians, they came up with this surprising turn of the One: being the State of the whole people, their machinery of old men knows of no other dissidence than that of the mentally insane. Whence the hospital as the sole place of the outplace.

But enough of these horrors.

To think correlation all the way through, we must bring out the whole enigma of the unity of opposites. It is only insofar as the opposites are heterogeneous or unalignable, that is, to the precise extent that there is no convivial place of the splace that solicits the outplace, that there exists a dialectical unity, one which does not make any Whole out of what it ties together.

To distinguish the One from the Whole: such is the simple and supreme proposal. Bear in mind that in this gap lies the whole question of the Subject.

This is why at this point we are faced with a severe expository problem: the correlation of the heterogeneous cannot be schematized. It can barely even be expressed. Every schema distributes a series of places and leads us back to structures; every discourse fixes the splace of the very thing that it passes over in silence.

The effects of the whole and of places, wherein the One of the contradiction, posited only according to one of its sides, becomes altered, undermine representation.

No injection of colours can make the schema of the dialectical sequence into a complete presentation of correlation, of A_p, through which the term (the outplace) is affected, or infected, by its specific contrary (the splace). Strong correlation, which the word 'struggle' remits to its practicality, depends on an indirect investigation and on a concept without any representable assignation.

It is with the name 'force' that we shall cover what overdetermines the exclusion from any place in which the outplace lies revealed.

2

What is it that can put two heterogeneous qualities into correlation? Only their reciprocal application as forces indifferent to anything other than their own expansion.

Correlation means force against force. It is the *relation of forces*.

Let us set aside right away the relapse or deviation of this still obscure idea. If one launches into the theme that an 'active' force restrains and obstructs a 'passive' (thus, re-active) force, one falls back into the statism of asymmetry. The abstraction of the pair active/passive once again dissolves the qualitative heterogeneity. The second (reactive) force is only determined, negatively, by the first: it is still the splace that fixes the place of the outplace.

A striking example of this relapse is the purely antirepressive conception of the politics of the people. People are 'mobilized' because they suffer too much mistreatment. Brutalized by what turns out to be, fundamentally, the only active force of the political field: the State, the boss, the cop. These wicked entities, suddenly, exaggerate their evil designs. The great battle cry 'Down with repression!' can be heard. The petit bourgeois is boiling with indignation.

Note that he is right and there is a good chance that in fact these 'exaggerations'—which the people permanently suffer in their depths—may bring the petit bourgeois out of his chronic dejection, or his complacency.

Yet the philosophy behind all this comes up short, because it denies at bottom any active autonomy, any real independence, any affirmative political virtuality, to what rises up in the guise of the enraged rebel of good faith. 'Down with repression' leads no further than to a *placed* reactive. The force of the people is here the flat shadow cast by the horrors of the State, and the conflictual correlation remains caught in the unifying weakness of the structural.

How, in the echo of the great antirepressive vituperation, will I be able to establish my capacity to *repress the repression*? Therein lies the key to understand everything that otherwise turns sour according to the theme of disenchantment.

We must come to understand that what raises me up reactively against the active of the Other must also be the active of a force in which the Other is no longer represented. Even if it is required by the adverse power in its repressive excess, the force that rises up in revolt against this repression is itself in interior excess over this requisitioning.

This is what Hegel understands with a definitive sharpness.

3

It will be appropriate here to read in its entirety one of the strongest passages from the Great Logic: the chapter titled 'The Essential Relation', which suffices to say that it concerns the enigma of correlation.

For starters, here is a passage where Hegel expressly develops the idea that the essence of the reactive must be the active interiority, unless we fall back on this side of the 'essential relation', that is, unless we fall short of the strong correlation:

> This process then in which an impulse is exerted upon one force by another force, the first force *passive* receiving the impulse but then again passing over from this passivity into activity, this is the return of force into itself. It expresses *itself*. The expression is reaction in the sense that it posits the externality as its own moment and thus sublates its having been solicited by another force. (L 523)

Everything is here: it is when force posits 'externality as its own moment' that it gains access to a qualitative correlation centred on itself, whose heterogeneity is irreducible to the face-to-face confrontation of forces. It is when the people erect their vision of the adversary as an internal figure of their own politics that they 'sublate' the antirepressive dependence, excluding themselves from any inclusion and proceeding to an affirmative scission.

To think correlation is to think force as acting and, thus, as grafted onto the other force, but according to its irreducible quality, for which henceforth the splace is no more than the mediation *to be destroyed*.

This whole chapter from Hegel, even if it is sometimes idealistically hesitant, can serve as a recapitulation of our endeavour.

Let us look at how it is constructed.

The three parts are successively:

1. The problematic of the whole and the parts
2. Force
3. The exterior and the interior

This is our plan as well, for the part-whole relation is nothing other than a theory of the splace, in which it turns out that, in structural terms, every contradictory correlation is only an exclusion, an out-place, whose principle of unity is inclusion (the part as that which is of the whole).

Force, as we have seen, comes to overdetermine the unifying impasse to which the structure of inclusion in the whole leads back, by the irreducible position of qualitative interiority in the confrontation of forces.

In a striking anticipation of Lacan, Hegel seizes this impasse in the form of the pulsation, the vacillation, and the alternating eclipse:

> Now in so far as this [existent] is a part it is not a whole, not a composite, hence a *simple*. But the relation to a whole is external to it and therefore does not concern it; the self-subsistent is, therefore, not even in itself part; for it is part only through that relation. But now since it is not part it is a whole, for there is only this relation of whole and parts present and the self-subsistent is one of the two. But as a whole, it is again composite; it again consists of parts, and *so on to infinity*. This infinitude consists solely in the perennial alternation of the two determinations of the relation, in each of which the other immediately arises, so that the positedness of each is the vanishing of itself. (L 518)

If one rules out force, this being-posited whose essence is to disappear in a perennial alternation, this vanishing term in which the dialectic of the whole is sutured, is the destiny of the outplace (here posited from the start as part), which only finds a place by excluding itself from it as autonomous, and it is equally the destiny of the splace (here, the whole), which only accepts the outplace by cancelling itself out entirely, since it is what governs the locations.

Thus it is confirmed that the only form of process tolerated by the structural dialectic is the infinite vacillation of what *is* only for the sake of nonbeing and of what *is not* for the sake of being. Such is the correlation conceived of as pure scission, since to say that the two are one makes them no longer two, and if there are two of them, it is as two times one, and thus the One is Two, and so on.

This is, by the way, a very important process. A consequential thinking of the vanishing term is the realistic apogee of the structural dialectic.

Yet, Hegel would not be able to stop there, much less so in that he seeks—this is the error of his truth—a circular completion. Hence, by suddenly adding on force, he pretends to engender it from the oscillation, whereas force is only the latter's essential, originary, and undeducible overdetermination.

Force is what keeps the parts in the movement of the whole. It is the non-numerical quality of the whole, its consistency that cannot be dissipated in the variety of the parts. Of the whole, it engenders no longer the functioning according to the regime of the splace—the distribution of the place of the parts—but the mobile consistency, the unification in the act.

The theory of force is tantamount to a theory of the historical side of the dialectical correlation, the side of its activity-as-one, anchored in (and not, as Hegel pretends to believe, deduced from) the correlation-in-eclipse of the system of places.

4

This historicity of correlation is deepened in an investigation of the Hegelian trinity, which posits *first* 'the conditionedness of force', that is, its pure essence of correlation. Force is only thinkable as activity relative to another force, and this in its very being: 'the conditionedness through another force is thus *in itself* the act of force itself' (L 521). The notion that the correlation is an 'act' or a 'making' is the unrepresentable knot of the question.[11] Scission as the locus of forces posits the radical anteriority of practical existence over the intelligibility of the correlation.

Secondly, Hegel clarifies, as we saw, the interpretation of correlation in terms of activity and passivity under the name of 'solicitation of force'. He shows its interior active basis, with passivity being only an appearance, a derived empirical correlation.

In the finest part of his analysis, Hegel posits that if force is essentially active in its correlation to the other, then the result is that what conditions it, which at first appears as the other force, the exterior, is in reality interior to it. The movement by which force unfolds itself towards the exterior, against the other force, is much rather governed by the *expansive wrenching away from itself*.

It is by realizing its interior unity, by purifying itself of its determination (of its division) by the bourgeoisie, that the working class projects itself expansively in the destructive battle against the imperialist splace. 'Solicited' by bourgeois oppression, it only acts as force, and only enters into a combative correlation with the adversary, by determining itself *against itself*, against the internal form of its former impotence.

And, likewise, an individual only arrives at his or her singular force within the given circumstances by entering into conflict with the network of inert habits to which these circumstances previously confined him or her.

The unrepresentable internal mainspring of the correlation is the pure capacity for expansive unity of a heterogeneous quality.

Or, as Hegel says, 'the activity is essentially [activity] reactive *against itself*' (L 523).

This dimension of wrenching itself away from itself, as interior exteriorization, if you will, is what Hegel calls—this is his *third* articulation—'the infinity of force'. To speak of force in its infinity is to speak of action as correlation; it is to name the primacy of practice. 'The infinity of force' is nothing other than the axiom of Goethe's Faust: 'In the beginning was the Deed.'[12]

This infinity of exteriorization leads to the final dialectic of the chapter, where the exterior and the interior become entangled:

> Outer and inner are determinateness posited in such wise that each of these two determinations not only presupposes the other and passes over into it as into its truth, but, in so far as it is this truth of the other, remains *posited as determinateness* and points to the totality of both. (L 525)

At this point, a Lacanian eye will discern the crucial arrival of the topology of the subject, figured in non-orientable surfaces, such as the Möbius strip. For us, this is tantamount to recognizing that in the logic of forces splace and the outplace are correlated in such a way that it is no longer possible to posit the second as the simple exterior-excluded of the first.

In the logic of forces, the unity of opposites is not an orientable correlation, and therein consists its historical essence, even though a subjacent (structural) orientation is precisely that with respect to which the non-orientable can be delimited.

Likewise, the proletariat as political class—as force—is linked to the bourgeoisie in a wholly historical unity-of-struggle, which cannot be distributed into the domains of the social whole and which structures the same being—the people—without prohibiting, but actually requiring, that we orient the class position in its *placed* groundedness, that is, in the social relations of production.

The fact that this topological unity of opposites, which under the rule of force brings about the correlation of interior and exterior, is for Hegel nothing less than 'the unity of essence and existence' (L 529), or what he calls 'actuality', which constitutes the pivotal transition in all of the Great Logic, is a telling sign of its importance.

For the materialist dialectic, when one is led astray in the labyrinth of force, inside and outside, shadows and fog, there where space provides for neither place nor lack of place, it is the Subject—this Minotaur bereft of any Theseus—that one comes across.

It is then that every subject surpasses its place by force, inasmuch as its essential virtue lies in being disoriented.[13]

Subjective and objective

April 15, 1975

Division of force—Spinoza and Malebranche—Stalin—The transmission
of the new in the sciences and the nonsciences—Nonlove among
politicians and psychoanalysts—May 1968—The bourgeoisie makes
politics—Periodization—The Hegelian opera

1

Force is its own affirmative expansion, but placed within the overarching
structural aspect of the other force: whether it rules over the unity of the
splace (force in the position of the State, or of the symbolic) or reveals
the outplace (force in the position of the revolution, or of the real).

This is our to and fro method. No sooner have we tracked down the
historicity of the contradiction, the unalignable quality of its terms, their
mutual strangeness to each other, than we must quickly ground all this in
the ordered soil of the structures, unless we let ourselves evaporate into
the metaphysics of desire, that is, the substantial and nomadic assumption of the outplace from which place itself comes to be inferred. This
assumption marks the boundary of the dialecticity of the dialectic 'to the
left' (lefty deviation, rather than leftist). Nothing new on this end ever
since Spinoza.

The rightists, for their part, have never left the splace, whose description fills them with joy. The most generous watchmaker in the family
is without contest Malebranche. Spinoza and Malebranche, at bottom,
are the great purifiers of force. The Jew posits its unity, which is not the

whole—and one is supposed to make do with that. The Catholic pronounces its exhaustive mechanism, with its weight and counterweight, so that God may hear arising from his Creation—that outplace for which he made place—the morning bells of his Glory.

And so you have the significant austerity of the One versus the mirroring delights of the Whole.

Being Catholic *and* Jewish, force is impure. This is what put an end to metaphysics (not for nothing was there the procession in honour of pure Reason led by a few guillotines and lots of popular committees) at the dawn of the second conceptual modernity (the first one was consolidated with caravels, Greek texts, telescopes, and infinitesimal calculus).

Force is impure because it is always placed. The new of historicality is infected by the continuity of the structures. Something of the quality of force becomes homogenized with the splace, at least so as to figure therein its own abstraction and support the law.

There is the infinity of force and there is its finitude. This is not even, as in the case of Hegel, the experiential and circular inference from the one to the other.

Our take on this will be as follows: in any contradiction, force manifests its impurity by the aleatory process of its purification. The mode in which the subjected character of force unfolds itself, in its scission from its affirmative infinity, is itself a movement, in which force concentrates (or not) its qualitative identity, thus expansively tearing itself away from that which nonetheless persists in fixing its site.

There is no other definition of the political class party except to say that, in what can be a situation of extreme weakness and dilution, it must concentrate the historical project that is the force-of-class in person, namely, that which emerges out of place and smashes the imperialist splace.

This gives us some philosophical background adjusted to Stalin's declaration, the use of which is otherwise well known, that 'the party is strengthened by purging itself of opportunist elements.'[14] To say 'strengthened ' is an understatement. Invested in no operation other than that of splitting the force of the working class from its subjected figure, 'concentrating the correct ideas' (Mao), keeping itself maximally out of place, and destroying in itself all that is not the destruction of the splace, the party *is* purification.

This does not mean that it is pure, nor that it tends towards purity—any more than cutting off heads defines the essence of its action. On this bloody path, Stalin arrived at nothing but disaster. But the party operates at the juncture of itself and its impurifying dissipation, being as it is that which gives direction, at the heart of the class, to the unstoppable battle between the two paths, without any claim to existence other than the manifest proof of a denser quality, a more compact heterogeneity, a newer destructive and recomposing power.

At this juncture, the internal expansion of force sketches out the history of a contradiction, whereas the impurity brings it into alignment by prescribing its place, so that the first speaks to the *hor-* of the *horlieu* ('outplace') and the *es-* of the *esplace* ('splace'), and the second, to the *-lieu* and the *-place*. Mao gave this juncture a name whose simplicity is bewildering: struggle of the old and the new—a struggle which, he assures us, especially when he is readying himself to endorse the second Chinese revolution (called 'Cultural'), will pursue its course, including violently so, up to and including the time of the fallacious communist pacification, beyond classes and the State.

2

Struggle of the old and the new. The purification of force amounts to the concentration of its newness. Those 'right ideas' of the masses, which the Marxist party must 'concentrate', are necessarily new ideas.

It is quite a step into the dialectic to understand, in a non-trivial sense, that every rightness and every justice are, in principle, novelties; and that everything that repeats itself is invariably unjust and inexact.[15]

And yet, it is pointless to try to live without repetition.

The best image for this turning point can be obtained by comparing taught mathematics to invented mathematics. While the first apparently is merely the ordered display of the second, from the point of view of the dialectic we must consider taught mathematics to be inexact, giving us no idea at all of what mathematics is as a subjective and historical process.

What is taught is not mathematics but only its locus. Pedagogy delimits a splace, it is up to you to be out of place with respect to it, that is, to produce were it only one decisive theorem, one that provokes a thorough reshuffling—which is the only title that can be claimed for the mathematician, who is not to be confused, as Lacan would say, with the university professor of mathematics.

In short, what is not transmitted is precisely the process of qualitative concentration of this bizarre force by which all splaced mathematics becomes shot through with holes.

It is, moreover, perfectly obvious that every great scientific discovery amounts to a purification. What ruled was the impure, chaos, trickery; in comes an order that cannot be brought in line with former customs.

Every science forms a party: just look at their congresses.[16]

Will you say that *nothing* is transmitted on this side of things? No, you only have to read those great correspondences of the seventeenth century between Descartes, Fermat, Pascal, and others, for which the valiant Father Mersenne all by himself served as the postal administrator, in order to see that some newness is caught in the act and transmitted therein. Nevertheless, very often this happens by the defiant slant of what is kept silent, in the margin of the text, by the purely particular appearance of a hidden general principle. God knows that these masters of thought carry mistrust and silence to an extreme. Here the lightning bolt of disruptive communication kindles the dry branch of evasion.

All by themselves, these letters demonstrate that if the splace propagates itself by zeal, confidence, and love (as 'modern' pedagogues are wont to say), as much as by coercion, contempt, and coldness (as is common practice among the whipping priest-pedagogues of old England), the concentration of force requires rather, for its singular transmission, the reliance on allusion, tension, and an oblique form of polite mistrust, whose art reaches its peak among the classics. Indeed, it is an understatement to say that Descartes and Fermat, or Pascal and the shadow of Descartes, did not like each other. It is through their essential nonlove that the force of truth circulated.

People do not like each other very much either in the great political parties, which is something that a few naive people take to be the despicable effect of 'power struggles', when it is actually the ontological axiom of purifying unity that is thus gaining ground.

People do not like each other at all in psychoanalytic societies, especially when one puts them to the question of 'How is psychoanalysis transmitted?' There is a profound logic to this nonlove. It is what conveys the process of force and is punctuated, as is only to be expected, by exclusions, scissions, and excommunications. In the case of the psychoanalysts, it is at every instant that one is strengthened or weakened by purifying oneself of the opportunistic or revolutionary elements in one's midst.

In Lacan's *Ecole Freudienne de Paris*, this nodal point of 'How does one here receive the title of psychoanalyst?' which is what this School with a perfectly chosen name calls the pass, currently produces ferocious battles whose outcome, beyond the unfortunately inevitable death of its gigantic despot, one must expect to be the decline of this School into the mediocre anarchy of its im-passe.

The individual does not escape this fate. If it pleases you to come into being *qua* subject, you will be forced, as you well know, expressly and against all existing customs to found the party of yourself: harsh, concentrating force and the power of abnegation to an extreme point, and following its condition of existence which is not to love oneself too much. This is something that the classical moralists said once and for all, and first among them Pascal, one of our four truly great national dialecticians—the others being Rousseau, Mallarmé, and Lacan: 'The self is detestable' (*Le Moi est haïssable*). There is no need to go back over this.

At least, that is, if one wishes to coordinate within oneself the mass dimension (anger, indignation, frenzy, surprise, encounter, revolt, joy . . .), the dimension of the State (ways and customs, repetitions, sociability, familiarities, meals and sleepovers, cats and dogs . . .), and the dimension of the party (concentration of force, heroism, innovating continuity, purposeful work, scission from oneself, unity of a new type, courage).

This is demanded of nobody, and it is moreover impossible to decide. It happens, let us say, that '*it* makes a *subject*'.[17]

3

A definition: we will call *subjective* those processes relative to the qualitative concentration of force.

Let me emphasize that these are practices, real phenomena. The party is something subjective, taken in its historical emergence, the network of its actions, the novelty it concentrates. The institution is nothing but a husk.

Correlatively, we will call 'objective' the process whereby force is placed and is thus impure.

Inasmuch as it concentrates and purifies itself *qua* affirmative scission, every force is therefore a subjective force, and inasmuch as it is assigned to its place, structured, splaced, it is an objective force.

More exactly, we will say: the being of force is to divide itself according to the objective and the subjective.

If you take a bird's eye view of May '68, you will see in it a new and qualitatively irreducible breath or aspiration; you will see in it this exceptional and radically new point of concentration, which is the establishment of thousands of young intellectuals in the factories, together with the minimal apparatus for this concentration (the Maoist organizations). You will also see in it the enormous weakness of this concentration and this apparatus, the insurmountable dilution of the revolt into peaceful, protesting, infrapolitical figures.[18] You will see in it the defensive manoeuvre, for the sake of the fixity of the splace, comfortably agreed upon between representatives of the government and representatives of the unions, between Pompidou and Séguy. May '68 is really only a beginning, and continuing the combat is a directive for the long run.

You can thus observe, at one and the same time, the objective strength of force and its subjective weakness. Everyone in the strike and in the street for a precious, and in its own way, immortal commencement. But seven years later we are very few to hold up the subjective future and concentrated restricted action of all this, in the midst of the sepulchral atmosphere of the *programme commun* and the prayers of Mitterrand the undertaker.

This amounts to saying that the subjective aspect of our adversary's force is itself still in a fairly good state. This is something the revolutionaries never managed to understand. Most of them think they are the only subject and represent the antagonistic class to themselves as an objective mechanism of oppression led by a handful of profiteers.

The bourgeoisie is in no way reducible to the control of the State or to economic profit. On this point, too, the Cultural Revolution enlightens us, insofar as it designates the bourgeoisie in conditions wherein the industry has been entirely nationalized and the party of the proletariat dominates the State. The bourgeoisie makes politics, it leads the class struggle, and not only from the angle of exploitation, nor from that of coercion, whether it is legal or terrorist. The bourgeoisie makes a subject.[19] Where then does it do this? Exactly as with the proletariat: in the midst of the people, working class included, and I would even say, since we are dealing with the new state-bureaucratic bourgeoisie, the working class *especially* included.

The bourgeois imperialists are a handful, of course, but the subjective effect of their force lies in the divided people. There is not just the law of Capital, or the cops. To miss this point is to stop seeing the unity of the splace, its consistency. It is to fall back into objectivism, whose inverted ransom, by the way, is to make the State into the only subject—whence the anti-repressive logorrhoea.

We must conceive of imperialist society not only as substance but also as subject.

Thus far, however, we have only dealt with the subjective, which is not the subject, but rather its element or its genre.

The objective and the subjective divide the dialectic. If you take the two antagonistic forces (without forgetting their underlying articulation into splace and outplace), you can delimit within them an objective dialectic and a subjective dialectic, which together constitute the dialectic of force.

See the schema below, applied to the canonical example of the contradiction bourgeoisie/proletariat:

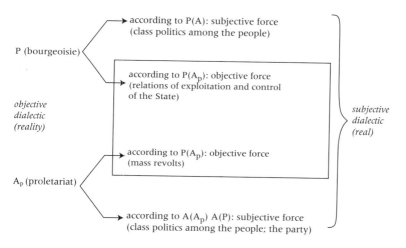

P (bourgeoisie)
- according to P(A): subjective force (class politics among the people)
- according to P(A_p): objective force (relations of exploitation and control of the State)

A_p (proletariat)
- according to P(A_p): objective force (mass revolts)
- according to A(A_p) A(P): subjective force (class politics among the people; the party)

objective dialectic (reality)

subjective dialectic (real)

The common objectivity subtends the life of the masses—oppressed and rebellious—in accordance with the axiom: 'Wherever there is oppression, there is rebellion.'[20] This is the objective dialectic, the way of the world, history—made by the masses, as we all know.

The subjective is politics, made by the classes in the masses.

Let it be said in passing: *to understand the distinction between history and politics, masses and classes, is exactly the same thing as understanding the distinction between the Whole and the One.* This is no trifling matter.

It is clear that the point of application of the bourgeois subjective force within the splace is intended to prevent the constitution out of place of the proletarian subjective force. The fundamental target of subjective activity is thereby to block the process of concentration (of purification) of the antagonistic force. It is a matter of maintaining the latter maximally diluted at all cost, even if this dilution is made up of innumerable revolts.

Here we must single out for condemnation the makeshift philosophy of the advocates of the 'convergence of struggles'. This geometric conception remains entirely within the objective assignation of force. You may 'coordinate' them as much as you like, but a sum of revolts does not make a subject. The geometric character of 'convergence' must be replaced with the qualitative character of concentration. A minimal and purified political heterogeneity is a hundred times more combative than a parliamentary armada of represented struggles. Convergence is the typical objectivist deviation, in which, once the work of subjective purification is spirited away, antagonism finds itself ill-advisedly dissolved.

Frankly, it must be said that convergence does the work of the adversary's subjective force.

At bottom, it is always in the interests of the powerful that history is mistaken for politics, that is, the objective is taken for the subjective. This is the natural element for the maintenance of their own subjective activity, which is applied so that no unaligned quality may come to concentrate itself to confront them.

There is no shortage of people under their thumb among the 'Marxists': All those who embroider their dispiriting niceties around a 'Marxism' reduced to the morose virtue of a 'science of history'.

Science of history? *Marxism is the discourse with which the proletariat sustains itself as subject.* We must never let go of this idea.

4

Let us return to this trait whereby the materialist dialectic sets itself apart from the Hegelian dialectic: it periodizes, while the other one makes circles.

We now have two tools in our possession to ground periodization, which is, after all, what defines the making of history—finding the right period could even be said to be history's exclusive task:

a) The terms of the contradiction are doubly determined: as to their place (splace/outplace) and as to their force.
b) Force is doubly determined: objective and subjective.

You will say to me: what does this have to do with periodization? Well, it does to the extent that we can formulate the twofold dialectical criterion of periodization:

- that splace be caught up in the destructive flagrancy of the outplace;
- that the subjective aspect of force attains a threshold in its qualitative concentration.

This is the double precondition for the advent of a subject-process.

Taking things from a distance, let us return to the Paris Commune, about which historians have always quarrelled to know whether it is the last of the 'archaic' workers' insurrections of the nineteenth century or the first of the 'modern' revolutions—which is prime evidence of the deficiency of their criteria.

As may be expected, given the existence of a double criterion, there are two assessments of the Commune in the Marxist tradition (aside from the possibility that a third is in preparation, via the Cultural Revolution: consequently, there will be four).

Marx's assessment (*The Civil War in France*) is in actual fact purely objective. It designates the Parisian action as the clarification of the immediate political objectives of the class *with regard to the State*. It is necessary to break the military and police machinery with their administrative appendix, without seeking to occupy them. It is necessary to put in place organs of power of a new type, and not merely to direct, by substitution, the old ones. In the Commune, Marx registers the heterogeneous quality of force as such, together with the limitation of a political dialectic articulated according to the sole logic of the dominant place, the place of power. Marx divides the expression 'taking power' according to place (one must dominate the adversary) and force (one must above all deploy the occupation of the dominant place in a different way and in accordance with a new quality). Thus we pass from the structural side of the dialectic to its historical side: the proletariat is not only the outplace of a place, it is the other force of a force.

Nevertheless, we still remain within the objectivity of force, or rather within the undivided unity of the objective and the subjective. Concerning the process of the concentration of force, whose weakness he evidently perceives (it is the weakness of the communard leadership, which is parliamentary and reactive), Marx does not propose any particular analysis susceptible of helping us move beyond such weakness. Marx goes no further than the first criterion of periodization (place and force).

It is Lenin's partisan activity, up to the victory of October, and even more so up to the crushing of the counter-revolution and its foreign support in the civil war, that brings about the second assessment. In this activity, starting with *What Is To Be Done?*, the subjective question plays a central part. Concentrating force is the very essence of Leninist work, which bases itself on the weaknesses and failures of the Commune, while Marx instead armed himself with the Commune's victories in order to modify, on a crucial point, the *Manifesto*.

Lenin draws a fourfold lesson from the crushing of the Commune:

1. It is necessary to practise Marxist politics, and not some local romantic revolt, whether workerist or populist.[21] The profound meaning of *What Is To Be Done?* is entirely contained in this difficult and original call: let us be absolutely and irrevocably political activists (meaning professionals, that goes without saying: who has ever seen amateur political leaders?).
2. It is necessary to have an overall view of things, in the national framework at least, and not be fragmented into the federalism of struggles.
3. It is necessary to forge an alliance with the rural masses.
4. It is necessary to break the counter-revolution through an uninterrupted, militarily offensive, centralized process.

And what of the party, the famous Leninist party, in the midst of all this? The party as the core of steel, an army moving with the rhythmic step of seasoned professionals? For Lenin, the party is nothing but the operator of concentration of these four requirements, the mandatory focal point for a politics. The party is the active purification of politics, the system of practical possibility for the assessment of the Commune. It is inferred from politics (from the subjective aspect of force). By no means does it come first. It is an aberration to read *What Is To Be Done?* as a theory of the party when it is a handbook of Marxist politics. With regard to the party as apparatus, what can be inferred is mixed and secondary. *What Is To Be Done?* is a theory of the subjective aspect of force, in the guise of a general call to political confidence.

It is not due to its institutional concerns but because of the demands of its Marxist political ambition that *What Is To Be Done?* entails a silent assessment of the Paris Commune.

Besides, it is curious to see that the explicit examination of the Commune carried out by Lenin in *The State and Revolution* follows an entirely different thread, which originates in Marx and is relative to the problem of the State: appearances notwithstanding, in that text we are dealing, through the return to objectivity, with a far less novel undertaking.

Every periodization must encompass its double dialectical time and thus—to stay with our example—contain October 1917 as the second and provisionally final scansion of the assessment. Whence the embarrassment of historians: according to the force/place relation, the Commune is new (Marx). According to the subjective/objective relation, it is October that is new and the Commune is that *edge of the old* whose practical perception, by purifying force, partakes in the engendering of its novelty.

It is highly probable that the Chinese Cultural Revolution has the same profile and that the question of the second time of its periodizing function is now open. The subjective question (how did the Cultural Revolution, mass uprising against the new bureaucratic state bourgeoisie, run into the problem of the reshaping of the party?) remains in suspense, as the key question for any Marxist politics today.

If Hegel makes a circle, it is because he always seeks a single time. As a matter of principle, he ignores the differed retroactions, even though he insidiously tolerates them in the details.

5

In Hegel's *Logic*, there is a chapter on objectivity. However, it is most instructive that this chapter should be located in the section titled 'Subjective Logic', where it follows the chapter on subjectivity and prepares for the one on the Idea. Objectivity, for Hegel, is the mediation between pure subjective formal interiority and knowledge. Here we see a flagrant idealist inversion, but that is not the essential point. The bottom line of the whole affair is that, in making objectivity arise from pure logical form, Hegel gives himself in advance the unity of the two criteria of periodization. Integrally referable to the formal subjective, which it dissolves and contains, objectivity all at once opens itself up to absolute knowledge. It is only the progressive filling of the exterior by the interior, the coming to light of the content of the form, according to the extenuation of form itself. The underlying conception remains that the subjective is the pure law of the splace by which the void exceeds itself into the outplace so as finally to become equal to the reflected totality. From that moment onward, place passes over into force according to the same movement by which the subjective passes into the objective, and the *unique* reflection of this movement is none other than the dialectic itself. Whence a principle of 'periodization' which, all in one piece, closes in on itself. It is the subject as circle who has the last word.

Thus the idealist dialectic fails to recognize the *discrepant double scission* that grounds any historical periodization.

Of course, Hegel is as always capable of locally forgetting his global forgetting. That the dialectical scansion implies the four terms of the double scission (place, force, subjective, objective), and not the three of alienation (position, negation, negation of the negation), is something he establishes in a famous passage from the chapter on the absolute Idea:

> If one insists on *counting*, this *second* immediate is, in the course of the method as a whole, the *third* term to the first immediate and the mediated. It is also, however, the third term to the first or formal negative and to absolute negativity or the second negative; now as the first negative is already the second term, the term reckoned as *third* can also be reckoned as *fourth*, and instead of a *triplicity*, the abstract form may be taken as *quadruplicity*; in this way, the negative or the difference is counted as a *duality*. (L 836)

To count the negative (or difference), which is the very principle of contradiction, not as simple universal, but as Two, and thus to establish the period as quadruple: such is the materialist intuition at this supreme point of Hegel's *Logic*. What is covered under the distinction between 'formal negative' and 'absolute negativity' is nothing less than the distinction of the subjective and the objective, as is to be expected, in inverted positions.

This intuition is immediately rescinded by the obsessive theme of the circular return to the beginning:

> It is in this manner that each step of the *advance* in the process of further determination, while getting further away from the indeterminate beginning is also *getting back nearer* to it, and that therefore, what at first sight may appear to be different, the retrogressive grounding of the beginning, and the *progressive further determining* of it, coincide and are the same. (L 841)

For the materialist, there is no beginning unless it is marked by a novelty that is undeducible from the periodizing closure. Progression and retroaction cannot be fused together. The position of the relation force/place does not permit one to deduce the scission of force according to the objective and the subjective: one must *wait* for the second time. But, precisely, Hegel is in no condition to wait for October 1917 in order to fix the eternal historical essence of the Commune. He must from the start take up his position at the end of time, whereby the circle is traced, in order to know who is who in the unity of the progressive and the retroactive.

One remains dismayed by the fine arrogance to which Hegel thenceforth bears witness. The transition from the subjective to the objective is one of the most tortuous exercises of the entire *Logic*. Since the subjective is purely formal (what else can it be before the objective?), one can find Aristotle's logic in it. It is thus a matter of deducing the theory of the physical world from the figures of the syllogism. The immediate reality of the existing thing, grasped in its scientific concept, must arise from the supreme formal figure, which is here the unfortunate disjunctive syllogism—the schema: A is B or C or D, but A is neither C nor D, therefore A is B—promoted to the status of nothing less than the supporting base of Hegelian circularity. The thickness of the fumes recalls those operatic stagings whereby the technicians blow smoke through the floorboard in order to allow for the fusion, in the midst of cloudy poetry, of the delicate passage from a military reception with chorus and elephants to a love-duo in nightgowns perched on the balconies of Venice. For example:

> The syllogism is *mediation*, the complete concept in its *positedness*. Its movement is the sublating of this mediation, in which nothing is in and for itself, but each term *is* only by means of an another. The result is therefore an *immediacy* which has issued from the *sublating of the mediation*, a *being* which is no less identical with the mediation, and which is the concept that has restored itself out of, and in, its otherness. This *being* is therefore a *fact* [*eine Sache*] that is *in and for itself—objectivity*. (L 704)

Subsequently, Hegel proposes his classification of the sciences, since objectivity, the suppression of the syllogism, quietly climbs the conceptual slope which goes from mechanics through chemistry to life as such.

Compared to this classification, Auguste Comte's is a miracle of materialist precision, especially if we consider that Hegel claims to deduce his without remainder from formal logic!

However, we will take comfort in this misfortune of the Hegelian circle, if we know how to draw our lesson from it with respect to the criteria for periodization and if we are able to think what is required in terms of divergence, between the opposition place/force and the opposition objective/subjective, for the clear arrangement of the paths of the subject.

And then, Hegel is certainly correct to write the following about the syllogism: 'If it is not thought a small matter to have discovered some sixty species of parrots, one hundred and thirty-seven species of veronica, etc., much less ought it to be thought a small matter to discover the forms of reason' (L 682).

In French 'Marxism', there is a plethora of people who, for lack of engagement with the syllogisms of action, insist on counting parrots. The result is that what they call 'ideological struggle' comes down to trying to take the place of those who count veronicas.

PART II

The Subject under the Signifiers of the Exception

Of force as disappearance, whose effect is the Whole from which it has disappeared

December 15, 1975

Definition of the structural dialectic—The Greek atomists—Logic of the clinamen—Chance—The vanishing term—What are the masses and what do they do?—The causality of lack

1

We confirmed that there exists no neutral dialectic that could be inserted into the eternal struggle between idealism and materialism. It is the dialectic itself that must be divided, according to the edge of its dialecticity, into its structural side and its historical side: logic of places and logic of forces.

In the pedagogy of this project—which disassembles and reassembles in its entirety the old fool's bridge of the relation Marx/Hegel—we propose that the formulation 'idealist dialectic', which one usually reels off to bad-mouth Hegel, be replaced by 'structural dialectic'.

It is first of all a matter of assigning Hegel's idealism (or Mallarmé's and Lacan's) not as much to the exterior perversion of a pure inner core so much as to the choice of the principal term in the correlation of opposites whose unity constitutes the dialectic's whole being.

Whence the following provisional definition of the structural dialectic:

a) The structural dialectic is certainly a form of dialectical thought (this is its materialist side) in the sense that, broadly speaking, it stems from two crucial ontological principles:

- the primacy of process over equilibrium, of the movement of transformation over the affirmation of identity;
- the primacy of the Two over the One (contradiction).

b) The structural dialectic has a tendency (this is its idealist side), first, to make the structural aspect of the dialectic prevail over its historical aspect, that is, place over force; and, second, within this very same primacy of the structural foundation, to make the theory of the splace, on the basis of its regulated universe, predominate over the emergence of the outplace.

As a result, we must register the perversion that from this moment on is introduced into the relation between the subjective and the objective, together with the tendency to undo every principle of periodization in favour of a circular closure.

The structural dialectic, by its choice of the prevailing terms, in the long run works only on one side of the concept of contradiction and, in my opinion, it is not the correct one.

I said before that there are three articulations to this concept of contradiction: difference, correlation, and position.

The structural dialectic privileges the weak difference over the strong difference. It tends to reduce any difference to a pure distance of position. This is its spatializing ambition, which works to the detriment of qualitative heterogeneity, for the latter, being as it is unschematizable, can be registered only in its temporal effect.

The structural dialectic prefers the correlation of pure exclusion, of split positionality, and of interchangeability, to that correlation which, under the name 'struggle of opposites', attempts to grasp the destruction that issues from a certain quality of force.[1]

The structural dialectic immobilizes the position of the terms into a symmetry, or into an invariant asymmetry, rather than seizing the becoming-principal of the secondary, the rupture of any splace by the explosion of its rule and the loss of principle of the initial position.

However, the structural dialectic does encounter the real as obstacle, which is the effective thought of the historical. It includes the latter, albeit in order to subordinate it and only when it is no longer a dialectic of the whole but a combinatory: a structuralism.

Structuralism is the internal 'rightist' temptation of such a dialectic, with the obscure and poetic effort of the likes of Mallarmé or Lacan consisting entirely in *not giving in* to this temptation—just as one does not give up on one's desire.

What characterizes the structural dialectic resides rather in the complex dissolving action by which, in the closest proximity to a contrarian real that rules it out, it is the authority of the structure that constantly ends up being re-established. What is essential lies in the lacunary incompleteness of the project and the pathos of silence in which the never-written Mallarméan Book meets the never-tied Lacanian knot. All in all, therein lies the never-abandoned respect for the real that, even at the highest point of its disavowal, comes through in these great idealists.

Here we find such a tension (whose hermetic cadence of writing, so often mocked by the envious reader, is the figure of a harsh sincerity) that it will never be a waste of our time to follow these heroes of nonbeing into the arcane secrets of their acidic dialectical alchemy.

Of the real, by dint of its torsion, they give us all the juice.[2]

2

From the start and then all the way to the end, they must all solve what we might very well call the three canonical problems of the structural dialectic—problems which, in many respects, make up the whole tradition of idealist modernity:

1. How to bring back a strong (qualitative) difference to its bare bones, the weak difference, or the difference of position, which undergirds it? This is the problem of the schematization of the unschematizable, of the flattening out, or of the chain effect.
2. How to make disappear whatever was needed, in matters of force, in order to proceed with this reduction? This is the problem of the vanishing term.
3. How can the nonbeing of the vanished force cause the movement of places and, better yet, their totality? This is the problem of the action of the structure, or the problem of the causality of lack.

Chain effect, vanishing term, causality of lack: let us add the splitting, which we will deduce later, and there you have a whole organized according to the sole clarity of a multiple of Ones.

The Greek atomists were the first in all this.

3

What difference can be stronger than the one between atoms and the void? The Greek materialists, to begin with, posit an absolute heterogeneity: on one hand, the discrete multiplicity of matter; on the other, the infinite continuity of the nothing.

Hegel admires the impetus that 'makes this simple determinateness of the one and the void the principle of all things, deriving the infinite variety of the world from this simple antithesis and boldly presuming to know the former from the latter' (L 166).

This impulse behind the structural abstraction, though, immediately comes up against its own force as the obstacle presented to it by the real.

If the atoms stand in a radical qualitative exteriority to the void; if no atom is nameable otherwise than by this exteriority of principle—to be an atom, and not part of the void—then it is clear that *nothings happens*. The atoms remain suspended, as the dust of identity, in that which serves as their ground, vain stars in the night sky devoid of any constellation.

Here the difference is so strong that no Whole can make its way in any process whatsoever.

Now, the atomistic hypothesis has no aim other than to compose the real of the Whole. So here it is running out of gas.

One will therefore argue—this is the second moment of the affair—that the void engenders the movement of the atoms. With this gesture, which breaks with the pure principle of qualitative and reciprocal exclusion, a correlation, or even a position, begins to be sketched out. The void is causal: it splaces, if not the atoms themselves, then at least their trajectories.

Hegel makes a big thing out this small move, rapidly drawing the blanket toward his own concept of the negative:

> . . . with the first thinkers the atomistic principle did not remain in this externality but besides its abstraction had also a speculative determination in the fact that the void was recognized as the source of movement, which is an entirely different relation of the atom and the void from the mere juxtaposition and mutual indifference of these two determinations . . . The view that the void constitutes the ground of movement contains the profounder thought that in the negative as such there lies the ground of becoming, of the unrest of self-movement—in which sense, however, the negative is to be taken as the veritable negativity of the infinite. (L 166)

Certainly, the appearance on stage of correlation is always the sign of dialectical and even, if you want, of speculative profundity. Hegel keenly observes that the most important operation of atomism lies in this relaxing of the strong difference of atoms/void, and not in their position as mutual obstacle.

If there are two, the principles leave entirely open the question of the One divided by them. This is where one awaits the dialectician.

Is movement this One of the correlation? Surely, for if the void is the cause of movement, then this applies equally to all the atoms. Otherwise, these atoms would have different relations to the void regarded as cause. But this is impossible, in light of the fact that, *qua* atoms, they constitute the opening principle, simply defined by not being the void, period. Therefore, all are in any case identical with regard to the void.

It is thus necessary to posit that the atoms all move together eternally and according to parallel trajectories, at variable speeds.

This rain of falling stars constitutes a disaster, which does not add up to a Whole either.[3]

It must even be admitted that this 'movement' is perfectly null, for lack of a reference point with which to mark it—the simultaneous and isotropic vection of an infinity of atoms, without the shadow of a doubt, being equivalent to their absolute immobility.

Once again, nothing happens. Even by subjecting the atoms to the efficacy of the void as motor, it remains the case that the differential heterogeneity of the principles is kept in a sterile rigidity. Strong difference (actually, absolute difference) serves at once as a halting point.

But there is something and not nothing. This is what the atomists turn into the obstacle of the real over and against the rigid duality of their principles.

In order to pass from the duality of principles (atoms/void) to the one of the world as system of wholes (things), one must obviously *filter the strong difference into a weak difference*. One must combine the atoms amongst themselves, instead of eternally launching them, like Mallarmé's unthrowable dice, into the void of their identical nonbeing.

Here we are approaching a crucial operation of the dialectic, namely: the linking together of a chain. This means passing from a strong difference, wherein the quality of the real *qua* force makes itself felt, to a homogeneous combinatory space, wherein a process becomes composed with terms of *the same kind*.

In ancient atomism, this is what is called the *clinamen*.

4

An atom is deviated, the world can come into being. The sudden oblique-ness of a trajectory interrupts the identical movement of the atoms and produces a collision of particles from which is finally born a combined multiplicity, a thing, sufficient to make up a world.

Here, a whole proceeds, as it should, from the fracture of an identity, namely, the parallelizing and paralysing identity of the movements of the atoms.

A whole is always the death of a One.

What is this clinamen? In the splace of isotropic trajectories, we can immediately recognize in it the outplace of an unlocatable, *deregulated* movement.

Actually, in order to deviate from its course, the atom must relate to the void in a singular manner, by excepting itself from the law which all at once arranges for the identical rain of particles under the unanimous effect of the void.

The deviating atom *marks the void,* since it is affected by it in a different way and not just in its generality as atom.

Let us closely follow the thread of the operation. If an atom relates to the void in a manner that is not the general rule for all atoms, it may func-tion as *atomistic designation of the void itself.* It is here that strong difference begins its involution into weak difference, since the opposition between the deviating atom (or rather of the clinamen as the act of this atom) and the atom as pure principle reinscribes from one atom to another, and thus within the same kind of principle, the absolute heterogeneity of the void and the atom.

This operation is entirely comparable to the one you obtain when you pass from the absolute opposition of principle between bourgeoisie/proletariat, to the division into two roads of the mass movement itself, if not to the internal struggle over the party line. The 'bourgeois road' of politics, such as it is active within popular action, is neither the absolute exteriority of the imperialist class nor the global domination that the latter exerts over society as a whole. It is neither domination nor hegemony. The first case corresponds to the strong static opposition of void/atoms. The second, to the undifferentiated setting in motion of the atoms. What inter-ests us, however, is rather the way in which the popular creativity, the revolt in action, marks the antagonistic element within their very midst. There you have a practical clinamen, which is not surprising at all, since in politics the world is called history and the masses make history just as much as, for Democritus, the atoms make the world. It is, so to speak, from people to people within one and the same people that, during any political storm whatsoever and even otherwise, the originary qualitative difference which radically separates the people from imperialism is reinscribed.

It is also certainly true that, in order to understand this reinscription which filters difference, we must admit the capacity of the masses to *deviate*. Besides, this is what is called their movement: the mass movement.

Of course, the clinamen presents us with a major embarrassment. It pertains neither to the void nor to the atoms, nor to the causal action of one over the others. It is also not a third component, or a third principle. It is only that which enables one to arrive, from the absolute qualitative difference so boldly posited as beginning principle, at the combination of atoms into a weak difference, which alone explains the world of things as it obviously exists.

The clinamen is the dialecticity of the principles, the weak differentiation of the strong difference.

This operator of involution matters more to us than the two boundaries of its efficacy: atoms/void, on one hand, combined world of atoms, on the other. (Notice that in the meantime the void has dropped out. Such indeed is its fate and the clinamen, which denotes this fate, must also vanish in its effect. We will see this in detail.)

The clinamen is the atom *qua* outplace of the void, which dialecticizes the void *qua* place of the atoms.

Let us say that in the long run and well beyond the Greeks, the clinamen is the subject or, to be more precise, subjectivization.

In this way, the structural dialectic seeks to do without force. However, this requires an outplace that verges on the miraculous, in opposition both to the monotonous fall of atoms, of which the void is the cause, and to the laws that will govern, subsequent to the clinamen, the composition of the Whole. The need for this outplace will be called 'freedom', or 'chance', since the massive action of the void *qua* strong difference as well as the combinatory process are, for their part, completely necessary and strictly put into the splace. The combinatory process in particular is nothing but the concatenation of atoms according to the figures of the real world. This means putting into a chain elements which are all of the same kind.

The clinamen is a-specific, beyond necessity, absolutely out-of-place, unsplaceable, unfigurable: chance.

It is not for nothing that chance comes back as a major category for

Mallarmé. Chance is a key concept in any structural dialectic. For Lacan, under the name of Fortune, it is nothing less than the real.

For us, it is true that history is the fortune of the event, never to be confused with politics, which is its *forced* subjective rationality.

It is fully in keeping with Marxism to say that history is the chance of political necessity.

Which does not mean introducing even one ounce of irrationalism.

The Greek atomists are respectful of the real. Right from the start, they postulate the strong difference, which is the flattened-out shadow of force. They know that strong difference does not change into weak difference all by itself. For this to happen, the void would have to be composed of atoms; it would have to be possible to *compose the void*, just as Descartes, in order to link up his 'subtle matter', needs an even more subtle matter. We know what infinite impasse results from this desperate operation of filling. Unless one posits two kinds of atoms, those of the void and those of the real, which would restore the strong difference without any gain.

Immediately someone will object: this is exactly what these Greeks do with their clinamen! For you have the deviating atom, first kind, and the 'normal' atoms, second kind. You have by no means established an inter-atomic combination. You have quite simply divided the atoms according to the strong difference, so that they finally may engender the thing.

It is from the One split by the clinamen that the multiple connection of the Whole is composed.

This is a decisive objection. Here Chance is separated from necessity so that the latter, unfaithful to the principle of its strong sterile beginning (atoms, the void, and that's all), may spread throughout the figural combination of weak differences. But chance always returns, as Mallarmé says, for 'in an act where chance is in play, chance always accomplishes its own Idea in affirming or negating itself. Confronting its existence, negation and affirmation fail. It contains the Absurd.'[4]

It is not enough to say that one has won by situating the real process henceforth within the sole concatenation of atoms, if it turns out that an absurd heterogeneous quality—deviation—has been brought in along the way. The putting into a chain requires that the rule of homogeneity be complete. Atoms and nothing else: that is what is wanted.

The structural dialectic depends on the idea that at bottom strong difference is unthinkable. Sure, it serves as opening principle. But everything that *exists* in thought is the result of weak differences: differences among atomistic positions for Democritus, among written signs of the Poem for

Mallarmé, among signifiers for Lacan, and, in a certain sense, among political class positions within the masses for Marxism. It is imperative that the investment of the opening principle into the process of the real restore the splace without any heterogeneous trace of the outplace.

Grounding the world in the difference between the deviating atom and normal atoms is a step forward, no doubt, from its impossible though real grounding in terms of the void and atoms. At least here the atom is repeated in its difference. It marks a minimal progress if the deviant atom is the singular mark of the void, to the point where it reinscribes the heterogeneous within the combinatory process of the world.

Whence the following crucial step in our dialectic: *it is of the utmost importance that the clinamen in turn be abolished.*

What does this mean? It means that no particular explanation of any particular thing whatsoever should require the clinamen, even though the existence of a thing in general is unthinkable without it. It means that no atom should ever be mappable as deviant, in any combination of atoms whatsoever, even though the existence of deviation conditions the very existence of a combinatory.

No sooner has it taken place than the clinamen must absent itself radically from all its effects without exception.

No sooner has it marked the void in the universe of atoms than it must be the absolute void of this mark.

The structural dialectic thus seeks to cancel out this imperceptible emergence of force in terms of its result, so that the outplace of the clinamen may give visibility to the splace of the combination of atoms.

This is the second major operation, the one by which, as Mallarmé says, 'chance is conquered word by word' ('The Mystery in Letters', D 236), the clinamen is abolished, the necessary deviation barred: the operation of the vanishing term.

5

Lacan develops the real as cut, which in a retroactive dispersion reveals the key of the order where it holds sway; Mallarmé devotes his poetic machines to set the stage for the abolition of the trace of lack ('aboli bibelot d'inanité sonore'); the atomists point toward the intracombinatory effacement of the clinamen.

What is a vanishing term? It is the one that, having marked the strong difference of the real within the homogeneity of terms of the process, must disappear so that the weakest difference possible—the difference of places—may alone govern the becoming.

The vanishing term enables the *passage* from the strong difference to the weak one, by marking the heterogeneous quality and abolishing itself straight away. It is the *passer* of force onto the places.[5]

It is the mark that is only de-marcated and never re-marks itself in its initial force.[6]

There has been a clinamen, an atom has deviated, but it is merely an unlocatable and atemporal batting of eyelashes, between the falling rain of atoms and the organizing collision of things. 'Subsequently', so to speak, the clinamen no longer has anything to do with what happens and it is in vain that you would search the world for an atom marked by the stigmata of deviation. All atoms are identical, the one affected by the clinamen no longer bears any trace of it, exposed as it is like all of them to the unanimous rule which governs the combinations and which, once again, is nothing more than the rule that demands that an atom, if it is presented with some void, move straight ahead in it, exactly as any other atom would.

The clinamen is outside time, it does not appear in the chain of effects. All effects are subject to the law. The clinamen has neither past (nothing binds it) nor future (there is no more trace of it) nor present (it has neither a place nor a moment). It takes place only in order to disappear, *it is its very own disappearance*.

The deviating quality has vanished absolutely. You never come across it in the whole field of the thinkable, that is, of real things. The weak difference (among atoms) rules undivided.

Except that by dint of the clinamen, whatever grounded and yet rendered unintelligible the fact that there is *this* world, that is, the strong difference of void/atom, has found itself, for the time of a lightning flash, at the surface of being.

In the structural dialectic, the qualitative difference in which force emerges is not a nothingness. It is a disappearance whose effect is the Whole from which it has disappeared.

It is for this disappearance, as point of the real and not at all real, that we reserve the name of the vanishing term.[7]

To think the real amounts to thinking the self-annulation of that which makes the real in general possible.

The atom affected by deviation engenders the Whole without any leftover or trace of this affection. Better yet: the effect is the retroactive effacement of the cause, since if you limit yourself to the real of the world—to the combinations of atoms—then deviation, which is neither atom nor void, nor action of the void, nor system of atoms, is unintelligible. That which grounds the possibility of thinking suffers a shipwreck in the unthinkable.

The dialectical thought of this point of the unthinkable, as vanishing term whose primitive category is that of the outplace, entails crossing the limit of the whole mechanism. It must grasp the fact that a completely unfolded reason carries out the active effacement of that which grounds it, leaving behind this erased remainder that is the shadow of force whose name it denies. Indeed, this structural reason is unwilling to recognize anything other than the transparent play among places.

Nevertheless, no matter how effaced it may well be, the vanishing term also leaves behind this enormous trace that is the whole. There is a world only by reason of the clinamen, even if no clinamen can ever be signalled in the world.

Nowhere placed, the vanished force sustains the consistency of all the places.

The vanishing term disappears only insofar as *nothing* is included that matches it, except the power of inclination in general, which it has grounded by breaking with the One. How? By means of a *coup de force*.

Perhaps I will surprise you by telling you that, for the Marxist, this clarifies the role of the mass movement, which is both absolute in terms of force and null in terms of place. Yes! The mass movement is the vanishing term of the evental concatenation that is called history.

The masses themselves, in their static being, their structural positioning, their statist placement, constitute the historical world. It is from their basis that any figure of the State draws its sustenance, and it is from the consensus that holds them together that any given social being receives its definition. These splaced masses do not *make* history so much as they *are* history.[8]

However, this being of history is a result, whose possibility invariably arises from the disappearing fury of the *deviating* masses, that is to say, the masses who, in the unpredictable storm of their confident revolt, stood up against the figure of the State that first served as their founding principle.

The fact that one can describe the mass movement, its memorable lucidity, its invincible courage, its particular division, its suspicious-looking assemblies, its fraternal terrorism, does not authorize us to believe that therein lies a stable term of socio-political being. Any attempt to institute in a lasting way the forms of its creative impatience, or to define its *state of affairs*, changes the mass movement into its opposite. All that the Soviets after 1920 or the Chinese revolutionary committees after 1970 accomplish is the statist disappearance of their historical apparition. The being of the mass movement is to disappear, and we must accept that it appears *without a trace* on the vast stages of the historical splace, to the point where so many exhausted nostalgics end up asking themselves: 'What happened there? What were we thinking?'

They only forget that the whole from where they speak, even if one recognizes in it nothing of the enthusiasm from before, and even if what dominates is the appearance of its opposite, draws consistency from the force unleashed by the movement. What is more, they forget that no political project has any future—no matter how impoverished its present appears to be once the storm has been splaced—except by keeping steady in the direction indicated by the founding disappearance of the mass movement.

In the relation of politics to the mass movement, it is the dialectical function of the vanishing term that we must take into account, by pegging it onto the force and, if possible, by avoiding its reduction to the sole atemporal clinamen from which the conservative mechanism of places is born.

It is according to the modality of their stable splacement that the masses are history, whereas it is in their appearing-disappearing that they make history.

They make what they are, but disappearing is what gives them being.[9]

Herein the following paradox is revealed: the essence of the vanishing term is to disappear but it is at the same time that which exists the most—as Whole, cause of itself.

Only that which is missing from a Whole can give it consistency.

Deduction of the splitting

January 5, 1976

Mallarmé and the theory of the crowd—The three figures of the
combinatory—Any term has a vanishing border—Theorems of the
structural dialectic—Structural definition of the revolutionary—
Mallarmé and anxiety

1

Last time I proposed to you that we split the existence of the masses
according to whether they present us with the *being* of history or, as a
vanishing term endowed with causal power, constitute the *making* of
history. Of these masses, the poet Mallarmé—that hermetic recluse—has
the strong awareness that they hold the silent secret of any art worthy of
its name.

While it is true that his poetic machinery assembles a rigged splace of
constellations, roses, credenzas, and tresses, arranged against the backdrop
of a bourgeois salon deserted by Midnight; and while it is true that the
vanishing term, from which these epochal ingredients draw the force of
joining together into a cold Idea, does not seem to go any further than the
setting sun (that Phoenix, that 'beautiful suicide', that 'pride at evening'[10])
or than the death of the Genius (logic of the 'Tombs', for Baudelaire, for
Théophile Gautier, for Verlaine, for Wagner, for E. A. Poe . . .), we would
be wrong to conclude that this prodigious dialectician has never done
more than making the mental rounds of his own room or worshipping
his ancestors.

Mallarmé wanted nothing less than to empower the City with a book and a theatre in which the infinite and mute capacity of the masses—which he names the crowd—would finally find what it takes to produce, by withdrawing from it, its complete emblem: 'The crowd which begins to surprise us so much as a virgin element, or ourselves, fulfils for sounds the function of guardian of mystery! Its own! It compares its rich muteness to the orchestra, wherein lies collective greatness' ('Sacred Pleasure', D 241).

The muteness of the crowd is that by which the latter produces, in the hushed secret of its historical greatness, the representative and illuminating concentrate of art.

Of this causality lost in the night of silence, the artist according to Mallarmé is only the empty mediator. The book is a process independent of any personal subject: 'Impersonified, the volume, to the extent that one separates from it as author, does not demand a reader, either. As such, please note, among human accessories, it takes place all by itself: finished, existing' ('Restricted Action', D 219, translation modified).

As 'finished' or 'made', *fait*, it is under the pressure of 'collective greatness' that art arranges itself, without being marked by it from within, that is, without being a politics. As 'existing' or 'being', *étant*, it forms a splace, which henceforth can be contemplated by the crowd from which it issues, without knowing it, since art exists 'theatrically, for the crowd that, unconsciously and obliviously, hears its own grandeur' ('Music and Letters', D 190, trans. modified).

The crowd is the vanishing term for art, the clinamen which from language as usual—trading currency without a concept—sets apart the poem—as the proper linguistic organization to render explicit 'the relations [. . .] few or many' and to 'simplify the world' (*ibid.*).

Of course, the crowd can never be grasped in its causal act, since it disappears in the same process. In the retroaction of art, it much rather seems to be abolished, a massive shadow that prior to the work itself projects its lost correlate. Mallarmé's key image here is fireworks: commemorating, on July 14, the foundational riot, they project onto the sky a splendour of which the crowd is only the nocturnal ground: '[. . .] a multitude under the night sky does not constitute the spectacle, but in front of it, suddenly, there rises the multiple and illuminating spray, in mid-air, which in a considerable emblem represents its gold, its annual wealth and the harvest of its grains, and leads the explosions of the gaze to normal heights' ('Conference on Villiers', *Œuvres complètes* 499).

What do the seething and destructive masses of the Revolution and this peaceful flock of official spectators have in common? Precisely the fact that 'the multiple and illuminating spray' of the poem—or of music—does nothing except make a Whole, in a stellar emblematic inscription, out of the productive wealth of the people, of which it nevertheless, in its compact absence, lights up only the self-estranged amazement.

In view of this function of art, Mallarmé—and this is his idealist bent—in a surprising text sends back to back the universal suffrage and the riot (with a slight conceptual preference, nonetheless, for the latter):

If, in the future, in France, religion comes back, it will be the amplification of the sky-instinct in each of us, rather than a reduction of our instincts to the level of politics. To vote, even for oneself, does not satisfy, as the expansion of a hymn with trumpets sounding the joy of choosing no name; nor can a riot be sufficiently tumultuous to make a character into the steaming, confounding, struggling-again-into-life hero. ('Music and Letters', D 195)

The force of the demand, which makes Mallarmé into an intellectual revolutionary, here consists in annulling the self-nomination in the crowd's ('steaming', 'confounding') force. Herein lies a vanishing 'tumultuousness' from which, struggling back into life, all heroic idealism proceeds. Let us understand the following: in order for a representative splace (a 'religion') to come into being, the subject must be carried away by its 'sky-instinct', which abolishes even its old nominal identity. Against the background of this striking lack, of which universal suffrage is the perfect denial, what installs itself, ceremonially, is 'the amplification in each of us'. After having disappeared in its act, the crowd, now returned to its substantial placidity, contemplates the emblem of its vanished force.

There is no approximation, in our own time, of what Mallarmé dreams of, except the colossal crowds dressed in red on Tiananmen Square at the peak of the Cultural Revolution. Such is the true theatre in which the people proceeds to 'hear its own greatness'.

The fact that the imbeciles have found this to be religion only does justice to the concept.

However, it is also proof of the fact that the riot, contrary to what Mallarmé says, is indeed the exact form of the crowd as vanishing term, which is 'sufficiently tumultuous' to cause the spectacular restructuring of time itself.

And this, even though it is true that art is the concentration of force.

Mallarmé, in those years between 1880 and 1890, suffered above all from a lack of riots which threw the crowd back on the stable floor of its statist being. He knew this very well: '[. . .] there's no such thing as a Present, no—a present doesn't exist . . . For lack of the Crowd's declaring itself, for lack of—everything' ('Restricted Action', D 218).

'There's no such thing as a Present' means that there is no clinamen, no creative disappearance of the crowd standing up in rebellion. There is only the placid combination of places according to the law's regularity—'the Law,' Mallarmé says, 'seated in all transparency, naked and marvelous' ('Music and Letters', D 195).

What is especially marvelous is that in these colonial and provisorily docile times, Mallarmé should have been able to detect, if only so as to assign its task to art, that everything that has splendour, everything that subsists and continues, results from the crowd's lack and bears witness to the fact that, by disappearing, the rioting masses have founded even the world that forbids them to exist.

2

The structural penchant consists in seeking to combine elements that are all identical. Therein lies something of an algebraic prescription, in which the repetition of the same letter, only different in terms of its place, and not even indexed according to its locus, provides the matrix of all elementary intelligibility. Let us call this the first figure, in which only the strictest minimal difference appears, the difference from the same to the same, from place to place, occupied by identical marks.

First figure: a a a a a a a a a a . . .

However, if one is a dialectician and not only a structuralist, one stumbles upon the obstacle proposed by the real: in order to distinguish itself, the mark (the term, the atom) must lift itself up against a background of blankness (the splace, the void), which now, with regard to the first, establishes an absolutely qualitative difference. One thus comes to posit two principles and not just a single kind of terms. In a second figure, we need the void and the atoms, the blank page and the signs. This need for a strong difference functions retroactively as the condition *a priori* of the logic of places. Let us write 0 for the heterogeneous term from which the homogeneous ones draw their identity by opposition.

Second figure: 0 // a a a a a . . .

Here we are blocked by an *excess of force*. From 0 to a, we do not even have, as in the case from the place P to the term A, the mediation of an index, A_p, the term-in-its-place. Here we have the incommunication of opposites, the Two of Manichaeism. Opposed to the continuous void, there is the dissemination of no whole whatsoever.

Certainly, the series a a a a . . . is qualitatively determined by its opposition to 0. But this applies to *all in one piece*. The strong difference makes the multiple into a One of opposition, without the possibility that anything combined emerges from it.

The clinamen, as we saw, finds the escape route of a causal indexation. One atom is marked by the void in a singular way, one sign is marked by the background, one signifier (the Phallus) by the symbolic, in that its movement (its scription, its representative function) interrupts the isotropism of the domain so that the combinatory *gets going*.

Whence the third figure: a_0 (vanishing term) / a a a . . . (initial chain instituted as place of all things).

This figure stays in the family (only a's) but this time around the combinatory consistency of the chain is guaranteed by the vanishing term.

This edging out of the void into an index touches upon the articulation of the thing.

The vanishing term is none of the elements of the Whole. The cause is thus nothing, since 'something' is only a combination of elements of the Whole.

Nevertheless, if there is something rather than nothing (which is the question for Leibniz and Heidegger), if the combinatory exists on the basis of which the immobile dispersion of Ones into powder, the milk for a milky way of nonsense, is overcome, then it is under the effect of the deviation of one One, vanished in the whole.

The vanishing term is therefore not nothing, but, as cause of the whole, it is consubstantial with its consistency.

Like a Democritus of written signs, Mallarmé says with clarity: 'But there is, and here I intervene with confidence, something, little—*some little nothing*, let's say explicitly—*which exists*, for example, *equal to the text*' ('Music and Letters', D 177). Some little nothing made for the express purpose of causing the whole of the poem, to which thenceforth it is equal: such is Mallarmé's vanishing term, the support of the causal effect of lack.

3

It remains metaphorical to say that the vanishing term is equal to the whole. *It is not* the whole, this little nothing from which all consistency results, nor is it this consistency itself, since the latter is so little nothing that it is distributed into things. Where then is it? Whereto goes the striking and irreparable deviation, out of which all order is made?

After the mutation of differences, the vanishing term, and the causality of lack, we need to deduce the splitting. This is the fourth concept of the structural dialectic.

Let us pick up the thread of atomism again.

The fact that a clinamen has taken place means that the atoms, whose movements are finally combined, from now on can link themselves onto one another. The deviation, though disappeared in the sense that no atom in the real world is its bearer in particular, is in fact omnipresent in any *linkage* of atoms.

The fact that an atom, instead of scooting by parallel to all others, can be linked to the point of entering into the consistency of a thing, is precisely the mark in it of the evaporated clinamen.

To include itself into the thing as a whole is what, in the atomistic act, is due to the deviation. Even though this concerns the epitome of its normality: to be an element of a combination.

That which thus links the term 'a' to its identical and distinct neighbour 'a' is, so to speak, the appearance-disappearance *between them* of the vanishing term, which is the support for any possible linkage.

Actually, *any atom* is the vanishing term, in that it is capable of linking itself to the others so as to make up the whole of a thing.

The upshot of this is that *no single atom* is the vanishing term, so that we can avoid—as is the goal of the structural dialectic—the return of the strong difference which is what would be entailed by the division of the stock of atoms into two kinds, the deviating and the normal ones.

Each atom must be regarded as being, on one hand, itself, that is, the indifferent 'a' distinguished only by its place, and on the other, its capacity to link itself onto the others, to include itself into the whole, that is, its internal marking by the vanishing of the clinamen.

Such is the equation of the splitting: $a = (aa_0)$, in which one easily recognizes, reconstructed from a different angle, the equation of the scission $A = AA_p$, to which we were led last year in our investigation of the Hegelian dialectic.

I say from a different angle, since after the indexation by the place we now obtain the scission by the cause.

In the structural dialectic, any term is split into its place, on one hand, and its vanishing capacity for linkage, on the other.

For us, this is as good as place and force. But, as I said before, the structural dialectic is reluctant to *name* the force, and breaks its back trying to keep it in place.

One element of the combinatory is included as singular but it is linked to the others only under the effect of a missing totalization, of which it presents the border; (a/a_0) latches itself onto (a_0/a) through the vanishing that is common to them via their border a_0, from which it results that they are totalizable.

Thus, the absent cause is always reintroduced into the whole of its effect. This is a major theorem of the structural dialectic: *in order for the causality of lack to exert itself, all terms must be split.*

Thus, the trace left behind in the social world by the great mass movements, about which we have shown that they were the vanishing terms of all things historical, resides in the fact that any form of consciousness, any point of view, any reality, in the final instance is split into the old and the new, categories by means of which history *produces movement* in the entities that make up its combination.[11]

As for the proletariat, it is the subjective name of the new in our time. If the working class defines its place in the structure, the essential point is for it to mark the border of the old, which explains that this proletariat can be, in China in 1966, the movement of the schooled youth, and, in Portugal today, the peasants from the South. The apparent mistake in terms of position overlaps with the truth of the opposition; the falsity of the place is the truth of the force.

No matter how stable, or even ossified, it may appear to be, a historical thing presents the border of the disappeared movement from which results its presence in the whole, that is, the actuality of its future destruction, just as on those stumps washed up on the shore the dried foam marks a border of the dead sea, which is also the tide's reversible imminence.

It is one of Mao's strengths to have insisted that the revolutionary Marxist is the lookout for the vanishing term, emblem of the new within the old. He or she is the active guardian of the future of the cause.

These great causes, in whose name sacrifice is sometimes the least of things, are in fact great causalities.

The fact that the vanishing term presents itself, a_0, in order to attach itself onto a; that we have the theorem of the thing: $(a=aa_0) \rightarrow (aa)$, which links the splitting to consistency: all this is nothing else than the general form of Lacan's theorem: 'A signifier is that which presents the subject for another signifier.'

A term is that which presents the vanishing term to another term, in order together to form a chain.

To function as a combinable element amounts to presenting the absent cause to another element.

4

Mallarmé thus sets out his programme: 'To evoke, with intentional vagueness, the mute object, using allusive words, never direct, reducing everything to an equivalent of silence, is an endeavour very close to creating' ('Magic', D 264).

The object, reduced to silence, does not enter the poem, even though its evocation grounds the poetic consistency. It is the absent cause. But the effect of its lack lies in affecting each written term, forced to be 'allusive', 'never direct', in such a way so as to become equal on the Whole to the silence by which the object was only initially affected.

The allusive is the vanishing border of the written term. It is that by which, under the effect of the object's absence, it combines itself poetically with other terms, in order finally to produce the evocation of the lack, that is, a poetic thing, an integrally combined universe.

The poem's word is split: it is word and nonword, speech and silence in equal parts, light and express shadow. This splitting alone is what supports the poem's manoeuvring, its inclusion into the chain of metaphors.

If it is silence that must be said, the poem must reduce each word to its vanishing side.

The poem as a whole, becoming the equivalent—according to Mallarmé's wish—of the silenced object, proceeds to the word's self-effacement. The difficulty lies in the fact that the exclusive instrument for this process of self-effacement of the word, based on its vanishing border, can only ever be other words.

Therefore, we must also efface the instrument of the effacement, otherwise the word gains the upper hand on the side of the oblivion of lack, on the side of its anonymous identity, wherein Mallarmé recognizes language's function of exchange, somehow monetary in nature.

The poem exchanges nothing. The annulment of exchange is its major outcome. For this to happen, the trace must disappear from that by which the words put in motion brought sparkle to their very own vanishing.

At the core of Mallarmé's dialectical machines we find not only the trinity: vanishing term, causality of lack, splitting; but also the *second degree* of its effect, that is, the lack of lack.

For reasons that we will have to investigate, Lacan names 'anxiety' the lack of lack. And, he says, it is that which does not deceive.

Mallarmé says nothing different:

The lampbearer, Anxiety, at midnight sustains
Those vesperal dreams that are burnt by the Phoenix
And which no funeral amphora contains,
On the credenzas in the empty room . . . (CP 69, trans. modified)

Indeed, of the void in which a subject eclipses itself, anxiety is the extinguished light in which this subject gave lustre to its scant reality.

'A la nue accablante tu'

January 26, 1976

Syntax—Inaugural metaphor—Metonymic chains—All the concepts of
the structural dialectic—The lack of lack: the poem does what it says—
The USSR and the siren

1

A poem by Mallarmé is a whole whose missing object is the structural
dialectic itself. It is, explicitly, 'a stilled, melodic encipherment, of the
combination of motifs that compose a logic' ('Music and Letters', D 188).
This goes to show the relevance of its unpacking.

Why is it a poem, if the theme enciphers a logic? One might also ask:
What fallen object is the cause of Lacan's style?

It is possible to answer this question in the form of a demonstration. The
syntactical governance of Mallarmé and Lacan's sentences is not in the
least futile or arbitrary. It is the language of the structural dialectic, always
standing on the edges of the flat precipice of structuralism, yet ready to
leap back like a young goat in order not to fall into it.

Here, poetry makes up for the force, which one seeks to deny.

Let us proclaim that Mallarmé's poetic machine, though opaque when
looked at from the outside, nevertheless possesses only a single meaning.

We must put an end to the laziness that has so many readers bypass the
obstacle in order to claim that the enigma's virtue consists in allowing a
hundred underlying answers. This absolute dialectician does not present
any 'polysemy'. One should not take for an erratic chaos whatever is given

multiple echoes, based on the firm and consecutive encipherment of the One-of-meaning, by those remarkable stampings with which the poem illuminates and extinguishes itself.

The guarantee of the unity of meaning, Mallarmé warns us, is none other than that which functions as law for the space of writing: 'What pivot, in these contrasts, am I assuming for intelligibility? We need a guarantee—Syntax' ('The Mystery in Letters', D 234–5).

Not to get lost in the grammar is a major guideline for anyone seeking to discover the poem's functioning and, consequently, to gain access to the elucidation of its lack, that is, the dialectical logic in person.[12]

To back this up, let me give the punctuated, stretched out, a-poetic and flattened version of the object that I propose to unpack today:

Stilled beneath the oppressive cloud
that basalt and lava base
likewise the echoes that have bowed
before a trumpet lacking grace

O what sepulchral wreck (the spray
knows, but it simply drivels there)
ultimate jetsam cast away
abolishes the mast stripped bare

or else concealed that, furious
failing some great catastrophe
all the vain chasm gaping wide

in the so white and trailing tress
would have drowned avariciously
a siren's childlike side (CP 79–81/83)[13]

So what shipwreck has swallowed even the mast, the sails torn off, which was the final debris of a ship? The foam on top of the sea, trace of this catastrophe, knows it, but says nothing. The ship's horn, which could have informed us, has not been heard, impotent, under this low sky and in this dark sea with its colour of volcanic rock, which imprisons the possible echo of the distress signal.

Unless, in reality, furious for not having had any ship to disappear, the abyss (sea and sky) has swallowed a siren, of which the white foam would no longer be anything other than the hair.

In sum, the poem reveals its architecture once we understand the following:

- *'tu'* in the first line is a past participle of the verb *taire*, 'to silence, hush, or still', referring to the shipwreck (*'quel naufrage, tu à la nue, abolit le mât dévêtu?'*: 'what shipwreck, stilled beneath the oppressive cloud, has abolished the stripped mast?');
- *'par une trompe sans vertu'* refers to *'tu'* (*'quel naufrage, tu à la nue par une trompe sans vertu'*: 'what shipwreck, stilled beneath the oppressive cloud by a horn without force');
- *'à même'* refers to *'basse'* (*'la nue, basse de basalte et de laves, à même*—in the sense of *'tout contre'* or 'flush with'—*les échos esclaves'*: 'the cloud, base of basalt and lava, flush with the enslaved echoes');
- the second quatrain is punctuated with a question mark;
- in the tercets, we must imagine a comma after *'furibond'* ('furious') as well as after *'haute'* ('high or exalted');
- *'furibond'* is said of *'l'abîme vain éployé'* ('the vain abyss outspread'), which is responsible for drowning the siren.

No other path is possible (you will test this for yourself) if one wishes to include all the explicit materials following the supposition, confirmed by the author, that the syntax serves as guarantee.

2

Last year I spoke of the splace, the legal place presupposed by any event. Mallarmé takes as his point of departure a splaced figural representative: sea and sky blended into the low-ceilinged oppressiveness of the nothing.

Metaphor of the splace, and more specifically of the white page where everything is inscribed. Decor about which it would be too much to say that it is a fragment of nature, since Mallarmé excludes with great precision the assemblage of sky and sea from nature: 'The sea—which one would do better to keep silent about than to inscribe in parentheses, if the firmament doesn't enter along with it—becomes disjoined, properly speaking, from nature. A certain exceptional drama works its ravages between them, and this has its rationale in no one' ('Bucolic', D 269).

Of this 'exceptional drama', our sonnet offers a sketch as 'impersonified reason' or 'rationale in no one' (pure logic) whose writing must fill the lack by practising the effect. To read such a sonnet means to become the mental equal to those for whom:

Satisfied by no fruits here, my starvation
Finds equal savour in their learned deprivation. (CP 81)

As for the dialectic and force, I propose that you, in reading Mallarmé, perceive the equal flavour of their absence.

In this regard, dialectical poetry is the reverse of dialectical politics, where the flavour, often quite acrid, is perceived in the real.

As a result, to this day, all political poetry pertains to epic, which is only obliquely poetic, namely, by whatever escapes its magnificence rather than by that which brings out its splendour.

If one admits that Mallarmé, as a poet, holds the virgin page to be the original metaphor for the splace-in-itself, we will at once see that the poem opens with a second metaphor, where the complex sea-sky replaces 'the blank paper guarded by its white' ('Sea Breeze', CP 25).

On the Mallarméan sea, split off from nature, reduced to its anonymity, a trace, the foam, holds the principle of a meaning ('*tu le sais, écume*': 'you know this, foam') which it does not give up ('*mais y baves*': 'but slobber on').

This is the poet's first written trace on the paper void, itself a metaphor, for us, of the outplace which any splace makes retroactively into a place. For the written 'in itself' has no assigned location and comes into existence only by contradicting the chance-like purity of the virgin page.

The metaphorical gesture by which the poem becomes possible is aimed at the contradiction of the trace and the blank space, metaphorized into foam and sea-sky.

Mallarmé's crucial problem resides in the process set in motion by the inscription of words that are out-of-place on the splace of the page. The theoretical statements that escort the poems do not leave us any doubt about this:

To lean, according to the page, on the blank, whose innocence inaugurates it, forgetting even the title that would speak too loud: and when, in a hinge, the most minor and disseminated, chance is conquered word by word, unfailingly the blank returns, gratuitous earlier but certain now, concluding that there is nothing beyond it and authenticating the silence. ('The Mystery in Letters', D 236)

Even before the poem, we obtain the following metaphorical line of entry (with M_o for 'metaphor'), as seen in the diagram below.

The interrogation of the foam, and consequently of the outplace and of writing, is the point from where the poem is arranged.

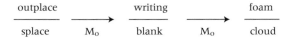

Two hypotheses, separated by 'or' or 'unless', *ou cela que*, resolve the suspense of a word that in itself is undecipherable:

a) the foam would be the trace on the marine void of a shipwreck;
b) the foam would be the trace of a siren's plunge.

These two hypotheses are in turn organized according to two metonymic chains. The ship is made up of a distress signal (the horn), then of a mast stripped of its sails; the siren, of its young flank, and then of its trailing hair.

Ship and siren are the two vanishing terms that support the fact that there is something (the foam) rather than nothing (the oppressive cloud).

Vanish they do, these terms, with the foam being only the trace of their disappearance. The ship has been wrecked, the siren has plunged underwater, and if the foam opens up the whole question of the thing, it is because the question concerns its cause, which is of the order of the movement of an absence.

The metonymical chains, veritable still for the Mallarméan concept of the negative, aim to bring absence all the way to the edges of nullity.

The ship is evoked only by the abolition, not even of its own massivity but of its mast, supreme jetsam; or by the hypothetical sound of an inaudible horn. The siren is reduced to its youthful head of hair—except that it is only a single white hair.

If we agree to mark with a slash, or an oblique bar, the disappearing act of the causal term, then the two chains, interrupted by 'or' or 'unless', present themselves as follows:

foam ↗ sh̸ip (wrecked) → ma̸st (stripped and abolished) → ho̸rn (ineffectual)
↘ sir̸en (drowned) → *hair*

Here we find ourselves back with all our categories. The strong difference (foam/blank), which opens up the problem of the thing; the network of weak differences, organized in metonymies (ship, mast, horn; siren, hair); the transition from one to the other by way of the causality of lack, supported by the vanishing terms: the ship's wreck and the siren's drowning, of which what is—the foam—is the mark out-of-place on the splace's desolation.

That the vanishing term is the mark of the void itself is sufficiently clear from the fact that the ship is engulfed, and the siren, 'stingily' or 'avariciously' drowned, as if these terms derived their substance and their effect only from being reabsorbed into the abyss of the sea, of which they are the disappearing delegation in the world.

Let us also notice the progress made over the whole course of the poem: if the wrecked ship is an external included, a heterogeneity engulfed in the homogeneous, then conversely the marine animal of the siren results from a dazzling expulsion out of its native element, a homogeneity in transit, just the time of a dolphin's leap, in the superficial heterogeneity of the visible, much to the regret of the avaricious abyss.

The place is so avaricious as to take back immediately whatever it gives out, the thin scar of the cause, so as to ensure that nothing takes place other than itself: 'Nothing will have taken place other than the place' (*A Dice Throw*).

As for the splitting, it too is manifest, with regard to the foam's double nature. The foam certainly is a trace, and thus it is captured in the network of mundane differences, as opposed to the unlimited nature of the cloud. But on the other hand, it holds out only thanks to a resemblance to the abyss, of which it indicates the negative power and the underlying effect of abolition. That which exists out-of-place, the poem says, finds itself

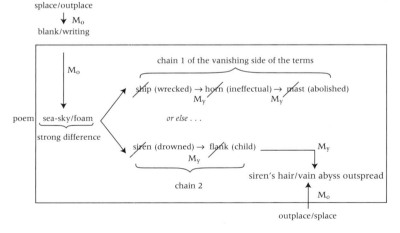

placed therein under the law of the place (of the splace). Ship and siren, returned to the nullity of the abyss, divide the foam according to the cause (the vanishing side) and according to consistency (the effective but really mute trace, which 'slobbers on').

We would thus be at the end of our troubles, having seen how the text works as emblem of the structural dialectic according to its metaphorical (M_o) and metonymical (M_y) operations.

Except that the diagram immediately suggests the following questions:

1. Why two vanishing terms (ship and siren)? Why this second cleavage which, cut in two by the enigmatic coup de force of 'or', *ou cela que*, arranges two metonymical chains?
2. Why this unusual closure, which at the end of the poem provokes the metaphorical re-emergence, in the guise of the relation hair/abyss, of that which apparently had been introduced from the start as foam/sea-sky? What have we gained, by moving from foam to hair?

3

Is it not enough to have only one vanishing term in order for its effect of lack, which divides any index of the real, to authorize the whole of the poem?

Nevertheless, it is twice that the ship does not take place.

First wrecked, the ship casts away its sails, shuts up its horn (its siren, already, but in the sense of an alarm), so that its supreme jetsam may abolish itself.

But the shipwreck in its turn is revoked and put into doubt. It would rather be a matter of a siren's plunge.

These two negations do not belong to the same species. The first offers a figure for the vanishing of the causal term; the second annuls the vanishing itself. And, against the backdrop of this revocation, the second and final vanishing term (the siren) takes flight.

You see, in Maoism, we also must produce the destruction of the bourgeoisie twice. First of the old bourgeoisie, the classical one, for which Leninism provides the means to destroy its apparatus. And then of the new one, the state bureaucratic bourgeoisie, which as Maoism teaches us sprouts up even among the instruments of the first destruction, the Leninist party and the socialist State.

The whole question consists in knowing whether the revolutionary masses, the historical agent that is the vanishing cause for the Leninist revolution, are the same as those that come and flush out, from that which at first had been their backbone (the party and the State), the wailing bourgeoisie that managed to impose itself in Russia, after Stalin had not been able to propose anything in order to defer it, except the sombre equality in the face of terror.

One or two vanishing terms? Is the 'revolution' that Lenin opposes to the State the same as that of the Cultural Revolution?

It seems rather that after the socialist wrecking of the bourgeois ship, we have to consider the communist plunge of the sirens of the State. Besides, these are sirens with a moustache. Only the temporary ascendancy of the new, monopolistic and state-bureaucratic bourgeoisie is able to account for the fact that its raucous and sinister song can seduce navigators of history that are as disparate as the Ethiopian colonels, the military in Vietnam, a few Arab intellectuals, technical experts in the Eastern bloc, bearded Latin Americans, or the simple-minded professional workers of the French trade unions.

In order to turn all that into the whole of a shipwreck, it is not surprising that strange novelties are needed, such as the mobilization of tens of millions of students and workers around affairs involving the theatre, movies, oil painting, and philosophy.

For Mallarmé, in any case, the second vanishing term inscribes itself based on the lack of the first. This lack is radical insofar as it no longer bears on the term (the ship) but on its disappearing (the shipwreck, the ship).

The poem exhibits the causality of lack in its effect, but also in its law, since it is governed from within by the lack of the first supposed causal term, the first vanishing term.

'Or else . . .' carries out the abolition of the abolished. What was presupposed in terms of the efficacy of absence now finds itself annulled.

Consequently, the poem is not only the metaphor of the dialectical categories. It is their concept. The reality of the categories is at work to move along the poetic thing.

We pass poetically from the ship to the siren, both of which are metaphorical figures of the vanishing term, by way of the vanishing of the first figure, whence the necessity of the second is engendered.

What the poem says, it does.

In this regard, it resembles the Marxist act, in which the written is never anything but the prop with which the political subject supports itself in its antagonistic unity. After Lenin, every Marxist text bears the title: 'The Current Situation and Our Tasks.'

Mallarmé interprets the structural dialectic less as the theme for a metaphor than as a directive for the poem.

That which was lacking, the ship, or the ship, must come to lack in its lack so that the siren, *qua* ideal, may come into being.

Mallarmé says: 'blow out the candle of being, by which all has been. Proof' (*Igitur, Œuvres complètes* 434).

The poem is this retroactive proof of blown-out being—of being—which in order to be provided requires the lack of lack.

If everything exists thanks to what is lacking from it, then the same applies to the cause. It is only by abolishing a first causality that you give consistency to the concept of causality itself.

This special operation, typical of Mallarmé's dialectical machines, by which they undertake from within the suppression of their first negative metaphor, in what follows will be called: annulment.

As for the question why the siren comes to a stop, immobilized as it is in the ideality of a lack which, for its part, cannot come to lack, we will not have time to answer it today.

There is no shortage of people who think that with the October revolution a 'workers' State' is put in place that no historical contingency, however repulsive, will ever separate from its essence.

It is clear that under the banner of the withering of the State, Marx imagined not only the lack of the bourgeois State but, progressively, the lack of its lack, called communism, in which any political causality is abolished. Of this abolition, the State of the dictatorship of the proletariat supports the plan. Lenin completed this by indicating that any State was at bottom bourgeois, so that, in coming to lack under the effect of the first insurrectionary assault, which clears the ground for the proletariat, the State—always bourgeois—must necessarily lack a second time, now clearing the path for the communist masses of the classless society, as the vanishing term of history in general, finally given in its concrete concept.

What the masses experience is that the socialist State and the party at its helm are a rat's nest of bourgeois bureaucrats.

This experience still had to be turned into a Marxist politics. It belongs to Mao's imperishable initiative to have at least pronounced its urgency.

Mao, in the guise of a long series of cultural revolutions, for the first time has designated and put into practice the return of the State's lack back upon itself—the 'or else' here being nothing less than his endorsement, in a sensational dazibao, for the riots of the youth and then of a segment of the workers, against the new bourgeoisie of the socialist State.

From that which put an end to the old tyrannies, we must also know how to liberate ourselves.

Those who, after that, persist in talking about socialism and its State as a stable entity certainly share with Mallarmé the hypothesis of a halting point. But they have failed to see its annulation.

Mallarmé has an alibi that they cannot produce. Contrary, alas, to the imperialist USSR today, the siren, even if returned to the abyss, does not exist.

Any subject is a forced exception, which comes in second place

February 1, 1976

Theatre—Catholicism and politics—Lack and destruction—The signifiers of exception, locus of the subject—On the role of tombs in Marxism and in art—The halting point—Analysis of the dice throw—The rose and communism

1

Who will measure what we owe to the theatre, from Aeschylus's *Oresteia* to Brecht's plays? Capital art, uninterrupted analyser of our history. Mallarmé pronounces a clear and distinct axiom about this: 'Theatre is, by essence, superior' ('Of Genre and the Moderns', D 142).

Mallarmé applies himself to establish the theatre of our time. What does our time mean here? It is the time when the foremost representational—theatrical—religion, Catholicism, has fallen in disuse.

In his analysis of the mass, our dialectician finds as much figurative truth as Hegel does at the level of the concept in the mystery of Redemption. The mass is a notorious theatre of the structural dialectic. See rather for yourself:

> Such, divided into the authenticity of distinct fragments, is the staging of a state religion, as yet unsurpassed by any framework, and which, divided into a triple work, proffers a direct invitation to the essence of a type (here, Christ), then proffers his invisibility, and then by vibrations outlines the enlargement of place to the infinite, strangely satisfying to a modern hope of philosophy and art. ('The Same', D 251)

The summons to appear, which is the theme of the 'real presence', ends in the invisibility of God, the fundamental vanishing term. Taken in the emblem of his absence, the latter functions as the cause for the thundering art of the church organs, which carries the place to infinity, just as in *A Dice Throw* the launching of the numbers, uncertain until the officiant's disappearance into the seawaters, lifts the gaze up to the constellations that enumerate a sum of stars.

The fact remains that, in 1890, one can no longer decently make do with Catholicism. The secularization of all theatre of superior essence leaves 'only two ways open to mental research, where our need bifurcates—aesthetics, on the one hand, and political economy, on the other' ('Magic', D 264).

Nothing has changed. To what should we devote our need for theatre, if not to art or to politics? Someone will allege science. Mallarmé's profundity here lies in not having said a word about it! Who will believe that truth, such as it is, may be that which causes a subject's desire?

It remains to be seen why it is the case that our need must bifurcate. This is the whole question of theatre as political art. Nevertheless, I can vouch that among those who were up and about in politics around May 1968 and who gave up in 1973—they are legion—the better ones returned to the artistic reference while the worst fell into the vacuousness of 'universal reportage', if they did not devote themselves to the cool cataplasm of monotheisms.

Politics is in a structure of fiction. This is not the least of Mallarmé's statements: '. . . the social relation and its momentary measure, condensed or expanded to allow for government, is a fiction, it belongs to the domain of Letters' ('Safeguard', D 290, trans. modified).

To have covered up the essential absence from which the social bond issues has been, for this bond itself, a grave error. It prevents us from relating to the political 'substructures', as we should, from the position of an involved audience whose elementary right is to hiss the play, or even to interrupt it, as soon as it proposes nothing more than a mediocre artifice, a vulgar fiction in which the crowd would not be able to recognize its own greatness:

Great damage has been caused to terrestrial togetherness, for centuries, by indicating to it the brutal mirage, the city, its governments, or the civil code otherwise than as emblems or, vis-à-vis our estate, as what necropolises are to the heavens they make evaporate: an earth surface, almost not bad-looking. Tollbooths and elections are not here below, though they seem to sum up democracy, what makes a popular cult,

even when such formalities are followed augustly, as representatives—
of the Law, seated in all transparency, naked and marvelous. ('Music
and Letters', D 194–5)

This is also an invitation to the politicians to take care of their representations, whose professional—that is to say, fictional—rule comes down
to exposing themselves absolutely in the transitory function of emblems,
without ever imagining that they themselves possess any substance
whatsoever.

In politics only one link is required: trust, which must be granted, as in
the theatre, in order for the fiction to work.

A politics relieved of everything except this revocable bond weighs no
more than the written trace on the page. Everything else, which is as yet
perhaps inevitable, weighs up to a 'great damage'.

In Marxism, this theatrical airing of politics bears the name 'withering
away of the State'. That just goes to show in what sense the State corresponds to a necropolis for the paradise that it makes evaporate! At the
final term of this, if we can still speak of a term, there remains only the
internal confidence of the masses, which is the reciprocal support of their
truth *qua* fiction.

Mallarmé, for his part, retains the task of caring for the Book, while he
waits for something better.

What is art? The arrangement of nature into a Whole, by its causal
retrenchment.

Nature has taken place; it can't be added to, except for cities or railroads
or other inventions where we change the form, but not the fact, of our
material.

The one available act, forever and alone, is to understand the relations, in the meantime, few or many: according to some interior state
that one wishes to extend, in order to simplify the world.

Equal to creating: except that the notion of object, escaping, is lacking.
('Music and Letters', D 187, trans. modified)

To occupy the lack of being puts some order in the symbol.[14] The equality
of elements and the final seal of verse concentrate, in rhythm and rhyme,
the satisfaction of the desire to create: '[. . .] the poetic act consists in seeing
that an idea can be broken up into a certain number of motifs that are equal
in some way, and of grouping them; they rhyme; as an external seal, the
final words are proof of their common measure' ('Crisis of Verse', D 206).

Our investigation is devoted to following, under the effect of the natural nonplace, the labyrinths of egalitarian fragmentation (the splace) and of that which is created therein in terms of the new under the hallmark of verse (the outplace).

I do not imagine, any more than Mallarmé does for nature, that we can 'add' to society—except nuclear plants. Marxist politics must know how to entrench, how to put the old social order at fault in order truly to create that which did not exist.[15] It seems that this requires destruction, which is more than lack—which is to lack what force is to place.

Even here, the poet does not abandon us: 'Destruction was my Beatrice' (Letter to Lefébure, 1867).[16]

2

The annulment never inscribes itself linearly in the poem. You have the metonymical chains, from the ship to the mast, from the siren to the hair of foam. You have the metaphorical substitutions, foam for trace, abyss for the splace. But in order to produce the lack of lack, you must leap from one hypothesis to another: ship? No: siren.

This leap in meaning or direction alone enables the annulment of a first vanishing term and the exhibition of the concept of the causality of lack.[17]

Do we not have here some stroke of force? A stroke of the force?[18]

But this also comes at a price. Mallarmé pays for the debt incurred for having broken the pact of the metonymical chain with signifiers of the exception. We saw 'or else. . . .' above. There is almost no poem, except—which proves the rule—the Tombs, that escape this need. 'What if . . .,' 'No, but . . .' (*A Faun in the Afternoon*). 'Unless . . .' (*Funerary Toast* and *Remembering Belgian Friends*). 'Were it not that . . .' (*Sonnet*). 'But . . .' (*Little Ditty, A Lace Vanishes . . .*). 'Except. . .' (*The Fine Suicide Fled . . .*). 'Though. . .' (*Her pure nails on high. . .*). 'Except perhaps . . .' (*A Dice Throw . . .*).

Such are, accumulated, the intratextual indices of what the law of the text's splacement would not be able to engender all by itself, since it is a matter of what, properly speaking, is an exception to it.

Once the first vanishing term is given, the poem follows a line of totalization. Whatever wants to interrupt it must stand out of place. But how, if no force comes to overdetermine, *qua* subject, the series of consecutive places?

Here the annulment of the vanishing, the shift to a second line of totalization, requires that instead of the metonymy of a supplementary effacement (after the ship, the pulled sail, the extinguished horn, the engulfed mast, why not the torn flag, the thread of this flag, the atom of this thread?) there comes—'or else . . .'—the qualitative break in which the strong difference, dismissed before, takes its revenge so that the repressed heterogeneity returns.

Let us say this in a straightforward manner: all the occurrences of 'or else', 'unless', and all the 'buts' and 'except that' are nothing less than the signifiers through which, as a caesura between two orders and in the time of a lightning flash, the subjective effect takes hold.

Appearance-disappearance of a new type, in which the exception clause makes for all the interpolated drama of the subject. Strong difference suddenly punctuated in the thick plot of metaphors and metonymies. Abrupt interruption of the ideal egalitarian fragmentation.

The lack of lack, which results from the annulment, is not twice the lack, according to the previously established law. It needs more, as witnessed in the grammar: an unknown lead, impossible to track according to the initial splacement, opens up to the poetic effect.

I provisorily call 'subject' this unpredictable bifurcation.

Any subject is a forced exception, which comes in second place.

Mao has posited for the first time that there is no hope in engendering communism in a linear fashion from the socialist State. From that which sufficed to knock down the old social order, we should not expect that it will go any further based on perseverance alone.

'Perseverare diabolicum' is a maxim for the socialist State.

The strong difference, which Mao calls 'antagonistic contradiction', must reappear to its full extent: Cultural Revolution.

In so doing Mao discerned the current agency of the communist political subject, the stroke of force that separates it from its alleged prior line of existence, the socialist State and the party that is all too involved in it.

Oh, but Mallarmé would much rather not show this subject that the structural will of his dialectic stumbles up against! If only all this could be kept within the homogeneity of the poetic operations! He voices his ambition in the programme for Igitur: 'The drama . . . is resolved in an instant, just the time of showing its defeat, which unfolds in a flash.'[19]

The time to say 'or else', 'except that', happens no sooner than the subject already has taken place, as dissidence to the place. Henceforth, once past the annulment, we are transitioning toward the idea of the cause, and again we only have at our disposal the familiar universe of metonymies.

Is not this thin forced splitting of two chains, this minimal interruption for which a few adverbs or a few conjunctions suffice, almost nothing?

Yes, but without this infimous and total gap, without this grammar of exception, there would only be the monotonous and infinite efficacy of the grinding of being under the law of an absence.

Any true dialectician, even a structural one who subordinates it to the play among places, recognizes in passing, 'in a flash', the emergence of force whereby the outplace includes itself destructively in the splace that excludes it.

In so doing, said dialectician produces a theory of the subject.[20]

The fact of having pushed his poetic machinery all the way to the implacable rigour of 'certainly this, if it was not perhaps that' ultimately saves Mallarmé from the flat precipice of structuralism. The latter is that which, in *A Dice Throw*, just before the 'except, perhaps, a constellation', he calls with precision 'the constant neutrality of the abyss' (CP 177), from which the unlikely stellar exception comes, for the time of a subject effect, to keep him apart.

As for the 'Tombs', if they do not require the grammatical exception, this is because the annulment of the first vanishing term (the deceased, Poe or Wagner, Verlaine or Baudelaire) is figured in them by the 'solid sepulchre', the 'calm block' which from the start partitions the earthly life of the hero and the ideal life of his work: he is dead, except that we honour his material tomb only for the mysteries of his spiritual eternity.

No other function is attributed to the mausoleums of Lenin or Mao: they are dead, the monument says, if it is not for the fact that the political subject, for whose tortuous path they henceforth occupy the position of polar star.

As for knowing whether it is not rather the star that is thus put in the mausoleum so that finally 'the time to show its defeat' may come for the subject, that is an affair for the State, which, after all, is never a subject.

3

Why does the poem come to a close? This is a question of pure fact and of pure logic. It is a fact that it comes to a close. A poem by Mallarmé even gives a special impression of closure, of an integral enframing. And yet, it would be logical for it to remain open-ended, since the combined operations of the vanishing and the annulment, by which the cause produces its effect and then delivers its concept, by themselves imply no halting point whatsoever.

The ship . . . or else the siren . . . if not Neptune . . . unless a conch . . .

And why not the circle of a reconvocation of the ship? Now that would be pretty!

Stilled beneath the oppressive cloud
that basalt and lava base
flush with the echoes that have bowed
before a trumpet lacking grace

O what sepulchral wreck (the spray
knows, but it simply drivels there)
ultimate jetsam cast away
abolishes the mast stripped bare

or else concealed that, furious
failing some great catastrophe
all the vain chasm gaping wide

in the so white and trailing tress
would have drowned avariciously
a siren's childlike side

left dead by the song's excess
except that hatred the mast annuls
from foam the plunging ride[21]

At the cost of a second subjective forcing ('except that'), we obtain the perfect closure, from which set theory had to guard itself by forbidding that one accept descending chains in the form of a loop of the type:

$$a \in \ldots\ldots\ldots \in d \in c \in b \in a$$

The simplest of these loops is $a \in a$, which posits that the set is an element of itself, which is something no intuitively graspable set can tolerate. Accordingly, such formal entities were called 'extraordinary' sets, so extraordinary in fact that to simplify, or even simply to make possible their metatheory, one forged their interdiction pure and simple, provided for by the special axiom called the axiom of foundation (or of regularity). And so too the axiom of foundation forbids that one descend to infinity, in the following way:

$$\cdots\cdots\cdots a_{n+1} \in a_n \in \cdots\cdots\cdots a_2 \in a_1 \in a$$

Delimiting the impossible, the axiom of foundation is properly named, in that it touches upon the real: the real of self-inclusion by way of being an element of itself.

So it is, in some regard, with the class party, at least in the way Stalin sees it: 'detachment of the working class', part of this class—element of its whole—it is also equivalent, identical to it: from the point of politics, the party is the class.[22]

Thus the Stalinist class contains itself as element.

This amounts to saying that it is unfounded—with regard to the axiom of foundation.

Mallarmé, for his part, is well-founded. The poem, which is supposed to be finite, does not end in a loop, nor does it suggest the principle of an iterative descending infinity.

I leave it up to you to judge whether my looping—defounding— addition which annuls the siren and re-establishes the ship produces a paradox for the operations accepted by the Mallarméan theory of poetic sets: metaphor, metonymy, vanishing, annulment. The latter, I repeat, articulate all the concepts of the structural dialectic: chain effect, vanishing term, causality of lack.

Mallarmé stops.

Mao does not stop. To Stalin's loops he prefers the other slope of the unfounded, of the real as impossible: the infinite descent. From the party to the masses, in which it installs and unlimits itself, the trajectory never crosses a stable frontier. Without the mass line, the party is null and void. Not to include the party disarms the masses in questions of politics. Whence the following two axioms: the party is 'leading nucleus of the people as a whole', rather than 'class detachment'.[23] It builds itself, and rectifies itself, 'open wide on all sides', rather than purifying itself according to its law of organization.[24]

Stalin's politics is closed, detached, frontier-like: algebraic; that of Mao is open, implicated, tendential: topological.

Topological, too, is the Maoist concept of political history. Periodize and pass beyond. No halting point. 'Success, failure, new success, new failure, and thus all the way to the final victory.' But the 'final' in question is only the one prescribed by the periodization. There is no final victory that is not relative. Every victory is the beginning of a failure of a new type. 'This is the final struggle',[25] the official song of the workers for a whole era, designates the mode of historicization prescribed by the current figure of conflict (of class conflict, as far as we are concerned). After which, new contradictions, new struggles, new failures, new 'final' victory.

And communism? Communism is the name for the other era of conflict. 'I don't believe that communism will not be divided into stages, and that there will be no qualitative changes. Lenin said that all things can be divided' (Mao, *Talk on Questions of Philosophy*, 1964).[26]

This type of statement amounts to the following, which is crucial for Marxism: history does not exist (it would be a figure of the whole). Only historical periods or historicizations (figures of the One-of-the-two) exist. This is why we communists postulate no halting point. When we determine the current stage, it is with regard to the preceding one and the coming one. We do not count further than three. Four at the most: an uncertain four is needed in order to obtain three certainties.

Mallarmé's poem, which is less the current stage of the Book than the waste of its impossibility, posits an implacable finitude. It 'may limit all the glum flights of blasphemy hurled to the future' (*The Tomb of Edgar Allan Poe*, trans. modified); it is that 'rock . . . which imposed a limit on infinity' (*A Dice Throw*).

There is a time to conclude. Is it the good old negation of negation? Many believe so. Chance having been denied a first time, the second negation produces the idea of chance itself. The siren is the absolute of which the ship is only the mediation. We can find something of this kind in *Igitur*:

At last he himself, when the noises are silenced, will forecast something great (no stars? chance annulled?) from this simple fact that he can bring about shadow by blowing on the light—Then, since he will have spoken according to the absolute—which denies immortality, the absolute will exist outside—moon, above time. . . .[27]

Latent Hegelianism, consolidated by what follows: 'The infinite emerges from chance, which you have denied' (*ibid.*).

4

There is certainly nothing wrong with this interpretation, which gives in to the openly idealist aspect of the structural dialectic. But I would like to raise two objections.

It is given the lie in *Igitur* itself by the following theorem, which Mallarmé calls a 'schema':

Briefly, in an act where chance is in play, chance always accomplishes its own Idea in affirming or negating itself. Confronting its existence, negation and affirmation fail. It contains the Absurd—implies it, but in the latent state and prevents it from existing: which permits the Infinite to be.[28]

Mallarmé's logic does not settle for negation any more than for affirmation. The causality of lack has nothing to do with the labour of the negative. The conceptualization (the infinite) of the real (chance) operates by way of the reciprocal neutralization of both affirmation and negation.

The dialectical procedures (vanishing, annulment, and, we will see, foreclosure), which moreover are irreducible to one another, have no other aim than the production of the concept. It follows that they expose themselves to chance only in order to inscribe its necessity. Therein lies the special interest of Lacan's paradox, for whom (formal and deductive) logic is the science of the real (pure happenstance, chance encounter). This paradox explains the negative semblance of the operations: they delimit within language (within *lalangue*, Lacan would say), more specifically within poetic language, the forbidding dictatorship under the effects of which the real can be said in its necessity.

A Dice Throw illustrates throughout the affirmative power of the dialectical sequences, without lining up the paraphernalia of negativity (but the lack, the void, the disappearing: yes. A subtraction is not a negation.)

The 'hoary maniac' who comes to 'play . . . the game in the name of the waves' disappears so as to bury himself in the 'original spray' while nobody knows whether the dice have been launched or not. Apparently: 'Nothing of the unforgettable crisis or else the event might have been achieved in view of all results null human will have taken place a commonplace upsurge is shedding absence other than the place a lowly splashing of some kind as if to scatter the empty act abruptly which otherwise by its falsehood would have founded the loss in these indefinite regions of the swell where all reality is dissolved' (CP 178–9, trans. modified).[29]

Except that there emerges a constellation, 'cold with neglect and disuse', which idealizes the wager on the real of which courage has the task of structuring the suspense. In this sense only: 'Every Thought emits a Dice Throw.'

The initial operations which clear the ground for the stellar exception—the inventive production with which the mental bravura is rewarded—present a formidable complexity.

The scene—a deserted ocean—brings out of its own void a wrecked boat, of which the foam is the sail, the marine abyss the conch. As the final piece of wreckage of this phantom ship in the process of abolition, there rises the captain's closed fist, containing the dice. The hesitation before their launching (that is, the equivalence of negation and affirmation) changes the aleatory gesture into a veil of engagement—between the old man and probability, a veil of illusion which 'will falter and fall' until it is no longer comparable ('as if', first subject effect) except to a hovering quill. The quill metamorphoses the ocean into a velvet cap, such that underneath this feathered headgear one guesses the presence of Hamlet, 'bitter prince of the reef', but above all, in the play, the master of the undecidable act. The Dane's rock is barely even evoked when it is to its being slapped by the tail of a siren that the quill's annulment is assigned, logically equivalent to the erasure of the dice throw.

Appearing suddenly out of the maritime void, at least six vanishing terms follow one after the other: the ship (wrecked), the arm of the dice thrower (hesitant), the veil of engagement (which falls), the pen/quill (hovering on the brink of the abyss), Hamlet (the undecidable act), the siren (terminal scales).

The system of metaphors continues unflinchingly, from the pair chance/necessity that serves as a directive for the poetic logic—science of the real—all the way to its idealization as halting point: sky/constellation ('at some last point that sanctifies it'), through the intermediate rungs, each of them carrying out the self-effacement of its predecessor: wing of foam/gaping depth; sail/shell; hand containing the dice/the master's corpse ('a corpse cut off by its arm separated from the secret it withholds'); probability/old man; quill/abyss; quill/velvet cap; Hamlet/reef; siren/rock.

Add to this a theoretical commentary, which is mixed in with the process and which underscores its equations. It informs us that in this theatre where there is no backstage, the play being performed is the one from which any dialectical adventure draws its formal legitimacy.

While the hero throughout has had the courage of disappearing into the operations aimed at the logical capture of the real, the final subject effect, marked by a magnificent 'except perhaps', occurs at the end of the journey, when an incredible network of metaphors, metonymic corrosions, and successive disappearances, has scraped to the bone the 'ghost of a gesture' where 'an idle chance' was attempted.

I would compare this hard labour of logic to partisan work, when politics tracks down the tiniest of antagonisms in the midst of a thick consensus, reduces the plenitude of the social to its conflictive bone, and, just when it is on the verge of having exhausted its resources, receives, if all is properly carried out, the subjectivizing exception of an abrupt collapse of the initial conditions under the imperious pressure of the revolts.

Our minuscule action may seem equivalent to inaction. But the courage to hold steady in this equivalence enables us to be the political subject of this new era.

Is our chance as Marxists 'idle'? Certainly! Who would bet a penny on the revolution in France today? Our thought, though, emits this throw of dice. This is because it has the required patience for it and, on its own scale, knows how to produce the radical logic of which the vulgar fortune of events is only the first chance.

Now we come to my second objection to the poet's alleged Hegelianism.

His halting points are not just about anything! The leading role is reserved for the stars: constellation of the dice throw, 'Septentrion' of scintillations; 'festive star' elsewhere ('When the shade threatened . . .'); 'of a star that no longer shines, but dies' ('Herodias: Overture'). This is a well-established tradition. Hugo already ends plenty of poems with the sight of this starry sky, concerning which Kant said that, together with the moral law in his heart, it completed the whole of Reasons.

The other endings? The swan, the rose and the gladiolus, the jewels ('the fire of a bracelet,' 'cold precious stones'[30]), a woman's tresses, the music instrument, the siren and the Amazon. The tomb.

It is not very clever to see how, beyond their cultural evidence (all this is poetic, isn't it?), the signifiers in question are in some way separable. No matter how worn-out they may well be, their qualitative intensity distinguishes them to the point where, by merely saying 'rose' (certainly not petunia), or 'swan' (duck, by contrast . . .), or 'mandolin' (avoid cornet), or 'tresses' (mop of hair won't do), I put myself at a precious distance in sharp contrast to 'table', 'room', 'passageway' or 'central heating system'.

Whence, despite the archaic *hoir* ('heir'), the uniquely preliminary nature of the following lines:

The heir apparent's ancient room,
Rich though fallen trophies bearing,

Would still be cold if he came faring
Through passageways back through the gloom.[31]

With these lines Mallarmé prepares from a distance the following graduated halting points (the first two being the underpinning for a retroactive annulment by the third): 'the console's lightning glow', 'some rose in the dark', 'there sleeps a mandolin forlorn'.[32]

The time to conclude overdetermines the dialectical laws in a play of pre-established intensities that the temporal depth of language draws back into itself.

Bootlegger of culture, Mallarmé, who pretends to generate the poem's ending from the strict resources internal to the dialectical procedure, injects some familiar connotations therein in order to achieve his goal. Because the floating language we inherit authorizes us to do so, we tolerate that a poem pauses at the rose of dark night or the swan's exile. We have almost arrived safe and sound, having been guided by the star.

That is where, after the 'and yet' of the exception, the second *coup de force* sneaks in, the bluff of intensity where we succumb to the subject.

The logic of places, even when handled by an absolute virtuoso, would be hard put to deliver anything other than the regular and virtually infinite iteration of that which vanishes and that which is annulled. This requires the historical miracles of art, all of them by the way with their special date attached, since this dying nineteenth century stands out like no other, Mallarmé included, for its wilted roses, its gilding, its gladioluses, its consoles, and its fans.

No aversion here, as far as I am concerned. Marked with the seal of inherited intensities, the poem attests that we must dialecticize the structural dialectic beyond itself. This would be a kind of force, if at the end we were to play with the fascinating and impersonal seduction of separable signifiers.[33]

This is also proof that the 'negation of negation' in all this is not what allows us to conclude.

The beautiful word of 'communism' has been entrusted to us, Marxists, as the misleading name for the halting point of our prehistory. Even that of 'revolution', though less openly melodious, often functions as the time to conclude, though it is clear that it concludes nothing, having no meaning whatsoever aside from the one conferred upon it by the *other* revolution, the second one, from whence the limit of the first becomes clear.

The word 'communism' has contracted some mould, that's for sure.

But the roses and the gladioluses, the tresses, the sirens, and the consoles, were also eaten by moths in that fin-de-siècle poetry which was given the name 'symbolism' and which all in all was a catastrophe.

Let us try to be no more communist in the sense of Brezhnev or Marchais than Mallarmé was a symbolist in the manner of Viélé-Griffin.

If symbolism has held up so gloriously well with the swans and the stars, let us see if we can do as much with the revolution and communism.

It is because one takes the exact measure of their power, and thus of their divided sharing, that words may be innocent.

Jewellery for the sacred of any subtraction of existence

February 8, 1976

Mallarmé and the class struggle—Sonnet in *ix* and *or*—Foreclosure—The subject as delay—Logic of the trajectory—Everything is true, but we must move on and go beyond

1

The heterogeneous exists as subject. This is what Mallarmé supports by way of the forced exception. There is also the fact that the rarification of the decor, driven by the insistence of the vanishing terms, enters into conflict with the poem's brutal concluding intensity.

'Conflict' is the dialectical title of a rarely quoted prose text, originally published with another title: 'A Case of Conscience'.[34] A case of the intellectual's conscience in the class struggle. Yes indeed! The latter is mentioned by its very name in the text.

Mallarmé is in the countryside. In front of his retreat, as an annex of industrialization, a 'mess hall for railroad workers' is being constructed. Four lines give us the equivalent of Germinal in order to present the working class of this building, that violent, trade unionist 'labour squad', full of alcohol and rage. Translation of the insults against property and exploitation. The hostility turns against the villa occupied by our witness: '"Piece of crap!" Accompanied by the sound of feet kicking the grate, suddenly bursts out.' He is hurt, irritated. His restrictive soliloquy, which at first attempted to exempt itself from the workers' hatred, is interrupted by a whim: the other class, unforgettably quarrelsome.

Pulling himself erect, he examines me with animosity. It is impossible to wipe him out mentally: I want to complete the work of alcohol and lay him in advance in the dust so that he will cease to be this vulgar and mean colossus; without my having to lose to him first in a fistfight that would illustrate, on the lawn, the class struggle. In the meantime, he overflows with new insults. (D 44)

Mallarmé finds no help in his opponent's obvious drunkenness. Rather, he sees in the latter's muteness a dubious destructive complicity. At this point he is 'racked with contradictory states, pointless, distorted, and affected by the contagion, the shiver, of some imbecilic ebriety' (*ibid.*).

What could be the structural artifice to which the shady intoxication of the class struggle pertains?

Only Sunday offers a controversial escape. After the political discussions ('Sadness', says Mallarmé 'that what I produce remains, to people like this, essentially, like the clouds at dusk or the stars in the sky, vain', this time it is the star which, tried by antagonism, comes up against its limit and is unable to conclude except with vanity), floored by the alcohol, the workers fall asleep.

Tempted to return to his daydreaming beyond the confusion of bodies, Mallarmé cannot make up his mind to do so. A powerful respect, which literally has come from elsewhere, renders him immobile.

In the alcohol-sleepiness, this 'momentary suicide' (45), he deciphers first 'the dimension of the sacred in their existence' (46), the provisory substitute of an interruption for the workers in which we should recognize, for lack of its higher form which would be the revolt, a derivative form of this access to the concept that is the annulment.

Then, 'constellations begin to shine'. Are we once more going to end on the note of their cold disuse? No. The experience of antagonism forces the intellectual to link his endeavour to the concept of this experience. You will say that they are irreducibly real, these workers 'whose mystery and duty', as Mallarmé declares, he in his capacity 'should understand' (45).

The body of workers, that is, class in its nocturnal detachment, presents an opacity far stronger than the stars. Rather than representing an obstacle for the poetic endgame, it becomes the latter's substance, rejoining centuries of creativity of the people all the way to the infinity of a social idea:

Keeping watch over these artisans of elementary tasks, I have occasion, beside a limpid, continuous river, to meditate on these symbols of the People—some robust intelligence bends their spines every day in order to extract, without the intermediary of wheat, the miracle of life which grounds presence: others in the past have built aqueducts or cleared fields for some implement, wielded by the same Louis-Pierre, Martin, Poitou or the Norman. When they are not asleep, they thus invoke one another according to their mothers or their provinces. But in fact their births fall into anonymity, and their mothers into the deep sleep that prostrates them, while the weight of centuries presses down on them, eternity reduced to social proportions. (46)

Given the limits of its time, what integrity is there, in addition to the beauty of the tribute, in submitting his intellectual task to the tenuous chance encounter of the real of classes, without conceding anything to populism, through the inner consent given to the idea that here the violent source of a different kind of concept must be grasped!

2

A second flattening of which the syntactical guarantee is the law of the splace:

Her pure nails on high displaying their onyx,
The lampbearer, Anxiety, at midnight sustains
Those vesperal dreams that are burnt by the Phœnix
And which no funeral amphora contains

On the credenzas in the empty room: no ptyx,
Abolished shell whose resonance remains
(For the Master has gone to draw tears from the Styx
With this sole object that Nothingness attains).

But in the vacant north, adjacent to the window panes,
A dying shaft of gold illumines as it wanes
A nix sheathed in sparks that a unicorn kicks.

Though she in the oblivion that the mirror frames
Lies nude and defunct, there rains
The scintillations of the one-and-six.[35]

In any empty room, at midnight, only Anxiety reigns, supported by the disappearance of the light. Like a torch in the form of raised hands which would hold only an extinguished flame, this anxiety of the void cannot be cured with any trace of the setting sun, not even with the ashes that one could have collected in a funerary urn.

The poet, master of the places, has gone to the river of death, taking with him a signifier (the ptyx) which refers to no existing object.

However, near the open window on the north side, there faintly sparkles the gilt frame of a mirror on which are sculpted some unicorns chasing after a nymph.

All of this is going to disappear, it is as if the nymph drowned in the water of the mirror, where nevertheless rises the reflection of the seven stars of the Great Bear.

Mallarmé was rather proud of this poem, which he qualified as 'null-sonnet reflecting itself in all manners'.[36] He considered that in this sonnet he had pushed self-sufficiency to the extreme in making a whole out of nothing. Think of the title of the first version: 'Sonnet allegorical of itself'.

The text appears to empty itself out non-stop. The burden of lack, so to speak, is at a maximum:

a) The 'vesperal dream', an allusion, classical for Mallarmé, to the setting sun, already burnt by the ending day—though called upon to be reborn, whence its metaphorization by the bird Phoenix, which always rises up again from its ashes—has not even left behind a trace: there is a lack of trace of that which has disappeared.

b) The decor (a salon) is absolutely empty.

- The master is at 'the Styx'. The poet, subject of the chain, always occupies the place of the dead. He sacrifices himself so that the text may come into being as a closed totality, strictly governed by the law: 'The right to accomplish anything exceptional, or beyond the reach of the vulgar, is paid for by the omission of the doer, and of his death as so-and-so' ('Restricted Action', D 216).

- He has taken with him the 'ptyx'. So many glosses have been written about this word that no dictionary consigns! Mallarmé, though, has said twice that it is a matter of a pure signifier, uninscribable otherwise than as the attribute of the dead poet. *'Aboli bibelot d'inanité sonore'*, null-object reducible to the sonorous void of the signifier; 'sole object that Nothingness attains', object withdrawn from being, subtractive object.

- If it is subtractive—minus one—this is because the ptyx stands in excess over the treasure of the signifier. Guardian of the possibility of meaning, it does not fall under this possibility. The ptyx is the plus-one of the signifier, whose denotation, no matter how long the chain may well be, never arrives.

– The master is absent, under the emblem of this perfect signifier of lack, which is also, much to the torment of copyists, the lack of a signifier, unattested for outside this poem, in which moreover it enters only in order to designate its exit.

c) The gilt frame of the mirror agonizes, it can barely ('perhaps') be deciphered.

d) The nix is defunct, buried in the mirror.

Aside from these effects of absence, we could rightly say that this time the splitting traverses—atomism taught us to recognize this necessity—all the elements of the poem.

The vesperal divides day from night. The Phoenix divides itself by fire into ashes and rebirth. Midnight is the supreme Mallarméan hour: last hour of the day that ends, or first one of the day to come? Divisible, split. Atemporal hour. It is at midnight that *Igitur* must realize its act (to throw the dice): 'This returned Midnight evokes its shadow, finite and null, with these words: I was the hour which is to make me pure' (*Igitur*, chapter 'Midnight'). The funeral amphora, which moreover is absent, like the tomb—another exemplary Mallarméan sign—would signal presence, but of that which is no more. The master exists, guarantor of the place, but he is dead. The ptyx, key to all meaning, has none. The gold of the mirror shows itself, like the setting sun, only in its disappearing. The aleatory nix is pursued, but defunct. The mirror contains both the waters of oblivion and the fixation of the seven stars.

Note also that nothing exists except in the form of a Greek tale, nocturnal mythology, fabrication of a dream. The Phoenix, legendary bird. The ptyx, signifying stamp tantamount to the Phallus for Lacan. The Styx, dead metaphor of death. The unicorns, medieval relays of the Phoenix. The nix, exclusive femininity for the faun.

We would never be done stating the annulment of inexistence, the nothing of nothing that this incredible machine makes into its subject matter.

This includes even the sonorities, to the point where we cannot believe our ears. How can one possibly construct a sonnet within the closure of rhymes in *yx* and *ore* (quatrains) and then, by inversion of the musical gender, in *ixe* and *or* (tercets)?

Jewellery for the sacred of any subtraction of existence.

All that is passed down to us is a single exception of certainty, the seven stars of the constellation which all of a sudden comes to pull us out of anxiety, brought forth in the mirror of our oblivion by the 'though' to which is linked, salvific, an impeccably delayed subject.

3

To those of you who have already been instructed by 'A la nue accablante tu', I propose that you hunt down the vanishing terms that sustain the function of causality. We obtained a good return when we found two, the ship and the siren.

Now here we get into a snag.

The nix is a good candidate. Her drowning restores her to the mirror. She is a nix. And this judicious vanishing term is subsequently annulled ('though') so that the constellation may be put in place, as always, with the value of a halting point.

If we stick to the tercets, the affair is easy enough.

The presupposition of the setting sun (the vesperal dream), the 'natural' vanishing term for the pair day/night (writing/page), is metaphorized in the empty room by the division of the mirror: gilt frame with unicorns, on one hand, dark glass, on the other. The waning of the frame's gold, horizon for a salon's setting sun, induces the nix as vanishing divisibility: pursued by the fire of the frame's unicorns, she plunges into the mirror's night. Her revocation ('defunct') would not leave any trace—it would generate only 'the oblivion that the mirror frames'—if the constellation did not come to relay her in terms of annulment ('though').

The annulling connection is all the more firm and affirmative in that, according to the legend, it is after all the nymph Callisto who was cast into the sky so that she would draw the Great Bear. Dying from its own vanishing, she is reborn, eternal and cold.

What is a good metaphor for the vanishing term in general? The (setting) sun? It is day + night.

What is the nix (defunct)? The same thing, restricted to the living room ('restricted action'): gold (waning) + mirror (dark).

Now, what is a good metaphor, in the night completed by the lacking sun, for the Idea of this lack (hence, of the lack of lack)? The stars, whose brightness revokes the vanishing term by producing its concept. By way of the star, the sun certainly comes to be lacking twice. The star presupposes the night, hence the causal vanishing of the sun, and yet, by bringing brightness, it annuls it.

The idea of the (setting) sun, which the (defunct) nix re-names, is the reflection of the seven stars in the mirror's night (in 'the oblivion that the mirror frames'). There we have the concept, the lack of lack, from which all anxiety is lifted, *since it is* anxiety.

It is the absence of sun that led to anxiety. The seven-star constellation is born from the annulment of the supposed trace of this absence: the nix. It thus grasps anxiety, not as effect but as essence.

Yes, but is there then only one vanishing term, the nix? And what about the quatrains?

4

There is first of all the poem's retroaction upon its conditions. What is it that takes place before the empty salon?

The inaugural pair is clearly that of day and night. It is given twice, in its vanishing juncture. The 'vesperal dream', scarlet illumination of the evening, and the Phoenix (the sun), consumed by its inherent fire in the promise of being reborn at dawn.

It is in the middle of the night that the poem proposes its wager, by way of the concept-star of the dead fire, on the solar promise. Between two presences, only the lack of the absence of any present, which has the value of an idea, saves the world from chance.

Between two imaginaries, only the symbolic guards us from the real.

Between two mass uprisings, only the politics of the party preserve the class.

Beware: though they can be stated at the same point, these three statements, the Mallarméan, the Lacanian, and the Maoist, are not isomorphous.

Does the empty and nightly room keep the trace of the golden promise? This is the question that commands the inspection of the places, according to the poetic regime of anxiety.

Something a bit strange happens. We can certainly see that, in their succession, the (funeral) amphora, the master (at the Styx) and the (inexistent) ptyx constitute the triple ban of nonbeing. The first one contains the ashes, the second is dead, the third is this word that says nothing.

But in addition, *none of them is there*.

These ghostly beings for sure would be vanishing terms, since they have no other being except to designate nonbeing, if we did not have to admit that to vanish is something they cannot do, affected as they are, in the decor, by a radical absence without any effect (contrary to the supposed ship, which could be inferred from the visible foam, or contrary to the divisible mirror, which we can discern).

Should we say that these terms are annulled? No, since for the annulment of a hypothetical term, its vanishing must be the cause of a trace with regard to which, as exception, another term is made to appear, such as the siren after the ship, or the constellation of seven stars after the nix.

The amphora, the master, and the ptyx have all the attributes of the vanishing term, except the vanishing, from which a trace of the lack should be evinced. They lack without a trace. On this account, they are irreplaceable.

Here, we have a new kind of absence: one that no longer operates within any representation, and on which the concept, the lack of lack, has no grip. Picking up a notion from Lacan, we should say that these terms are foreclosed.

I must distinguish three operations that work on absence:

– the vanishing, with causal value;
– the annulment, with conceptual value;
– the foreclosure, with null value.

We owe it to Mallarmé's genius to have posited, with regard to the ptyx, that the pure signifier of lack tolerates to be evoked only when struck by foreclosure. It is not that it disappears: it *is not there*.

Unalterable support of the 'there is not', it makes for a tangency of the real, of which is said only the 'there is'.

That is why the word itself had to be carried to the shores of death.

There is something unconceptualizable. That is what, based on the foreclosures, this sonnet's quatrains declare. What is this unconceptualizable? The pure fact of there being some concept—which is the reality to which the tercets are devoted. What makes that there is some concept is the master, death, and the pure signifier: the poet, the amphora, and the ptyx.

This is something you will never be able to deduce: this triangle of the subject, death, and language. For all deduction happens from there.

To deduce means to substitute. The 'rules of substitution' lie at the basis of mathematical logic. The amphora, the master, and the ptyx are unsubstitutable, held as they forever are in the 'there is not', symbolic correlate of the 'there is' of the real. The symbolic trinity as such.

Is this true? I mean, that there is some unconceptualizable? Mao did not seem to believe so. He said: 'We will come to know everything that we did not know before' (SW IV, 374, trans. modified).

In this regard, the Marxist axiom: 'It is right to revolt' is ambiguous. Is it meant to indicate that the revolt has its reason, its concept? I don't think so. The revolt is what founds rationality, and it concentrates a thousand reasons to revolt. As popular subjectivization, however, neither can it be reduced to its reasons (which belong to the structure or to the event), nor does it wholly abolish itself in the positivity of its political future. Here there is a factor of historical fortune, of illuminating chance, which is not that of language and of death, but that of courage and justice.

Of the revolt, the State can only say that 'there is not' any. Political revolutionaries, for their part, stick to the 'there is'. Exquisite chance to intoxicate the revolutionary, the revolt is the ptyx of the State.

5

We are almost at the end of our troubles. Let us mark x the foreclosure, and / the vanishing. The annulment is punctuated with 'but' or 'though'. We thus obtain the following constructed schema:

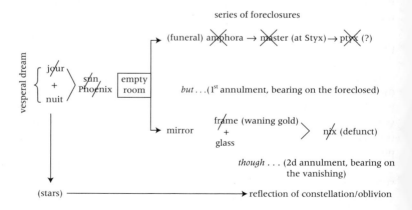

Where then is the lightning strike of the subject in this case? The two annulments do not have the status of a *coup de force* that elsewhere we recognized in them (and that one can discern in the majority of Mallarmé's poems: practise yourselves!).

The 'but' in the first tercet is opposed only to the nullity of foreclosure. It opens a line of totalization onto the gilded frame, without breaking up any other, since the amphora, the master, and the ptyx give consistency only to the radical lack of existence, to the nonplace.

The 'though' eternalizes the nymph Callisto, rather than destroying her. Defunct and naked, she is a new Herodias: 'Mirror, cold water frozen in your frame' (CP 30), which the stellar exception stops on the edges of the nothing.

This poem is more subtly structural than many others. Leaving aside the foreclosures, which have no effect other than to intensify the void, the heterogeneous is almost unreadable in it. What slides under the 'though', sutured onto a legend (Callisto) which bridges the nymph and the star, is only a subject of diminished force, almost folded back—finally!—onto the even surface of the metonymical operations.

Except for this singular delay of perception that saves the day within the night only in the final instance, when obviously the sky's reflection in the mirror was present from the start.

The construction's detour via the waning gold and the generation of the revocable vanishing term (the nix) only serve the purpose of differing the time to conclude.

The foam in 'A la nue accablante . . .' was traced for us from the start. Hence, the leap of the hypothesis, the 'or else' of the subject, imposed itself without any possibility of escape. Here the ruse, which justifies Mallarmé's basking in it, consists in postponing the stellar trace as if it could *result* from the nix, whereas it is actually consistent, or coexistent, with it.

What is the function of anxiety? To divide the night. The opposition day/night is in and of itself an antidialectical metaphor, a pure strong difference. Day and night succeed one another without releasing the movement of the unity of opposites. They are disjointed alternating entities: metaphysical, as is their invocation in the devastating mythology of amorous fusion—the most radical attempt at disavowing sexual difference—in Wagner's *Tristan*.

The first dialectical step consists in grasping the succession of two terms in strong difference from the vanishing of the causal term that articulates them, here the (setting) sun. If, however, the restricted night in which one operates—that of the empty salon—is indivisible, this step is only a semblance. What matters is to salvage the trace of the day as internal scission of the nocturnal void. That is why anxiety is said to be a 'lamp-bearer', carrier of light. This is not so much its reality as much as its *duty*. Its dialectical duty, which requires that at the point of anxiety the other subjectivizing figure comes in, the one which breaks up the order of things and tolerates its scission: courage.

The poem's energy corresponds to what Hölderlin names 'the poet's courage', to which the following is prescribed:

Is not all that's alive close and akin to you,
Does the Fate not herself keep you to serve her ends?
Well, then, travel defenceless
On through life, and fear nothing there!

All that happens there be welcome, be blessed to you,
Be an adept in joy, or is there anything
That could harm you there, heart, that
Could offend you, where you must go? (PF 201)

For Mallarmé, though, there is no temporal advent of the new. Courage, for the structural dialectic, is devoid of historicity. Whence the great difficulty in distinguishing it from anxiety.

For a militant Marxist, there is the anxiety of the night of imperialist societies, the anxiety of the ashy Phoenix of May '68, or of the Cultural Revolution—can we not ask whether even the amphora remains? The last Master is so old! As for 'communism', that ptyx, who takes hold of it, for what purpose? It is also a duty to divide what is obscure, to hold fast to the worker's promise even at the heart of its deepest denial.

We are lamp-bearers. Just as the poem does with the deserted salon, we inspect the political place in order to discern therein the staking out of antagonism that will relay the promise and organize the future.

Wherein then lies the difference? In that, a structural sectarian of weak differences who rejects the aspect of historical force in the scissions, Mallarmé can only deliver anxiety over to a logic of trajectories.

Time is extinguished by space. The solution to the lamp-bearing problem (here, the reflection of the Great Bear) must be there from the start. Only the poet's dead eye spins the subtle threads that link one object to another so that, in a tricked perspective, the illusion of a surprise may come about.

See what Mallarmé writes to Cazalis to guide the possible illustration of the sonnet (he is referring to the first version, from 1867):

For instance, there is a window open, at night, the two shutters fastened; a room with no one in it, despite the stable appearance provided by the fastened shutters, and in a night made of absence and questioning, without furniture apart from the vague outline of what appear to be tables, a warlike and dying frame of a mirror hung up at the back of the room, with its reflection, a stellar and incomprehensible reflection, of Ursa Major, which links to heaven alone this dwelling abandoned by the world.[37]

The composition of the whole is prior to the operations, and the poem does not have recourse to anything other than what it latently presupposes.

To the logic of the trajectory, which the structural dialectic comes up against and which announces the new only in the retroactive operation of its *mise-en-scène,* we oppose the logic of tendencies, of currents, of vanguards, wherein that which is barely at its birth, though placed and subjected, links up with the most terrible force of the future.

The Mallarméan subject who is given over to the space does not exceed anxiety. He formulates its law of exception, which he deduces from the place.

Here whatever amounts to the subject of anxiety is nothing but the delay of perception.[38] Had the constellation been initial, it would subjugate the subject. Coming in the conclusion, it saves it. Nothing new occurs, except in terms of position in the language.

6

We find no fault with the Mallarméan operations. The chain effect is taken to its peak by the unprecedented use of metonymical sequences. The vanishing term is the centre of gravity of the whole mechanism of the poems. The causality of lack is reduplicated, as lack of lack, into its concept. Thus, a new operator is introduced: the annulment. The splitting affects all the terms of a given poetic splace. The terms that are foreclosed convey the theory of the unconceptualizable.

Here the complete structural dialectic is present, active, displayed in the vibrating marvel of language, submitted to the unifying touch of verse. Lacan will not add to it.

Dialectic, yes indeed! For the other (historical) aspect, which is here subservient and devoted to the sheer lightning flash, by force frees the subject from the chains that keep it *in the same place*.

All this forms a precious legacy: the articulation of the subject-effect under the signifiers of the exception; the cunning use of the signifying forces of poetry that leave us wide open as to a time to conclude; and, finally, the delay in the trajectory, by which the subject of anxiety throws the dice.

The exception in the signifier, the word that shines, the delay: Lacan will go very far along these same trails.

No, I find no fault with all this, except that I am not swayed by an order of things in which all thought is devoted to the inspection of that which subordinates it to the placement of an absence and which brings salvation for the subject only in the already-thereness of a star.

The fact that in this famous and fatally unknown author everything is true only commits us to scrutinize the welcome de-emphasizing to which we should treat him.

This will lead us to Lacan, and, I hope, to some assurance from Marxism as to its lamp-bearing powers for the theory of the subject, which will determine whether it, and it alone, can carry the light of courage into the adventure of this century, in which it is claimed to have provoked only anxiety.

Part III

Lack and Destruction

The new *one* forbids the *new* one, and presupposes it

January 10, 1977

Lacan's amphibology—That of Marxism—Two sexes,
two classes

Let us enter, without further delay, into Lacan's ambiguity: '. . . when one makes two, there is never any return. It never amounts to making one anew, not even a new one. *Aufhebung* is one of those pretty little dreams of philosophy' (S XX, 90/79, trans. modified).

The settling of accounts with Hegel, coming from the one who for us French Marxists is today's Hegel—the only one whom it is our task to divide—in a single phrase gives voice to the distance that separates two centuries in the history of the dialectic.

Lacan is speaking about history—in this case, as behoves him, the history of love. It is a question of elucidating the absolute novelty of the event named 'courtly love' in the thirteenth century. His answer is that something gets split there—something whose vividness cannot be altered by any superior resorption.

Here we are in the midst of our dispute. Lacan, the theoretician of the true scission, of which the Maoist maxim 'One divides into two' sought to preserve the irreparable force, against those repairmen of flat tyres, the revisionists, to whom is suited the syrupy conviction that 'Two fuse into one'.

As for the strict dialectical logic, Lacan outperforms Mallarmé, who was fixated on the stars, in the precise extent to which he is made to recognize:

- the novelty of the real, attested to by the tearing apart of the discursive link;
- the precariousness of the One, obliterated by the new, whose essence is the division.

In so doing, the Hegelian reconciliation, wherein everything is devised so that the pangs of time are nothing more than the presence of the concept ('*Die Zeit ist der Begriff selbst, der* da *ist*', 'Time is the concept itself that *is there*', the *there* that sets the tone[1]), is reduced to the imaginary alone—a 'pretty little dream of philosophy'.

However, the subtlety, in which the analyst's experience is an educator beyond reproach, lies in the syntactical amphibology that Lacan will use relentlessly—contrary to what I held to be Mallarmé's essential univocity—as an operator by which the sentence, having neither recto nor verso, holds together the two sides of one and the same reversible blade.

Which sides? Let us be clear: those of the dialectic, in its structural aspect and its historical aspect. The side of place (the symbolic, in the Lacanian terminology) and the side of force (the real).

Consider our opening line: 'It never amounts to making one anew, even a new one.' Does this cunning strategist of *lalangue*, as he puts it, mean that the division of the one makes for no novelty? The emphasis of the negative, in that case, would fall on the new: not even a *new* one. We are in the logic of iteration, wherein that which splits off is absolved without any return of its unified form—but we are unable to say that anything happens except the Law of this splitting.[2]

Or rather does he mean that from the division of the one there arises an affirmative novelty, which we would only have to consider outside the form of the one that previously could be assigned to it? The emphasis of the negative, in that case, would be on the one: not even a new *one*. Something new, therefore, beyond the signifying law from which any prior form of the one drew its evidence. And, consequently, an irreversible disaster of this very law, the symbolic ruined by the real, the one ungraspable except in the process of its destruction.

The entire genius of Lacan's elucidation on the subject hinges on the fact that in sentence after sentence, and in seminar after seminar, he says both things at the same time.

So do we. Because we had better admit that, insofar as it divides itself into proletariat and bourgeoisie, the field of politics only gives rise to its iterative law, from whose point of view its novelty is less clear than its permanence throughout the eras. Especially if we follow Mao in admitting that this division remains intact under what is called 'socialism' and that it will last, in Mao's own terms, 'for a very long period of history'. But we equally admit that as the political inducer of nonpolitics (of communism), the proletariat causes the breakdown of the one that it divides to the point where it can no longer take on this form, not even by inscribing itself as *one* of the terms of the contradiction.

For Lacan, the analytical theory holds on to this equivocation as the lesson of desire from where the subject is apprehended.[3] For us, Marxism holds on to it in the political practice whose subjective point is the party.

Lacan, an involuntary theoretician of the political party? Marxists, unenlightened practitioners of desire?

This is a false window. The truth is that there is only one theory of the subject. Lacan is ahead of the current state of Marxism and we must take advantage of this advance so as to improve our Marxist affairs.

Why do we draw this undivided and masked theory of the subject from Marx-Lenin-Mao and from Freud-Lacan? Should we climb the fool's bridge—the horror!—of Freudo-Marxism?

No, because not even for a second is it a matter of reconciling doctrines. Everything depends on the real, but the real that is ours, in turn, depends only on the following:

– there are two sexes;
– there are two classes.

Make do with that, you subjects of all experience!

On the side of the true

Philosophies on the blackboard—Four corners of truth: coherence,
repetition, totality, torsion—On para-being

1

Any good polemic is always supposed to require a zoology of deviations. State
Marxism, which in general is to Marxism what in the world of prose a sentence from a district court is to Rimbaud's *Illuminations*, excels in this manic
manipulation of typologies. There is the left in appearance only, which in
reality is on the right; the revisionism which is symmetrical to dogmatism;
the petit-bourgeois anarchism which is the counterpart of half-bourgeois
bureaucratism; the economism whose reverse side is voluntarism . . .

The Chinese say: 'Giving labels'. Can we do without them? I doubt it.
Sometimes we must know how to simplify the world.[4] What memory
obscured by innumerable singularities would afflict us if we were forbidden to enumerate the poison flasks? The fact remains that neither politics
nor the Party have as their vocation what Mallarmé called the 'atlases,
herbariums, and rituals'.[5]

As for philosophy, the—simple—combinatory comprises four notions,
taken two by two: idealism and materialism, and then dialectics and
metaphysics.

From here we infer that there are four philosophical types:

1. Metaphysical idealism;
2. Dialectical idealism;

3. Metaphysical materialism (sometimes also called 'mechanicism');
4. Dialectical materialism.

Furthermore, we know that in order to be a correctly calibrated Marxist, it is bad to be idealist or metaphysical and honourable to be materialist or dialectical.

We thus have at our disposal one serious insult (piece of metaphysical idealist), two moderate insults (idealist dialecticians and mechanical materialists: you are on the right track but on one leg only), and one form of praise (materialist dialectician: excellent, you passed the exam, Stalin prize for the peace of concepts).

What is the meaning of these primitive terms with which we Marxists compose our scale of insults?

Materialist is whoever recognizes the primacy of being over thinking (being does not need my thinking in order to be). Idealist, whoever posits the opposite.

A dialectician is someone who turns contradiction into the law of being; a metaphysician, whoever does the same with the principle of identity.

Today we will not fuzz over these robust distinctions. Except with a table in which the complete typology refers to a single contradiction (that between thinking and being-in-itself) and in which, by the perversion introduced by every supplement, we will distinguish five philosophical types—which is something Lenin already does, to tell the truth, in *Materialism and Empirio-criticism*, by separating the 'frankly and plainly' argued idealism (Berkeley) from Kantian relativism.[6]

TYPE		THINKING	BEING-IN-ITSELF
subjective metaphysical idealism	1	↻↗	✕
objective metaphysical idealism	2	↻↗ - - - - - - - → ●	
dialectical idealism	3	⟲ ←	
metaphysical materialism	4	✕	(● ——→ ●)
materialist dialectic	5	⟿	

The preceding diagram links the distinctions to the trajectory of the process of knowledge.

This table should be considered a philosophical topology. Why? Because it is based on the position of inside and outside, on the question of the border of thinking, on a logistics of frontiers. And because it is from this vantage point that it illuminates the question of truth, whose papers we are here requesting before its *passage through customs*.

Thesis 1, let us say that of Bishop Berkeley, has always seemed fascinating due to its radical appeal. It posits that thinking has no sensible outside. No matter how far you go, you will never be any farther than that somewhat reactionary hero who travelled around his bedroom.[7] It is properly impossible for thought to expatriate itself, since it never deals with anything but the images of images that populate it. Truth, which is the name of an agreement of thought with itself, of an immanent adequation, is identical to that which ordinarily fixes the formal status of its inscription: coherence. 'Truth and coherence reciprocate one another': every time you read this aphorism, or one of its derivatives—and they proliferate—you can bet that you are in the company of the bishop.

This topology seals its closure by foreclosing the real which, hallucinatory, comes back in the form of the cross, in the divine errancy of closed thinking.

Yes, the decisively modern award for metaphysical idealism does not go to whoever recites *'esse est percipi'* but to whoever argues, on the basis of the right of forms, that the criterion of the true, giving up on adequation coherent with being, is coherence adequate to itself.

Positions 2 and 3 distribute the reasonable idealisms. Here the outside is recognized as such, the topology arranges a border of thought.

However, the process of crossing the threshold and the driving principle behind the process of knowing continue to follow the law of the idea. The trajectory starts out from the mental place. How does it pass over, or not, into its objective outside? Two paths:

a) That of Kant, in position 2 in our table, excludes the being of knowledge. Required in its pure mention by the very fact of experience, the in-itself remains unknowable to it—an empty term which grounds the unity of knowing only in the extent to which it absents itself from this very operation.

Being-in-itself for Kant is the placed inexistent from which it follows that it possesses force of law for the transcendental subject.

Whence the return to coherence as the guarantee of truth.

In exiting the bishop's palace, what does Kant gain by recognizing that there is an outside, if the constituent legislation of the inside suffices to gauge experience? What he gains by doing so is, first, the opening of a territory for morals and religion that is in excess over the delimitation of knowledge. And, second, a minimal productivity, as soon as the true judgement, instituted by the void and thus decentring the place of being that it lacks, finds the force to link together terms that *are not* the analytical repetition of one another. The 'synthetic *a priori*' judgement names this topological ability of generating the new according to a trajectory in which the real exteriority, even though it cannot be traversed, nonetheless imposes from afar upon the subjective interior the strangeness of a production on itself.

b) Hegel's path, in position 3, declares that the interior produces its own exteriority. It is an expansive topology, in which the passing-outside-of-itself constitutes the whole act of a place. We could say that all Hegelian sets are open, were it not necessary, in order to posit their malleable frontier, to close the whole once again and to program from very far the transgressive opening as return-to-itself, so that the local exteriorization is never anything but the effectuation of a global interiorization.

This goes to show that the Hegelian truth never exists except integrally. This is what Lacan inverts when he makes the half-saying into an absolute condition for stating the true.[8]

Before we get to this point, let us observe that our doctor of the split has hesitated, and even flirted, like all of us, with the Hegelian chimera of the integral, swaying it as close as possible to the dialectic in which the true circulates as its own falseness:

[. . .] as long as the truth isn't entirely revealed, that is to say in all probability until the end of time, its nature will be to propagate itself in the form of error. [. . .]

In other words, in discourse it is contradiction which sorts truth from error. From whence the Hegelian conception of absolute knowledge. Absolute knowledge is this moment in which the totality of discourse closes in on itself in a perfect non-contradiction up to and including the fact that it posits, explains and justifies itself. We are some way yet from this ideal! [. . .]

So we are led, it would appear, to a historical Pyrronism which suspends the truth-value of everything which the human voice can emit, suspends it in the expectation of a future totalization.

Is it unthinkable that it might come about? After all, can't progress of the system of the physical sciences be conceived of as the progress of a single symbolic system, to which things give sustenance and substance? [. . .]

This symbolic system of the sciences tends towards the *well made language*, which one might consider to be its own language, a language deprived of all reference to a voice. (S I, 263–5/289–91)

Who does not measure Lacan's honesty on this point, the care given to rendering the trajectory? Let this be a lesson in ethics, as far as the logic of contradictions is concerned. Nobody seriously takes on the dialectic without evoking the shadowy part that enables the dream of its coalescence. Should it be such a cause for joy that error is the commercial agent of truth? Let us beware of those people who are all too hasty to consent to the noonday of the half-said.[9] They cowardly lean toward the wrong side.

I like it that one abdicates the Whole only when forced and constrained to do so.

Hegel, on his part, is not very prone to abdicate. There are no truths, in his eyes, no matter if they are absolutely special, that cannot be stated as guaranteed by the integral of the true.

What is the issue all about? It is about the topological status of truth which, as is the case in mathematics, involves the very difficult apparatus for passing from the global study to the local study.

We learn rather early on in school that being able to give the profile of a function does not automatically mean mastery over whatever bungling or confused aspects may surround such a particular value.

Truth is a function, a variety, a surface, a space. This is what is so immensely burdensome for philosophy, which would gladly want it to be nothing but a commercial code.

Marxist philosophy is no exception. For the whole business of the 'primacy of practice', not to say anything about the even more obscure affair of the 'class character of truth', all this is meant to demarcate, with regard to the real—with regard to the event—that which functions as general structure from that which functions as singular tendency.

The most abstruse topological statement of our vulgate is the one that declares that 'the universal exists only in the specific'.[10] This is where we produce the joint, as close as possible, between the local and the global. How about the universal impact of a particular revolution? Of which worldwide variety do the elements called 'Commune', 'October', and 'Cultural Revolution', which are French, Russian and Chinese as far as their localization is concerned, constitute the fundamental group? To answer this question, we must force an entire topology of history, with its orientation, its singular points, its curvatures, its knots, and all its gear.

In any case, if Hegel makes a passage and a function out of the local threshold crossings, he sees no guarantee of the truth except in the Whole.

Which is to say that he guarantees nothing at all.

Position 4 in our table does not bother itself with these frivolities. For Lucretius or La Mettrie, the subjective time of knowledge is null. What does this mean? That a region of the general mechanism can be 'named' knowledge, in the same way we name a cow or spinach. What distinguishes this region of reality? Undoubtedly, that it transfers, or transports, a material assemblage from one point to another, that is, from the real to its 'image'. To know means to busy oneself, by a physical effect, with a re-production of something. The guarantee of truth attaches itself to the correct mechanism of this transportation. A dream or hallucinations are only outages in the refrigerated truck that transports images, or imprints. It is rot that gets to us.

The materialist criterion of truth fits in one word: repetition. I escape the dazed dream of atoms insofar as that which marks repeats at a distance that which is.

Position 5, that of the materialist dialectic, admits—not without having to pay a price which we will evaluate below—that we must distinguish thought from sensible being. This is its objection to the radicality of mechanicism. What it retains from the latter—against Hegel—is that what is already there in the process of knowledge is taken from being, and not from the idea. As for the trajectory, it disposes in it the spiralling discrepancy of the new, whereby it excludes the idealist integral: from the Whole, no guarantee whatsoever follows.[11]

All truth is new, even though the spiral also entails repetition. What puts the innovative interruption into the circular flexion? A certain coefficient of torsion.

Therein lies the subjective essence of the true: that it is twisted. 'The true, then, of course, is that. Except that it is never reached except by twisted pathways' (S XX, 95/87–8).

2

The inventory gives us four philosophical names for truth: coherence, repetition, totality, torsion.

There are no others. The 'adequation' of Aristotle and Saint Thomas has never been anything but a nicety out of a dictionary. To say that there is truth when the spirit agrees with the thing does not dispense anyone from looking for the effective law of the agreement in question. Aristotle and Saint Thomas offer their solutions to this problem, which, like all others, are distributed in the system: coherence, totality, repetition, torsion.

Lacan never fails to lash out against adequation: 'Thus Truth draws its guarantee from somewhere other than the Reality it concerns: it draws it from Speech. Just as it is from Speech that Truth receives the mark that instates it in a fictional structure' (E 684/808).

Sure. But the fact that reality engages no truth is the point of departure for any philosophy. Adequation misleads no one, nor does it pass for an illuminating stroke regarding the enigma of the true.

This enigma can be read off the diagram of truth:

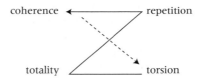

Aiming at the whole, the subject-process of truth repeats its difference, under a new law whose hidden coherence can be situated only by a torsion of the initial rule.

Lacan, on this topic, has said it all, albeit with an insidious slippage.

What he did not say is something I leave to you as a (difficult) exercise to figure out. It is a question of demonstrating that, as far as Marxism is concerned, the schema of truth becomes the following:

Those of you who, at this stage, solve the problem can move on to the last chapter: they are ripe for the ethics of Marxism, except for the explicit supplementary condition of engaging, here and now, with the partisan torsion.

'Torsion', even if the word does not belong to the common parlance of Marxism, can be inferred from it by combining the notion of the circle and that of the leap. The torsion of the true designates a circularity without a unified plane, a discontinuous curve. See Mao: there is a circle, since the point of departure of truth is practice, which is its point of arrival as well, and theory is the mediation by way of a curve from p_1 to p_2. There is torsion by the double unhinging that, as an integral part of truth as trajectory, grounds the practical novelty, the local index of p as the division into p_1 and p_2, which is not a temporal division but a cognitive one: the law of placement.

Why a *double* unhinging? Because in order to guarantee the circularity, even if it is a broken one, we need two discontinuities.

Whence the 'two leaps' of knowledge: from sensible to rational knowledge (a leap in the practical identity of the trajectory) and from rational to revolutionary knowledge (a leap whereby p divides itself). Read *On Practice*.

One will recognize that from the sensible to the rational, we move by way of a break along the axis of truth: totality → repetition. Whereas from rational to revolutionary knowledge, we move horizontally: repetition → coherence.

This is precisely what interrupts the repetition, since the perceived coherence is new.

In his pedagogical language Mao the Marxist states two theses that are essential for our understanding of the true:

1. All rationality structures the Whole by way of repetitive series.
2. All perceived coherence interrupts a repetition.

One can go very far with this. But I imagine the objection, which I will quote: 'You are clouding the issue! After all this, is it still possible to treat Lacan as an idealist? At least admit that he is guilty. Let us add to the dossier one of his declarations, which is devastating':

For it is still not saying enough to say that the concept is the thing itself, which a child can demonstrate against the Scholastics. It is the world of words that creates the world of things—things which at first run together in the *hic et nunc* of the all in the process of becoming—by giving its concrete being to their essence, and its ubiquity to what has always been: *ktèma es aei.* (E 229/276)

'Do you recognize, my Marxist prosecutor will continue, the primacy of thinking over being-in-itself, of the subject over the object—idealist axioms to which Lacan assigns their modern form, in which it is a question of the anteriority of language over the thing itself?'

If I ask my sagacious opponent: 'Is there primacy of capitalism over the proletariat?' I am not sure that he will be much better equipped to provide an answer. It will prove useful at this point to meditate on a crucial thesis from Lacan: 'The subject is, as it were, internally excluded from its object' (E 861/731). It is difficult, in this internal exclusion, to pinpoint a primacy.

A torsion, yes.

Like Marx, and like Freud, Lacan is vividly aware of the fact that he is bringing about a (Copernican) revolution. Not in the sense of an inversion but rather a slanting: what we saw as straight, we must see as twisted.[12] What we believe to be in front of us, as Lacan puts it brilliantly, is being-to-the-side, para-being, par-appearing:

> It is at the very point at which paradoxes spring up regarding everything that manages to be formulated as the effect of writing (*effet d'écrit*) that being presents itself, always presents itself, by para-being. We should learn to conjugate that appropriately: I par-am, you par-are, he par-is, we par-are, and so on and so forth. (S XX 45/44)[13]

Let us agree to call dogmatism any Marxism that pretends to restore the line, without anything aleatory, right in front of us.

To name this line 'just' is only a smokescreen for calling it 'right.'[14] Read in the heavy hand of history, it is the line of truth of which we recognize the foldings.

'Let us para-be', that is our war cry.

And better yet: 'We are nothing, let us para-be the Whole.'[15]

There are no such things as class relations

February 14, 1977

Christ, Marx, and Freud, (re)founded by Saint Paul, Lenin, and
Lacan—The revolution as the impossible proper to Marxism—An
exercise in torsion—'Destroy', he says

1

I spoke to you about periodization. I told you that the materialist dialectic
undoes the circle of the Hegelian dialectic in certain ruptures whereby
every phenomenon comes to inscribe itself two times (at least).

The double seal is the price of History for all novelty.[16]

Of course, Marxism is a phenomenon and, as such, it is periodized.
It thus begins two times: with Marx and then with Lenin. 'Marxism-
Leninism' is a name for this double seal—for the double name. The doc-
trinal One of the historical Two.

Christianity, too, begins two times: with Christ and with Saint Paul.
Note that the certainty of the first beginning is attached to the truth of
the second. Without the founding militant activity of Saint Paul, without
the idea—against Peter—of universalizing the message, of leaving the
Law, of exceeding the Jewish universe, what would have become of
this millenary power, from which alone we can read a beginning in
the tangled history of that sectarian leader liquidated by the Palestinian
establishment under the protection of the neutrality of the Roman State?
The political time of the universal Church, of which Saint Paul is the brilliant and ill-humoured Lenin, retroactively grounds the Incarnation as

fact. Let us understand: as the discursive fact of this militant, conquering apparatus.

Must we argue that organization alone can make an event into an origin? Yes, insofar as a political subject requires the historical underpinning of an apparatus and insofar as there is no origin except for a determinate politics.

However, the event, once it is thus assigned, takes on an inexhaustible value of critical anticipation with regard to what the retroaction fixates as origin, scansion, or border.

Consider the suspense of retroaction and anticipation that links the Third International to the October Revolution: Marxism truly comes into being during this period, in particular—anticipation—as capable of heresies and—retroaction—as capable of a foundational epic. It is only from victorious Leninism that we can date the existence of Marxism as the originary discursive designation of a new political subject.

Indeed, there can be no question of a subject as long as the language is still missing in which to pronounce a verdict about heresy or to remit to the epic.

Will we say that it is only from Lacan that we can date, strictly speaking, Freudianism *qua* theory of the subject? Or even Freudianism *qua* epic? As for heresies, they appeared soon enough. Will we argue that, before Lacan, there existed only an open doctrine and a scientific ambition no more accomplished, in matters of 'psychology', but also no more mediocre, than that for which we can credit Marx, through *Capital*, in matters of economy?

Without a doubt. A line of demarcation had to be drawn between the I and the ego so as finally to isolate the process of which 'unconscious' is the name, just as it was only a question of vague objectivities until Lenin energetically revealed that in matters of Marxism, 'politics is the concentrated expression of economics', and partisan activity, the concentration of politics.[17]

It is not for nothing that Lacan wages war against every relapse of psychoanalysis into the energetic of drives, or what we would call economism.

What is, in the final instance, the 'primacy of the signifier'? It is the primacy of the ethical, of the ethics of well-saying.[18] And for Lenin, that is the primacy of politics, which is an art—'Insurrection is an art'—much more so than a science.[19]

Lacan is the Lenin of psychoanalysis. He says it himself, and justifiably so, in a passage that has not yet made a lot of ink flow:

Marx and Lenin, Freud and Lacan are not coupled in being. It is via the letter they found in the Other that, as beings of knowledge, they proceed two by two, in a supposed Other. What is new about their knowledge is that it doesn't presume the Other knows anything about it—certainly not the being who constituted the letter there—for it is clearly on the basis of the Other (*de l'Autre*) that he constituted the letter at his own expense, at the price of his being, which, by God, is not nothing at all for each of us, but not a whole lot either, to tell the truth. (S XX, 97–9/89–90)

Here we see that the binomial of names corresponds universally to the double seal of the origin.

So the problem of our time would be the following: Where is, yet to come and making three, the Mao of psychoanalysis?

But our Lenin in question is alive and well: he can accumulate the numbers, like a king succeeding himself.[20]

2

As far as our topic is concerned, which is that of truth, I read Lacan's materialism in his steady uprightness about torsion from which it turns out that, indexed according to the Whole, a perceived coherence interrupts the repetition that structures it.[21]

Let us illustrate the torsion of the true, which constitutes the topology of its coherence, the caesura of its repetition, and the fissure of its whole, with our good old fool's bridge: the 'relation' of proletariat/bourgeoisie.

I say 'relation', and not relation, on the grounds that, if the real of psychoanalysis is the impossibility of the sexual *qua* relation, the real of Marxism can be stated as follows: 'There are no such things as class relations.'

What does it mean to say that there are no class relations? This can be stated differently: antagonism.

The bourgeoisie/proletariat antagonism designates the relation of classes as impossible, whereby it delimits the real of Marxism. This is not the same as its object, for the object of Marxism, I said so repeatedly, is none other than its subject: the political subject.

The real is what the subject encounters, as its chance, its cause, and its consistency. I will come back to this triplet: chance, cause, consistency.

For the subject of which Marxism is the theory, this real is the bourgeoisie/proletariat antagonism as impossible relation among the people. The shape that this nonrelation takes is valid for any Marxist politics, in the register of chance (to seize the bull by the horns), of the cause (it is from this nonrelation that politics as such, which is to say mass politics, is born), and of consistency (the sustaining of antagonism is what gives Marxism its staying power, as well as defining the principle of unity of its stages).

Do we then adopt, such as it is, Lacan's maxim that the real is what is impossible? Yes, without any quibble. The real of Marxism is the revolution. What does the revolution name? The sole historical form of existence of the relation of class, that is, antagonism, which turns out to be *the destruction of that which did not exist*.

The revolution is the existential of antagonism. It is therefore the name of the impossible that is proper to Marxism.

Does this mean that revolutions do not exist? Quite the contrary! That they are real means precisely that they exist, and that's all. The Marxist status of the revolutions is their having-taken-place, which is the real on the basis of which a political subject pronounces itself in the present. Nothing has taken place except the revolution. It is an impossible event, like all true events, of which Marxism ensures the subjective guarantee by the retroaction of its concept.

'Paris Commune', 'October '17', 'Cultural Revolution' are not empirical configurations of which some 'Marxist' historian or other would provide the narrative. They are Marxist concepts that enable us to think the relation of the political subject to the real, that is, to the existing impossibility of the revolutions.

These concepts are otherwise crucial and foundational than those that one is misled into taking for Marx's primitive concepts, such as 'mode of production', 'productive labour', 'surplus value', and others.

For Marxism, seized from any point that is not its effective operation which is entirely of the order of politics within the masses, does not deserve one hour of our troubles. Nor would it be worth investing this hour in a Freudianism reduced to the dreary doctrine of sexual determination, adjusted to some therapy or other meant to reinforce the ego.

In these times marked by the 'common programme' of the Left, those who imagine that anything whatsoever of Marxism can subsist if one pretends to do without the impossible revolution are just good for the absolving talent quest of academia.

Marxism is the practical discourse for sustaining the subjective advent of a politics. What practice?[22] I approve of the definition Lacan gives to praxis: 'What is a praxis? [. . .] It is the broadest term to designate a concerted human action, whatever it may be, which places man in a position to treat the real with the symbolic' (S XI 6/11).

Marxism seeks to change the real of revolutions through the symbolic grip of which it assures the political subject of such a real, a subject for which, as we all know, it reserves the name 'proletariat', which is neither more nor less appropriate than the (dubious) word 'unconscious'.

This is also where Marxism must ordain its torsion.

3

In a topology from which we might think the pair exterior/interior, what is the site of these two terms, 'bourgeoisie' and 'proletariat'?

Economism, which is fond of distinctions, posits the exteriority: bourgeois is whoever owns the means of production. Proletarian, whoever is separated from them and has at his disposal only his labour force, which he sells.

Now there is something that is certainly not wrong!

We know what follows. This topological exteriority changes over into a functional interiority. This is the revenge of the place, which we saw in the case of Hegel. If the proletariat is only this productive (exploited) exteriority, it would be better to name it—with Marx—'labour force', or even 'variable capital'. Indeed, it is nothing but a piece of capital. You have made a distinction governed by the rule of a structured set, in which 'distinction' is actually only a law of composition, that of the cycle of enlarged reproduction. What you have is *Capital*. Here the working class is even the most precious capital, since it is the only active principle of its regeneration. You may do away with the capitalists, all the while maintaining the law of capital. This is what the Russian functionaries manage to do quite well. The workers, by contrast, cannot be subtracted from the overall configuration. From this we can infer that their initial distinction from the bourgeoisie, purely from the point of view of exploitation, of the extortion of surplus-value, came down to the following statements of inclusion: the bourgeois world splaces class, capital is the place of the proletariat.

Paradoxically, in order to come to think of the proletariat as being—or as possibly being—the outplace of the bourgeois splace, *we must first think the bourgeoisie's interiority to the proletariat.*

This is where truth appears to stand in a torsion, whereas the coherence of the economists gave us only the repetition of capital as place-whole.

In the beginning, the 'proletariat' is indicated as a particular figure of the bourgeoisie, the split figure of the latter's politics. What started Marxism was nothing else than the popular and workers' insurrections of 1830–50, themselves grafted onto the bourgeois democratic movement in Europe. An exceptional disorder. Just as psychoanalysis began only by listening to this singular disorder of speech that is the *fin-de-siècle* hysteric. The historical symptom whence to track down the subject originally can be read off the bourgeois political disorder. What is this disorder? The scission introduced into the subject by its assignation to a heteronomous order. It is the expulsion, the purging, of the internal infection by the subjective proletarian emergence, whatever the degree of its consistency, that first constitutes it.

We might as well say that it is the emergence of bizarre practical organisms in the henceforth-confused domain of bourgeois politics that constitutes the proletariat's par-appearing.

What is the proletariat? All that is historically in the process of curing itself of a mortal political disease. It is a surviving body, borne from rot. Never cured, we should note, always in the process of being cured.

As a symptom of health, which from any other point of view except Marxism reads as a symptom of incurable illness, the politics of the proletariat certainly stands in internal exclusion to bourgeois politics, that is, to its object.

Does the bourgeoisie make a subject? I affirmed as much in this very place, in April 1975. Let me contradict myself, it is a trick of par-appearing. The bourgeoisie has not been a subject for a long time, it makes a place.

There is only one political subject, for any given historicization. To ignore this major observation gets one tangled up in a vision of politics as a subjective duel, which it is not. There is one place, and one subject. The dissymmetry is structural in nature.

The proletariat exists everywhere where some political outplace is produced. It is therefore by purging itself that it exists. It has no anteriority over the organization of its political survival. To expel the bourgeois politics by compressing its own organism-support and to bring into existence the proletarian politics, apparently, are one and the same.

Does this allow us to wager the existence of *a* political subject? No, I do not agree with the view that it would suffice to have the multiplicity of the revolts, the outplace of pure subjectivization, the eruptive given of the popular political concentration.

The torsion is more radical. It is not only as the place-out-of-place of self-expulsion, as heteronomous politics, that the proletariat *qua* subject comes into being in the world. Within the continuity of the purification, one can always take the proletariat for an unnoticed card of the bourgeoisie itself, a return of its subjective competence, a pitfall of the place. This is what we are taught by the appearance in the USSR of a *new* bureaucratic state bourgeoisie.

The subject's measure demands that the strict logic of the outplace, governed in wholly Mallarméan fashion by the causality of lack, exceeds itself in the *destruction of the place*.

It is not an empty place, not even that of power, that conjures the emergence, in the political disorder, of the subject of its occupation.

'Destroy, he says': such is the necessary—and prolonged—proletarian statement.[23] This barbarous statement forbids us to imagine the political subject in the structural modality of the heritage, the transmission, the corruption, the inversion. But also in that of the purifying cut, of the world broken in two.[24]

Destruction means torsion. Internal to the space, it ravages its places, in a laborious duration.

To what interiority pertains that which exists only by destroying the rule of delimitation by which the exterior functions as a border?

And yet, the proletariat certainly emerges *in its place*.

Here we must produce a topology of destruction. That of the lack (of the hole) alone cannot by itself fulfil the thought of ruins.

Our entire dispute with Lacan lies in the division, which he restricts, of the process of lack from that of destruction.

Lack and destruction: This gives us focus, all the more so in that this dialectic is transversal to the one of algebra and topology, which commands all of materialism.

Every subject crosses a lack of being and a destruction

February 21, 1977

Lacan–Hegel—The subject of the chain—The communist effect—
Ontology—Lacan's four axioms—Destruction as mastery of loss

1

Lacan, I said earlier, is our Hegel, that is, he presents the (idealist) dialectic of our time. With our time comes the requirement that one pretends to oppose this dialectic to Hegel's machines, and Lacan does not shirk this duty.

Provoked by Jacques-Alain Miller, on May 27, 1964, into saying 'Lacan *against* Hegel', he approves with delight but also with the polite prudence of denying that it could—'at all'!—be a matter for a 'philosophical debate' (S XI, 215/240).

What happens is that ten years earlier—I invite anyone to look at the index of the *Ecrits*: Hegel takes the lion's share, after Freud (who is not part of the competition and thus does not appear in the list) but before anyone else—it was a question of deciding 'if there is still something prophetic in Hegel's insistence, which reveals the extent of his genius, on the fundamental identity of the particular and the universal', that is, in the dialectical torsion itself, and to inscribe in it the retrospective label of psychoanalysis, which provides this torsion with 'its paradigm by revealing the structure in which this identity is realized as disjunctive of the subject, and without appealing to the future' (E 292/242, trans. modified). This is the operation, applied to Hegel, of the double stamp of dialectical modernity. Consequently, of the double jump.[25]

Like Hegel for Marx, Lacan for us is essential and divisible. The primacy of the structure, which makes of the symbolic the general algebra of the subject, and of *lalangue*, its transcendental horizon, is countered ever more clearly with a topological obsession in which what moves and progresses pertains to the primacy of the real.

There are, broadly speaking, two successive Lacans, the one of the lack of being and the one of the ontology of the hole, of the nodal *topos*, and, consequently, of the being of lack.

From the primacy of the symbolic to the consistency of the real.

The rational matrix tied to the effect of lack, by which Lacan continues the Mallarméan effort, is concentrated in the articles in which Jacques-Alain Miller in a clear step-by-step manner sets out the logic of the signifier, and then the theory of *lalangue*. Miller's conclusions sum up the formalism of the structural dialectic, under the thematic heading of the vanishing entity, of the inconsistent totality:

> It is only when the mark disappears that its place appears, and therefore the mark as such. Is this enough to justify our saying that it attains its being only in its disappearance—that it takes hold only on the border of its lack—in a flash? [. . .] the being of the mark, just like that of lack, 'exists' only in the in-between, incorporeal, ungraspable, or in the difference between the one and the other, in the movement, in the passage, and it is always either too early or too late. [. . .] This process—this entity—presents itself as untotalizable—or, as a contradictory totality, which is to say, a totality with its contradiction, or with its nonintegrable element, multiplicity irreducible to a unity. [. . .] The mark [. . .] doesn't *consist* (it is inconsistent), it persists, it insists, it is a process.[26]

The subject here is revealed in the eclipse of the marking, caught in the pulsating movement, the flashing at the edge of that which articulates it.

Thus, the proletariat, trapped in the political law of the bourgeois world, is only—as Lacan says of the object of fantasy—an 'unspeakable vacillation' (E 550/656). Whoever wants to declare its substance is a swindler.

Of the proletariat, we never obtain anything except the body (the party), except the traces: popular historical facts whose nominal evidence strikes us with uncertainty.

Whence its subject-making.[27]

Prescribed by the loss of its object—thus sutured onto the real by the lack of being—desire divides the subject, being inextensive to the 'nothing' from whence it proceeds. The only mode of existence of such a division is the law of alternation on which, in Lacan's case, no star comes to put its stamp.

The subject follows throughout the fate of the vanishing term, having the status of an interval between two signifiers, S_1 and S_2, which present it one to the other. Just as the proletariat is only that which a (named) revolution presents to another (nameable) revolution. Just as the wrecked ship (S_1) presents the subject of writing to the siren (S_2) while nothing consolidates this presentation, not even the Mallarméan dream of a cipher of the universe, confined in the Book in which this universe should logically culminate.

For Lacan, the subject leads to nothing,[28] which is not negligible, but it makes no sense in that it must slide over absence without any grip, for 'desire is the metonymy of the lack of being' (E 534/650, trans. modified).

In this way, Lacan gives himself an access road, which suits us, into ontology: the unconscious is that being which subverts the metaphysical opposition of being and nonbeing. For it is the effect of the lack of being (effect which has a name: transference).

To that extent, as we will see, the unconscious resembles the proletarian politics according to the Marxist, which *is its effect (its ef-fact) of not being* (ef-fact whose name is 'communism').[29]

J.-A. Miller, still him, goes after Lacan with the question: 'What is your ontology? What is the unconscious?'

Oh, the ordeals to which one thinks that Marxists are subjected when one throws at them point-blank the burning question (this happens a thousand times over, so that we carry incombustible protective gear): 'Where is your proletariat? Is it not an imaginary signifier?'

Woe to those who believe that they must follow their loquacious tormentor onto the terrain of existence to which he has provoked them. Whether they search on the side of the workers and factory exploitation, or whether they bring up the existing States, the result will always be either too much, or too little. It is futile to want to hand out the certificate of existence of an empirical set (be it a social class) or the ideal nonbeing of a project for society (be it 'socialist') to that which gives a political subject the force of its name.

Neither the sexual drives nor the International Psychoanalytical Association have ever proven the existence of the unconscious. Let us not expect anything more, in terms of the proletariat, from the factory strike or from the Chinese State.

Lacan, when put to the question, immediately heeds the good advice of oblique cunning. Thus, he spreads out his answer, announcing first that 'of course, I have my ontology—why not?—like everyone else', but that as far as his discourse is concerned, it 'makes no claim to cover the entire field of experience' (S XI, 72/69).

On February 19, 1964, it would seem that he overdoes it in terms of modesty: No, 'Psychoanalysis is neither a *Weltanschauung*, nor a philosophy that claims to provide the key to the universe. It is governed by a particular aim, which is historically defined by the elaboration of the notion of the subject' (S XI, 77/73).

Yes, but this subject is precisely the ultimate secret weapon[30] (ours, which shows a similarly dubious modesty, is the political actualization), since its concept reshuffles nothing less than the idea of all possible science—just as ours, that of all practical apperception of the social bond. Until Freud, epistemology as founded on the trajectory which goes from perception to science wanders off in the wrong direction, because it 'avoids the abyss of castration' (S XI, 77/73). Let us understand this as saying that you have no access to the right idea of truth if you circumvent the effect of lack. This would amount to giving oneself the coherence without the torsion, which will push you repeatedly into the mirage of the whole.

Ontology or not, psychoanalysis according to Lacan imposes a general rectification on philosophy, which touches upon nothing less than the way in which truth leans up against the real.[31]

And so, two months later, despite his 'refusal to follow Miller's first question on the subject of an ontology of the unconscious', our trickster bustles about letting go of 'a little rope' (S XI, 134/122). What little piece of rope? That which dodges the opposition of being/nonbeing:

At this point, I should define unconscious cause, neither as an existent, nor as a ὀυκ ὄν, a non-existent—as, I believe, Henri Ey does, a non-existent of possibility. It is a μη ὄν of the prohibition that brings to being an existent in spite of its non-advent, it is a function of the impossible on which a certainty is based. (S XI, 128–9/117)

This 'prohibition that brings to being an existent in spite of its non-advent' conveys the causal prematurity of the subject, the too-early/too-lateness of its fortune. Who is not familiar, in politics, with the futility of linear accumulation? Of exact prediction?

Neither being nor nonbeing, the political cause, which always fails to show up if announced as just cause, is the real, at once abolished and dazzling, by which a hole is punctured in history so that the proletarian subject, its body divided, may fasten itself onto it.

Its name? 'The masses.' This is the real that the partisan subject retroactively encounters in any break in historicization.

The masses are not the substance of history but *the prohibition to repeat*, which brings to being the aleatory subject that Marxism puts into discourse.

2

The 'first Lacan', in terms of what matters to me and which does not concern psychoanalysis, boils down to four theses, the system of which covers the four names of truth (coherence, repetition, totality, torsion).

This axiomatic arrangement in my eyes gives structure to the essence of the *Ecrits*, as well as the *Seminars* until the end of the 1960s.

Beginning in the 1970s, which one can mark by the primacy of the knot over the chain, or of consistency over causality, it is the historical aspect that gains the upper hand over the structural one.

Psychoanalysis, in my view, suffers a shipwreck in the process, while ethics comes to rule, absolutely. But this is only the opinion of a distant amateur.

I would deduce the four constitutive theses of the first doctrine as follows:

1. *Thesis of the empty place, at the source of repetition*

    . . . what is repeated is a product, not of nothing from the real (which people believe they have to presuppose in it), but precisely of *what was not* [*ce qui n'était pas*]. (E 32/43)

2. *Thesis of the vanishing term, at the source of torsion*

    Where it was just now, where it was for a short while, between an extinction that is still glowing and an opening up that stumbles, *I* can come into being by disappearing from my statement [*dit*].

    An enunciation that denounces itself, a statement that renounces itself, an ignorance that sweeps itself away, an opportunity that self-destructs—what remains here if not the trace of what really must be in order to fall away from being? (E 678/801)

3. *Thesis of the imaginary fixation, at the source of totality*

However, the notion of unconscious fantasy no longer presents any difficulty once it is defined as an image set to work in the signifying structure.

Let us say that, in its fundamental use, fantasy is the means by which the subject maintains himself at the level of his vanishing desire, vanishing inasmuch as the very satisfaction of demand deprives him of his object. (E 532/637)

4. *Thesis of the phallus, at the source of coherence*

For the phallus is a signifier, a signifier whose function, in the intrasubjective economy of analysis, may lift the veil from the function it served in the mysteries. For it is the signifier that is destined to designate meaning effects as a whole, insofar as the signifier conditions them by its presence as signifier. (E 579/690)

This latter signifier is therefore the signifier to which all the other signifiers represent the subject—which means that if this signifier is missing, all the other signifiers represent nothing. For something is only represented to.

Now insofar as the battery of signifiers is, it is complete, and this signifier can only be a line that is drawn from its circle without being able to be counted in it. This can be symbolized by the inherence of a (-1) in the set of signifiers.

It is, as such, unpronounceable, but its operation is not, for the latter is what occurs whenever a proper name is pronounced. Its statement is equal to its signification. (E 694/819)

Thus, from the quadrangle of truth, Lacan extracts, as far as the algebraic doctrine of the subject is concerned, the following trajectory:

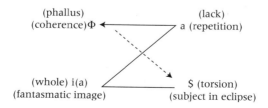

In this trajectory, the subject is governed by the ignorance of the loss that constitutes it. It follows that there is no truth which is not mutilated, and no subject which is not subjected.

The operations of the splace are substitutions (metaphors and metonymies). It is therefore impossible to recognize the loss as such. The subject glides between the successive partial representations of that whose radical lack institutes it as articulated desire.

Needless to say that politics has only the very mediocre interest of a blindness that causes a racket about its false substitutive insights: 'What is social is always a sore' (Conférences 19).[32] And better yet, in answer to the following question which reveals a good amount of frontal optimism: 'The political implications of your psychoanalytical investigations?', which is a truly American question, addressed to Lacan in the winter of 1975 at Yale University: 'In any case, there is no progress. What one gains on one side, one loses on the other. Not knowing what one has lost, one believes to have won. My "twisted brains" suppose that this is narrow-minded' (Conférences 37).[33]

A balancing, in an unclarified half-saying, of gain and loss: such is the outcome of any structural concept of the political subject.

If it is possible to say anything more about it, it is only insofar as there is an effective *mastery of loss*.

The objection being that it cannot be question of a form of knowledge, much less a recollection.

So what is the mastery of loss? Marxism teaching us that it is destruction.

The destroyed real is not reducible to its disappearance in the hole of the lack. It surely drops in it, and sometimes without any leftover, but thenceforth it is divided between its causal effect of pure lack and what we will provisorily call the secondary effect, whose mainspring consists in delegating a virtuality of *excess* over the repetitive placement set in motion by the lack of being.

Destruction divides the effect of lack into its part of oblivion—of automatism—and its part of possible interruption—of excess over the place, of the overheating of the automatisms.

By this thin gap, another mastery can be said to come into being, together with an asymmetrical balancing of loss and gain.

Contrary to common opinion, which sees perseverance in being as the ground of all conservatism, it is in effect—as Lacan claims—from that which is lacking that conservation secures itself. But we must add that, from what comes to be destroyed, at the very least the precariousness of conservation is secured, as well as that part, inherent in all repetition, which insists in interrupting it.

Every subject stands at the crossing between a lack of being and a destruction, a repetition and an interruption, a placement and an excess.

The subject's antecedence to itself

April 18, 1977

Destruction—The more-than-real and the interruption of the
repeatable—Cure and re-education—Two subjective allocations of force:
anxiety and superego

1

Destruction is that figure of the subject's grounding in which loss
not only turns lack into a cause, but also produces consistency out of
excess.

Through destruction, the subject latches onto that which, in lack itself,
survives the lacking and is not the repetitive closure of the effect to the
presence of the cause.

If the *structural* concept of contradiction (the splitting) points to the lack
as its mainspring and to the law as its horizon, the *historical* concept of
contradiction is forged on the basis of destruction whose sphere of action
lies in the nonlaw.

It is true that one pole of the contradiction, the one that constitutes the
law of the splace as the place's evil genius, plays on its own absence as on
that which, by founding the repeatable, guarantees the perennial conservation of the world.

Such is the definition of the ruling class, which thus can never be made
present except by that which, in the antagonistic subject, is subservient
to repetition.

It would be rather fitting, moreover, to name this absence 'society'—for example, French imperialist society—so as to avoid falling into the trap of its subjectivization.

As for the 'private' subject, it is indeed to the law of desire, and more specifically to the pair of perversion/neurosis that we must ascribe the unforgiving effect of its vacillating identity. Neurosis and perversion: such is the society that each of us makes for him or herself, as the primordial *element* of the subjective.

However, the fact that the other pole of the contradiction from which the subject arises can be considered destructive invites us not to reduce the subjective dialectic to its aspect of socialized (or neurotic) repetition.

It remains true, though, that *the social is the neurosis of politics.*

This is what trade unionism, with its doleful compulsion, its teary allegiance to the State, and its strict subordination to all imperialistic repetitions, incarnates 'in the raw'.

The logic of trade unions stems from lack alone, and thus from the law: their vindication is by definition 'legitimate'.

Politics, even though it is structured in the same way, originates in the self-destruction of its legitimacy.

We must reserve the name *subject* for that which cannot be inscribed on the splaced ground of repetition except destructively as the excess over that which keeps it in place.

To define the subject as 'the metonymy of the lack of being' only identifies half of its essence, the other half being *that which gives being to the lack,* that is, destruction, which is irreducible to the act of pure substitution.

Thus the subject, as the placed product of the law of lack, brings out a 'more-than-real' in its domain through which lack itself, in the tracks of destruction, comes to lack.

It is actually this 'more' that I call *force.*

However, this point needs some rectification. In the booklet entitled *Theory of Contradiction*, which I wrote two years ago, the notion of force is not really dialecticized. There force complements, or even compliments, place insofar as it is conceived of as a 'placed force'. At bottom, it is nothing else than the quality of the process that provides the threshold, or the period term, for the overthrowing of the system of places.

Today I would say that it is still in vain, however well intended and pedagogically sound it may be, that we seek to 'fill' the structure with the qualitative. It is not only because of their qualitative heterogeneity that the two terms of a contradiction turn into a 'relation of forces'. If we remain at that level, we are back in a duel.

The conservative term can be identified with the law of lack and subordinates the other to itself as repeatable. Force is nothing but that which, by concentrating in itself, out-of-place, a term that was assigned to repetition, jams up the mechanism of repetition and thus triggers the possibility for the destruction of its law.[34]

There where the old coherence prescribed a mere sliding displacement, an interruption arises through a purification that exceeds the place. This is the history of force.

From this point of view, just as there is only one subject, there is also only one force, whose existence always surfaces as an event.

This event, trace of the subject, crosses the lack with the destruction.

Such is the case when a revolution crosses the rising curve of the price of wheat, or the number of war casualties, with the insurrectionary crowd taking the Bastille, or with the Bolshevik political order.

The subject-support is inescapably divided between the part of itself that is subjected to repetition (since it is placed) and the part that interrupts, blocks, and brings about the nonrepeatable.[35]

You thus obtain something far more complex than the simple distinction force/place. You do not have two concepts for one and the same process, but rather two processes (repetition/interruption and lack/destruction) for one concept (that of the subject).

Force is what, on the basis of the repeatable and dividing itself from the latter, comes into being as nonrepeatable.

In order to shed some light on this crossroads, I would ask you to compare the aim of the psychoanalytic cure and that of political re-education, no matter what the obvious and universal failures of either may well be. It is the intention that counts.

We will turn a deaf ear to those who argue that a couch is after all not as serious as a camp. To them I say without hesitation that this remains to be seen. The axiom of the *nouveaux philosophes*—'A camp is a camp'—is just as false as what the Chicago therapists wanted to promote through the excommunication of Lacan: 'A couch is a couch.'

The truth is that the psychoanalytic cure has no real aim other than that of the readjustment of the subject to its own repetition. Hence Lacan shows extreme moderation in relation to his own power as an analyst: 'An analysis should not be pushed too far. When the analysand feels that he is happy to be alive, it is enough' (Conférences 15).

What does political re-education seek to provoke? A radical toppling of one's subjective position, that is, the interruption of the repetitions induced by the subject's previous (class) position. The 'happiness to be alive' definitely leaves this subject indifferent.

The psychoanalytic cure does not claim to exceed the law of lack. In fact the opposite is true: through the resolution of the symptom—which is, according to Lacan, 'that which many people have that is the most real' (Conférences 15)—the labour of truth is directed at recreating the dependence on the cause through its very oblivion. For 'every successful symbolic integration involves a sort of normal forgetting', and the 'integration into history evidently brings with it the forgetting of an entire world of shadows which are not transposed into symbolic existence. And if this symbolic existence is successful and is fully taken on by the subject, it leaves no weight behind it' (S I, 192/216).

The aim of the psychoanalytic cure is the slightly smoother exercise of the efficacy of lack.

Political re-education, or revolutionarization, entirely deserves the humanist charge made against it of 'wanting to change people', 'brainwashing', 'destroying individuality', or, as Mao says, of wanting to 'change man in his innermost being'.[36] This is the avowed goal of the cultural revolution; it presupposes the conviction that the old man can or may die.

Look at the reverse side of these accusations: they are nothing but a plea for the eternal ignorance of the loss that constitutes the I. They are a mere defence of the right to repetition.

The paradox of this line of defence is flagrant. When asked about the expectations of someone who enters into analysis, Lacan answers that for this person it is a matter of getting rid of a symptom. 'A symptom is curable', he says. But what is a symptom? 'The so-called neurotic symptom is simply something that allows them to keep on living' (Conférences 32).

So then should we be delivered from what is most real for us, from that which allows you to go on living?

To live with one's own truth causes a symptom because that which should be too little is instead too much.

In this regard, the cure does not really aim to bring the whole into alignment with the true. Such an excess of restitution to the rigour of truth opens the risk of psychosis: 'Thank God, we don't make them (the analysands) so normal that they will end up psychotic. That's the point where we must be very cautious' (Conférences 32).

The point is rather to remit the real to the oblivion of its oblivion, from where its causal force is purified in the lack: alignment of the true onto the whole. This type of work requires moderation.

The process of revolutionarization, for its part, calls on history, in vain, as it should be, and often treats it to a beating, in order to 'spill the beans' of the true in the integral of its schize. Its ambition is to make a symptom out of the old totality, and a total truth out of the symptom—out of the crisis.

Here we are nearing the domain of ethics, and of the strictest kind of ethics to boot. Is it at all possible to make sense of any resistance whatsoever if the identity of the subject derives only from the repeatable and from the obscure rights of the lack of being?

Conversely, however, can one measure the price of destruction to be paid for any mastery of loss and for any opening of a space of novelty?

The cure or the revolutionarization: as always, the facts in themselves decide nothing either way. Between those who survived the couch and those whose militant politics, in the forced marching style of the *Gauche Prolétarienne*, put them there, we really cannot say that the Western debate of the 1970s has brought much that is of value.

Instead, let us try to grab hold of the two faces of the notion of the subjective—whose articulation will require great efforts from us—in order to graft onto it the fruitful destruction, together with the happiness of falling short of it.[37]

2

If Lacan is a dialectician, he must notice what he does not notice. I mean: no matter how far he pushes the structural primacy of the law of lack, we will not recognize him as our Hegel unless he at the very least points at the other aspect, that of destruction, of the more-than-real, of force.

'Force', however, is a term for which he feels an intense dislike, busy as he is fighting the deadly arrogance of the American economicists.[38] 'Psychic energy', quantity, flow: all this is *ignorantiae asylum*. Lacan proceeds in no uncertain terms from epistemological mistrust—'How often, in the course of history, have the notions of energy and force been taken up and used again upon an increasingly totalized reality!' (S XI, 163/149)—to the significant verdict—'in general, force is used to designate a locus of opacity' (S XI, 21/24).

From this side we should not expect to obtain any satisfaction.

I propose that there are two themes in Lacan that indicate everything that, beyond or shy of lack and mark, in a breaching of the algebra of the subject, comes into being as the more-than-real of destruction.[39] These two themes are anxiety and the superego.

The principal reference when it comes to the superego is the following:

> The superego has a relation to the law, and is at the same time a sense-less law, going so far as to become a failure to recognize [*méconnaissance*] the law. That is always the way we see the superego acting in the neurotic. Isn't it because the morality of the neurotic is a senseless, destructive, purely oppressive, almost always anti-legal morality, that it became necessary to elaborate on the function of the superego in analysis?
>
> The superego is at one and the same time the law and its destruction. As such, it is speech itself, the commandment of law, in so far as nothing more than its root remains. The law is entirely reduced to something, which cannot even be expressed, like the *You must*, which is speech deprived of all its meaning. It is in this sense that the superego ends up by being identified with only what is most devastating, most fascinating, in the primitive experiences of the subject. It ends up being identified with what I call *the ferocious figure*, with the figures which we can link to primitive traumas the child suffered, whatever these are. (S I, 102/119)

The superego gives access to the root of force of the law itself, to that which is no longer of the order of language but which nevertheless lies at the core of the commanding character of the law.

If the law can bear the advent of destruction—the excess over the repetition that the law itself dictates—it is because the very order of the law, grasped as pure commandment, is in itself essentially excess and destruction.

This is the first signal of what I will describe as the eternal antecedence of the subject to itself. Witness the law, which the subject must both follow and break in order to come into being in its specific splitting.

Regarding this signal, Lacan says that the superego functions as an opening, no matter how sinister. The nonlaw is what manifests itself as the affirmative side of the law; for this reason the superego can be simultaneously the sign of the law and of its destruction. The superego originates as an instance where there is something out-of-place in the commandment concerning every place, that is, where there is a nonrepetition of the prescription to repeat.

It is precisely there that some light is thrown on the paralysing (and thus, in effect, disruptive) function of the superego, as is shown examplarily in the senselessness of obsessional neurosis and, in the case of the political subject, alas, in everything that takes comfort in the presence of the State.

In neurosis and in the universe of irrational regulation, the superego sustains a destructive morality, a commandment stripped bare, which forces every symbolic placement and sends it into syncopation.

Let us put aside for the time being that all this has been registered negatively (the 'senseless' and so on). Here interruption as such begins to stand out.

Now as far as anxiety is concerned, it is from the point of view of the real in excess rather than from that of the failing law that it functions as interruption—and therefore as revelation.

> [A]nxiety is a crucial term of reference, because in effect anxiety is that which does not deceive. But anxiety may be lacking.
>
> In experience, it is necessary to canalize it and, if I may say so, to take it in small doses, so that one is not overcome by it. This is a difficulty similar to that of bringing the subject into contact with the real—a term that I shall try to define next time. (S XI, 41/40–41)

Anxiety is the submersion by the real, the radical excess of the real over the lack, the active failure of the whole apparatus of symbolic support provoked by what reveals itself therein, in a cut, as unnameable encounter.[40]

Here, again, it is necessary to 'channel' its effect, since anxiety destroys the adjustment to the repeatable. It short-circuits the relation of the lamp-bearing subject to the real.

Anxiety, then, is the sign of that which in the subject forces the legal splace.

As in Lacan's superb expression, anxiety is nothing but the lack of lack.

But when the lack comes to lack, its metonymic effect is interrupted and a mastery of real loss begins, paid for by the ravaging of all symbolic points of reference.

Hence anxiety never deceives. Destruction must reach the law of lack in order for the lure of deception, semblance, and the oblivion of oblivion to be swept away.

Anxiety and the superego are therefore two fundamental concepts of the subject (there are two others), if by this we mean to designate that which lies at the crossing of the inert and civilized law of lack and the barbaric interruption of destruction.

These two concepts have been recognized by Lacan, one in the paralysing horror of obsession, the other in the ravaging truth of the plunge into the real. Although this was not his theoretical guiding thread, it was nonetheless right in line with the rigour of his experiment—accomplished athlete of the dialectic that indeed he was. . . .

Torsion

May 2, 1977

On a certain dialectical use of the mathematical text—Torsion—
Subjective formulas—First mentions of justice and courage

1

I would like to talk about a certain use of mathematics that is properly my own, without seeming proper to anyone else: neither to mathematicians, who find it metaphorical, nor to others, who are intimidated by it.

Briefly put, it is a matter of short-circuiting the dialectical analysis by examining the way in which mathematics treats a word, so that without losing anything of its rigour, this treatment is nonetheless from the start considered to be an interpretation of this word.

Indeed, an interpretation, or rather: a realization, or even a representation, as in the theatre.

The postulate is that no signifier finds its place in a mathematical text by random chance, and that even if it is true that its mathematical character derives from its role within the formal texture of the demonstration, this texture should also be considered, in its overdetermination, as the retroactive analysis of this very non-random character.

This is tantamount to saying that we consider the mathematical signifier a symptom around which the deductive text, without knowing this at all, attempts an auto-analysis.

That is, we take the mathematical text to be in the position of the analyst for some of its own words—as being symptomatic of itself.

This type of analysis will then have to be confronted with the one that opts for different paths, such as the dialectical and materialistic theory of the subject, in order to accomplish the convergence of a necessity, or to investigate the apparent abutment in a chance-like coincidence.

The backdrop for all this is the understanding that, in grappling with language, the mathematical formalisms perform a desubjectivization only at the cost of exploiting to the maximum—to death—the signifiers to which the subject is sutured.

Consider also the fascination that Marx and Engels feel for differential calculus and their somewhat naïve intent to seek therein the matrix of the 'laws of the dialectic'; or Marx's fallacious conviction, displayed in his numerous writings on mathematics, that he was a mathematician because he was a dialectician. These are all signs that the enigma of writing is tied to the fantasy of a formalized dialectic, with mathematics being its restricted specialty from which, upon close scrutiny, it would be possible all the same to extract the universal principle.

We should abandon this path in favour of the one I am indicating, which holds that words resonate within a demonstration well beyond the level of inferences for which they serve, even though this echo is nowhere to be heard except in the actual understanding of the chain of adduced proofs.

I give you an example.

We have already seen that the term 'torsion' designates the subject-point from which the other three classic determinations of truth come to be coordinated: totality, coherence, and repetition. This then reminds me that, besides its topological use (as in the torsion of a knot, following Lacan's lead), the word 'torsion' is also used in algebra in a very simple way.

Take a group, which, I recall for you, is a set defined by a law of composition among its elements. Let us mark '+' this law, which has the 'good' canonical properties of being associative $(x+(y+z))=((x+y)+z)$; of having a neutral element, '0', such that $(x+0)=x$; and of associating each element with its inverse (that is, $-x$, with $(x+(-x))=0$). One calls 'torsion' of an element x of a group the smallest whole number n, if it exists, such that x added to itself n times equals zero:

$$\underbrace{x + x + x + \ldots + x = 0}_{n \text{ times}}$$

149

For the sake of convenience in writing up what follows, let us agree to use the notation nx for the addition:

$$\underbrace{x + x + \ldots + x}_{n \text{ times}}$$

An element which presents a torsion is a torsion element: in sum, a contorted element. A group in which every element has a torsion is a torsion group. For every element x of this group, there is a whole number n such that $nx = 0$.

This name is not due to me. Mathematicians have used it for at least fifty years. Regrettably, I have not studied the history of this signifier.

Observe the way mathematicians analyse the choice of this word, that is, in what way the mathematical chain represents 'torsion':

1) First the definition. Who fails to see that torsion is connected to repetition, that is, the repetition of the operation characteristic of the group, applied n times to the same element? The element itself insists, so to speak, in the addition $x + x + x + \ldots + x \ldots$, it becomes serialized through repetition. Every partial addition is particular, but when there is torsion, after the designated number of repetitions is reached, the sum is nil. At this point we will say that *torsion interrupts the repetition*, which is what defines its dialectical status.

Torsion interrupts repetition in the qualitative character of the different additions. For if torsion were surpassed, one would find once again the partial sums from before its effect. If $nx = 0$, we will have $nx + x = 0 + x = x$, and $nx + 2x = x + x$, and finally $nx + nx = 0 + 0 = 0$.

This justifies our saying that, in this case, it is per force that those sums will return, owing to the fact that they present a *null excess* over what preceded them, before the torsion brings us back to zero.

Of all the past additions in which the element insists, algebraic torsion wipes the slate clean.

2) Is there a qualitative distance between the logic of torsion and the ordinary laws of groups? This is what one would expect since, by discovering a new type of coherence, torsion refuses to be collapsed back into the various repetitive series that make up the fabric of the Whole. This is its crucial function as an interruption. In Marxist terms, it is also the paradoxical status of the party.

In mathematics, this point is analysed through a very simple and very strong theorem which states that the axiomatic theory of torsion groups is not presentable in a first-order logic.

A first-order logic is one in which the quantifiers ('there is', $\exists$, and 'for all', $\forall$) are applied only to individual variables. In this type of logic, for example, you can write: 'There is an element having the property P', that is, $\exists x\ (P(x))$. But you cannot write: 'There is a property p having a characteristic A.' First-order logic is generally sufficient for normal purposes, although it employs an infinite number of axioms for the theory in question.

There is one case that interests us in particular, precisely because it holds no interest for us. It is the case of groups in which no element different from zero is subject to torsion. In English, these are called *torsion-free*: groups with absolutely no torsion that are, in other words, perfectly 'straight'.[41]

Such 'straightness' troubles the dialectician. In these groups, x is added to itself without ever interrupting the process of repetition.

Now, the theory of torsion-free groups, that is, the theory of algebraic straightness, is fully presentable in first-order logic. Take the infinite list of axioms that say that, no matter how far you go, for every element x different from 0, the repetition of additions to itself will amount to a sum that is not nil:

Ax. 1: $(\forall x)\ (x + x \neq 0)$
Ax. 2: $(\forall x)\ (x + x + x \neq 0)$
....   taking as the domain of the quantifier
Ax. $(n - 1)$: $(\forall x)\ (nx \neq 0)$ all x different from 0
....

If you add this to the three fundamental axioms of groups, you have the first-order theory of torsion-free groups.

However, the same procedure cannot function for torsion groups. Why? Because you do not know, for each number, which whole number presents its torsion. You only know that it exists. Thus, you would have to be able to write: 'For every element x, there is at least one whole number n such that $nx = 0$', or: $(\forall x)\ (\exists n)\ (nx = 0)$.

But $(\exists n)$ applies the quantifier, not to an individual variable, but to the property 'being a whole number', that is, to a predicate. In this way, we exceed first-order logic. Thus, the theory of torsion is indeed qualitatively in excess, in terms of logical complexity, over the theory of straightness.

This is what definitely convinces the dialectician. In fact, she will be happy to see that it is the existential uncertainty looming over the effectiveness of torsion that hinders the alignment of the theory onto first-order logic. Notice that if the axioms of algebraic straightness fall short, it is because they are all universal, determined by $\forall$, that is, by the 'for all' whose logical effects of simplicity and masculine character are well known. A theory in which the axioms are all universal has good or robust properties. In particular, every substructure of a model of this theory is itself also a model of this theory.

In contrast, the existential that the theory of torsion runs up against—figure of the aleatory nature of the interruptions, the indeterminacy in any rupture—exceeds the logical plane where the universal could hold up.

Mathematical justice for the clean slate of successful revolutions.

3) Torsion groups (infinite ones, it is understood: finite groups are all torsion groups, but little do we care for the finite) can, nevertheless, present pleasant algebraic properties, provided they are commutative. A group is commutative if regardless of the value of x and y, we have: $x + y = y + x$.

In this case, we can easily establish the following:

- The elements that have the same torsion n form a subgroup.
- The group can be broken down as the direct result of subgroups, with each of these subgroups being composed of elements whose torsion takes the form p^q, where p is a whole number.

I do not want to take up too much time explaining these statements. They tell you, albeit vaguely, that in a universe of communication, of reversibility, torsions draw up well-ordered subsets, breaking down the initial set into substructures whose principle of identity is clearly established.

The subversive value of torsion thereby is watered down into an analytical law, becoming a conceptual vector that allows for a reasonable partitioning of the Whole.

Here, in sum, torsion tends towards the segmentation of the Whole into local coherences in which repetition is, so to speak, minimal.

It is as if, seen from afar in a reversible historical space, revolutions had no other function than to serialize events, to classify the epochs and to reconnect and re-group the heterogeneous.

Or as if the party had no other destiny than to bring to light the partitive repetition of history, through that spectacular element of commutation that we call the 'restoration of capitalism'. Alas, this is what happens, as we all know, when the party conflates itself with the State.

But in the final analysis, history is not commutative. This is even the founding principle of its inexistence, the secret of which is torsion.

What, then, does the algebraist tell us about non-commutative infinite torsion-groups?

4) Well, not much. He hands the question over to us.

The only hope was that a non-commutative torsion group generated by a finite number of elements would itself be finite.

Why was this the—antidialectical—hope? Because one thus would have connected the values of two finitudes: the finitude of torsion, which blocks the infinity of the repeatable, and the finitude that engenders the group, which masters, in some way, the twisted dialectic that puts the aleatory finite suspense of torsion to work within the non-commutative infinity of the group.

A finite-generated group is one whose elements can be presented as the sums (with possible repetitions) of elements taken from a finite stock. If, for example, your stock contains three elements—a, b, c—every element of the group will be of the type (a + a), (a + b + a + c), (c + b + a) . . .—these are only arbitrary examples.

Obviously, two combinations can be the equals to one another (that is, they can yield the same element). Thus a finite-generated group is not necessarily infinite.

Since in a torsion group any additive repetition of an element to itself is interrupted (that is, it lapses back to zero[42]), and since this is true in particular for the elements of the finite stock that generate the set, one can have the impression that it is not possible to find an infinity of different combinations of additions. Intuition tells us that there is a chance that a finite-generated torsion group may itself be finite.

For the sake of our dialectical convergence, this would represent a snag.

Marxism's field of operation, for its part, has three analogical properties: it is infinite, it involves torsion, and it is finite-generated. Why? First, because the eventual element, which is the raw material of mass politics, is infinite. It is even infinite at every moment because its theoretically countable nature, from the point of view of politics, is only a fiction. Second, because repetition is thereby interrupted in favour of the advent of another coherence, from the standpoint of torsion, within the whole. And finally, because the elements for the presentation of all politics—classes—are definitely finite in number.

The deductive analysis of the term 'torsion' from an algebraic point of view would show an abrupt divergence, an exploratory chance, if every finite-generated torsion group were finite. With regard to the dialectic, the mathematical interpretation of the term would be in a position of mastery over the excess.

But this is not at all the case. The theorem of Shafarevitch (1964) shows that it is not true that all finite-generated torsion groups are finite. It demonstrates this by way of a counterexample, through a group generated by three torsion elements that is nonetheless infinite.

The existence of such a group brings the analysis of the term 'torsion' to its closure in a context of dialectical convergence.

Thus, infinite and non-commutative torsion groups turn out to have only rare and unhealthy properties. They stand, as algebra shows, at the outer edges of the algebraic unnameable.

Torsion functions as the border-limit of algebra. Torsion is perverse: subject.

Note that we have not presented a model of anything here, nor attempted to 'mathematize' anything whatsoever. We have only tried to restore a sort of surplus brilliance whose sole means of expression remains the mathematical text, understood as the objective elucidation of the symptom provoked by the contrived chance of the word.

What happens, however, when the deductive analysis of the mathematical signifier that we have isolated diverges from its dialectical interpretation? In this case, let us have the audacity to say that an unexplored mathematical lead must force the divergence. We maintain that no term comes into use by chance.

This is as good an approach as any other, though certainly unorthodox, to search in existing mathematics for those places that hold in reserve the means to take a step beyond and thus to find what is everybody's dream: an unknown theorem.

For mathematics is the science of the real, and its signifiers, whatever they may be, are accountable for it.

2

What algebraic notation will we use for the superego and anxiety to indicate that these two concepts refer neither to subjective experiences nor to parts of the subject, but rather to two processes whose combination defines that region of practical materiality that we would do better to call the 'subject-effect'?

No subject pre-exists anxiety or lasts beyond the superego, if anxiety is what subjectivizes and the superego is one of the modes of consistency of the subject-effect.

Here we construct the concept of the subject starting from much more general dialectical categories: force (F), place (P), truth (T), locus (L), destruction (d), and lack (l).[43]

Anxiety is that excess-of-the-real (excess of force) over what can be symbolized (placed) thereof in a certain order, from whence a subject emerges already divided, crushed from its birth by its own truth, whose saying, under the rule of lack, comes itself to lack.

Thus, if $\not\vdash$ indicates the excess, then this is the cipher for anxiety:

$$F \not\vdash P = \frac{T + l\,(l)}{\cancel{S}}$$

The sign '$=$' indicates that it is at the moment of excess, within the differential form of subjectivization, that S ex-sists as split.

As for the superego, which names the part of nonlaw that adheres destructively to law itself, if we posit that L is for law (or for locus, or for the splace) and d for destruction, we will have to write it down as follows:

$$F \not\vdash P \rightarrow \frac{L + d}{\cancel{S}}$$

Here '$\rightarrow$' must be read as indicating that it is in the realm of the consistent effect (of the subjective process), which is integral and not differential, that S endures in its eclipse, under the terrorizing call of the law purely linked with its native ferocity.

As you can see, it is a question of Oedipus and of Sophocles.

To say that anxiety serves as a guidepost for truth amounts to saying that it is in the guise of an unplaced force—and not in the logic of places, though the latter is presupposed—that a sufficient quantity of subject-effect splits off in order for new knowledge to appear.

This is the enunciation of torsion (it is from torsion and for torsion that the other three names of truth—coherence, the whole, and repetition—are generated) for which Mao, at the peak of the Cultural Revolution, provided a crystal-clear translation: 'Troubles are an excellent thing.'[44] An excellent thing, that is, if we want to see clearly.

This could be a definition of anxiety: the trouble with seeing things clearly.

We will see that it is also, and from the same point, the definition of courage, but in order to see this we will have to find our way through the scission presented in Greek tragedy. It is certainly true that truth in the register of anxiety is unliveable because of its essential complicity with lack: Mallarmé gave us its latent structure. It is unliveable to the extent that—demanding an interruption of the efficacy of the symbolic, the effect of a hole—it can never be domesticated into an integral saying. Being only half-said, the truth is ill-said.[45] This is why the truth—that of Oedipus, that of Sophocles, the truth that demands the bloody sacrifice of the gaze—is indeed tragic.

There is, however, another truth and another tragedy: that of Orestes and of Aeschylus. Here, destruction assures the subject of a certain mastery of loss. It is no longer $\frac{T}{\cancel{S}}$ but $\frac{S}{\cancel{A}}$. What does this mean, if not that in this way we come out of the radical impasse to which the unity of the place, that is, the insurmountable fixity of the symbolic confines us? Destruction becomes dialectically linked to loss in the unrepresentable supposition that *the splace is divisible*—a supposition that itself is almost unsayable, even though it is the foundation of the uni-saying of the truth.

Hence, the subject as the excrescence of the revolt of anxiety is born in the violent internal distance of the law to itself, and it names the process through which the order that the subject sustains in its truth comes into being as other than itself.

Neither the other of Lacan nor the Other can conceive of this type of alterity, which is the only one that allows us to think of the advent of revolutions, the only one that allows us to understand in what sense, as Marx says, the communist revolution involves 'the most radical rupture with traditional ideas' (*The Communist Manifesto*). The only one, finally, that can name the heteronomy of politics.

Indeed, within this divided law, this broken symbolic, we deal with a trans-Other which is such that what is at issue is the transformation of the very framework for deciding the other and the same.

In this sense, we must say that, historically, there where a subject arises at the crossroads of lack and destruction, and at the point of anxiety but in the inversion of its truth, there is truly found something the existence of which Lacan denies—an other of the Other, from which it follows that what functioned as the first Other now appears as nothing more than an unenlightened mode of the Same.

This is precisely the process for which Athena serves as a name at the end of Aeschylus' *Oresteia* when, in order to interrupt the archaic family vendetta, she institutes a tribunal such that, as the chorus—anguished yet on the path toward courage—announces, the new laws overthrow the old ones.

The courage of the scission of the laws, the anxiety of an opaque persecution, the superego of the blood-thirsty Erinyes, and finally justice according to the consistency of the new: these are the four concepts that articulate the subject.

As early as in 1954, Lacan implicitly indicated the necessity of these four concepts when he anticipated the ethical reach of his discipline:

Once the number of cycles necessary for the subject's objects to appear have been accomplished, and his imaginary history is completed, once the successive tensed-up, suspended, anxiety-provoking desires of the subject are named and reintegrated, all is not, for all that, brought to term. What was initially there, in O, then here in O', then again in O, has to be referred to the completed system of symbols. The very outcome of the analysis requires it.

Where could this adjournment come to a stop? Do we have to extend the analytic intervention to the point of becoming one of those fundamental dialogues on justice and courage, in the great dialectical tradition?

That is a question. It is not easy to answer, because in truth, modern man has become singularly unused to broaching these grand themes. He prefers to resolve things in terms of conduct, of adaptation, of group morale and other twaddle. (S I, 198–9/223)

Anxiety does not lie and the superego gives legal consistency to destruction. But the 'fundamental dialogues on justice and courage' open the way to that aspect of the 'dialectical tradition' in which, by virtue of a completely different take on the irruption of the real, the subject placed as force can force the excess over the place.

Theory of the subject according to Sophocles, theory of the subject according to Aeschylus

May 9, 1977

Justice and the superego: nonlaw as law and law as nonlaw—Joseph Conrad—Courage and anxiety—Sophocles according to Hölderlin—The decree of Athena in Aeschylus—Reversal of the native place and reversal of exile

1

'[O]nce the successive tensed-up, suspended, anxiety-provoking desires of the subject are named and reintegrated', says Lacan: psychoanalysis operates as the reduction of the too-much of the real; it reintegrates within a splace of nomination that part of excess over the place which kept the subject in the suspense of anxiety.

Thus, force is put back in its place.

Yet, Lacan also says, 'all is not, for that matter, brought to term'. In what sense? The question carries considerable weight, since what is at stake therein is the dialectical extension of the theory of the subject, that is, the recognition, on the solid material basis of the effects of the structure, of their excessive reverse side through which history returns as subjective novelty.

The excess-of-the-real, then, detached from its obscure readability in the truth of anxiety, might be able to support the extension of the symbolic order and not simply to put back into its place what functioned as outplace therein.

Here Lacan mentions a grandiose perspective: 'It is in as much as the subjective drama is integrated into a myth which has an extended, almost universal human value, that the subject brings himself into being' (S I, 190–91/215).

There thus seems to be an extensive and universalizing productivity of the 'subjective drama' to which in the end the psychoanalytic work, via the 'fundamental dialogues on justice and courage', could hold the key.

Why justice and courage?

Justice is that by which the subject's nodal link to the place, to the law, takes on the divisible figure of its transformation, whereas the superego expressed the ferocious archaism of the fixity of the law. Justice makes no sense as a constitutive category of the subject if the symbolic operates as indivisibility whose kernel of terror founds the consistency of the subjective process, in the repetitive fabric of obsession. Justice requires a dialectical precariousness of the law, susceptible of being shaken up in the process of its scission. This is not the precariousness of this or that particular law, but of the very principle of commandment itself.

More radically, justice names the possibility—from the standpoint of what it brings into being as subject-effect—that what is nonlaw may function as law.

In Marxism, this is well known. Here the counterpart of the superego is the fact that the essential and constitutive core of the State, the domination of one class, is always dictatorial. Under the pretence of defending the legal apparatus and parliamentary democracy, the State is essentially the illegal being of all legality, of the violence of right, and of the law as nonlaw. On the other hand, the communist theme is justice, for it claims that, under the category of the withering away of classes and of the State, nonlaw may become the last law of proletarian politics. Communism, as the sole modern theory of revolution, effectuates the partisan subjectivity of the universal principle of justice, that is, the nonlaw as law.

Therefore, what extends itself (Lacan's 'extended, almost universal' value) must be rooted in what is in excess (over the place, the locus, the symbolic, the law).

Poetry may serve as our guide in this matter insofar as it is only by breaking up all ordinary prose that it extends the limit of the communicable and pushes back the inaccessible frontiers of *lalangue*.

It is wholly consistent that Joseph Conrad, the supreme novelist of anxiety and the superego—as *Heart of Darkness* and *Lord Jim* testify—should nonetheless give art the strategic task 'to render the highest kind of justice to the visible universe'.[46] In order to do so, he also in one and the same movement had to become the exceptional novelist of courage that he is: see *The Rover* for men and *The Arrow of Gold* for women.

Courage is insubordination to the symbolic order at the urging of the dissolutive injunction of the real. As based on the excess-of-the-real, courage is identical to anxiety, but as a disruptive force within the splace, it functions as its inversion. Courage positively carries out the disorder of the symbolic, the breakdown of communication, whereas anxiety calls for its death.

Since courage is not an attribute of the subject, but rather the divisible process of its intrinsic existence, it is more appropriate to compare it to *fortitudo* (fortitude or strength of mind) than to *audacia* (audacity or boldness). For the opposite of courage is not fear, but anxiety. On this topic, see Spinoza's *Ethics* (Part III, beginning with Proposition 59). *Audacia* is entirely defined by the mediation of the Other; it is 'the desire by which someone is led to do something which involves a danger which his equals are afraid to undergo'.[47] *Fortitudo* is intrinsic because it sustains itself only from the true, $\frac{S}{T}$ meaning '[a]ll the actions which follow from emotions which are related to the mind in so far as it understands'.[48] But the truth at issue, by the thrust of the real, produces a deficit in the symbolic whereby the subject, as courage, turns the radical absence of any security into its force. In this process, the subject truly loses its name. Besides, it is also one of Spinoza's theorems that security desubjectivizes (in his language, security is not a virtue): '*Securitas* [. . .] *animi impotentis est signum*' (Scholium to Proposition 47). Security is the sign of a subjective impotence.

Anxiety means deficiency of the place, while courage is the assumption of the real by which the place is split.

Anxiety and courage share the same divided causality, in a reversible articulation of the point impacted by loss.

On the necessary and indestructible basis of anxiety and of the superego, courage and justice thus articulate the subject-effect as the division, by the excess, of the symbolic order—of the splace—in which this excess is un-placed.[49]

This makes clear why a political subject comes into being only by tying the revolt to a revolutionary consistency, and destruction to a recomposition. Such is the real process which bespeaks the fact that for every order and every principle of legal commandment, however stable they may seem, their becoming coincides with their internal division. The Other must give way to its very own scission into that unprecedented Other which it never was and that Same whose identity it had never prescribed.

2

There is a theory of the subject according to Sophocles and another according to Aeschylus. The latter (which is historically the first, but still the second for Freud and, though invisibly, the first for Marx) entirely dialecticizes its other because, besides anxiety and the superego whose structure it retains, it postulates that courage and justice are necessary operators of the subject-effect.

It goes without saying that Sophocles and Aeschylus here serve as signifiers, or even as concepts, and not as names or as literary works. It is true that they are texts, but these are meant for the theatre, which changes everything.

The whole purpose of our critical delimitation with regard to the psychoanalytic contribution to the theory of the subject can be evaluated by asking the following question: why is its theory of the subject essentially based on Sophocles, that is, predicated on the Oedipus complex?

I propose that we must be Aeschylean. Lacan sides with Sophocles, but points at Aeschylus, which is where we want to get.

Hölderlin opens the debate over the real issues in his dazzling 'Remarks on "Antigone"', where he describes the essence of Sophocles in the following way:

1. The type of contradiction put into play by Greek tragedy is that of the originary versus the formal, of what is native versus what is learned (the 'natively Greek', says Hölderlin, is opposed to the 'native form'). In other words, we see a division of the native place, an internal contradiction that opposes the simple foundation of the law to the law itself. In terms of splace, tragedy is the *parousia* of an intimate scission, namely, the one that sets apart the One of the splace from its function, which is that of regulating the multiple. Let me add in passing that this is an avatar of the contradiction, which makes the subject, between the One and the Whole.
2. For the Greeks, this contradiction sets in opposition:
    –   on the side of the originary One, its infinite and orgiastic, 'Asiatic' consistency;
    –   on the side of the regulated (civilized) splace of which this One is the origin, the firmness of its finitude, its power of representative closure, which can be found in the formal perfection of Greek art, mathematics, architecture, and the politics of the city-polis.

Let us translate: if the Greek law is finitude and closure, then the nonlaw that is the foundation of this law, its native violence, is multi-form Asia. Thus, the realization of the Greek superego, which gives the subject its consistency—the law as nonlaw—is *elucidated* in tragedy.

3. In Sophocles' *Antigone*, this elucidation of the tragic contradiction is set in motion by insurrection. The fratricidal rebel violently turns against the city and, as a result, he is radically excluded (he is killed and his body is left unburied). But the attempt at exclusion fails: the shock spreads throughout the polis, not in the form of a political insurrection, but as the result of an infinite unlimitation within the native form.

4. This infinite form-giving process produces a reversal—it is a subjectivization thanks to which the place allows its contradictory origin, its illegal unity, to return within the inflated framework of regulations.

5. The reversal takes on the (theatrical) figure of an antagonism:
   - The very unlimitation of the native form gives rise to a *formal too-muchness* (Creon). The law is revealed as being in excess of its own restorative figure. Creon is the superlaw.
   - In reaction to this excess of form, the latent *formlessness* in its turn is set ablaze and calls upon the infinity of the sky against the finite law of the polis (Antigone).

'Creon' is the name of the superego: the law deregulated—destroyed—by its very own native essence as it returns in excess of the place that it circumscribes.

'Antigone' is the name of anxiety, that is, the principle of the infinity of the real, unplaceable within the regulated finitude of the place.

From this point of view, Antigone and Creon, although they are antagonists in the play, in my eyes accomplish the same process, which defines the Sophoclean tragic subject. Such is the foundation of this tragedy as textual One: to present the subject-process through the combined categories of anxiety and the superego.

3

We can formulate the problem as follows, by isolating two major theses in Hölderlin's account:

- The effect (the course) of insurrection is that of a reversal, by which the road of the new is barred.

– The internal engine of the tragic comes from the excess of the law over itself, from the figure of Creon. The formless is set on fire only as a reaction, in a second time. As for the figure of the rebel, he cannot be put in any camp. He is simply an algebraic term, an absent cause subtracted from the polis. Those who stand up against one another are the excess of form and the formless, the superego and anxiety—intertwined figures of the primordial One, the One of the reversal.

Thus, we ask: what is the link between these two theses? At stake are the politics underlying Hölderlin's poetics. The possible modernity of the tragic is a political question—as a question for the theory of the subject.

For Hölderlin, the contradiction is tragic insofar as it leaves no way out other than death. Why? Because it is not governed by any new right. In the two terms (Creon and Antigone), it is the infinite form that pervades everything, that is, the real that submerges the symbolic, the native force that dissolves the place. The unity of opposites prevails over their division, in direct proportion to the extent to which the essence of the process lies in the already-there of the origin. Hence the Sophoclean name of every subject-process is reversal. This is what Oedipus incarnates with all the clarity of his blindness. And indeed I believe that this subjective figure, whose dialectical edge is limited to that of anxiety and the superego, must always prevail in times of decadence and disarray, both in history and in life.

This is precisely where we must take hold of the division between Aeschylus and Sophocles.

In Aeschylus' *Oresteia*, the tragic is set in motion by the murder of Agamemnon. Orestes, forced to kill his mother (who has in turn killed his father), is somehow predefined by the infinite dynamic of revenge and counter-revenge. This is the repetitive splace in which a murder shall be punished by another murder, as the chorus says. Here the unlimited is the debt of blood. The (future) Sophoclean categories are clearly present, connected to the splace itself: that palace dripping with blood from where Orestes flees after the murder that subjectivizes him through anxiety and where he is pursued by the pack of Erinyes, watchdogs of the superego and cruel custodians of the repetitive totality constituted by the family vendetta.

But the true orientation of the trilogy is the rupture that allows for the advent of the new. What is at stake is the *interruption* of the infinite debt, of the repetitive chain of murders, by way of the torsion—imposed by an ex-centred decree of Athena—which allows for the advent of a new right, capable of completely recomposing the whole logic of the decision.

For in the tribunal that is thus set in place, it is indeed a new coherence that is instituted by the interruption of the repetitive series that made up the whole previous social order.

The result is that the two antagonistic positions are no longer articulated by the unity of the native as in Sophocles/Hölderlin. Instead they are the internal division of that which constitutes them, a division beyond the law of everything that can have a legal value. It is the locus itself that is shown to be in principle not one, but two.

In the course of this dialectical process, the new prevails over the old. In Hölderlin's lexicon, we could call this, not the reversal of the native form, but its advent.

These two positions are made explicit in the trilogy. We can see the first one in the chorus of the Erinyes, the divinities of revenge:

Catastrophe now is coming from new ordinances, if a justice which is harm to justice shall prevail for this man here, the matricide. This day's work will at once accustom all men to licence. [. . .] Justice's house falls. There is a place where terror is good, and a watch on minds by fear seated above. It is well to learn wisdom through grief. Would any that nurses no terror in his heart's clear light—both man and city the same— revere Justice still? [. . .] the man who defies out of boldness, transgressing [while he carries] his great cargo, one randomly got without right; in violence, will lower sail with time, once trouble catches him up and his yard-arm shatters. He calls on those who do no hear, from the whirlpool's centre so hard to struggle with; and god laughs over a hot-headed man, when he sees one who was confident that he would never be caught impotent in helpless torment, and not surmounting the wave-top. His prosperity, life-long till then, is dashed upon Justice's reef; he dies unwept, unseen.[50]

Thus, the dialectic between anxiety and the superego is the sole foundation of some form of measurement in the chain of revenge. Justice is subordinated to the superego, to the structural regularity of punishment, whereas subjectivization occurs through the trouble of anxiety, under the sign of death.

Athena, the founder of the new right, of course states the second position:

Athena: Now hear my ordinance, people of Athens, who are judging the pleas in the first trial for shed blood. For the future too this council of jurors shall always exist in Aegeus' people [. . .]. Untouched by desires for gain, revered, quick to anger, the land's wakeful guardian of those asleep, this council I now establish. This has been my lengthy exhortation to my citizens for the future; and you must rise and take your votes for casting and decide the case with respect for your oath. My speech is said . . . And Orestes wins even if in the judgement he has equal votes. Empty the votes from the urns at once, you jurors who have this duty put on you! [. . .]

Apollo: Count the emptied votes correctly, strangers, with reverent care against a wrong determination! When good judgement has gone away, great harm happens; but if a single vote comes in, it can set a house upright.

Athena: The man here goes free on the charge of bloodshed. The numbers of votes are equal.[51]

Thus, against the unlimitation of the old rule, the dispute must be settled by instituting the new one. Such is the divisible courage of the council, which intrinsically refers to the justice of number. The fact that it takes equally divided votes to seal the decision symbolizes a radical change in the very concept of what a decision means or possibly can mean. It is a scission in the very essence of right.

Athena's decree produces an egalitarian torsion from whence the new juridical coherence—that of the majority deliberation beyond appeal—once it is apprehended and put into practice, interrupts the mechanical seriality of revenge.

Thus we see that there exist indeed two Greek tragic modes: the Aeschylean one, the direction of which is the contradictory advent of justice by the courage of the new; and the Sophoclean one, the anguished sense of which is the quest, through a reversal, for the superegoic origin.

4

What does Hölderlin say?

The true language of Sophocles, since Aeschylus and Euripides know more how to depict suffering and wrath, yet less how to depict man's understanding as wandering below the unthinkable. (ELT 110, trans. modified)

My first objection is that it will not do to pair up Aeschylus with Euripides. But this is only the sign of a much deeper distortion: a partially unexplained predilection for Sophocles, which is not entirely absent from Freud either—for who will argue that the native logic of the unconscious is exempt of reversals?

If Aeschylus excels in anything, it is rather in grasping, on the super-ego's firm ground, the moment of the *institutive disruption*. There is never a return to order in his theatre, but rather the recomposition of a different order. Aeschylus excludes the presupposition of a unity of the originary. This is why the Aeschylean hero indeed does not wander under the unthinkable. His excellence assuredly is on the side of the thinkable. It consists in *turning away from any return*, or rather: his virtue lies in the ability to expose a non-native reversal.

As a result, it is no longer the formal excess that serves as the engine, but rather the courageous refusal. Although devoured by anxiety, and in fact *precisely because* he is devoured by anxiety, Orestes does not internalize the law of the debt of blood with its endless allocations, nor does he turn against it in a blind fury. Instead, he demands a discussion based on facts; he stands firm and does not give in to the murderous seduction of the Erinyes.

'Orestes', who is first the name of anxiety, is the name of courage. 'Athena' is the name of justice.

Antigone, Creon, Orestes, and Athena name the *complete* range of subject-effects within Greek tragedy: the formless, the formal excess, interruption, and recomposition.

In a tragedy by Aeschylus, the dynamic course of insurrection, as Hölderlin would say, does not coincide with the propagation of death. It is what founds justice through the internal division and withering of the old right. Far from being tied to the exclusion of the absent cause, the rebel—Orestes or Prometheus—is the immediate agent of this dynamic course.

Hölderlin clearly opts for the Sophoclean tragic, that is, for the structural part of the theory of the subject.

The dividing line depends on the native limitation of the reversal. Because of this limit, Sophocles' tragic history circumscribes antagonism in the power of the One.

The crucial point for Sophocles/Hölderlin is the retrogression toward the origin in its double aspect: the formal excess and the fire of the formless. In this case, the tragic hero who owes his subjectivization to anxiety and his consistency to the superego follows the involution of the splace to the point of death.

The key point for Aeschylus is completely different—it is the interruption of the power of origin, the division of the One. This interruption also has two aspects. The first is that of the courageous refusal, which questions the law under the effect of an excess-of-the-real and transcends anxiety in the mode of a *dispute*. This moment is reached when Orestes demands that a decision be made on the question of whether he was right or wrong. The other aspect is that of the recomposition which, on the basis of the interruption, unfolds a new order of justice.

Neither of these two forms amounts to a return of the origin in the rule. Both name the dimension of the subject which, while always being realized under the law (anxiety and the superego), nonetheless at the same time also exceeds it so as to bring into being the novelty of its being—in this case, for Aeschylus, a subject of law.[52]

Like any great dialectician, Hölderlin at times recognizes in passing the virtuality of Aeschylus' side: 'And in the native reversal where the entire form of things changes, and where nature and necessity, which always remain, incline toward another form—be it that they turn into chaos or pass into a new form' (ELT 115, trans. modified).

However, the virtual novelty, the 'new form' that tragedy could generate, comes about only through the force of death. Why? Because this new form, as is subsequently shown, is nothing more than the formal excess— it is only the law itself caught in the vortex of terror—and because chaos is nothing but the unlimited, the blaze of the formless. Besides, how can one fully gain access to the novelty of an effect if one presupposes, in the mode of the native, the absolute unity of the cause? Therefore, Hölderlin must make explicit a principle of limitation: a *total* reversal, he says, is not granted to humans. It is clear indeed that a total reversal could not be native. In order for that to be possible, we would have to be delivered from superegoic *fixity*. Aeschylus' path, in which courage and justice dialecticize anxiety and the superego, allows for divisibility and elucidates the possibility of deliverance.

It is not that we have to leave the beautiful word 'reversal' behind. Instead, I want to distinguish two forms of what this word designates for the theory of the subject. There is the native reversal, which takes place in anxiety and pretends to cure it, both through the terror of restoration and through its opposite, the mystical stupor. But then there is also the reversal of exile, in which it is from the denegation and scission of the old law that stems the illumination, in the guise of the new, of the torsion inflicted upon the real. The reversal of exile revokes the original in its scant reality, while restoring the real in justice.

In this regard, it is a total reversal: let us make a tabula rasa of the past.

This is not simple, because it is vain to hope that the process of the reversal of exile will take place without the structural anchorage of the native. Indeed, it is from the materialistic impasse of the latter that the practical existence of the former proceeds. It is one-sided to declare the subject tragic; nevertheless, tragedy exists.

To sustain exile, or as Rimbaud says in *A Season in Hell*, 'to hold on to a step once taken', is what Hölderlin could not bear.[53] Exile for him never stopped being the crucifying mediation of the return.

There is no other definition of courage: exile without return, loss of one's name. But Hölderlin wants to maintain the nomination of what is near:

> And no wonder! Your native country and soil you are walking,
> What you seek, it is near, now comes to meet you halfway. (PF 277)

I claim that we must pass or overtake nostalgia, as one passes or overtakes a special convoy; we must exceed the pregnant form of the return by way of courage.

Sophocles stands for the returning quest of the near in what is remote, the infinite patriotism of pure proximity, a truth so intimate that one has to die in order to uncover it in oneself.

Aeschylus stands for the remote in the near, exile closest to one's skin.

An action anchored in that whose logic is most forbiddingly foreign to everything that is familiar to us: such is the subject of antagonism.

Even though we have to return—and it is this return that makes the subject—there can arise an enlightened overcoming of what no longer entails any return.[54]

Of the strands of the knot, to know only the colour

May 23, 1977

Notes for a diagram—The crisis has matured—Classes, the State, masses—Mathemes—At the blackboard

1

I went a bit fast these last times. In order to counter the enigma, let us exaggerate it. My goal is to draw up a table of what we have accomplished. But I will do so by going through a series of random annotations.

1. Lacan's terms and our own

We began, in 1975, with the splace (or the place of the subjective), the outplace, concentrated into force, and the double articulation of the two: placement and excess.

We have corrupted this lexicon of force and place with Lacan's trinitary version: symbolic, real, truth, imaginary. That three makes four is clear.

'Subject' is common to both of us, and commonly evaded.

Deceitfully, I propose to you the following two ordered lists. Are they isomorphous? Let's see.

Lacan: symbolic, real, imaginary, truth, law, signifier, knot.

Here and elsewhere: place, force, ideology 1 (totality-repetition), ideology 2 (torsion-coherence), State, logic of places (algebra), logic of forces (topology).

2. We are dealing with the theory of the subject as such

With the productive rationality of the subject-effects. It is said neither that a subject requires a (sexuated) individual as support nor that it belongs to a (social) class. We are only giving an overview. Whence the possibility of the aforementioned lexical corruption.

3. Force and destruction

This is one and the same concept, divided according to the structure and according to the process.

According to the structure, force remains defined in terms of the place, as purification in excess, as too-much-of-the-real. It continues to be referred to the lack.

According to the process, force is what interrupts the repetition. It is this moment of interruption that makes lack stray into destruction.

In Marxist politics, one knows this difference only too well. 'Being a force' to be reckoned with means counting for too much—from the point of the adversary—in terms of the tolerable place of the oppositions. It is an interiorized repressive definition. Now, this fascination with lack is almost the rule among 'revolutionary' political parties. They measure their own force against the quantity of tolerable excess, that is, against the threshold of destruction. Above all, they do not want to take the place of being out of place. If necessary, they weaken or divide themselves. This tendency to deploy force only according to the structure makes the revolutionary impatient, anxious to exceed the excess in the act of interruption.

The exemplary historical figure of this subjective drama is Lenin's fury in 1917, when the party, Zinoviev and Kamenev, *essentially* balk at the notion of forcing history by way of the insurrection. They want to have nothing to do with this 'art', which is the name Lenin raps about to describe the insurrection in the dignity of its uncertain power. For them, the force of the Bolsheviks lies in waiting; it is a cumulative given.

The essence of politics indeed consists of waiting. On one hand, this is insurmountable. But when Lenin says that the insurrection is an 'art', he means precisely that it violates the essence of politics.

What does Lenin say? We must read all these texts from the fall of 1917, for example 'The Crisis Has Matured':

What, then, is to be done? We must *aussprechen was ist*, 'state the facts', admit the truth that there is a tendency, or an opinion, in our Central Committee and among the leaders of our Party which favours *waiting* for the Congress of Soviets, and is *opposed* to the immediate taking of power, is *opposed* to an immediate insurrection. That tendency, or opinion, must be *overcome*.

Otherwise, the Bolsheviks will cover themselves with eternal *shame* and *destroy themselves* as a party.

For to miss such a moment and to 'wait' for the Congress of Soviets would be *utter idiocy*, or *sheer treachery*. [. . .]

To refrain from taking power now, to 'wait', to indulge in talk in the Central Executive Committee, to confine ourselves to 'fighting for the organ' (of the Soviet), 'fighting for the Congress', is *to doom the revolution to failure*.

In view of the fact that the Central Committee has *even left unanswered* the persistent demands I have been making for such a policy ever since the beginning of the Democratic Conference, in view of the fact that the Central Organ is *deleting* from my articles all references to such glaring errors on the part of the Bolsheviks as the shameful decision to participate in the Pre-Parliament, the presentation of seats to the Mensheviks in the Presidium of the Soviet, etc., etc.—I am compelled to regard this as a 'subtle' hint of the unwillingness of the Central Committee even to consider this question, a subtle hint that I should keep my mouth shut, and as a proposal for me to retire.

I am compelled to *render my resignation from the Central Committee*, which I hereby do, reserving for myself the freedom to campaign among the *rank and file* of the Party and at the Party Congress.

For it is my profound conviction that if we 'wait' for the Congress of Soviets and let the moment pass now, we shall *ruin* the revolution. (SW II, 417–20)

I hope that you will discern the nomination, almost unbeknownst, of an unprecedented subject-effect. That which splits off here rejects the 'waiting', as a closed figure of force, so as to tip over into the immediate destruction of its conditions.

This moment of pure torsion—of resignation as a mission[55]—in which the cumulative is inverted into loss, into the squandering of force, is the temporal sphinx of the subject.

Here we see the crossover, in a raging vacillation, between the lifeless straightness of what is missing and the vital risk of interruption.

Here the subject awakens to the decision, which is purely its mode of existence. To decide always amounts to disjoin, in the determinant unity of the serial lack, the point of destruction. This is why it is extremely rare that anything whatsoever pertains to a decision.

4. The double articulation of force and place

Either it is the case that one is the loss of the other, when the excess, being destructive, cannot be located in its assigned place, or else it is the other way around, when, by keeping at its place, force is squandered in the wide-eyed opening of the superego.

This is Marx's great discovery, especially during the Paris Commune:

> If you look at the last chapter of my *Eighteenth Brumaire*, you will find that I declare that the next attempt of the French Revolution will be no longer, as before, to transfer the bureaucratic military machine from one hand to another, but *to smash* it, and this is the preliminary condition for every real people's revolution on the Continent. And this is what our heroic Party comrades in Paris are attempting.[56]

It is a question of destruction, as a tendency of heroism—subjective quality if ever there was one—so as to give rise to the popular dimension of the insurrection.

Marx theorizes the link between destruction and the 'really' popular extent of the historical phenomenon in question. The being of the working class may very well appear as subject, as it did in June 1848, in the defensive, mute, tragic aspect of anxiety. But the interest of the people as a whole, for its part, lies in the general interruption of the series of the place, that is, in the destruction of the intimate mechanism of the State.

The more the revolution is capable of being radical, and not stuck in the bloody outburst governed by the anxiety of repression and the superego of terror, the more it participates in the courageous tipping of the scales into destruction and the just audacity of recomposition, and the more it turns out to be the act of a people, of which the proletariat only names the One, as the One of politics.

5. Classes, the side of the truth

The dominant class derives its position from keeping the splace as is. Its truth is half-said, by claiming to be all. It manages the repetition. All perceived coherence is unsustainable in its eyes.

The revolutionary class defines itself as the subject that sustains the truth in its division. Based on its political existence, which is highly aleatory, the half-saying becomes One-saying according to the torsion from the point of which the new coherence is put into practice.

The Marxist analysis in terms of class is isomorphous with the Lacanian analysis in terms of truth. Both cases require torsion, since the truth cannot be said all (Lacan) and there is no truth that is above class (Marxism), hence it cannot, in effect, be said all.

This means that it must be said not-all. That is, it must be said in the guise of the subject: hysteric for the one, revolutionary for the other.

'Proletariat' is the political name of the truth that is not-all.

6. State and masses, the side of the law

The State is the violent core of the law's commandment. Its specific effect lies in the annulment of the antagonistic subjective force.

The masses, by making history (good as much as bad), can be registered on the side of the nonlaw. They are the only antistate force, which is their very definition.

The masses can irrupt onto the stage of history only in a destructive excess over and above the State. This is their communist invariance. They may also, in their identity as substance, dictate the thickest, and even the most abject, statist consensus. But this is their placed being, their forced being. Their being-in-force falls under the law of nonlaw.

We call 'masses' the historical interruption as such, the real of the cut.

7. Four mathemes

Our algebra is composed of L (the locus or place), F (force), P (place), T (truth), l (lack), and d (destruction). The sign = marks a differential time; the sign → an integral process. ⊦ is the fork of the excess over the bar of the placement.

I have already written out for you the mathemes of anxiety and the superego:

Anxiety:

$$F \not\vdash P = \frac{T + 1\,(l)}{\cancel{S}}$$

Superego:

$$F \not\vdash P \rightarrow \frac{L + d}{\cancel{S}}$$

Courage is the destructive tipping of the scales in which the truth is sustained in its division:

$$F \dashv\!\!\backslash\; P = \frac{S + d}{\cancel{T}}$$

Justice recomposes the space under the mark of a law which henceforth is lacking in that which attaches itself to it. It illuminates and consolidates the division of the place:

$$F \dashv\!\!\backslash\; P \rightarrow \frac{S}{\cancel{V} + 1}$$

These four mathemes constitute the effect-of-the-subject.

2

Let me recapitulate this for you in space (see diagram below).

Regarding the double division which determines the subject effect, it would be fair to say that Lacan has exhaustively named only one half.

To the first division, the horizontal one in the table, corresponds the dialectic of law and truth, whose correlate would be that of the State and class. Freud named it.

The second, vertical divide receives no analytical name. It passes between the one of the law and its division, between the State and the

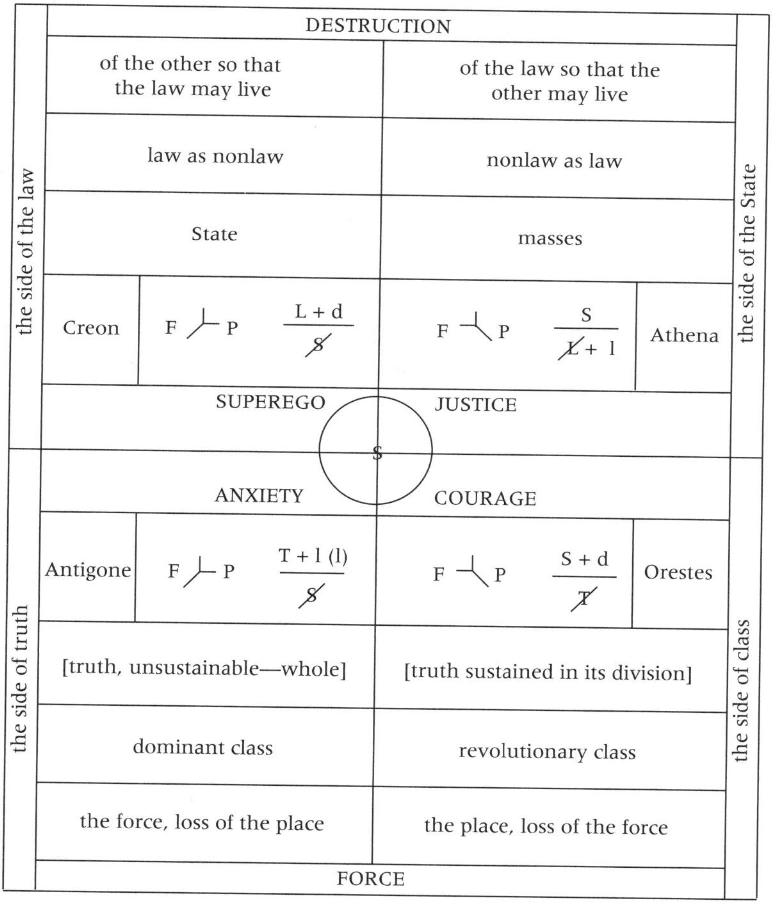

		DESTRUCTION		
	of the other so that the law may live		of the law so that the other may live	
	law as nonlaw		nonlaw as law	
	State		masses	
Creon	$F \vdash P \quad \dfrac{L+d}{\$}$		$F \dashv P \quad \dfrac{S}{\$+1}$	Athena
	SUPEREGO	$\$$	JUSTICE	
	ANXIETY		COURAGE	
Antigone	$F \vdash P \quad \dfrac{T+l\,(l)}{\$}$		$F \dashv P \quad \dfrac{S+d}{\$}$	Orestes
	[truth, unsustainable—whole]		[truth sustained in its division]	
	dominant class		revolutionary class	
	the force, loss of the place		the place, loss of the force	
		FORCE		

(Left side, top to bottom: "the side of the law", "the side of truth". Right side, top to bottom: "the side of the State", "the side of class".)

masses, between the two antagonistic classes. Marx has named it. It is through this division that historicity circulates.

As a result of the knot of this double splitting, a knot which so far we know only by the colour of its strands, there are four fundamental concepts of the theory of the subject.

This exhausts the critical powers of our algebra. We know what, under the effect of the unnamed destruction, escapes Lacan in the determination of the subject. But we do not know what it is in courage that retroacts on the unavoidable anxiety, nor what it is in justice that resonates in the prescription of the superego, nor finally how the recompositions, whether they are terrorizing or dissolving, articulate themselves onto the interruptions, other than in the false empirical evidence of succession.

The matheme of the four mathemes defines our current impasse. To ensure its materialist guarantee will require a vast detour. From the latter, we expect a framework with which to elucidate our singular lives, and the art that imbues them, as well as the existence of politics, and the history that is plotted in them.

At all times it is from an ethics that action gains a premonition of its risk and its success. From the widespread conviction that action is impossible, the most ravaging desubjectivizations are borne.

What can we expect from a theory of the subject, if not to shed some light on the mystery of decision?

Part IV

A Materialist Reversal of Materialism

The black sheep of materialism

November 7, 1977

The subject of tradition—Fall glumness—To defend Marxism is to defend
   a weakness—On idealist domination—From God to idealinguistery

1

'What is a subject in politics?' For good reasons this question torments
us, memorable leftists and leftists of short memory. We carry this obscure
question, almost without knowing it, to a point of even greater obscurity,
into the class of factory workers and its obtuse history. But can this question be materialist? Can it be Marxist?

   Would it be a matter of adding a convenient 'psychology' to dialectical
materialism, in the way Politzer wanted, to the point of suppressing itself
in the process? I say many times no. It is not the case that Marxism, having
occupied itself—let us suppose in general satisfactorily—with classes and
the State, with history and with politics, would have left blank the suspicious domain of the individual, the fury of sex or the emotion of love—
leaving them for other cooks of the concept.

   It has never led to anything, nor will it ever lead to anything, to imagine
that there is some lack to fill in Marxism, some regional discipline to
which its powers ought to be extended—a psychology, for example, which
people have prided themselves for dreaming up on the Russian side, with
the help of a few canines blessed with educational saliva.

   Our question, which is much more radical, does not take the figure of a
region of the concept. We ask: 'What makes a subject?'[1] and it is in the best

constituted domains of the tradition—class action and its party—where this question resonates most abruptly.

Besides, this tradition does not fail to shelter our problem. Perhaps it even gives it too much shelter. It is an entirely orthodox distinction to oppose the 'class-in-itself', which is the pure existence of the worker collective, and the 'class-for-itself', subjectively constituted in its revolutionary goal.

It remains to be seen whether this Hegelian arrangement is illuminating.

The track that lies open before us consists in the notion that the organizational phenomena of politics depend, in any historical process, on the subjective. They are its matter.

This argument finds echoes throughout 150 years of history in the hair-splitting debates over the question of who are the *agents* of history: The classes? The masses in revolt? The State? The revolutionary leaders? Who then makes history as subject? Who is the subject of the verb 'to make'?

Mao on this topic flirts with theology: 'The people, and the people alone, are the motive force of world history' (SW III, 207).

The people here occupy a transcendent subjective position.

Leninism certainly has marked a major stage in the focusing of Marxism on subjective action. Here the theory of organization as practical subject dominates the class analysis.

With Marx, we rather have a theory of the self, a critique of the illusions of consciousness. Class positions are explained as part of ideological apparatuses that are not far from evoking the function of the imaginary in the ideal edification of this self that for every subject constitutes its Whole.

There is also the recurrent debate about the role of the individual in history. Related avatars are Khrushchev's thesis on the 'cult of personality' to conjure the phantom of Stalin, and Lin Biao's Icaric fall when in light of the 'theory of genius' he tried to project Mao into the inactive heaven of proletarian Buddhas.

You see the disparate nature of this legacy.

In any case I exclude all attempts to put the subject back into the saddle as simple centre, as point of origin, as constitutive of experience. The theory of the subject is diametrically opposed to all elucidating transparency. Immediacy and self-presence are idealist attributes for what is introduced only with the aim of relinking the dialectical division.

Concentrating the dialecticity of the real, the subject-process essentially touches upon scission. The subject does not overcome itself in any reconciliation of itself either with the real or with itself. Lacan is our current teacher with regard to this major precaution.

2

What is all the fuss about during this fall of 1977? The despair over History, the idiosyncratic aestheticism, the taste for special constructions, the conviction that the monstrous figure of the State looms over and defines our destiny and that Western rationality, of which Marxism would only be the modern outcome, is caught up in this definition. The media echo the news that with the Gulag and the Vietnamese boat people, with Pol Pot and the Soviet armada, we would finally have what it takes to put an end to the abomination of Marxism.

The ethics behind this trend is divided between a morals of rights (to defend the life of the individual against the deadly abstraction of the State) and a politics of the lesser evil (to defend Western parliaments against the totalitarianisms of the East). The communist ambition is judged criminal for preferring mass politics over humanist and juridical negotiating. Against ideological violence, we hear pleas for the stubborn regularity of institutions, insofar as they would erect a bulwark around the insular conscience.

The radical socialist Alain already spoke of 'the citizen against the powers that be'.[2] This French modesty now makes a comeback in an anti-Marxist diatribe served up by a key character: the leftist renegade, the repentant Maoist, whose sales pitch—like that of a whole generation of 'Stalinist' intellectuals already in the 1950s—is that nobody will catch them red-handed again.

Hand over education to those who got tired of antagonism, to all those who, after joining their fate to that of the workers, have since then come back to their prescribed place as intellectuals, and you will make the wish of state functionaries come true by keeping thought for the next two decades within the narrow confines of the usual course of affairs. It will be everyone for him or herself, nobody will pretend to speak for anyone whatsoever.

This is the surest road towards the worst. When one abdicates universality, one obtains universal horror.

With regard to this mediocre challenge, I see two attitudes among the different people I know: to defend oneself or to change oneself.

'Defending' Marxism and politics leads only to deafness. Do you really believe that our anti-Marxists could scream foul play and announce our debacle if we were able to defend ourselves victoriously? I claim that, devoid of all novelty, the anti-Marxist propaganda of the repented and the realigned, of the champions of human rights and the amateurs of Helvetian peace of mind, only has the effectiveness of our own weakness.

Yes, let us admit it without detours: Marxism is in crisis; Marxism is atomized. Past the impulse and creative scission of the 1960s, after the national liberation struggles and the cultural revolution, what we inherit in times of crisis and the imminent threat of war is a narrow and fragmentary assemblage of thought and action, caught in a labyrinth of ruins and survivals. That which we name 'Maoism' is less a final result than a task, a historical guideline. It is a question of thinking and practising post-Leninism. To measure the old, to clarify the destruction, to recompose politics from the scarcity of its independent anchoring, and all this while history continues to run its course under the darkest of banners.

To defend Marxism today means to defend a weakness. We must *practise* Marxism.[3]

Whence the paradoxical statement that I would propose to you: Even though it is evident that our anti-Marxists have it in above all for the dialectic, it is materialism that we must found anew with the renovated arsenal of our mental powers.[4]

If we were to let go of our grip, limiting ourselves—as we did during the militant years—to positing that the movement is everything and that it divides itself into two, while the anti-Marxists demand a return to rights and laws worthy of theologians, we would remain with our backs against the wall, blind to ourselves and to our time.

True, it is not by chance that the petty attacks of the likes of Glucksmann and others are aimed at Hegel and at the role of Reason in history. The supreme target is the dialectic.

Like the rused tacticians of ancient China, we grant the adversary these abrupt changes of terrain that turn their ravaging flights into cavalries for windmills.

We demand of *materialism* that it include what we need and which Marxism, even without knowing it, has always made into its guiding thread: a theory of the subject.

The inaugural text was titled *The Communist Manifesto*. What were these communists, in 1848, if not the new subject about whom the founding fathers said:

The Communists do not form a separate party opposed to other working-class parties.

They have no interests separate and apart from those of the proletariat as a whole.

They do not set up any sectarian principles of their own, by which to shape and mould the proletarian movement.

The Communists are distinguished from the other working-class parties by this only: 1. In the national struggles of the proletarians of the different countries, they point out and bring to the front the common interests of the entire proletariat, independently of all nationality. 2. In the various stages of development which the struggle of the working class against the bourgeoisie has to pass through, they always and everywhere represent the interests of the movement as a whole.

The Communists, therefore, are on the one hand, practically, the most advanced and resolute section of the working-class parties of every country, that section which pushes forward all others; on the other hand, theoretically, they have over the great mass of the proletariat the advantage of clearly understanding the line of march, the conditions, and the ultimate general results of the proletarian movement. (SW I, 119–20, trans. modified)

Communists: they are, in the movement of history, the political subject.

That is the point from which we must start again.

3

The materialist thesis is not simple. It is even less simple, appearances notwithstanding, than the dialectical thesis.

Marxists have always posited that ever since its Greek origin, the contradiction that defines philosophy is the one that opposes materialism and idealism. This is the axiom of the battle of the clerks:

The philosophers split into two great camps. Those who asserted the primacy of spirit to nature and, therefore, in the last instance, assumed world creation in some form or other [. . .] comprised the camp of idealism. The others, who regarded nature as primary, belong to the various schools of materialism. (Engels, *Ludwig Feuerbach and the End of Classical German Philosophy*, SW III, 346)

What is the source of this structural invariance according to which philosophy seems to stage a skeletal battle on whether A precedes B, or B, A?

What supports this in the real is that the ruling classes are invariably prone to claim that thought precedes being (nature). All this is rather curious, is it not? And Engels at bottom does not explain himself further on the topic.

Let us give two provisory motives for this idealist compulsion.

A ruling class is the guardian of the place, the obligatory functionary of the splace. Its aim, both violent and hidden, is to guarantee repetition and prohibit the political subject, through the blockage of interruption.

To rule means *to interrupt interruption*.

In the language of the politics of the State, this is called 'restoring order'. Order is what is re-established while keeping silent about what establishes it. Like the subject it denies, order declares that it comes in the second place.

The conservative posture requires that the law be named as indivisible: it can only be un-established, but never divided. From subversion to conspiracy through destabilization, the State's lexicon is replete with words to refer to the un-establishment of the law, but not a single one to name its division.[5]

The indivisibility of the law of the place excepts it from the real. To link up this exception in the domain of theory amounts to stipulating the radical anteriority of the rule, which, in fact, is defined (established) only retroactively, through the torsion in which its coherence appears as disjoined from the new coherence.

The position of this antecedence is elaborated in philosophy as idealism. It is necessary to ground the place of the repetitive series in the absolute.

Idealism is the nominal parousia of the splace as such. Plato, as behoves a founder, designates it as *topos*.

Idealism necessarily dominates, being the obligatory language of conservation.

On the other hand, it is true that to this very day every ruling class on its own account has kept in place the social division of labour. Cutting transversally across class conflicts, we find these great millenarian structural invariants, these three 'great differences'—city and countryside, industry and agriculture, intellectual and manual—whose abolishment is the very aim of communism.

It is in this sense that communism is concrete. Specified with exactness by the most tenacious social differentiations, it takes up the question of politics only as the angle required for its access to the real. Naming as it does, through popular violence, the need to measure the stages reached with regard to the resorption of the three great differences (hence of students engaged in the process of production, cities stopped from growing, the small industrialization of popular communes, the workers' technical innovation, etc.), the Chinese Cultural Revolution deserves in turn to be named the first communist revolution in history.

Whatever fails keeps its name. If not, what exactly is it that failed?

For those classes of which communism is the spectre, it is important to consolidate the distinctions. Albeit in a variety of formulas, whose extension is almost devoid of common measure, they all monopolize intellectual labour and systematize its 'superiority' over its manual counterpart.

We will recognize that idealism is transitive to this social axiom. In the final analysis, it subordinates nature to the concept, much like the specialized worker of the assembly line is subordinated to the engineer, or the slave, that 'animated tool', to his mathematician master.

Do not think that the vulgarity of this argument is an obstacle to its truth.

In the handbooks of philosophy, you will see that like the epithet of a two-bit Homer, the adjective 'vulgar' almost invariably attaches itself to the noun 'materialism'. Well yes! There is something trivial about reading the abject secret of a speculative permanence in the densest of social hierarchies. But that is how it is.

Whence the materialism of the bourgeois revolutionaries of the eighteenth century—against the clerical-feudal establishment—and that of the proletarians of the nineteenth—against the barons of finance capital converted to spiritualism.

Thus, too, with the onset of the old age of conservatism one easily forgets the irascible materialism of one's political youth. The same ones who feasted on priests and academics end up subsidizing the mission of the good fathers in Africa, or distributing to the Central Committee the icons of a 'Soviet humanism' through which we can easily glimpse the well-heeled dachas and the black Mercedes.

4

Materialism, if it is not a dead dog, attests within the concept to the purifying emergence of force. It is an assault philosophy. With its dissolving purpose and simplifying courage, it makes the fissure of the symbol shine at the farthest remove, instructed as it is by an out-of-place.

Materialism stands in internal division to its targets. It is not inexact to see in it a pile of polemical scorn. Its internal makeup is never pacified.

Materialism most often *disgusts* the subtle mind.

The history of materialism finds the principle of its periodization in its adversary. Making a system out of nothing else than what it seeks to bring down and destroy, puffed up in latent fits of rage, this aim is barely philosophical. It gives colour, in often barbarous inflections, to the impatience of destruction.

The first materialism of our era, that of the rising bourgeoisie—that of the eighteenth century—exists only with reference to religion, which it proposes in a violent and even repugnant manner (what more mediocre fable than Voltaire's *The Maid of Orleans*, the versification of those sordid bar stories where one looks avidly underneath the frock of the village priest?) to abolish immediately. This materialism, though it refers to the clockwork science of the world, calculatedly close to Newton's mechanics, seeks to organize as quickly as possible a single directive: 'Crush the infamy!'

However, this time of offensive subjectivization produces no stability. We see this as early as in the French Revolution, when the anti-Christian excess of the provisory allies, the plebeians of the cities, is broken by Hébert's execution on the guillotine, whereas the regeneration of spiritualism of the great idealist systems connotes the possibility of a universal concordat.[6] Bourgeois secularism, established through the State, will sometimes be anticlerical, never materialist.

Let this be retroactive proof of the fact that materialism organizes the assault, not the takeover; the uprising, not the repression.

The bourgeoisie, taken to be the guardian of the modern place, must obey three conditions, once the old regime is overthrown and the path is open to its worldwide rule:

- tolerate this minimal part of materialism that is adequate for the rationalized lift-off of the productive forces, as accredited by science;
- reorganize idealism, which makes a symbol and a rule out of the subordination of the manual to the intellectual in the hierarchical division of labour;
- sustain in philosophy the juridical and moral order that names the prescription of the places, and assigns the repetitions.

The product of all this is a specific idealism, centred on Man, and no longer on God. Consciousness as the focal point of experience, the subject as guarantee of truth, morality as atemporal formalism: this average Kantianism lasts, on a massive scale, to this very day.

The second figure of materialism is thus made out of the assault against humanism, and especially against the petty Kantian teachers of the university.

They pushed their pawns very far, those pawns of the transcendental, all the way into the ranks of the new politics, as we can see in the Leninist diatribe that is called *Materialism and Empirio-criticism*.

The battle in the background of the second materialism, of which the bourgeoisie is already no longer the bearer, comes down to taking sides with Hegel against Kant.

Ask yourself in passing if every materialism is not the *stiffening* of an old idealism.

Where did the materialists of the eighteenth century get their superflat machines, if not from Descartes? And Lenin brings Hegelian immanence to bear against the transcendental. And we, against Althusser's 'process without subject', invoke Lacan.

A new figure of materialism announces itself in a division of idealism. Its subjective mainspring is what introduces the break.

The second materialism, after that of irreligion, will be historical because its task is no longer to undo God, but to undo Man. Nature—which is what one opposed to grace and miracles—ceases to function as referent. Taking its place is the historical becoming of the world, in which the class position turns out to divide humankind and there is not one simple term capable of functioning as the centre of either experience or truth.

Whence its name, 'historical materialism', and its surname 'dialectical materialism', with the second elevating into generality that which the first guarantees in its temporal precariousness and its divided being.

Yet, today, I do not see how 'antihumanism' could be the particular mark of Marxism. From the 1960s onward, it was universally held that we had to be done with Man, and such was the task for Foucault and Lacan as well as for Althusser.

Does this automatically mean that we enter that orphanage of being that gives materialisms their shelter of charmless truth? Far from it! All antihumanists of the period held on to a constituent function in the last analysis, namely, that of discourse.

Language is that of which experience is the effect, and it is from that which makes his speech possible that Man derives the power not to exist. There you have the axiom of all our best thinkers.

There are three materialisms, for the excellent reason that there are three idealisms: religious idealism, humanist idealism, and then—the fruit of this historical cul-de-sac in which imperialism casts its last rays of languishing modernity—linguistic idealism.

'Linguistic' here imposes itself, insofar as 'the structure [can be] recognized as producing, as I say, language out of *lalangue*.'[7]

Language = structure: such is the constituent statement, which we should not confuse with this or that statement in the scientific discipline named linguistics, or better yet the one named—by Lacan—'linguistery'.[8]

Even so, to the extent that it claims to expand all the way to the thesis: the world is discourse, this argument in contemporary philosophy would deserve to be rebaptized: 'idealinguistery'.

Today it is idealinguistery that the materialist assault makes into its cause.

It is exactly for this reason that the essence of active materialism, by a Copernican inversion, demands the position of a theory of the subject, which previously it had the function of foreclosing.

At its worst when it reduces itself to the description of vast discursive configurations that characterize the entire mental and practical process of an era, idealinguistery excludes any subject. This is the thesis, which I will call fixist, of Foucault, that Cuvier of the archives who with some bookish bones examined with genius gives you the entire brontosaurus of a century.

At its narrowest, the subject that idealinguistery tolerates is anything but simple centre, translucid focal point, transcendental disposition. It is a question of a decentred subject, a subjugated subject, in whose eclipse the law reveals itself to be reciprocatable to desire.

As such this subject is close to us, after all, due to the modesty of the effect that signals it.

Insofar as we recognize a political subject in a class actor, the latter too will be severely bound to the distance to itself prescribed to it by the form of the principal contradiction. The working class is forever unable to resorb the scission, which gives it being, between its social immediacy and its political project. Of such a political subject—finally restricted to the action of its place-holder, the party, body made of an opaque and multiple soul—we will never say that it constitutes history, not even that it makes history.

As for positing that its desire (communism) is reciprocatable to the law (the dictatorship of the proletariat), therein lies the whole stroke of genius of Marxism, with the party being the enigmatic subject-support of this reciprocity.

This doctrinal proximity forbids us the soothing vulgarity of yesteryear's materialisms. We say and we think that it is—vulgarly—idealist to posit that language precedes the world. True! But the *reversed* thesis (that the world precedes language) reveals, for what is at stake, an enormous weakness.

Neither God nor Man, in modern idealism, has the function of the organizer of being. The constituent function of language, which excentres every subject-effect, deactivates the materialist operator of the inversion—of the inversion in the sense in which Marx spoke of putting Hegel back on his feet.

To claim, by a 'materialist' inversion, to go from the real to the subject means to fall short of modern dialectical criticism, which separates the two terms—subject and real—so that a third, the symbolic or discourse, comes in to operate as a nodal point without for this reason becoming a centre.[9]

Barred from the path of a simple inversion and summoned to hold onto the scission in which the subject of idealinguistery comes into being as an effect of the chain, we Marxists find ourselves on the dire road of a procedure of destruction-recomposition.

To pierce through the adversary's line of defence requires this heavy ramrod whose idolatrized head bears our subjective emblems.

That a conceptual black sheep—a materialism centred upon a theory of the subject—is equally necessary for our most pressing political needs, which involve drawing up a balance sheet regarding the question of the party, no doubt proves something.

But what?

The indissoluble salt of truth

November 21, 1977

Thesis of the One, thesis of the Two—Am I Kantian?—The two metaphors (reflection and asymptote)—Asking forgiveness for the duck-bill—The Same except for its remainder—The party at the thresholds—The axiom of crossing

1

Under the name materialism we understand two perfectly contradictory theses. One states that there is the One, the other that the One precedes the Other, and thus that there is the Two.

'There is the One' is the monist thesis about being, for which 'matter' in reality is only the signifier. Every materialism posits the primitive unicity of being, with the implication that its intimate constitution requires only one name. Matter is this name.

It is only the nonderivable nature of the One-of-being that is designated by this signifier of matter. One can illustrate this nominating power with a variety of scientific considerations to make it seem attractive and convincing: mass, electrons, atoms, energy, waves, various particles, and so on.

Thus, if you want to name the name of the One, you instantly obtain the multiple. This has always been how negative theologians objected against any one predicate for God.

Materialist a-theology is necessarily negative.

Theological idealism is founded on the firm grasp of the Two. For the

Greeks, the intelligible responds to the sensible. For the Christians, the infinite and the finite are as incommensurable as the Creator and creatures. Two regions of being, whose reduplication splits every One caught in the finite. So it is for humans, made up of a soul and a body, or for Aristotle's anything-whatsoever, made up of a form and a matter.

The key concept of a religious idealism always operates at the juncture of two regions of being, whether it is (Platonist) participation, (Jewish) creation, or (Christian) incarnation.

Shall we say that, for Lacan, this dialectical extremity can be found in the knot, or to be more precise, in the *tying of the knot*? That is how it would seem: 'The knot does not constitute consistency, it ex-sists in the element of the cord, in the consistent cord.'[10]

In this ex-sistence of the knot I see a function of juncture. Because it is through transcendence within immanence (ex-sistence within consistency) that we recognize the operator of the connection by which all idealism—and idealinguistery cannot be an exception—deduces the unity of that of which it posits the gap of being. You can verify this for participation, creation, and incarnation. I will personally handle the knot.

As for materialism, you will see that it is rather a question of breaking the unity of nomination with which it blocks being. That does not make the task any easier or clearer.

And humanist idealism, you will ask, since we jumped absent-mindedly from Saint Paul to Lacan?[11] Its purpose is to make a subject out of an ontological region. To the constituent subject, to consciousness, to the for-itself, it opposes the flux of representations, the object, the in-itself. Similarly, via the concept, its fine brush traces the border of experience. Look at all those Kantian exercises, marked by a baneful obscurity, that are, for knowledge, schematism (law of the applied imagination by which sensible being enters into the field of the transcendental subject), and, for morals, respect (law of sensibility in order to move exclusively according to the intelligible).

I can see that there are some of you who think that since 1975, with splace and outplace, or with place and force, I got off the wrong foot in terms of materialism. They lie in wait for me at the juncture, and they ask themselves whether I do not call 'subject' the effect of the border where Kant and others get themselves into trouble.

You should note that already this would be better than to make *one* of the terms into the subject. And, moreover, I could invoke our ancestors for support. Indeed, what is that party about which Kautsky, praised high by Lenin, said that its 'task [. . .] is to imbue the proletariat [literally: to fill the proletariat] with the *consciousness* of its position and the consciousness of its task' (SW I, 156) if not, between the intelligible of Marxism and the sensible of the spontaneous workers' movement, a subjective schematism of a new type?

No doubt, the party is a being of the thresholds, an operator of the break-juncture in history's materialist One.[12]

And yet, we are materialists. Our trouble, no matter how great, is not the same as that of the idealists.

2

The second constitutive thesis of materialism affirms 'the primacy of matter over the idea'.

Is this thesis obligatory? Undoubtedly. If you stick to the One, you have only the name. Hegel is there to signal to us that the idea will do, in terms of the One. Absolute idealism and strict materialism are indiscernible as far as the real is concerned, being merely two designations for monism.

The monotype of being bears two possible marks.

In order to 'invert' Hegel, we need the Two of the inversion. The head and the feet, the idea and matter. How else could we posit the antecedence of the one over the other?

Therefore, for the materialist, who signifies the One of being, it is nonetheless necessary that matter not be the idea.

Seeking to distinguish his own One from that of the integral idealist, the materialist must accept that there are two names for the real, that both of them are valid, and that their order differs.

This amounts to saying that two sets with only one element are always isomorphic, no matter what their structure may well be. When a combines with a, if there is *nothing else*, the result is always a. The names matter very little.

If you want the minimum of algebraic difference conceivable, you need the pair (a, b), which can be ordered in two ways, $a < b$, or $b < a$, and which supports all sorts of algebraic structures (thus, $a + a = a$ as a law is not isomorphous to that which prescribes $a + a = b$).

In order to distinguish itself from idealism, materialism is forced to abdicate its essential axiom, which is monism, and to posit the thesis of all major idealisms, namely, that there are indeed two regions of being.

However, it does so only with the aim of annulling this thesis. For in truth there is only one region of being for materialism.

What does this mean, if not that thought for materialism is the vanishing term from which it follows that there is only matter?

Indeed, in order to name the One as such-or-such-a-One (in this case, matter), what is needed is the real of the Two. Two signifiers, in any case (matter and the idea).

This is what Marx summarizes as follows: 'Thinking and being are thus certainly *distinct*, but at the same time they are in unity with each other.'[13]

We posit that materialism exists in the recognition of two theses, one of which names being and the other its order—an order whose being lies in a vanishing nominal overhaul:

– The thesis of identity: being is exclusively matter.
– The thesis of primacy: matter precedes thought, and not the other way around.

We can say, in short, that the thesis of identity names the place (of being), and the thesis of primacy the process (of knowledge) under the rule of the place.

'Primacy' does not mean ontological hierarchy, or pre-eminence, since there exists *only* matter. It is nothing like the Platonist superiority of the intelligible, subject to inversion. 'Primacy' means that, in the process of knowledge that founds the thesis of identity, the eclipse of thought stands under the law of being, and not under that of thought itself.

The two theses of materialism give structure to the *metaphorical division* of the process of knowledge. Therein lies the real efficacy of their opposition.

Here we are at the arcane heart of the famous 'reflection theory', which, in matters of theory, proposes one out of two metaphors whose coupling shapes the baroque poem of materialism.

The other metaphor is that of the asymptote.

3

There have been mountains of glosses written on 'reflection theory', whether with Stalinist density or with idealizing irony. A typical product of materialist 'vulgarity', it now lies on the floor without showing any sign of life, as if a victim of critical lapidation. Even its very name, as soon as it is invoked, arouses laughter about something from the past that is over and done with, a sin fallen into the oblivion of its expiation.

What does this so-called 'theory' amount to? To the fact that it turns the homogeneous into a metaphor. Sustaining the One requires that we unify the known object and its knowledge in an ontological arrangement, said to be 'material', without any asymmetry other than that of causality (it is the object that causes the reflection).

The theory of reflection, by arranging the knowing part as a pure passive image, sustains in sensible repetition what otherwise it would have to impute to the constituent action of the subject.

What is important in this 'theory' has to do with the mirror—fairly Mallarméan, after all—which has the peculiar virtue of being a fragment of matter in which, at the same time and by a material effect, a sensible double of the object can be read.

At bottom, the reflection theory sets up the experimental chamber of Mallarmé's poems, the one in which—such is the decisive gain—the master is absent. By master, let us understand the Kantian subject.

Remember the way in which, in the afterword to the second German edition of the first volume of *Capital*, the origin of the metaphor is fixed:

> To Hegel, the life-process of the human brain, i.e., the process of thinking, which, under the name of 'the Idea', he even transforms into an independent subject, is the demiurgos of the real world, and the real world is only the external, phenomenal form of 'the Idea'. For me, on the contrary, the ideal is nothing else than the material world reflected by the human mind, transported and transposed into forms of thought. (SW II, 98, trans. modified in accordance with the French translation Badiou uses)

Here the operations of knowledge are named three times, as 'reflection' (which institutes the mirror), as 'transportation' (which indicates the spatial distance between the thing and its double, the place of the repetitive series), and as 'transposition' (which will open the path to the second metaphor, that of a difference within the repetition).

This triple ban is that of the sensible homogeneous against the productive self-development of the idea.

Let us say that for materialism reflection is the metaphor of the thesis of identity. There is only one region of being, in which mirroring doubles produce, under the name of knowledge, the repetition of the Same.

The second metaphor mathematizes the thesis of primacy into an asymptote.

'Reflection' names the One, 'asymptote' the Two. Materialism orders into the same phrase the asymptote and the double, the point of flight and the reduplication.

Let us read, if you wish, the letter from Engels to Conrad Schmidt, dated March 12, 1895:

> The identity of thought and being, to express myself in Hegelian fashion, everywhere coincides with your example of the circle and the polygon. Or the two of them, the concept of a thing and its reality, run side by side like two asymptotes, always approaching each other yet never meeting. This difference between the two is the very difference which prevents the concept from being directly and immediately reality and reality from being immediately its own concept. But although a concept has the essential nature of a concept and cannot therefore *prima facie* directly coincide with reality, from which it must first be abstracted, it is still something more than a fiction, unless you are going to declare all the results of thought fictions because reality has to go a long way round before it corresponds to them, and even then only corresponds to them with asymptotic approximation.[14]

If one holds fast to identity, which is how the fragment begins, one *must* end up with the insuperable gap. The essence of reflection is the asymptote. Every mirror (every concept) throws into a tendential abyss the object which it is its fiction to reduplicate. That is what the classics tell us.

Supposing that in terms of truth one demands pure repetition (of the reflection), then one will have lost coherence; supposing that one sticks to the whole (the image), then what dissolves is the torsion (the tendential reversal).

Engels experienced this for himself the day that, being a bit too rigid in the adequation of his concepts of zoology, he had mocked all fictions of egg-laying mammals, only to find himself forced later on 'to beg the duck-bill's pardon for'.[15]

This could be a proverbial saying for the militant materialist: 'Trust the mirror too much, and the duck-bill will defy you as such.'[16] That is: beware of sacrificing the asymptote to the reflection, the thesis of primacy (of being over thinking, of practice over theory) to the thesis of identity (the monotype of being).

Beginning in 1964–5, we reflected the fact that the PCF had abandoned all class objectives, and we named the image 'revisionism'. The adequation of the concept with the thing—the thesis of identity—amounted to tightly covering the political practices of this party, most notably its flagrant trade unionist counter-revolution of May–June 1968, under an ideological blanket: the revision of Marxism. We drew great hopes from this operation of deciphering, since all doctrinal revisions are weak and mortal—being only the decomposing of that which had the power of the universal on its side. We were thus able to imagine that the *immediate* relay, by the true Marxism and the 'true masses', was reserved for us in terms of the revolutionary ideology of Class. From there it was only a step to suppose that we were the latter's organizers in the short term. Because between the bourgeoisie and the working class ideologues of the PCF (their revisionist servants) on one hand, and the revolt and its Maoist baptism, on the other, what more could there be than between an egg-laying bird and a viviparous mammal, that is to say, nothing?

What lay in between was precisely the duck-bill of class that is the *new* bourgeoisie, the monopolist and state bureaucratic bourgeoisie, of which revisionism is only the transitory ideological production and whose historical rise to power, anchored in the imperial power of the Soviet Union, is only just beginning.

It thus became necessary to measure the tendential gap between our first—ideological—concept and the political real. To measure it, we should add, in the experiment of a weakness, which brought us back to the primacy of political practice over the arrangements of thought.

From the reflection of history, by conflictively asking forgiveness from the duck-bill of the 'common programme', we had to transit into the asymptote of a stubborn political duration.

Very few have withstood this experience, which consists in traversing the metaphorical division of materialism. 'To ask for forgiveness from the duck-bill' for the vast majority represented the dramatic choice between duck-billing themselves or else shouldering the old fur hunter's rifle.

History is the fine sift of gross approximations. That is its materialism and its austerity.

Reflection serves as a metaphor of the fact that thinking and being are one and the same thing. To this Engels adds—via the asymptote—that it is the same thing *except for something*, something to which the process of knowledge refers endlessly as *its remainder*.

In the order of the structure, the metaphor of reflection posits the identity, while that of the asymptote turns this identity into a historical process, exceeding itself by the conceptual insubordination of its remainder.

Materialism operates as the unifying scission of a structure of reduplication and an effect of approximation. It posits the Same, plus its remainder.

To say that materialism is dialectical is an understatement. It is entirely traversed by the dialecticity of the dialectic, its double occurrence as structure and as history.

I propose to name 'algebra' the first type of dialecticity of materialism (under the metaphorical law of the reflection, as logic of the thesis of identity), and 'topology' the second (metaphor of the asymptote, logic of the thesis of primacy, causality of the remainder).

4

Materialism dialecticizes the metaphors of reflection and of the asymptote, thus positing the whole in the exception of its remainder. Lacan bears witness to this as regards the division in which the subject comes into effect. I leave it up to you carefully to gloss this text:

> The jubilant assumption of his specular image by the kind of being—still trapped in his motor impotence and nursling dependence—the little man is at the *infans* stage thus seems to me to manifest in an exemplary situation the symbolic matrix in which the *I* is precipitated in a primordial form [. . .]
>
> But the important point is that this form situates the agency known as the ego, prior to its social determination, in a fictional direction that will forever remain irreducible for any single individual or, rather, that will only asymptotically approach the subject's becoming, no matter how successful the dialectical syntheses by which he must resolve, as *I*, his discordance with his own reality. (E 76/94)

Specular and asymptotic junction: that says quite a lot. The dialectical success of the *I*, that is, its identificatory resolution, is relative to the asymptote of which the imaginary of the ego names the limit-reflection.

The ego is a figure, for the *I*, of that unproductive whole of which the real unifications realize the provisory coherence.

Freud's materialism finds its foothold in the scission of the ego and the I, and it is to the latter's restitution that Lacan from the start devotes himself against the American idealists. Thus, in matters belonging to the theory of the subject, the logic of the process breaks with the investigation of a substance as well as with the intuition of a coincidence.

No matter how strongly I identify myself with the ideal figures of the ego, it is never true that, in *my* image, I am/is lost.[17]

It is rather appropriate that Lacan would reassert this certainty in his statement on 'the mirror stage'.

No materialist, neither Mallarmé nor Lacan nor Lenin, can afford to do without this metaphorical engine of the mirror.

For us, when politics amounts to making a subject, the most stringent condition demands that we conceive of it as neither substance nor self-consciousness. The party, as the subjective materiality of class, must be distinguished from its Ego, which adopts the figure now of the institution and now of the will. It is the polarizing fascination for this imaginary political Ego that led many to state that 'the party was always right' or that it was the accomplished substance of class.

But the party is never the class except according to the asymptote of the form of politics that it carries out in the midst of the people. If it makes sense to posit that it reflects a class position in such or such tactical episode in which two camps can be traced, we should immediately consider that strategically it rather finds itself 'in a line of fiction'—which is the true name of a political line, inasmuch as the truth of politics, like any other truth, stands in a structure of torsion.

The process of the political party never takes the form of identity either with itself or with class without at once involving a tendential remainder, which demands that it practise nonidentity. This is why the party is always historical, conjunctural.

Its law of existence is linked to the assessment of this law: torsion.

The act of knowing, as both asymptote and reflection, is constitutive neither of the object nor of itself.

What makes the thing that I have to come to know enter into the field of knowledge remains itself unknown to the knowing.

Indeed, the process of knowledge does not constitute the becoming-knowable of its object. The system from which it follows that such or such is the real to which I hold true cannot be figured in the process of this truth.

Look no further for the meaning of the famous line from Marx according to which man only poses those problems that he is capable of solving.

For it does not depend on man, insofar as the animal named 'man' exists, that a problem befalls him *qua* problem. Problematization is how the real makes a hole for the truth.[18] It is the remainder proper to the solution, the indissoluble salt of truth. Whence the asymptote.

However, the fact that man can solve a problem, inasmuch as in the retroaction of the solution it turns out that this problem posed itself to him, and that he can solve it *entirely*, guarantees the metaphor of reflection.

This is the famous paradox of the *Anti-Dühring*: knowledge is relative (asymptote) insofar as it is absolute (reflection). It is mutilated insofar as it is sovereign, especially as to the production of 'eternal truths':

> In this sense human thought is just as much sovereign as not sovereign, and its capacity for knowledge just as much unlimited as limited. It is sovereign and unlimited in its disposition, its vocation, its possibilities and its historical ultimate goal; it is not sovereign and it is limited in its individual realisation and in reality at any particular moment.
>
> It is just the same with eternal truths. If mankind ever reached the stage at which it should work only with eternal truths, with results of thought which possess sovereign validity and an unconditional claim to truth, it would then have reached the point where the infinity of the intellectual world both in its actuality and in its potentiality had been exhausted, and thus the famous miracle of the counted uncountable would have been performed.[19]

Cipher of the real, knowledge posits as the remainder of number the uncountable, whose excess over number makes counting into an exact operation.

We would not know how to fix the act of knowing into a simple trajectory without immediately having to divide the latter into that on which it operates and the condition of *this* operation itself, which stands in a position of remainder.

Knowledge crosses two processes: the process, in the real, of its conditions, and the process, in the subject-effect, of its seizing, of which the other is the retroactive underside.

> If it [the subject] knows something, it is only by being itself a subject caused by an object—which is not what it knows, that is, what it imagines it knows. The object which causes it is not the other of knowledge [*connaissance*].[20]

I myself will cross this Lacanian statement, but I will nevertheless reserve myself the right to voice a judgement on one precise point, which is that, for Lacan, the object-remainder of knowledge, which is not the other-object of the known, is the cause only of the subject.

As for me, dividing the theory of the remainder which, once again, is only the Marxist juncture of the reflection and the asymptote, I will posit that it is equally on the side of the real that we must designate the unknown cause of knowledge.

To reduce the latter to the cause of the subject puts us in the whole frame of idealinguistery.

We will therefore give preference to the axiom of the crossing, in which the subject does not appear: the knowing makes a knot out of a relation of thought to the real (within which there is adequation-reflection) and the becoming-knowable of the real, putting the two terms *vis-à-vis* one another, from whence the limit of the first relation comes to be determined as its condition-remainder (its purely asymptotic value).

The exhaustion of a field of knowledge presupposes the inexhaustion of that which, in the real and in history, supports its existence as One.

Answering—to the Sphinx—demands from the subject not to have to answer—for the Sphinx

December 4, 1977

There exists no unknowable—Oedipus, the sphinx, the pedestal—The irrational in a position of the subject for whole numbers, and for Pythagoras—The Cultural Revolution in the same position for the October Revolution and Lenin

1

No, the doctrine of the remainder, through which the two cognitive metaphors of reflection and asymptote are put into tension, is not Kantian.

I posit that there exists no intrinsic unknowable. To speak with Mao's clarity: 'We will come to know everything that we did not know before' (SW IV, 374, trans. modified).

Except to add that what we did not know *before* was determined as a remainder of what has come to be known, at the crossover between the nameless movement through which the real appears as a problem and the retroaction, named knowledge, which provides the solution.

It is not by chance that Oedipus answers the Sphinx at the crossroads.

However, if he knows how to answer the question 'What is Oedipus?', he must leave as a (dead) remainder the question of this question: Who is the sphinx, having made Oedipus—man—into his problem?

Let us not forget that the sphinx is in fact a sphinge.[21]

Kant's thing-in-itself would rather be the pedestal on top of which the sphinge is perched. No one will ever detain the question for which this stone is the answer.

But I hold that the sphinx is nameable, once the questioning limit from where Oedipus's answer provisionally appeared to be well adapted, through a forced event, comes into the light of history.

As a reflection of the question, this answer was right on target, were it not the asymptote of an omitted real, that of the sphinge whom Oedipus, by killing her, caused to fall into the anonymity of the remainder that is the price to pay for all exactness.

When materialism puts into question 'man', that obscure problem for which Oedipus states the clear solution, it resuscitates the sphinge and turns her from questioner that she was into the theme of its questioning.

The remainder is thus what periodizes knowledge, affecting all cumulative and linear hope of progress with an index of nullity.

There is no unknowable, even though all knowledge demands its position.

The real of knowledge is at all times that which is impossible to know. But that is precisely what asymptotically fixates the future of the reflection. This impossible, therefore, will be known, all the while being placed in the position of possibility (of reflection) by the new add-on in its field.

2

Pythagorean mathematics posits that the countable or denumerable is made up of whole numbers, or of relations among whole numbers. This is a prescription with regard to the possible. Whatever would fall outside of these assignations defines the impossible proper to number: the undenumerable.

That only whole numbers and their relations (the *logoï*, which later will be called rational numbers) count as 'numbers' is not, you will admit, an intramathematical result. Rather, the whole field of Pythagorean mathematics is prescribed by this latent decision—which precisely is not a decision but rather the unknown real movement through which mathematical problems, problems of numbers, whole or rational, come to exist.

You thus obtain a constitutive remainder of the field in which the mathematical knowledge of the era operates. This remainder is the undenumerable, posited as inexistent, according to the norm of the denumerable.

Knowledge means reflection as far as number goes and asymptote as concerns the inexistent that is proper to it.

Here one stipulates, by way of an answer-reflection to a problem, that within this domain a geometrical relation (that of the diagonal of the square to its side) can be measured neither by a whole number nor by a rational number.

It is evident only to us that this demonstrative event opens a crisis. According to the law of the place to which the demonstration conforms, there follows only one thing: that the relation of the diagonal of the square to the side is not a number.

After all my barstool is not a number, nor is the circumference of said barstool, which is round, in relation to its diameter.

If there is a crisis, it is insofar as it becomes a problem *to make a number out of an undenumerable*. This is what we are invited to do in the philosophical imaginary of the Pythagoreans, who want at all cost that being—thus the Whole—be made out of numbers.

The epistemological fable at issue here serves to draw up a table of the famous Lacanian 'instances'. It is very simple: the symbolic, in our case, posits as law that the denumerable be composed of whole numbers. With that you have what it takes to count and combine all that is. The (philosophical) imaginary figures the totality of the world according to what the law stipulates as the rule of (mathematical) words. It states: 'Being is number.' The real is the impossible, that is, the resistance of the undenumerable, of *that which is not* a natural number. The subject presents, at the point of the imaginary's deficiency, the numerable to the undenumerable: it takes effect as the mathematician's desire to number the undenumerable, to legalize the impossible.

At this point, you must force the law of the place, which prescribes no place whatsoever for such a 'number'.

It is a matter of naming the remainder within the field by which its lack is sustained.

In other words, it is a matter of making a reflection out of an asymptotic segment.

When, with Eudoxus, Greek mathematics engaged in the geometricalization of the denumerable establishes in its theory of proportions a classificatory arrangement that includes the irrational 'numbers', it forces the impossible, it symbolizes the real.

As such, you have destroyed the previous system of reflection through the injection, in excess over the place, of its asymptotic remainder. The field of the denumerable is enlarged. A new legal system, breaking up the old constraints, forges a concept of number on new grounds.

It is not wrong to state that, under the name of number, the relation of the diagonal of the square to its side comes in the position of the subject for the old place of the denumerable.

Whereby you find the outplace, force, destruction, and excess.

Whereby you find justice, the revolutionary recomposition of the theory of number according to an order in which forms of knowledge previously considered absurd can now function as reflections.

You have displaced the principle of the crossing that ties the asymptote to the reflection, the remainder to the place, the impossible real to the legality of the possible.

Does this mean that all that is left pertains to the order of reflection? Not at all. In such a space—which admits irrational numbers—there remains (for example) the impossibility of any solution for the equation $x^2 + 1 = 0$. The undenumerable (the unnameable) remains as asymptotic support for the solving retroaction of problems whose possible existence it prescribes.

When the Italian algebraists of the sixteenth century posit the existence of 'imaginary' roots (so well-named! the fantasmatic fury of number as Whole!), of the type $\sqrt{-1}$, they perform the second forcing of the arrangement of the denumerable.

Every un-crossing of the knot of knowledge makes for a revolution, by positing a name of the impossible for the subject.

3

The revolution of October 1917, you will agree, opens onto a new stage in the history of Marxism.

This stage is defined by the adequate solution, the solution-reflection, of a problem handed down by the failure of previous revolutions, specifically by the Paris insurrections of June 1848 and March 1871.

This problem can be formulated as follows: what type of organization does the proletariat need to really and enduringly break the enemy state machine? What becomes of a *victorious* insurrection?

The Leninist party resolves this problem. The field of possibilities prescribed by this organizational form is called the Third International. Pretty much everywhere, political class organizations in conformity with the Bolshevik model are set up. One reflects Bolshevism, universally practising the Bolshevization of parties.

There are successes. The Chinese party seizes power; and so do the Korean, Yugoslav, and Albanian parties.

Soon it appears—from within the Leninist investigation through the scission in the international communist movement of the 1960s—that the Leninist parties in fact have been capable of becoming bourgeois parties that oppress the working class and peoples in an almost fascist manner.

What can we say about this demonstration? Without resorting to the doctrine of the remainder, one will be content with little, that is, with affirming—like a right-wing Pythagorean summarily expelling the diagonal into nothingness—that these degenerate parties *are not* Leninist parties, that they inexist for that domain. This conservative posture amounts to speaking the closed language of orthodoxy. The task is one of restoration: to redo (repeat) the lost Leninist parties.

But if one is an audacious Pythagorean—or Bolshevik—one will instead pose the blasphemous question: what then was the asymptote of Bolshevik knowledge? Where then is its remainder?

The Leninist party is the historical answer to a problem that is wholly inscribed in the State/revolution contradiction. It treats of the victorious destruction. What happens then to this party with regard to the State/communism contradiction, that is, in relation to the process whereby the State—and classes—must no longer be destroyed but must wither, through an effect of transition?

The history of the USSR is by and large the historical demonstration of this point: the Leninist party is incommensurable to the tasks of the transition to communism, despite the fact that it is appropriate to those of the victorious insurrection.

But what testifies by way of forcing to the necessary extension of the 'partifiable'—like the denumerable in Eudoxus—is the Cultural Revolution in China, which, having stumbled on the party in the fire of a communist uprising, puts on the agenda the fact that the Leninist party is over.

The domain of Leninism makes no real place, when it comes to the party, for the problem of communism as such. Its business is the State, the antagonistic victory. The Cultural Revolution begins the forcing of this uninhabitable place. It invites us to name 'party of the new type' the post-Leninist party, the party for communism, on the basis of which to recast the entire field of Marxist practice.

Thus it is retroactively proven that the problems of Leninism—the 'questions of Leninism', as Stalin put it—left as a remainder the problem of these problems, the problematic of communism, only reflecting as they do the previously prescribed task, that of the taking of power.

The asymptote of the Bolshevik reflection is nothing other than communism.

What makes the State/revolution contradiction into a constraint must be destroyed and recomposed by the historical nomination of its remainder, which is relative to the State/communism contradiction.

Whence a revolution in Marxism, the Maoist revolution.

4

If knowledge is process, it must in principle follow the Hegelian matrices, which we have schematized in 1975.

We should expect that from the crossover two deviations, two relapses separate themselves.

What are the heresies of materialism?

The mechanicist one isolates the metaphor of the reflection. It imagines adequation without remainder. It sticks to repetition.

The dynamicist one does the same with the asymptote. Universalizing the doctrine of the remainder, it poses that all is flux, tendency, approximation. For this heresy, every unified configuration is an illusion, or even a 'totalitarian' threat.

Here you have the table:

DYNAMICIST MATERIALISM	DIALECTICAL MATERIALISM		MECHANICIST MATERIALISM
multiple of variable intensities	crossing		combinatory of undecomposable units
←	• thesis of primacy	• thesis of identity	→
	• asymptote	• reflection	
	• relative knowledge	• absolute knowledge	
	• remainder	• place	
leftists			rightists

The deviation on the right knows only the law of the place. It makes no problem of the problems it resolves.

The deviation on the left follows a perspective of flight. It is a radicalism of novelty. It breaks all mirrors.

Deleuze on the ultraleft; Lévi-Strauss on the right. Two materialisms that treat of idealinguistery by way of a drift. One into the combinatory of signs, the other into the cancerous molecules.

Materialism is always in the position of having to resist the temptations that found it: neither atomic deciphering nor liberation of flux.

Algebra and topology

December 19, 1977

Dogmatists and empiricists—Law of composition, or elementary belonging (algebra)—Neighbourhood, or adherence by inclusion (topology)—Hegel, the One, the One One (*das eine Eins*)

1

The Gnostics of materialism—the mechanicists—posit the adequation without remainder. Satisfied with the Same, cloistered in repetition, little do they care that the crossing of two processes is needed for any object whatsoever to come to be known.

Their logic is merely one of exactitude. Metaphorically, they stick to the mirror.

In politics, they dogmatize: 'What is said says what is.'

It should be noted that we need the dogmatists. Guardians of principles in the frozen surface of the mirror, they keep us from confusing the law of the remainder with the abandonment of the place. They are the ones who alert us to the fact that this or that 'novelty' in Marxism (from Bernstein to Khrushchev) or Freudianism (from Jung to Reich), far from forcing the unoccupyable place that specifies the current state of our problematic, simply leaves and goes off *elsewhere*.

The fact remains that the forcing turns them off. The conservative function of the mirror—of the looking glass—makes of the dogmatist a reluctant materialist. Ignorance of the remainder makes the dogmatist remain—in place.[22]

The Arians of materialism—the dynamicists—posit the ubiquitous remainder, the multiplicity of variable intensities. They are people who believe in the insoluble tendency. Satisfied with the Other, stretched out all over the torsions, it matters little to them that a splace and its rule are needed for anything real whatsoever to be in the position of an object (of knowledge).

Metaphorically, they stick to the asymptote, to the flow. Their logic is only one of approximation. In politics, they empiricize: 'What is matters more than all that is said.'

The empiricists lack neither flavour nor usefulness. Lying in wait for the movement, they keep us from reducing the need for exact reflection to the oblivion of novelty. The empiricists are the ones who alert us to the fact that this or that constraint of the place (from Lassalle to Stalin, or from Jones to Anna Freud) dissimulates for us the unoccupyable place from which any break could proceed.

The fact remains that they are turned off by the partisan taking of sides. The asymptotic perspective of flight makes of the empiricist a wandering materialist, a vagabond philosopher of natural substances. Ignorance of the mirror turns the empiricist into the mirror—of the world.[23]

These two army flanks of consequential materialism are the symptom of the latter's very own scission, whose metaphorical knot they untie. These preservationist discourses, cut off from their own life, point out that there are *two* processes that make up *one* materialism—and not only two theses (that of identity and that of primacy).

In an opening onto a new metaphor, we will say that there is the algebraic disposition and the topological disposition.

Active materialism crosses these two dispositions.

As for the subject, its—materialist—argument is inscribed in this intersection. Any subject effectuates the operations of a topological algebra.

2

I imprudently expose myself, first, to the mathematician's condemnation if I borrow metaphorically from his vocabulary and, then, to the philosopher's objection, if I give up on the idea of making the borrowed words shine in the light of pure science.

This path of split interpretation is my own. Please refer to the chapter 'Torsion'. I hope that I say nothing imprecise in mathematics, but also nothing that is mathematically proffered. My ambition here is to adorn materialism with a few signifiers whose sustained rigour will be that of precious stones, with the diversion of its end goal contributing to its force.

Precision put into the razor of the Marxist barber, mathematics is that unalterable blade with which one ends up bleeding the pigs to death.

Besides, as names for certain domains of mathematics and not for objects of these domains, neither algebra nor topology is a scientific name. They rather participate, as geometry or set theory, in the classificatory anatomy into which any discipline reduplicates itself in order to describe itself according to a few selected pieces.

What does the mathematician call 'algebra'? Let us trivialize, as they say. Supposing a given set—provisory figure of the Whole—algebra proceeds to the systematic study of the 'interesting' relations between the *elements* of this set. Its most general concept is that of the law of composition: to two elements of the set one associates a third, in a ruly fashion—just as to two numbers one associates their sum or their product.

What defines an algebraic species (a structure), which is that for which the mathematician reserves the key concepts of algebra, concerns the constraints upon the law of composition. For example, of being associative $((a+b) +c=a+(b+c))$, or of being commutative $(a+b=b+a)$.

The exercise of algebraic nomination presupposes homogeneity, in that all that is taken into account, as far as the elements are concerned, is their behaviour according to the law, once their identical belonging to the original set is accepted. An element is not defined algebraically by its location in the set. It suffices for it to belong to this set. In terms of place, the algebraic identity is one of belonging. The place is in some way universal. The force is lacking. The law imposes distinctions onto the indistinguishable. Such or such element, say e, will for example have the property of being 'neutral' in that, if $+$ is the law, for any element a (including e itself), $a+e=a$.

In the previous table, it is possible to say that algebra is registered 'on the right': it excludes all thought of tendencies and asymptotes. Homogeneous identity of belonging, elementary structuring, species distinguished in terms of types of legal constraint: the algebraic universe is limited to combinatory materialism.

Topology stems—via the requirements of analysis—from the need for a mathematical guarantee in order to grasp movement. It lies at the origin of primitively vague notions such as location, approximation, continuum, and differential. It is not aimed (as algebra is) at what happens when two distinct and homogeneous events end up being combined under certain constraints, but at what happens when one investigates the site of a term, its surroundings, that which is more or less 'near' to it, that which is separated from it in continuous variations, its degree of isolation or adherence.

If the master concept of algebra is that of the law (of composition), topology is based on the notion of neighbourhood.

The objection of the technicians? That an effective axiomatic starts from the definition of open sets. This objection has no historical validity. For the dialectical interpretation, it is clear that an open set is one that serves as neighbourhood for each of its points.

Topology works perforce on the *parts* of a set, considered as families of neighbourhoods of an element (of a point, one will say, thereby marking that this time it is the location that is crucial). It does not associate to each element an *other* element, but rather imposes upon it the multiform configuration of its environments.

The algebraic legislation produces difference based on the other (element) as the same. The topological disposition makes identity of the same according to the multiple-other of its neighbourhoods.

All in all, the element by itself has no interest for topology. It is a discipline of the heterogeneous, in that it tends to determine the point by families of parts, the included by what lies around it. Its aim is to make a rule out of approximation. Much more so than the being of a term, it seeks to establish its system of proximate differences.

The algebraic alterity is combinatory; the topological identity is differential.

You can read these features at a glance in the founding axioms of an algebraic or topological species. The first fixate the constraints for the productive associations among elements. Thus are specified groups, rings, bodies, and so on. The second determine the conditions for families of parts (of subsets).

Topology tends 'toward the left' in the previous table—on the side of dynamicist materialism—for it thinks the (elementary) One according to the primacy of the multiple (of parts).

Advanced mathematics deals with the topologies that are 'compatible' with a particular algebraic structure.

Any consequential materialism articulates an asymptotic (topological) process and a reduplicating (algebraic) process.

3

In Hegel's *Logic* there is an astonishing passage in which the becoming-real of the One guarantees the transition from quality to quantity.

This is nothing less than the speculative birth of number.

What is quantity? Hegel answers: the unity of the continuous and the discrete (L 199). That is, the dialectic of adherence to the neighbourhood (continuity) and of elementary belonging (discreteness). 'This act of distinguishing or differentiation is an uninterrupted continuity' (L 188). Algebra is tied to topology.

It is therefore the categories of materialism that Hegel sets about engendering, starting from the pure concept of the One. That is to say, on the basis of the placed element as such.

This artifice has great interest for us. Why? Because in politics the constant task one sets about accomplishing is to infer the materialist prospecting of a situation on the basis of the concept of the One. The unity of class, the unity of the people: such are the reference points from which it follows that the materialist analysis, at the farthest remove from inactivity, prescribes to the political actors their task in the given circumstances.

What is it that unifies, in the antagonistic action, a social force in revolt? What amalgamates this first unity with the One of the overall political process, from which the subjective logic of the party type can be inferred? It is not exaggerated to say that therein lies the mainspring of the militant intervention.

It is thus from the One that the materialist theme of action must sustain itself.

The bourgeois version of this requirement that is inflicted upon us today, and by which it is short-circuited into the idealist mirage of submission, also finds its emblem in the unity of the 'Left'.

Algebraic manipulation of parliamentary places, it bars the people, that supposed unity, from the topological path of the continuous, of active consistency.

Hegel introduces two operatory mediations in order to accomplish, according to the One, the engenderment of algebraic discreteness and topological continuity: *repulsion*, by which the One posits itself as distinct from the multiple-of-Ones; and *attraction*, by which the One amalgamates the multiple with itself.

All this is quite judicious. Repulsion draws its theme from division as the essence of the One. It is 'the self-differentiating of the one, at first into many, and then, because of their immediateness, in others' (L 173). We, too, approach the One according to its 'differentiating'. The social-real, for which the revolts and the forms of consciousness are our guide, can be read off the untying of its previous link. Any One is effectuated therein as innovating punctuality within a unity of atomicization, of a One tired of living in that it is nothing more than 'a becoming of many ones' (L 167).

In this passive algebra, the repulsive One, the first One to rise up in revolt—or in disjunction—is readable only on account of its contradictory virtue of attraction. If its immediate aspect is the dissidence within the homogeneous multiple—this multiple of ones about which Hegel brilliantly affirms that in the place sketched out by it, the one 'becomes only one' (*ibid.*), its act consists in polarizing the entire field by an attractive *unification*: just as a localized popular uprising, if it carries the proposition of a new unity, disturbs the algebraic homogeneity in the topological direction of a regenerated consistency.

This is what in the class struggle is called to form a camp.

The essence of the repulsive One is therefore to differentiate itself from repulsion, to purge itself attractively in order to forge, starting from the idea of dispersion, the real of the unification of the multiple.

In this way, the new popular camp, the structure of which is the process of proletarian politics, is no longer determined (algebraically) as One-in-the-multiple-of-ones, which is the status, let us say, of the voter in the voting booth, but determines *itself* topologically as One heterogeneous to the multiple of equality.

This is what Hegel concentrates as follows: 'Thus the One exercising the attraction, as returning to itself starting form multiplicity, *determines itself* as One; it is One as being not multiple, One One' (L 174, trans. modified). 'One One': (topological!) approximation of the German: '*das eine Eins*'.

The One One is that One which, from having emerged as subject under the law of repulsion-attraction, establishes itself at the crossing point between an algebraic constraint—which makes it One *One*—and a topological, attractive, coagulating consistency—which makes it *One* One.

Thus, class, in its divided but sometimes eruptive social existence, is the One from which it follows that the One One, the party, can come into being as politics.

The whole question for the party is to remain attractive, since attraction is precisely 'the One that is One One' (L 174, trans. modified).

Trade unionism is the intrinsically repulsive form, whence its organization copied from the productive branches of capitalism, in which the One becomes only more of the One. Its dominant is algebraic.

Proletarian politics is the moving system of repulsion-attraction by which the One becomes One One.

In this regard its ultimate site, following Hegel's analogy, must encompass both the continuous, which is the effect of attraction, and the discrete, effect of repulsion.

Indeed, if the attractive unity—the popular consistency of a camp—spreads, what is needed to mediate this propagation is for the antagonistic repulsion to be operative, that is, the class conflict by which the continuous One One distinguishes itself in turn (as One) within the discrete system of opposite forces:

> In continuity, therefore, magnitude immediately possesses the moment of *discreteness*—repulsion, as now a moment in quantity. Continuity is self-sameness, but of the Many which, however, do not become exclusive; it is repulsion which expands the self-sameness to continuity. Hence discreteness, on its side, is a coalescent discreteness, where the ones are not connected by the void, by the negative, but by their own continuity and do not interrupt this self-sameness in the many. The difference of the repelling is therefore present only as differentiability. (L 187, trans. modified)

Though affirmative in essence, attraction holds within itself the 'differentiability' from which it proceeded to begin with, when its existence (like that of us, a handful of Maoists) remained subordinate to the law of punctual existence, in the place of multiple-ones.

Any material subject, One for the One One, and One One according to the Ones, articulates the algebra of its placement and the topology of its novelty.

Neighbourhoods

February 6, 1978

Belonging and adherence—Cantor's theorem and the inexhaustion
of history—Relative scarcity of proper names—Materialism and set
theory—The axioms of neighbourhoods in their dialectical legibility—
The matheme of the cult of personality

1

Let us relaunch with a summary.

One can obviously state that algebra is the metaphor of the *calculable* in
materialism. In it, the relation to the real stems from the procedural possibility of knowing the behaviour of such or such a term, in its difference
and its combinatory capacity, under the effect of such or such an explicit
rule.

Topology takes things 'by the pack'. It metaphorically translates the
functional in materialism, insofar as it is the neighbourhood, the families of
belonging, the local variation, which constitute its domain.

Two different relations to the Whole: algebra explores it under the aegis
of the individuals that belong to it and the rules according to which they
relate to one another. Topology, under the aegis of the varied subsets of
which each individual makes its site within the Whole.

With regard to the Whole, the term of algebraic materialism is isolated.
The only relation it has to the set is one of singular belonging, $e \in E$. The
term of topological materialism is apprehended in the local modality of its
presence within the Whole, through the mediation of the families of parts

215

that surround it. What is thus specified is the particular way in which it *adheres* to the Whole. The fact that it is one of its elements is a necessary but insufficient requirement. One seeks to know from where it belongs to it, how, in what geography, with what collective physiognomy.

Algebra is a logic of belonging; topology, a logic of adherence.

Think of the difference between being a member of a political party and having adhered to it.

To register—to possess the card—pertains to algebra; to unite pertains to topology.

2

Hilbert said that mathematicians would never let themselves be chased out of the paradise that Cantor had opened up for them.

Hilbert is perhaps the last of those great subjective technicians of subservient writing who constituted a second golden age of the concept (the first being that of the Greeks). This age, like its predecessor, lasted for three centuries, and Gauss, in the middle of this time span, gathers all its prestige. Here you have an incomparable series of figures of anticipation and mastery, from which even the inexplicable adolescence, in the style of Rimbaud, is not absent—since it is provided by the figure of Evariste Galois.

The paradisiacal aspect of set theory, created in one fell swoop by Cantor, lies in the fact that it provides a unifying language of such powers of generality that in comparison the ancient objects of mathematical denotation must appear as contrived artefacts.

One will not be surprised that, establishing this calculable disposition of infinites in the harsh solitude of a positive theologian, Cantor slowly should have slipped toward the delirium of grandeur.

The notion that everything can be stated under the sole name of the set, and within the logic of belonging, is equivalent, as far as I am concerned, to the materialist recognition of the One of the name of being. 'Matter' here serves, for being, as universal signifier, just as the set does for mathematics. Besides, like the set, it can only receive an implicit definition, governed by axioms, whether latent or actually formulated.

'Set' and 'matter' are as a result subordinate to the principle of limitation that restricts the usage of any master signifier, namely, that it cannot be referred to the Whole. It is well known that the notion of a set of all sets is inconsistent. Similarly, the concept of an integral material totality is only the porous fantasy of materialism, its dejection turned back into idealism.

For the mathematics of set theory as much as for the true materialist, all totality is particular. That which belongs to the whole requires the position of the other, which is not of the whole.[24]

From this, one concludes among other admirable modesties that universal history, conceived as the actual totality of political events, for example, is an inconsistent notion. There is an inevitable historical dispersion. This is one of the reasons that invalidate the definition of Marxism as 'science of history', since history is not an object.

'The concrete analysis of a concrete situation', which is the Leninist formulation of active Marxism, has the virtue of detotalizing the referent and indicating that no Marxism is in a position to survey any totality at all.

When one ventures to enumerate 'the great contradictions of the contemporary world', of which there are four (between the proletariat and the bourgeoisie; between imperialisms and the dominated people; among the imperialisms themselves; and between socialist States and imperialist States), it is clear that this formal apparatus does not lend itself to being unified into the global perception of a course of history, and that it has no efficacy other than to map the types of process whose local overlapping *places* a situation with regard to that which surrounds it.

The algebra of the four fundamental contradictions thus prepares the topology of the concrete situations. Besides, none of the terms subsumed by it has any historical existence: these are pure concepts for the homogeneity of places. Imperialism is at least double (classical, on the American side; social-imperialist, on the Russian side); *the* world proletariat does not exist any more than *the* dominated people, and so on.

The structure of the proof of inconsistency for the set of all sets—for absolute multiplicity—operates at the juncture of algebra and topology.

Its mainspring lies indeed in establishing that one cannot bi-univocally correlate the set of the *parts* of a set and the set of its *elements*. The first multiplicity necessarily exceeds the second.

Suppose that you have U, the set of all sets, at once you will have to reject it as absolute, for being lesser than the set of its parts.

What a marvel of dialectical materialism is this famous diagonal reasoning from Cantor by which that which is left over grounds that which has the value of excess!

Take a function of correspondence which to each part P of the total (imaginary) universe U makes correspond an element u of this universe, in such a way that two different parts have two different corresponding elements. I tell you that one part drops out of this supposed correspondence.

In order to establish this, it suffices to distinguish those parts that contain the element that is assigned to them from those that do not contain it.

One could also say that the attempt consists in distinctly *naming* each part of the universe with an element from this universe. It is the attribution of a proper name to its parts, attribution supposed to be immanent to the resources of U, that here provokes the impossible.

I call 'autonymous' a part whose name figures, in the guise of an element, *within* the named part, and 'heteronymous' that part whose name is external to this part itself.

Let us investigate the set of all the correlates—of all the proper names— assigned to those parts which do not contain this name: of all the proper names of heteronymous parts. Since it is a set of elements of U, it is no doubt a question of a *part* of U, which therefore has its distinct proper name: we suppose indeed that all can have one.

Is this part autonymous? No, because by definition it contains *only* names of heteronymous parts, and therefore it cannot contain its own name, which as a result would be a name of an autonymous one. Is this part heteronymous? Every name of a heteronymous part belongs to it, by definition always. *Qua* heteronymous, it would thus have to contain its own name, and thus, be autonymous!

We must agree that the part that is thus construed, neither autonymous nor heteronymous, purely and simply is neither named nor nameable. It institutes itself in excess over the supposed correlation.

We touch upon the impossible of the bi-univocal correspondence between the parts of U and the elements of U. The resource of multiplicity of the parts overflows the elementary multiplicity in which it is rooted. U stands in a virtuality of being, by its parts, more numerous than itself.

Any elementary multiplicity induces an overtaking of itself.

I have always looked upon this algorithm, I add in passing, as the refutation of the isomorphism that is presupposed in so many doctrines between that which is of value to the individual and that which is of value to the collectivities. The resource of the collectives necessarily surpasses the type of structural multiplicity in which the individuals are resolved.

The point of the impossible of the correlation between elements of U and parts of U marks the real—of what? Of the fact that the power of U cannot go so far as to include the immanent nomination of all its parts. At least, that is, if you seek to distinguish two different parts by different elementary names—*proper* names.

Either the universe is closed, total, and then there is something strictly indistinguishable, since you do not have enough proper names at your disposal in the universe to distinguish its parts, or else one can always distinguish, but then the universe does not form a whole, there is some excess, by which you give rise to a proper name beyond the supposed totality.

The universe always contains more things than those it can name according to these things themselves.

Whence its inexistence.

Proletarian politics, when it exists, which is not so common, is one of the unnameables of any closed statist space. According to the law of the day, it remains without a proper name.

This lack of civil status is precisely its political status. It indicates communism as non-State, as non-whole.

3

Inasmuch as topology proceeds by way of families of parts and algebra, by way of combinations of elements, the impossibility of U can also be stated as follows: excess of topology over algebra.

Here, once a set is fixed, you have two types of multiplicity. One is defined according to belonging, $e \in E$; the other, according to inclusion, $P \subset E$.

Inclusion, it should be carefully noted, does not undermine the set-theoretical unity of language. What is a part? A subset all of whose elements also belong to the fixed initial set. $P \subset E$ means by definition that $e \in P \rightarrow e \in E$. However, the virtuality of the parts overflows the initial multiplicity. There is a scission of what 'being-in' means. The part, just like the element, is 'in' E. In another sense, *the* parts exceed E, whereas *the* elements compose it.

Do not look any further, as far as abstract generality is concerned, for the ground of your conviction as to the 'micro-revolutions' of the desiring individual. They stay in their place. No individual has the power to exceed the era and its constraints, except by the mediation of the parts, and, let's say it, of parties.

I would recapitulate this as follows:

MATERIALIST THEME		MATHEMATICAL ANALOGY	
unity of being (matter) principle of detotalization: neither universe, nor history – reflection—absolute knowledge – asymptote—relative knowledge the collectives are a force superior to the structural frame in which the individuals are placed		unity of language (sets, relation $\in$) principle of detotalization: no set of all sets $e \in E$ (elementary belonging) $P \subset E$ (partitive excess) the set of parts of a set has a cardinality greater than that of the initial set	
topological point of view	*algebraic point of view*	*topology*	*algebra*
becoming of a process excess force	elements and results of a process position place	families of parts (neighbourhoods) topological structures (spaces)	laws of composition among elements algebraic structures (laws)

Who will fail to see, in the dialectic of elemhentary multiplicities and partitive multiplicities, the poor allegory of what I said above regarding the scission of materialist knowledge? The algebraic composition of terms refers to the reflection, to the grounded correlation of the concept and the real. What is known is effectively so, the power of nomination is complete, absolute. It is furthermore relative, asymptotic, if one refers to the overflowing partitive multiplicities that support it and that constitute an obstacle to the fixity of the whole.

4

The mathematical notion of neighbourhood establishes a link between the elements of a set, which is the basis of belonging for algebraic materialism, and the surrounding adherence by which the elements are locatable, basis for topological materialism.

Let us practise the exegesis of the four axioms that govern the usage of this notion.

1. Any neighbourhood of a point contains this point.

This is to say that the set close to you includes you. Here we have in an exemplary fashion a principle of adherence: in topological thinking there exists no neighbourhood in exteriority. This materialism is an inclusive operation, wherein the singular is approached according to that of which it is a part. The element is the point of flight for a series of collectives. The individual has no other name than its multiple adherences. By contrast, you know that algebra, as separating materialism, arranges the external connections of the singular onto the singular.

2. Any part that contains a neighbourhood of a point is itself a neighbourhood of this point.

Therein lies the extensive value of topological thinking. A proximity that is looser than another is nonetheless a proximity. The 'farther', which can be measured only by the 'nearer', sketches out a movement of expansion of the local. By ever-hazier approximations, the element touches tendentially upon the totality, which is the limit neighbourhood, the neighbourhood of any point that has a neighbourhood. This axiom is that of the inverted asymptote: to seize the element requires the movement of its different horizons, it imposes the trajectory of distancing.

You have a double pace at work in the analysis of a concrete situation. On the solid ground of an algebraic framework, principle of the distinguishable and of legal connections, it is a matter of looking for the tightest neighbourhood, the closest collective, in sum, the one that is just-to-the-body. In order to do so, we must practise the expansion, accept that the local be dialecticized by ever vaster surroundings.

This topological law of expansion-constriction gives its active meaning to the classical pair of the universal and the particular. There is truth to these fixed categories, the truth of algebra. Their real effectuation spins out the topological inclusion of adherences, both the nearest and the farthest.

3. The intersection of two neighbourhoods of a point is a neighbourhood of this point.

There you have something with which to tighten the approximation, an asymptotic instrument. If you are part of two processes, you are part of their crossing, from the place sketched out by what they have in common. The working class may be the first neighbourhood—already very vast—of a factory revolt. You will thus obtain, according to axiom 2, wider neighbourhoods, the belonging of class to the general process of the contradiction proletarian revolution/imperialism. The intersection of these two neighbourhoods is nothing less than the form of internationalism immanent to the term 'revolt'. Does it unify the French and the immigrants? Or is it chauvinistic? Does it affirm, with the PCF: 'Made in France only'? It is a new neighbourhood, at the intersection of the national and the worker's, which demands a special topological taking of sides.

You obviously have other series in the political topology. The revolt, though of the *workers*, leads to a logic in its *popular* surrounding (support, behaviour of women, etc.). It is an expansion (axiom 2) and also an intersection. According to which principles are the leaders assuming the workers' adherence to the people? Are they workerist, locked up in the factory? Do they have proposals of a party type, explicit principles of the workers' immanence to the politics of the people?

You may also ask: which dominant historical memory saturates them? This is the temporal expansion-constriction. Do they act according to the dream of June 1936? The echo of May 1968? The sense of an isolation, of a beginning?

Of course, these questions are anchored in the consistency of the Marxist algebra, which arranges into a structure the elements of class, the people, imperialism, the strong moments of ideological history, and so on.

The concrete analysis of the situation traverses, within the conceptual legality of analytical Marxism, the collective adherences, their inclusions, their intersections. The political subject is *found*—or not—in these materialist crossings of the reflection and the asymptote.

4. Given a neighbourhood of a point, there exists a subneighbourhood
of this point such that the first neighbourhood
(the 'bigger' one) is the neighbourhood of each of the
points of the second (the 'smaller' one).

This axiom mathematically translates the asymptotic idea according to which what is near a point is near everything that is near this point. The category of neighbourhood does justice to the neighbours' neighbours.

Once again it is a question of tracking down the collective adherence, the excess of any localization over the singularity of the term. The axiom states: if materialism determines the approximate environment of a point, one knows that this environment will also be that of several other points, of a collective of points, which themselves compose a (tighter) environment of the first point, which itself, moreover (axiom 1), resides among them.

One sees how topology is *disidentifying* in nature. That which in topology applies to a term, a point, an individual, by way of the determination of its site, its local adherence, must also always hold true for others, for a collective, to which this individual belongs.

Any topological predicate is plural. The topological nomination is common, dialecticizing the proper names of algebra.

It is the materialist destiny of the subject to have to subvert its proper name in the approximation of its common names.

Or to have to identify its common names in the algebraic subsumption of the proper.

To reflect upon this point is what in materialism grounds the force, as well as the errancy, of the 'cult of personality', which in truth is the cult of a name.

Having to constitute the topology of its adherence is what exposes the political subject—the party—to the anxiety of disidentification, from which it is excepted by the terrorizing return of an algebra of the name.

Consistency, second name of the real after the cause

February 20, 1978

Psychoanalysis and Marxism in 1960 and after—Stalinists?—Two concepts of the real—Masses, classes, State, party: chains and knots—The double real of the Commune—Weak and strong consistency—*Hic Rhodus, hic salta*

1

The extreme form of the subject's algebraicization can be found in the first Lacan, for example: 'At the outset, subjectivity has no relation to the real, but rather to a syntax which is engendered by the signifying mark there' (E 38/50).

The 'without-relation' to the real is the slanted way, subordinated to the algorithmic rule, for saving materialism in the midst of the arcane mysteries of its subjective black sheep. If you determine the process starting from its structure, you obtain at least the structural materialism. You avoid the constitution of the real by the subject; you short-circuit the phenomenology of the data of consciousness.

However, does a syntax amount to a matter? The era (1955) begins to believe so without as yet knowing it. We are not so certain. Ten years later, the syntactical mode of thinking is retained, as far as Marxism is concerned, in Althusser's argument that the class is the nonsubject resulting from the articulation of the different instances in the overdetermined social totality. There is therefore an undecidability between, on the one hand, the combinatory and its mainspring as lack, which throws the materialist tension back to the signifying inscription, and, on the other, idealinguistery.

Lacan's eminent force consists in anticipating (by ten years), and even in anticipating upon the future of his anticipation.

He never confounds the algorithm of the chain and the flat combination of the terms, so that his algebra is maximal, to the point of effectively being its own border.[25] What interests Lacan is less the law than the illegal, chance-like principle of determination that the law puts into effect. He holds steady with regard to the subject effect, when all the others will understand that it must be relegated to the museum of dying humanist ideology.

When, around 1960, the Chinese communists started the ideological crisis with the USSR, they subjected themselves to three principles:

- To restore the scientific and conceptual rigour of Marxism-Leninism, in which sense they were algebraic, against the bland topology of peaceful coexistence, interpenetration, 'realism without borders', and goulash communism.
- To maintain that the revolutionary theme remained active (hence, algorithmic, and not a stable combination) in the figure of the wars of national liberation. In this sense, they pushed the algebra of world-wide contradictions to its topological border, under the sign of a point of condensation (of a limit-point) of all the factors put into play.
- Never to give up on the proletariat as universal political subject.

Consequently, they manifested the current of Marxist scientificity—the worldwide movement of Leninist orthodoxy against the revisionists of the Kremlin—beyond itself, all the way to its reversion in the Cultural Revolution. Just as Lacan, under the banner of the return to Freud and against the American empiricists, subverted both the common theme of antihumanism and the desubjectivization advocated by the structuralists, all the way to its reversal into a theory of analysis in which it is to its real that the subject exposes itself in the anguishing risk of losing both its image and its law in the process.

Even more was at risk, to be sure, in the Cultural Revolution.

And yet, something is hinted at by the minor fact that the suicide of a few intellectuals is invoked as an argument against both Lacan and Mao. Some day it will be the least of things to label Lacan another Stalin. With things as they stand today, a Stalinist is whoever seeks, on some major point of doctrine or ethics, not to give in.

However, that neither Lacan nor Mao are Stalinists is something you know, for the second, from the fact that he was the Buddha of communist disorder (the other being the socialist commander of special heavy metals) and, for the first, from the following text, among others, in which the algebraic metal mentioned above, returned to its algorithm, comes to melt in the furnace of the topologist:

> You know how, by means of axioms, Peano articulates it [the series of numbers]. It is the function of the successor, of the $n+1$, that he puts into relief as structuring the whole number—which nevertheless presupposes at the outset a number that would not be the successor of any other, which he designates as the zero. All that these axioms produce, in conformity with the requirements of arithmetics, will therefore be homologous to the series of whole numbers.
>
> The knot is something else. Here, indeed, the function of the plus-one is specified as such. Omit the plus-one, and there no longer is a series—simply from the section of this one-among-others, the others are liberated, each as one. This could be a way, fully material, to make you grasp that One is not a number, even though the series of numbers is made up of ones.
>
> It must be admitted that in this series of numbers there is such consistency that one is hard put not to take it for being constitutive of the real. Any approach of the real is for us woven out of number. But wherefrom stems this consistency that lies in number? It is not natural at all, and this is precisely what brings me to approach the category of the real inasmuch as it is tied to that to which I am also inclined to give consistency, the imaginary and the symbolical.
>
> If I find some service in the knot, it is because in these three *somethings* which I originalize as the symbolic, the imaginary, and the real, it is a question of the same consistency. It is on this account that I produce the Borromean knot, and this, with an eye on doing justice to my practice.
>
> To isolate consistency as such is something that has never been done. Me, I isolate it, and by way of illustration I give you—the cord.[26]

Here the topological intervention is specified. It is made from the One, as was to be expected.

The Mallarméan side of the real pertains to the vanishing object, cause of desire—or of the text—here the zero, from which it follows that there is succession.

As Lacan says explicitly, 'the knot is something else'. Let us translate: topology is not the same as algebra.

About the Borromean knot, we need not know more here than its elementary property: linking three closed loops in such a way that each is tied to the other two, it is nonetheless such that the cut of any one loop undoes all the links and disperses the whole.

If, for example, you have the following:

you see that loop 2 constitutes the One of the chain. It is a chain precisely insofar as only the cut of the intermediary term 2 (the 'weakest link') disperses the whole. If you cut 3, there remains the link of 1 and 2, and if you cut 1, then 2 and 3 remain linked.

By contrast, if you have either one of the following (they are the same!), the cut of any of the three undoes the whole:

 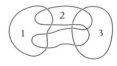

The One of the Borromean knot is that of a consistency that affects the whole, it is a One of adherence, the collective property of the terms, whereas the One of the chain prescribes the places of the connection, which have a separating function.

What is it that makes the knot into 'something else'? It is because the One does not have the same assignation therein as in the algebraic order. The One of numbers is sustained by the zero in order to repeat itself by addition. The One of the knot holds together the terms of the series.

In one case: algorithmic principle of the iteration of the Same, ordered algebra of succession. In the other: topological principle of partitive cohesion, of knotted interdependence.

We must therefore advance that in Lacan there are, adequate to the division of the One, two concepts of the real: the real of the vanishing, which is in a position of cause for the algebra of the subject; and the real of the knot, which is in a position of consistency for its topology.

From the real as cause to the real as consistency one can read a trajectory of integral materialism. Once the numerical succession is engendered in the efficacy of the vanishing term, we must still know what it is that makes all these numbers hold together.

Once it is understood that one succeeds the other, in the causality marked by the zero, and that they all *belong* to the domain of number, we must know which is the One-of-numbers, the general *adherence* in which the succession consists.

The algebraic linkage of atoms of the denumerable cannot in and of itself ground the continuity of their common maintenance.

There is the chain and then there is the knot.

Thus, in the space of the theory of the subject Lacan rises up to the challenge of the supreme problem of materialism, which is correctly to tie together its own division according to algebra and according to topology.

The 'real', for having to support under a single name the fact of being both the cause as object and consistency as third term, comes to the place that since always is prescribed to it: to ensure with regard to any dialectical process that there is the one of the two, which therefore makes three.

The destructive counter-proof is clear enough. If the real as cause fails, if the lack comes to lack, you have the anxiety of the too-much-of-the-real, which no longer makes sense; if the real as consistency fails, if the Borromean knot is cut, you have the dispersion of the too-little-of-the-real, which unmoors the law, henceforth terrorizing, and the imaginary, inflated to the point of the delirium of universal similitude.

See 'the masses' which, for the Marxists that we all are, I hope, are the historical name of the real. I have already had the chance to say that by 'masses' we never understand a substance. What then? That which a historical cut comes up against in an encounter.[27]

In general, the masses are neither thought nor thinkable. The 'there is' of the masses is the vanishing mode of the historical real, which can be perceived by the fact that there is some defect, some chink, in the state's armour—what is called, with Lenin, a 'revolutionary situation'.

However, we must also recognize that the masses are the sole principle of political consistency. The State, as the concentrated guarantee of an established political algebra, and the classes, as the point of assignation of social identification and as such imaginary (the point of view of class in its state form, the intelligible form of the social ego): all this holds together only within the *massive* regulation of general public activity. The State is unable to guarantee itself from anything other than the consent of the masses, whether snatched up or peaceful. As for the classes as principle of distribution, as imaginary disjunction, their immediate subject matter is massive.

The masses are therefore the real to which are tied both the State and the classes; they are the guarantee of consistency which, if undone, restores the State to the dead and closed being of its apparatus, and the classes, to the historical imaginary.

Materialism indeed affirms that 'the masses make history', it says so according to the algebra—as vanishing revolutionary cause—and/or according to the topology—as general consistency of the political place: Borromean knot of the State, the classes, and the masses themselves.

As for the political subject, it is what ties the knot made up of the State, the classes, and the masses, in the figure inscribed in the party, which draws its occasion from the revolutionary real, its duration from the link to the masses, and its aim from the State.

What remains to be seen is how this linkage, this linking, takes its order from the subjective consistency detained by the articulation, in the masses, of the point of view of class upon the State.

For politics is only the subject-effect of this articulation.

Thus, there certainly is a division of the concept of the real (of the masses).

To seize the moment is what defines the algebraic talent of the revolutionary. It is a matter of not missing the signifier of that which vanishes as real.[28] But to hold up the principle of consistency is what defines the topological genius of the communist. It is a matter of braiding the cord by which the State can come untied, insofar as the knot that ties it to the class (the dictatorship of the proletariat) is, by the mediation of the masses, Borromean.

When Mao says: 'Get yourself mixed up in the affairs of the State',[29] and when he launches the Cultural Revolution, he makes himself into a cord weaver, even if the party—the subject-effect grasped in its cause and in its consistency—must suffer dearly in the process.

Let us say that being both and at the same time revolutionary and communist, this subject in the throes of the real is eclipsed in the alternated angle of the monumental State and the class delivered up to rioting.

To consist in one's cause is not easy. Some, in the party, will always prefer the benefits of the State.

These preferences, which undivide the real for the benefit of the algebra, are what define the appearance of a special historical entity, the anticommunist fusion of the State and the masses, under a 'proletarian' class name that is henceforth absolutely imaginary. This entity has a name: the new bourgeoisie, born from within the party itself.

To be one of the new bourgeoisie, it suffices to give up in politics on one's communist desire. Which is, by far, the easiest thing to do.

Under these conditions, the State alone promises a consistency of which we say very little if we say that it is the consistency of those soups in which the ladle remains standing.

· The cause is lost. The loss is lost.[30]

2

To think the one of the two without a connection that would be external: this clearly requires an effort in topology.

Topology is this point of materialism where the dialectic supports its division. 'On the basis [. . .] of rings of string, a wedging [*coinçage*] occurs, since it is the crossing of two continuities that stops a third continuity. Doesn't it seem that this wedging could constitute the initial phenomenon of a topology?' (S XX, 119/131–2).

Wedging, crossing: we have seen these terms, which are constitutive of materialism in the process of knowledge. The real, in addition to its identity as a missing causal object, comes to the surface in consistency as the stopped crossing of two processes.

This shows the extent to which the real is the unity of the algebraic and the topological, unity of the cause and the consistency.

It is object, but *not only*.

In what sense do we say that the Paris Commune is real? Certainly not in that it has taken place, which is merely the index of its reality.

It is real, first of all, in that it breaks with the framework of the State, and even more so with the Marxist theory of the State. It is by putting into effect a point of the impossible in this theory that it reveals its status as real, so that Marx, who logically disapproves of the triggering of the insurrection, can only *encounter* in it the vanishing Parisian masses. Whence the obligation, to which he remains faithful, of being wholly on the side of that of which he disapproves in theory, so as to find the new and retroactive concept of his practical approval.

It is real, in the second place, in that the Commune enters into the consistency of any prolonged proletarian politics, to the point where Lenin is brought to dance in the snow when the power that resulted from the October Revolution surpasses the duration of the poor Parisian State of 1871. To the point also where the workers' insurrection in Shanghai in 1967 declares the founding of a Commune, and that moreover, as early as 1966, in the solemn declaration that tries to organize the Cultural Revolution, the Maoist leaders affirm: 'It is necessary to institute a system of general elections, like that of the Paris Commune.'[31]

We thus pass from the algebraic punctuality, by which a materialist domain opens itself up to knowledge, to the topological adherence, which saturates the recurrence of conflict with memory and neighbourhoods.

For us all, the Commune is the reflection of the revolutionary break it illuminates, while we stand in an asymptotic rapport to its communist vocation.

It consists, for having disappeared. This same object with its vanished precision, which is commemorated in the Père Lachaise cemetery, is co-present, as inexhaustible concept, nearest to our action.

It is the wedging of this double mode of being that makes up the materialist real of the Commune.

This obviously requires the current political subject: that of the Cultural Revolution, that of the Maoists.

3

Does Lacan push the dialectic of the real this far?

Here we are in the vicinity of a legitimate and nameable divergence. Why? Because the Lacanian concept of consistency is too restrictive. By failing to oppose and conjoin explicitly the algebra and the topology, he exposes himself to the risk of thinking of consistency only as an attribute of algebra.

Like those who in politics would see in the masses, once past the revolt that is the causality of lack, only an attribute of the class State.

For his own needs, Lacan does not have to push the issue beyond that which, at the level of formalization, lets itself be recognized as consistent homogeneity of the symbolic:

The nature of the mathematical language, once it is sufficiently isolated in terms of its requirements of pure demonstration, is such that everything that is put forward there—not so much in the spoken commentary as in the very handling of letters—assumes that if one of the letters doesn't stand up, all the others, due to their arrangement, not only constitute nothing of any validity but disperse. It is in this respect that the Borromean knot is the best metaphor of the fact that we proceed only on the basis of the One. (S XX, 116/128)

Who fails to see that consistency, in its Borromean figure, is here dangerously close to being a simple principle of existential interdependence?

This is not by accident. Engels—and Stalin—made this principle, erroneously, into the key of dialectical materialism.

The unilateral reference to the One, without the scission which even in Hegel opposes the ones to the One One, makes what is proper to the topology disappear, that is, its rootedness in inclusion, the partitive, the neighbourhood, the multiple.

To say that if the One is lacking, everything disperses, comes down to *deriving consistency from the cause.*

I venture that the primacy of algebra has the effect of reducing the field of topology to the sole consistency of the algebraic location.

As I did for difference, here I posit that there are two concepts of consistency.

Weak consistency is resolved in structural cohesion. *It makes a knot of what is only a chain.*

All Lacan's tracking of the real is subordinate to the study of strings, series of knots, Borromean chains.

Strong consistency overdetermines the algebra, as consistency of neighbourhoods. Though anchored in the cause, the object, the structure, it names the principle of the real in the collective excess and the adherence, letting itself be summed up neither in the lack of a term nor in belonging.

The consistency of interdependence is the elementary form, barely set apart from the algebra, of that which must be pushed all the way to the point of conflictual consistency, heterogeneous consistency, the consistency that is independent of all interdependence.

You know that this requires the concept of force.

Let us say that the Lacanian relation of the cause to the consistency, which makes up the whole divided name of the real, wants to remain in its place.

The truth is that destruction is required, at the heart of materialism, in order to ground in it the real unity of the logic of neighbourhoods and that of lack.

As for the subject, it finds in this unity that which in Lacan is only the eclipse of its inscription: the wherewithal to carry out the excess over the law, without needing to surpass materialism.

For it is materialism, divisible unity of algebra and topology, that under the primacy of the second such as it is induced by a subjectivization, enters in an excess over itself.

The two paths are clear, after all. Either the material locus of the subjective is made up of an algebraicization of the topological (Borromean chains, consistency of interdependence); or it is made up of a topologization of the algebraic (matrices of destruction, conflictual consistency).

Hic Rhodus, hic salta.

So little ontology

March 3, 1978

Heidegger—The guaranteeing of communism by the socialist State is not worth more than that of consistency by the cause—The three consistencies of the working class—Being is said in three ways

1

The notion that being is said according to the cause and according to consistency is actually the oldest theme of philosophy.

As such, philosophy touches upon the real, and upon materialism, by the indirect and urgent recognition of the pair algebra/topology, no matter what speculative clothing it comes in.

I do not approve, frankly speaking, of the disdain with which Lacan's sectarians regard philosophy, which they inscribe univocally in the register of the imaginary.

They boast about being daring antiphilosophers. I rather see them protect the algebraic indivisibility of the object. Besides, here they are at a loss as soon as the ontological tracking pursuit of the master, edging on silence and indifferent to the subtle and vain games of metaphor and metonymy, wants only to keep on weaving—norn of his own errancy—the real cord of destiny.

Consistency supports the question: what about the being of what is? Causality, the problem of the supreme being, by which the world is the form of what is.

Ontological question, theological question.

Heidegger intends to deconstruct metaphysics, previously defined as the concealment of the first question by the second. I say that he seeks to dissipate the algebraic precision of God, localization of simple belonging, placed being from which all beings take their place. It is a question of opening up onto the topological unlimitation of being, for which it is not for nothing that Heidegger evokes ad nauseam the dialectic of the near and the far.

Heidegger would like to put an end to the philosophical idea of a *guarantee of consistency by the cause*.

You will be able to shed some light on this point if you know that what we contemporary Marxists want to put an end to is the theme of a *guarantee of communism by the socialist State*.

The State, as causal result of the vanishing of the masses, establishes the algebraic disposition of politics. We declare that, socialist or not, and though invariably needed for the intelligibility of action, the State guarantees nothing with regard to the subjective effectuation of communism.

In order to believe the contrary, one must imagine this socialist State as an exception—as state of the exception, capable by itself of an algorithm for its own withering away, whereas Lenin already knew that any modern State, including the socialist one, is intrinsically bourgeois and hence pertains, with regard to the communist topology, to the category of the structure and the obstacle.

This status of the exception can be deciphered in philosophy among the crucial operators that allow one to crush consistency under the cause, or being under God. See Aristotle: all nature lies in movement, such is the law of the world. The supreme mover, who is being *par excellence*, is certainly the object-cause of movement in general, but it is excepted from it, being itself immobile.

The socialist State, supposed cause of communism, is exactly this immobile mover.

There is no more imperious demand than to keep the distance between cause and consistency as the dialectical division of the effects-of-the-real. What is thereby at stake is the subject.

If a philosophy has no other definition than to provide for the closing up of this distance through its immobile movers, its transcendental subjects, its negations of the negation, its beings-that-are-not-what-they-are, then it is true that we cannot be philosophers.

Let us say that philosophy lies on this side of the artifices with which it attempts to ensure its grip on the neighbourhoods and the adherences by the solidity of the object and the regulated efficacy of the causality of lack. It is neither its virtue nor its essence to want to ground the unity of being in the One of the object. Even in the most subtle of the concepts forged for the sake of this consoling mistake, we can always read the laborious recognition of the fact that the real, nominally split, proposes both the object-cause and the process-consistency, and that, for the subject of any knowledge whatsoever to face up to this, what is needed is the exploration of a conflictual compatibility between the elementary networks of algebra and the intricate partitions of topology.

2

To think the working class.

First, the algebra. A worker is whoever sells his or her labour force to be included in a production process controlled by capital. Legitimately, one will announce that the class is defined by its *place* in the mode of production. This is the infallible sign of the reflection, of the algebraicization. In addition, this is an obligatory passageway.

Is there consistency at this stage? Yes, if one retains the weak consistency, that of the algebraic location. It is an objective consistency, reducible to a similarity of belonging, to a law of the Same. The noun 'worker' designates this.

Do these 'workers' form a class? Yes, the sociologist will be pleased to find the special attributes, the similarities in clothing, attitudes, tastes, voting habits, and so on. The sociologist, in his bookkeeper's inventory, does not have to know about the exclusively differential nature of these similarities. It is clear that they regulate the same by way of the other, by way of the bourgeois, the professor, the farmer. The consistent interiority is missing. That which links the workers as class obviously cannot be summed up by the effects of their position. 'They' prefer *The Blue Danube* to Wagner? As a result, I consider them only as object *for another object*—the one who likes Wagner, the petit bourgeois; I do not exceed the algebra.

Rigorously speaking, one should say that here consistency is inconsistent. For the structure of belonging of the workers to the labour market puts them in competition with one another. It disjoins them more so than it brings them together. You know what is *one* worker, you ignore what are two workers, as One.

This is the zero degree of the neighbourhood.

The first degree is provided to us by the consistency of demands or trade unionism. The fact that adherence is not null and void in them becomes manifest with the appearance of organizational phenomena. Here the topology introduces a distance into the algebra of competition.

That which authorizes this gap is, strictly speaking, the possible bargaining about the price of the labour force. The salary disperses the workers, but the fact that it is negotiable organizes them.

Here you have a tendency: the actual salary fluctuates slightly around the value of the labour force. The surrounding of this fluctuation, though restricted, brings forth a whole topology of protests and demands, which relates *the* workers of a factory or a sector to the salary, no longer as a fixed contract but as an asymptote. What the unions call 'the fair salary', which governs the 'legitimate demand': these are all concepts whose property is that they know no sufficient satisfaction, since they fix only an imaginary limit point.

You can measure to what extent this consistency remains subservient to the algebra of exploitation. It is only in the margin opened up by the competition among capitalists, the industrial restructuring, the imperialist expansion, that the trade unionist demand endows the workers with a reality of partitive inclusion, elevating them above the atomization of the market.

As vacillation around a fixed point—the objective value of the labour force—that the revolt itself in the end comes up against as its absent cause, the consistency of demands knows only the poorest of neighbourhoods, the adherences that are the least distanced from the belongings, the most trivial topologies.

It is not surprising that the trade union ends up by becoming rigidified in the algebra of the great imperialist States. At its peak, as in the United States, this subservient role confers upon the union the monopoly of employment. In the strict sense, the unionist adherence, since it is obligatory simply in order to find a job, fuses with the worker's belonging.

The fact remains that what we have here is the precious acquisition of the gap as such, at least in the heroic phase of the unionization of the workers. The unionized class, without being subject, no longer stands under the law of the object. It brings into being the abstract element of the subjective.

The political antagonism gives rise to a principle of consistency that is radically heterogeneous to its underlying algebra. As a result, belonging henceforth is only a vague criterion. The (topological) position of class must be distinguished from the (algebraic and social) being of class. The political leaders of the workers are intellectuals. In general, this provokes the indignation only of the bourgeois, or of those for whom the mysteries of the real are unfathomable.

In the partisan political topology, the stakes lie in exceeding the algebra all the way to its limit point, where it can break. The destruction is articulated upon the maintenance, there where the trade union persevered.

The party is the support of the complete subject, by which the proletariat, built on the working class, aims at the dissolution of the algebraic frame in which this class is placed.

If consistency #1 is inconsistent, according to the very law of the algebra of competition, consistency #3 destroys the principle of consistency of the place. It is thus equally inconsistent, in that no *object*, on the side of capital, can function as cause of its consistency.

In the proletariat, the working class has disappeared. Realized as vanishing cause, it consists in the party, whose existence has no other aim than to suppress that which made possible the causality.

The objective existence of the class collects dispersed workers. Its political existence gathers communists. In both cases, the scission of the cause and of consistency is asymmetrical. The real of class is a specific imbalance of algebra and topology.

Only trade unionism seeks a balance. This is because it purports to make consistency out of the capitalist cause.

Ah, the tedium it unleashes! Between the hardship of work and the labour of the revolution, neither one nor the other, and priding itself on its 'realism', it is a hidden algebra and a submissive topology!

3

These distinctions are general.

Being—so little ontology!—is said in two ways, hence in three. Cause and consistency are the primitive concepts, whose combinatory, recognized in the asymmetry of dialectical divisions, gives us:

1. The primacy of the cause over consistency (of the algebra over the topology): being-placed, in a position of vanishing as to the object, and of dispersion-repetition as to the subject.
2. The equilibrium of the cause and of consistency: being-structured,

in a position of variation as to the object, and of similitude as to the subject.

3. The primacy of consistency over the cause: being-forced, in a position of destruction as to the object, of excess as to the subject.

As an exercise, I propose that you confront the triplicity of being, established in this way, with the Lacanian nominations:

- insistence, in which the effect of the symbolic governs the repetition;
- consistency (in the weak sense), into which the imaginary identification is resolved;
- ex-sistence, wherein lies the real.

As for me, I will only tell you that, seeing how people live and think, one may conclude that there are indeed three visions of the world: the ordinary, the trade unionist, and the political. Each gesture, each word, pertains clearly to one of these three types. Classify yourselves on a daily basis, you will be better off.

Is there not a source of happiness, in the ancient sense, in the ontological ground behind these mundane evaluations?

From this journey through materialism, I infer that already two definitions of the subject oppose one another:

- the subject is a consistent repetition in which the real ex-sists; (Lacan)
- the subject is a destructive consistency, in which the real ex-ceeds.

PART V

Subjectivization and Subjective Process

The topological opposite of the knot is not the cut-dispersion but the destruction-recomposition

March 13, 1978

Double occurrence of the subject—Crucial concepts—A Lacanian embarrassment—In praise of the party

The subject, if such an effect exists, is material—like everything else that exists. It follows that it can be grasped both by way of reflection and by way of the asymptote, through algebra and through topology.

What are the divided specifications of the subject-process that circumscribe the two conceivable orders of its materiality?

Let us recall that the political subject is the class party. The empirical side of it shows us its intermittent brilliance when it is a question of insurrection, and its lasting consistency when it belongs to the State.

The act of tying together—the Borromean effect—is not the same in these two circumstances. I will argue that, first, as the cut that ruins the link that ties the old class to the old State, it avers the real of the masses in the dispersive vanishing of its effect. The State falls to ruin, the class seizes hold of the mass, the party is resolved into the flow that carries it, politics coincides with history. Then, the re-tying causes the One of a different kind, the new class State, organizing a mass consensus.

What ties the knot depends either on its cut or on its linkage.

What does it mean to come to know a knot? Untying it is not enough, because it might be a matter of chance. It is also necessary to tie it.

The subject crosses these two operations.

The time of insurrection is essentially algebraic, as I said. It is by dint of what it causes to disappear that a revolution deserves to be gauged. The time of direction is topological. It is in the name of what it builds that a party appears before the tribunal of communist evaluation.

But the subject is not yet nameable in the separated abstraction of these moments.

Lacan was clear about this, as can be seen in a note added on the occasion of the publication of his *Ecrits*, in which he tempered the dominant algebraism of his first period. The text is from 1955, the note from 1966. In it Lacan comments on the introductory exercises of the 'Seminar on "The Purloined Letter"', where we can find the densest formulation of the algebra of the subject:

> The introduction of a structural approach to the field in psychoanalytic theory through such exercises was, in fact, followed by important developments in my teaching. Concepts related to subjectivization progressed hand-in-hand with a reference to the *analysis situs* in which I claim to materialize the subjective process. (E 48 n. 29/57)

These concepts of 'subjectivization' and 'subjective process' are crucial to me insofar as to the first we can attach the algorithmic explorations of the chain, and to the second, the *analysis situs*, the localization by neighbourhoods.

I also hold that without destruction—and its obverse, recomposition— you cannot think the subjective materiality of their coupling all the way to the end.

This is why Lacan has studied them one after the other: subjectivization, until the mid-1960s, and, subsequently, the subjective process, especially after 1968.

Subjectivization raises the question of its cause, to which Lacan responds with the real as object; subjective process, that of its consistency, to which Lacan henceforth still responds with the real, but in what guise? This is where he leaves us behind, because the Borromean knot such as he conceives of it remains haunted by the logic of loss and of dispersion.

Lacan's embarrassment with regard to consistency stems from the fact that he holds the cutting (of the knot) to be the proof of its truth. Now the opposite of tying the knot is not to cut it but to destroy it. The cut is only the algebraic abstraction of the destruction. Just as the revolution is only an abstract moment of communism.

This embarrassment is transparent in Lacan's texts. Consider the following:

The real is that there is something common to all three in consistency. Now, this consistency lies only in the capacity of forming a knot. Is a mental knot real? Therein lies the question. [. . .]

We are forced not to put the real into consistency. Consistency, to call it by its name, I mean by its correspondence, is of the order of the imaginary. Something which is largely demonstrated in all of human history, and which should inspire a singular type of prudence in us, is the fact that all consistency that withstood the test of time is pure imagination. [. . .]

If we can ensure that the imaginary ex-sists, it is because it is a question of another real. I say that the effect of meaning ex-sists, and that in this sense, it is real. It is not a matter of apologetics, but of consistency, imaginary consistency, no doubt, but there certainly does exist, it seems, a whole usual domain of the imaginary function that lasts and holds up.[1]

Consistency, inasmuch as it is real, is here reduced to ex-sistence, and thus to whatever withdraws itself from what is inscribed, to the absence of that which whatever consists makes into its presence. As to consistency properly speaking, here it is reascribed to the register of the imaginary, whose tie to the real consists in ex-sisting.

This fragment contains an essential equivocation, whose symptoms are clear enough:

- the real is at the same time present in the Borromean knot, as one of the three loops, and ex-sistent with regard to that same knot, because 'even if I do not trace the figure of my Borromean knot on the blackboard, it ex-sists, since no sooner is it traced than anybody can see clearly that it is impossible for it not to remain what it is in the real, namely, a knot.'[2] The real is thus this vanished element represented in the One that it causes to exist. It is object-cause, the One-of-the-knot, wherein any one whatsoever of the three loops marks its lack. We would be reduced to Mallarmé, except that

- consistency, the topological form of the One, is at the same time 'that which is common to the three' and that which can be figured in the one-of-three, the imaginary, which is the historical key to all totality and to all similitude. Thus, the one-of-the-knot would find the guarantee of its consistency in the imaginary rather than in the real, except that

- the real causes the imaginary consistency to ex-sist, whereby it touches upon the scission of the very being of consistency into object-cause (object-knot), on one hand, and ex-sistence, on the other.

245

You must not think for a moment that this inconceivable circle is pure sophistry. To tell the truth, it is what we witness every day. Everybody claims that if in a revolution there is this real of the cut that can be found in the impulse of the masses, the imaginary takes its revenge by being the only thing that guarantees, in the guise of some communist or egalitarian utopia, the terrorist consistency of society. Such is in essence the anti-Marxist war machine of these recent times. What does this mean, if not that the real is held out to be only a vanishing cause—some would call it with the bad name of the 'plebs'—and that the only consistency of communist politics makes for an imaginary recollection wagered by exsistent masses, that is, masses who are out of play, even though they are constantly invoked as an abstraction of the State?

Missing from this argument are the thought of an effective destruction of the old law and the observation that what recomposes itself can no longer in any way be *the same*. In this way, the real of the subject guarantees consistency *without the mediation of the imaginary*.

Even the impasse of the political subject does not restore the old rule. This is what the Maoist debate is all about. In the USSR, we have neither an 'interrupted' revolution nor I-don't-know-what totalitarian rendition of the bourgeois world, under the universal and repetitive concept of the modern State. We have a *new* bourgeoisie.

But to lay the groundwork for a new way of thinking of this novelty, we must make sure that the real is anchored in consistency as much as in causality; we must determine the subject in the subjectivizing differential *and* in the being of the subjective process.

At stake here is nothing less than the thinkable and practicable existence, though empirically unapparent, of a communist revolution.

A revolution, I say, 'uninterrupted-by-stages', whereby 'stages' should make you think of subjectivization; 'uninterrupted', of the subjective process; and the dashes, of the political subject.

The complete concept of these dashes is missing from Lacan, due to the fact that, under the idea of existence, he lets consistency drop into the imaginary, communism into utopia, and revolution into the structural vacuousness of an algebra of the Same.

Implicitly, Lacan states that the party is the Master. Now, I will argue that, insofar as it exists, which is rare, the communist party (the opposite, therefore, of the PCF) is certainly the discourse of the Master, of the State, but it is also that of the hysteric, in reality insurrectionary and following the pirouettes of the moment, as much as that of the university (Mao only laid claim to the title of teacher), and of the analyst, because in letting politics wither by stages, the communist masses must come to despise the party: liquidation of the transference.

I love the idea of the political party, just as one loves what consists as subject, for having been, because once lost, the leader-to-come of its own termination.[3]

Subjectivizing anticipation, retroaction of the subjective process

April 3, 1978

The prisoners' apologue—The scansion of the subjective process—
Subjectivizing function of haste—A logician's refutation—The nonsaid

1

Here, for the sake of the text's self-sufficiency, I must recount to you the anecdote whose exegesis will fixate our irreducible distance from its inventor, Lacan.

The following should be taken as the inference of the infimous gap through which the same passes over into the other.

All the while trying to keep a respectful sense of proportions, I admit that the function of the reading put to work here is comparable to the one that Marx, in order to identify his future, applied in 1843 to Hegel's philosophy of right.

At issue is the text 'Logical Time and the Assertion of Anticipated Certainty', which you will find in Lacan's *Ecrits* between pages 161 and 175.

Here you have three prisoners to whom a warden, of the sadistic kind promoted by 'enlightened' despotisms, promises that he will liberate only one of them, provided that he is the one who emerges victoriously from a mental test in which nothing but the pure resource of the subject is at stake.

The material for this test comprises three white disks and two black disks. One disk is fastened to the back of each prisoner in such a way that he can see what sign marks the two others but ignores his own. The task consists precisely in deducing his own from the other two, with each competitor being informed that there are a total of five disks, three white ones and two black ones. A prisoner will signal that he has found the answer by moving toward the exit door. Of course, he will be interrogated afterward as to the strictly logical nature of his deduction.

We can see that this test amounts for an individual to complete the differential trait (black or white) that marks him, and thus to achieve, by the symbolic act of exiting, the status of free subject.

It is important that this solution occurs from the point of the Other (the two others), who alone is in possession of every premise.

This puerile game is fascinating. Is it not fundamental, in order for the working class to make itself into the subject of communist politics, that it knows how to deduce from its experience alone the trait of universality that comes to mark its misery? And must we not, at every decisive step in our lives, take it upon ourselves to wager on a name, an act, a glory whose coefficient of existence we can obtain only from the others? Then is the time when we must outstrip them starting from the conviction that they are *the same* and drawing our inference of what marks us based on the way in which these same ones will practise an identical inference.

As though to underscore that it is from the Same that the eventual superiority of one-among-others must proceed, the prison warden fastens a white disk between the shoulders of all three prisoners.

Each one thus sees two white disks.

The central reasoning is then the following: 'I see two white disks. If I had a black disk, the others would necessarily see a white one and a black one. They would then say to themselves: "I see a black one and a white one. If I had a black one, the one who bears the white one would see two black ones. Since he knows that there are only two in total, he would conclude at once that he has a white one. He thus would already have started walking toward the door. But nobody has moved, therefore I have a white disk." And they would have started walking toward the door. But they didn't move. Therefore, I have a white disk.'

Move past the potential obstacle of your confusion. All this will become clear step by step.

Let us retain that this reasoning, based on the premise 'I see two white disks', is the same for all three prisoners, all of whom see two whites. Thus, they start to walk at the same time.

What does Lacan then tell us? That this beginning walk annuls their conclusion. Why? If A, at the time of putting one foot ahead of the other, sees that B and C do the same, he can no longer conclude, since his reasoning included the immobility of the other two as conclusive argument.

All of them will thus stop in their tracks, with the same restlessness of having jumped ahead of the conclusion.

But each one, seeing that the other two stop, will immediately annul the supposed annulment of his hypothesis. For if they had seen a black and a white disk, the two others would have no reason to stop. If they do, it is for the same reason as I: they have seen two whites, and they are restless because of the possible anticipation of their certainty.

All of them thus start walking again.

Here you finally obtain—according to Lacan—five constitutive times in the engendering of certainty, which periodize that which fully deserves the name of *subjective process*, which, as expected, is intersubjective:

1. The immobile wait during the lapse of time necessary for the deduction, and which I also suppose to be required for the other to formulate the reasoning at the end of which, if I had a black disk, he would aim for the door. This is the time to understand.
2. The step forward by which I decide as to my own mark. This is the time to conclude.
3. The representation of a possible haste, given that the others have also started to move. Retroactive discovery of a possibility to anticipate certainty.
4. The scansion: suspended moment at which all stop again. The attitude of stopping of the others objectifies the premise of their reasoning.
5. The reinitiating of the walk, governed by a certainty that this time is fully grounded.

You can see clearly that the subjectivization involved in this process lies hidden in the moment to conclude, which retroactively turns out to be marked by a possible hastiness. This is where the act surfaces in excess over the algebra. I can only wager on the time of the other (on his time to understand), hurried as I am by the real of the situation, which will set free only the first one to exit: 'The "*I*" in question here defines itself through a subjectification of *competition* with the other, in the function of logical time. As such, it seems to me to provide the essential logical form (rather than the so-called existential form) of the psychological "*I*"' (E 170/208).

According to the logical constraint, which defines the splace lorded over by the prison warden, the outplace here is an outtime, a time of possible advance, by which the act, the step forward, anticipates—perhaps!—the well-founded certainty. It is precisely this 'function of haste' that distinguishes the subjectivization from the subjective process, all the while chaining it to the latter under the law of the Other.

Consider the fact that without exception, a popular insurrection, even one that is finally victorious, is always premature with regard to the political process that prepares it.

There is no subjectivization without anticipation, which in turn can be measured by the subjective process. It is absolutely right that 'what makes this act [of concluding] so remarkable in the subjective assertion demonstrated by the sophism is that it anticipates its own certainty owing to the temporal tension with which it is subjectively charged' (E 171/209).

Consider also that the subjective process amounts to the retroactive grounding of the subjectivization in an element of certainty that the subjectivization alone has made possible. For at the time of the scansion, when all three halt, it is the haste of the others that I put into question and that sends their identity back to me.

Now all this is very true. Marx judges the Commune to be precipitated—subjectivizing in its political haste—and blames it for not marching onto Versailles. But this is in order to indicate retroactively the nature of the certainty (of victory) of which this haste itself could be the bearer, insofar as it can be deciphered in the other: in the initial disorder and surprise of the inhabitants of Versailles, and in the possibility of changing the lack into reason by a second haste, that of the military offensive against Versailles. The latter would then finally be caught up in the subjective process, that is to say, in a consequent political direction, which is the only validation of the vanishing algebra of the Parisian masses into a consistent subject.

In subjectivization, certainty is anticipated.

In the subjective process, consistency is retroactive.

To put into consistency the haste of the cause: therein lies the whole enigma of the subject.

2

However, the Lacanian exegesis cannot suit us. Its flaw consists in presupposing that which renders it impossible: an absolute reciprocity, a strict logical identity between the three prisoners.

I claim that if all three are identical logical machines, things cannot happen the way Lacan says. By thus forcing on the side of the algebra, we annul the topology. There can be then neither haste nor retroaction nor suspended time.

The title 'Logical Time' is a marvel in that it seeks to cross the asymptotic effects of time, anticipation, suspension, retroaction, and the reflection-effects of pure logic.

In order to legitimize this title in the course of a set of theses on the subject, something else would actually be needed than the axioms with which Lacan regulates his game.

I will demonstrate this.

Let us distinguish three reasonings, R1, R2, R3, according to the three premises that are virtually possible according to the rule of the game (I see two black disks, I see one black and one white, I see two whites).

R1: I see two black disks. Now there are only two blacks. Therefore I am white.

This is the reasoning that we could call immediate. The time of the glance.

R2: I see one black and one white. If I am black, the white one sees two blacks. Therefore, he reasons from the start according to R1. In the time of the glance, he should have taken off. If he did not, I am not black, I am white.

Notice that at this stage R1 is entirely contained within R2. It is by assuming that the other will accomplish R1, whose intuitive brilliance I am able to invoke, that I infer that he should have left the room.

R3: I see two whites. If I am black, the two others see one black and one white. They thus reason from the start according to R2. They should have concluded. If they have not left, I am white.

Once more, R2 is contained within R3, which is articulated around the fact that R2, if begun at the same time, would end before R3 can reach a conclusion, by giving a signal due to the fact of the other (the competitors who start to move).

As you can see, the three reasonings are by no means identical in terms of their demonstrative 'expanse'. In fact, they constitute a chain of inclusion:

$$R1 \subset R2 \subset R3$$

If, as is the case in our anecdote, everyone reasons according to R3, it is clear that the 'duration' of R2 has run out when R3 is completed, since R2 is an internal piece of R3.

At least, that is, if the 'speed' of reasoning of the three prisoners is the same. Now Lacan explicitly presupposes this logical identity: 'each of them [. . .] *is* A insofar as [he is] real—that is, insofar as he resolves or fails to resolve to conclude about himself—each encounters the same doubt at the same moment as him' (E 164/200–201).

But under this presupposition, the reasoning R3 is entirely conclusive, given the fact that if the other reasoned according to R2 *he would have started moving before I could finish R3,* which contains R2 as one of its parts, and he would thus have given me an abundant signal—but too late!—that I am indeed black.

By contrast, the fact that the other does not move except when I do cannot lead me to doubt. It is even the exact opposite. For it only indicates that he reasons, like me, according to R3. As a result my conclusion, which was already certain, is purely and simply confirmed: surplus certainty, and not suspended doubt.

Under the hypothesis that the subjective calculations are isomorphous and that we are dealing with algorithmically identical subjects, there can only be a single simultaneous motion forward of all three toward the door, overdetermining the certainty that each of them draws from the completion, without any kind of signal, of reasoning R3.

From then on you have only one time, that of the unfolding of R3, transitive to the act of concluding.

Both the periodization of the subjective process and the subjectivization thus come jointly undone.

For haste there is none.

Of course, the periodization is exact and the subjectivization is existent.

Therefore, there must be something *that Lacan does not say.* This silenced supplement is precisely the point where, in order to cross the temporal topology and the algebra of calculation, in order to account for the haste, it is necessary to posit that the heterogeneity of force exceeds the connection of the places.

By granting too much to the algebra, there ends up being no more place for the outplace nor any time for the outtime.

'Hurry! Hurry! Word of the Living!'[4]

April 10, 1978

Qualitative function of the supposed knucklehead—Force returns to the scene—Neighbourhoods and subjectivizing interruption—Four concepts, two times, two modes

1

We now know the following: *either* the subjective calculation follows the algebraic rule through and through, in which case there is neither anticipation nor retroaction, *or* there is a hasty subjectivization of certainty, but then we must presuppose some element of originary nonidentity. Which one is it?

If, when the other begins to move, I stop, aware as I am of perhaps having jumped ahead, it is because I suppose that while I reasoned according to R3, the other *may* not have been able to complete more than the reasoning R2, even though R2 is part of R3.

The experiential field thus includes the fact that each subject recognizes the possible nonidentity of the other. In this case, the fact that there are different 'speeds' of reasoning.

My awareness of haste is here dependent on the possibility that the other is perhaps a knucklehead.

You see that what is at stake, while measurable by the algorithm (its speed), cannot be reduced to it.

My haste and thus the entire periodization of the process stem from the perception, which is inseparable from the act, that there is a qualitative element in every subjective determination.

My haste, my halting. If you eliminate the element of doubt as to the differential heterogeneity of the other, then you'll have no conceivable haste whatsoever.

It is here, of course, that grafted onto the algorithm, there arises something whose principles cannot be reduced to the latter's rules: the question of my *proximity* to the other, here assigned to the difference R3-R2, in which the possible inferiority of my colleague's intellect in matters of deductive velocity warns me about the need to be wary when he starts to walk.

Thus, I must filter the experience of his starting to walk, certainly through the algebra, which relates it to *my* reasoning, but also through the topology, which around this reasoning determines a set of subjective neighbourhoods (of speed, haste, stupidity . . .) through which I proceed to evaluate the other.

We must observe how the 'competition' mentioned by Lacan imposes on the subject, in addition to the test of the algorithm, a qualitative attention to be paid to the play of differentiated *force* that sutures itself onto the reasoning as soon as it is a matter of an act properly speaking.

Better yet, I must conceive of the subject—we have been saying this from the start—as the result of a purification of force in the tension to resolve the algorithm.

Subjectivization operates according to the element of force by which the place (the conclusion I draw from R3) finds itself altered.

The story unfolds in the way Lacan says only under the hypothesis of a field of possible neighbourhoods that, by diffusing a qualitative certainty throughout the algorithm, forces the periodization of the subjective process—the suspended time.

Whence arises this immanent topology, which comes to interrupt an algorithm that without it would unerringly lead to its mechanical and true consequence? From the fact that the splace is always *already* the locus of the subjective.

By supposing that the other stands in a position of a possible difference of force, I subordinate my experience to the notion that every occupation of a place restores the law on the basis of the outplace.

The mark of this difference of intellectual force would be my salvation if the prison ward freed me at the end of my victorious and reasonable exit. But this difference must structure the entire field *from the start*, as the necessary concept of the subject, in order for my rivals' steps to take on the value of an alarm.

The subjective, in the differential of forces, always pre-exists itself.

That subject that I come to be in certainty is something I could only anticipate, based on its supposedly being already there, through the evaluation of the other. And I can ground that subject retroactively only insofar as, through the effects of haste, it gains mastery, in its very place, over the contradiction of forces.

2

In the end, I read haste as the interference of a topology in an algebra. The subject is consistent for having situated its cause in the element of disorder as much as in that of order.

For a knucklehead is a disorder in reasoning, no?

As Mao says: 'Disturbances are an excellent thing.'[5] We should understand that therein lies the secret of consistency.

However, if haste cannot be inferred from the algorithm; if there exists no purely logical function of haste, as Lacan claims, due to the fact that its function is topological, then where should we situate its possibility?

If it is the other's step that urges me to be distrustful and that reminds me of the fact that he possesses perhaps *a different force* from mine, then it is actually because I did not think of this before, because I could not think of this.

How could I have, since the extent of my difference from the other, topologically constituted, does not fall under any stable temporal measure and always leaves me guessing when it comes to knowing whether the supposed knucklehead may not be about to get lost in the most straightforward premises?

During the first moment of my reasoning suspense, no conviction regarding the different forces involved serves any purpose, for lack of falling under some reasonable calculation of its inscription in duration.

It is thus fitting to take off as soon as I have completed R3, *so that the logic of the neighbourhoods is active only according to the steps of the other.*

We will posit that the logic of the neighbourhoods is inseparable from the real. Haste, which cannot be inferred from the symbolic, is the mode in which the subject exceeds the latter by exposing itself to the real.

First of all, the real of the other's motion, rather than accelerating me, makes me stop.

But, more crucially, the real defines the stake, that is, the subject itself *qua* free subject.

I hurry for the simple reason that being the first to exit is the only real that matters. The act takes precedence over the reasoning.

You see: in this primacy lies the whole secret of subjectivization. When the popular insurrection breaks out, it is never because the calculable moment of this insurrection has arrived. It is because it is no longer worth doing anything else except to insurrect. This is what Lenin said: there is revolution when 'those from below' do not want to continue as before, and when it is everywhere imposingly evident that it is worth more to die standing than to live lying down.[6]

Our anecdote reveals that it is the interruption of an algorithm, and not its execution, that has a subjectivizing effect.

As for the subjective process, it exists only in the recomposition of consequences in light of the interruption. It is never the pursuit of the algorithm, since the entrance of force onto the stage breaks with the law to which it owes the fact that it exists in its place.

So it is with the party, whose political consistency, put to the test of the mass uprising, is modified forever.

3

Haste is divisible.

I can exit, without giving any thought to the qualitative difference of the other, because the real subjects me to an intolerable pressure and because the space of topological mastery is null. My passion to be free leads me to trust only the shortest algorithm, without tolerating any interruption.

Here is how it looks: because the real overwhelms me, in the guise of the vital importance of the stakes involved, I exclusively call upon the law, which fails to sustain me to the end.

If I short-circuit the ambiguous message of the other's departure, in order to run with a heaving chest toward the door, without evaluating this message's divisible significance, I no doubt subjectivize but purely according to the effect of a stiffened and lifeless algebra. I cling to R3, without considering the logic of the neighbourhoods.

From a different perspective, what we obtain here is anxiety, whose major concept we already have introduced.

The correlated subjective process represents the prison warden as the key to my very being. It is toward him that I run recklessly to beg for my release. If the knucklehead reasoned according to R2, there would be a sombre truth to it if he were to put me back in the hole.

Anxiety—subjectivization—calls upon the superego—the subjective process.

There is another side to haste, which finds support in a strategic anticipation without having managed to reach a well-grounded certainty. I take a moment's advance, by a wager on the real.

If, for example, I think as a good topologist that my competitors are more or less my peers, the only way to get away is by *not waiting* for the end of the reasoning, which they would otherwise accomplish at the same time as I. The possible undecidability of the outcome is what I calculate must be broken, through an essential subjective confidence in the fact that I will complete the reasoning in front of the prison director.

After all, that's the only thing that counts.

Victory belongs to the one who gains the upper hand by thinking on the go.

We have already encountered this sudden balancing movement by which I expose myself to the real without resorting to the immobile temporality of the law: its name is courage.

The two generic forms of subjectivization are anxiety and courage.

Notice that the act is the same. Haste is the form of the One for the scission courage/anxiety. But the subjective modes are opposed, insofar as one blocks a rigid law under the effect of too-much-of-the-real, whereas the other bets on the real under the effect of an anticipated calculation.

As for the prison warden, in the case of courageous subjectivization, it is not from him that I expect any salvation. I propose, rather, that my excess over all calculation, wagered by a bet on the real, subjects the law to itself. Confidence allows me to relate to myself in the conviction that, in the long run, the subjective process will recompose a world in which the law must wither.

Courage appeals to justice.

Thus, the double subjectivizing occurrence receives its names, as well as its connection to the double identity of the subjective process.

There are four fundamental concepts (anxiety, courage, justice, superego), two temporalities (subjectivization, subjective process), and two modalities: the mode ψ, which links anxiety to the superego, and the mode α, which links courage to justice.

As the topological upheaval of an algebra, the subject accomplishes itself in the act of dividing the mode ψ and the mode α.

The inexistent

May 8, 1978

Cumulative definitions of the subject—Cantor's theorem and the
regulation of nationalities—Prescription of the empty place

1

A subject is such that, subservient to the rule that determines a place, it
nevertheless punctuates the latter with the interruption of its effect.

Its subjectivizing essence lies in this very interruption, by which the
place, where the rule is deregulated, consists in destruction.

A subject is equally the process of recomposing, from the point of the
interruption, another place and other rules.

The subject is subjected, insofar as nothing is thinkable under this name
except a regulated place—a splace. And also inasmuch as what the subject
destroys is at the same time that which determines it in its being placed.

The fact that the subjective process occurs from the point of the interruption indicates the law of the subject as the dialectical division of
destruction and recomposition.

This is what guarantees that the subjective process in part escapes
repetition. The effect of the Same is destroyed, and what this destruction
institutes is an *other Same*.

The topology alone is capable of measuring the fact that one consistency
comes after another, in the causal ordering of the interruption.

The subject materializes the division of materialism, insofar as it cannot
be conceived without the support of an algorithm overdetermined and

confounded by the subjectivizing anticipations and the retroactions of the subjective process.

2

A subject is that element of an algebra from which the law of composition that determines it becomes open to chance.

As the power of the rabble always asserts: 'We can never know what these people are thinking.'

I know some ex-colonialists who were haunted by the regulated calmness of their servant, his perfect and smooth belonging to the racist system of servitude. They could not stop—and rightly so—being convinced that, at the first signal, that is at the first effect of vicinity, this affable man, this excellent cook, this child-lover, would unload right on their chest the scrap metal of an old gun usually reserved for Mister's morning hunt (besides, the little devil was diligent enough to bring the game and the snack to the occasion).

This is the old colonial subjective theorem of the impassiveness of the Chinese.

The topological disturbance of an algebra is the precise name for these fears whose roots lie in the extreme algebraicization of the splace.

All this still gives you only the *causal* location. The subject exists only insofar as that which perturbs comes to put its own order on another place.

'Great disorder under heaven creates great order under heaven': Mao was very fond of this proverb.[7] The support of this engendering is the subject-effect as such. A subject is engendered when the uprising gains access to the consistency of the war of liberation, and the aleatory of the place becomes articulated upon the differential of force.

You have four lemmas:

1. A subject stands in the algebraic position of internal exclusion. Even though it can be assigned to the law, it focalizes the interruption of the latter's effect.
2. A subject stands in a position of topological excess over the place. Even though it belongs, as a singular term, to the splace, it co-adheres, as a collectivizing term, to a series of neighbourhoods that blur the places.

3. A subject is destruction/recomposition, for there is never a nonplace.[8] The excess over the place dictates a re-placement.
4. Subjectivization designates the subject in the principal dimension of the interruption; the subjective process, in the dimension of the recomposition.

3

The crucial point is to understand the topological concept of excess. As far as the (algebraic) internal exclusion is concerned, we owe its concept to Lacan.

Both concepts present themselves at the same spot. Therein lies precisely the difficulty.

The theory of the subject is complete when it manages to think the structural law of the empty place as the punctual anchoring of the excess over the place.

The secret of this anchoring lies in the materialist-dialectical division of the very inexistent whose product is the existence of a whole.

Two concepts, and not one: this makes all the difference between the dialectical logic and the logic of the signifier.

Let us return, if you please, to the central example of the disjunction between algebra and topology: the excess of parts over elements, that is, Cantor's theorem.

A set E, considered as a whole, belongs to a type of multiplicity that the operations of set theory allow us to specify and that they call the cardinality of this same set, Card (E). Grosso modo, 'a set F has "more" elements than a set E' is written as follows: Card (E) $<$ Card (F).

Cantor's theorem comes down to this: The cardinality of the set of parts of E is always superior to the cardinality of E itself.

Let us consider the type of multiplicity of E, Card (E), as a law of the multiple. Let us say for instance that it is forbidden that a multiplicity be greater than the one that results from belonging to E:

$$\sim (\exists F) \; [\text{Card (E)} < \text{Card (F)}]$$

By the effects of pure logic, $\sim (\exists F) \; [\text{Card (E)} < \text{Card (F)}]$ can also be written as follows: $(\forall F) \; [\text{Card (F)} \leq \text{Card (E)}]$, which is the inscription of the fact that all cardinality is limited by that of E.

What you have here is the dialectical division of the whole, *depending on whether you link it onto the universal* ($\forall$ F) *or onto the inexistential* ($\sim$ ($\exists$ F)).

If, in formal logic, ($\forall$ x) (P (x)), all x is P, and $\sim$ ($\exists$ x) $\sim$ P (x), no x is not P, are equivalent, then the logic of the signifier establishes itself in the gap in writing this equivalence, which is where the dialectical logic follows it most willingly.

Lacan draws from this double linkage the formal logic of the sexes. Man on the side of 'for all x, this'; women on the side of 'there exists no x such that not this'. Which implies that 'the' woman, indeed, inexists in the whole.[9]

Hegel already declared this: Woman is the irony of the community.

On all this, read Lacan's 'L'étourdit' (*Scilicet* 4) and the crucial exegesis by Jean-Claude Milner (*L'Amour de la langue*, Le Seuil).

Notice, as is only fitting, that the universality of the proletariat postulates both and at the same time that a certain form of politics is valid *for all* (the emancipation from class will be the emancipation of all of humanity) and that this politics, which is communist, is the inexistent that is proper to the political *Whole*, which has meaning only from the point of the State.

'The' communist politics does not exist. There will only ever exist communist parties.

There was something irreducibly masculine about the Third International.

By positing that ($\forall$ F) [Card (F) $\leq$ Card (E)], we make E into a splace.

Consider that this is what a State decides through its regulations regarding nationality. The fact of belonging to the nation-state, which is algebraically codified by these regulations, fixes the type of multiplicity of the French: prohibited to designate as 'French' any superior multiplicity. The immigrant workers, for example, though empirically internal to this essential component of the whole that is the productive class, remain those without-rights in the national multiple. By holding them to be politically internal to this multiple, through the concept of 'the international proletariat of France',

- you interrupt the national law;
- you destroy a stronghold in the imperialist consensus, which knows only 'immigrants';
- you recompose a different rule for the multiplicity; for instance, whoever works, or whoever practises the politics of revolution, has the rights that are attached to being a member of the nation.

From this it follows that the immigrated workers are at the centre of the current process of political subjectivity, and that the political unity of the French and the immigrants, in its enactment, is its crucial point of subjectivization.

The immigrant proletarians are the inexistent proper to the national totality.

Our abstract splace E also has its inexistent: the type of multiplicity that is immediately superior, the set F which would contain E and which would nevertheless be its *successor* in the ascending order of cardinalities. This superior limit is properly speaking that of which the law forbids the existence: it is the immediate null-object of the law.

Among us, this is taken care of by the laws and practices of expulsion against immigrants, which remind the latter at all times of the prohibition of interiority within the national multiple, and thus of the impossibility, with regards to the whole, of a multinational composition of the nation.

How should we conceive of the legal inexistent that limits the whole? It is, in the first place, the place of the empty cardinality prescribed by the law that distributes and closes the places of possible cardinalities. Beyond Card (E), the rule states, there is *nothing*. This nothing is placed by the splace as the clause of its closure. It is the conceptless limit point that guarantees the splace its firmness in terms of the multiple.

Lacan and Milner are very clear about this. All totality requires that there in-exists at least one term which is not of the Whole, which does not belong to it. This impossible belonging sets the empty frontier of the Whole. It inexists with regard to the Whole, but it also ex-sists, in the extent that it is designated as the impossibility from which the possibility of every being of the Whole derives its rule.

Our society—imperialist society—is defined as a whole by the declaration that immigrant workers are not of this society, that it is impossible that they ever be.

This existential marking of the boundary by way of the empty place organizes the algebraic place of the out-place.

The rebellious demand of the immigrants, at this stage, has a name: 'Equal rights'.

It is a matter of occupying *the* unoccupyable place.

Here we have the first concept of the inexistent as the subjective polarity for the interruption of the law and the destruction of the whole. It is the *forced* occupation of the unoccupyable place.

A protest struggle in which the immigrants, represented as a particular social force, demand the same political rights as the French, forces the inexistent whose national multiplicity determines its closure as imperialist, that is, it forces the immanent popular internationalism.

Similarly, if I posit that there exists a cardinal immediately superior to Card (E), I detotalize, by occupying the empty place, the cardinality of E splaced as the maximum cardinality. Henceforth, it is only one cardinality among others, in the new closure marked by Card * (E), the cardinality that *succeeds* Card (E).

Whatever the $\sim$ ($\exists$ F) of the law created in terms of the void now finds itself filled.

In all cases, the subject proceeds from a subjectivization by forcing the empty place, which a new order grounds retroactively *qua* place, by having occupied it. Multinational people and cardinal successor are the process anticipated by the forced existence of the inexistent.

Any splace is thus the after-effect or *après-coup* of the destruction of another.

Subjectivization is the anticipation whose structure is the empty place; the subjective process, the retroaction that places the forcing.

The subject *is* the splace, as that which has become, through the inexistent, from what has been destroyed.

Logic of the excess

May 15, 1978

That the immigrants, aside from the empty place, induce
neighbourhoods everywhere—Cantor once more—The continuum
hypothesis as desire for algebra—The constructible (Gödel) and the
generic (Cohen)—The incalculable impact of the gesture of the dice
thrower

1

Is this all? In matters of the subject, is the inexistent all that exists?

What we have neglected is considerable. Are those immigrant workers
determined in their being by the recourse to the empty place alone? If we
want to define the angle by which they touch upon the political subject,
does it suffice to say that they stand in internal exclusion to French
society? On that account, the unity of the French and immigrants would
be limited to the show of solidarity granted by a few reasonable have-
rights to the rebellious without-rights. It is the feeble unionist politics of
'support' for a social force.

From the point of their practical immanence within the class
struggle, there is more, much more. The topology of the revolt of
immigrant workers qualitatively disrupts all the political neighbourhoods. Those who undergo the most important modification are not so
much the immigrant workers themselves, even if they snatch up the
right to vote, so much as the French: the French workers for whom
the subversion of their national identity, provided they are swept up

in the process, subjectivizes another vision and another practice of politics.

The political construction of a multinational class unity defines a topology that exceeds from within the law of imperialist society and that by no means can be reduced to the forcing of the empty place, or to provoking the failure of the laws of prohibition and the practices of expulsion that are part of the nation's regulations concerning citizenship, even if this forcing and this failure mark an obligatory tactical scansion.

There exists a recourse of excess which is immanent to the whole, and of which the occupation of the unoccupyable place is only the structural constraint, or the prescribed occasion.

Set theory gives us the abstract scheme of this scission of force.

If you posit that Card (E) is the maximum cardinality, you will certainly obtain the structural resources to pinpoint the empty place of its successor. But already E holds within itself the excess over this prohibition, since Cantor demonstrates that the set of the parts of E has a cardinality that is superior to that of E.

Conceived topologically, by the inclusion of its parts, E destroys the totalizing law of the maximum of multiplicity that it is supposed to be.

Now it so happens that the desire of the mathematician—and Cantor's desire to begin with—can guide us toward the recognition of the dialectical stakes that are involved in this.

Those who want to *limit* the revolt of the immigrants to the subjective element of trade unionism declare that the equality of rights, that is, the occupation of the unoccupyable place, is all that the action is about. They neglect the real of the neighbourhoods; they restrict the alterity of the Same to its algebraic filiations.

Mathematicians, though often mad, feel the pressure of the sword of order against their back. They would like to be able to posit that the immanent excess of multiplicity, which is that of the set of parts of a set, falls squarely in the empty place of its upper limit. In short, they would like to posit that the cardinality of the partitioned is exactly the successor of the elementary cardinality. That is, if P(E) indicates the set of the parts of E, and Card * (E), the first type of multiplicity superior to E, they would like to posit the following: Card P(E) = Card * (E).

This is the famous generalized continuum hypothesis, the primordial concern of specialists in set theory, for whose impossible demonstration Cantor used up his final years.

What is at issue is nothing less than the fusion of algebra (ordered succession of cardinals) and topology (excess of the partial over the elementary). The truth of the continuum hypothesis would make it a law that the excess within the multiple have no allocation other than the occupation of the empty place, or the existence of the inexistent proper to the initial multiple. This would maintain the filiations of coherence, in the sense that what exceeds the whole from within goes no further than to name the limit point of this whole.

But the continuum hypothesis cannot be demonstrated.

Mathematical triumph of politics over the unionist logic of realism.

2

Where do we stand?

In 1939, Gödel demonstrates that the continuum hypothesis is consistent with the axioms of set theory. If we want, we can add it to these axioms.

For the sake of this reassuring demonstration, Gödel uses a model that is internal to set theory, the class of *constructible* sets. This signifier is exemplary. It indicates to what point the aim is to obtain an operational mastery over the resources of multiplicity, to infer through procedures of ordered expansion the stage-by-stage construction of ever more complex sets. The potential anarchy of the excess of the parts is thus subdued, at the cost, it is true, of an extreme limitation of the set-theoretical resources. Gödel's model is characterized by an extreme narrowness of the multiple.

Logicians show great lucidity about this. Consider K. J. Devlin (in *Handbook of Mathematical Logic*):

(. . .) the notion of the power set of an infinite set is too vague; we know that P(x), the power set of x, consists of *all* subsets of x—but what does *all* mean here? The axioms of ZF [Zermelo-Fraenkel] and ZFC [Zermelo-Fraenkel plus the axiom of choice] do not help us much. The *constructible universe* is obtained when this looseness is removed by taking the power set of any set as small as possible, without contradicting the ZF axioms. More precisely, we notice that any subset of a given set which is first-order definable (. . .) from other given sets must 'exist' (in any 'universe') if the given sets 'exist,' and define the constructible hierarchy (with the constructible universe as its limit) by taking, at stage α, not *all* (?) subsets of what we have so far, but only those subsets which are first-order definable from what we have so far. This *minimality* of the constructible universe has the result that for any cardinal k, 2^k [the cardinality of the set of parts of k] is as small as possible (hence the GCH [Generalized Continuum Hypothesis] holds in the constructible universe). (HML 454, version adapted in accordance with Badiou's translation)

This text clearly proposes to put some order in the partitioning of the multiple. The fact that, for Devlin, the notion of 'all' the subsets of E is 'too vague' denotes his perplexity in the face of the unassignable resources of excess. The proposed path consists in keeping in existence only that whose definition, from within the whole, is explicit according to this whole itself.

The fact that one ends up in minimality shows what it is that he turns away from.

Long before the ecologists with their flourishing beards, the logicians posit that, in the face of the 'vague' spillages of topology, it is appropriate to proclaim: '*Small is beautiful*'.

Smallness is hierarchy: the constructible universe is built in strata in such a way that each stratum contains only objects that can be defined canonically on the basis of the preceding strata. Of course, the object to watch over is the one in which the excess is rooted, that is, the part carved out in the whole. Gödel's construction entails a veritable domestication of admissible parts—or of admissible parties. . . . One proceeds by way of an algebraic rarefaction of what is tolerated in terms of the subsets of a given multiplicity.

Let us simplify, so as to penetrate the antidialectical essence of the proof in question.

Given a set of sets, M, a part of M, say X, is declared definable in M if there exists a statement with a single variable, φ (x, a, b, c . . .), where a, b, c . . . are sets of M that are already defined, a statement such that the elements of X are the only ones to satisfy, in M, this statement.

Put differently, X is that subset of M such that an explicit statement, built according to the parameters that belong only to M, describes a property common to all its elements and to these alone. Such a statement characterizes X. M, so to speak, controls linguistically its part X. It detains its *formula*.

From there, you will pass from one set-theoretical stratum to another through an ordinal enumeration in a recurrent structure.

Broadly speaking, each stratum will allow all the parts from the preceding stratum that are definable according to the latter ('definable' in the rigorous sense used before). We can phrase this point in a definition of transfinite recurrence whose first term is the empty or null set.

Subsequently, you will accept only those sets that belong to a determinate stratum.

The constructible universe that is built in this way proceeds by stages in imposing the self-limitation of immanent multiplicities, whose formula must be able to be given according to the parameters of the whole.

One could for example demand that any political organization be definable based on the exclusive parameters of parliamentarism (participation in elections, clear classification 'on the right' and 'on the left', and so on) and that any worker's group be able to inscribe itself in a unionist formula. Besides, this is exactly what tends to be done. The notions of the extraparliamentary and of autonomy are quickly criminalized. The dominant political universe that is our own, no doubt, seeks to remain constructible.

In this universe, the excess of the multiple is ultimately reduced to whatever the algebra of it tolerates: it fits *just* under the concept of the inexistent that delimits the whole. In this way, the continuum hypothesis is satisfied.

The price to be paid for this is an extraordinary poverty of the multiple, as shown in the dismal spectacle of parliamentary elections and of asthmatic crowds that bless us with the gift of their personality during the 'meetings' of the major unions.

Indeed, the algebraic encoding of the excess, which submits it to an ordered enumeration, reduces what is subjectively too-much to what for this order is too-little.

Whatever a place holds virtually in terms of subjectivization, once it is realigned exclusively onto the empty point of its boundary, falls back on the equilibrium between place and excess, which does nothing more than repeat the fact that a place has the power of being the place of the subjective, without the qualitative break by which the subject-effect in a torsion escapes the local measure.

A truly astonishing theorem (Rowbottom) stages the force of interdiction by which constructibility mutilates the multiple.

In order to grasp its significance, we must understand that Gödel's outcome does not at all satisfy the regular mathematician. What the latter wants is for the doctrine of multiplicities to prescribe the continuum hypothesis as a necessary result, and not as an allowable supplement.

His or her goal is not the hollow freedom to add or not the continuum hypothesis to the axioms of set theory.

The underlying idea is that it is not possible to make an axiom of the identity between the excess and the occupation of the empty place. What is needed is for the real to impose on us *the impossibility for it to be otherwise*. If not, the integral dialectic prevails: there is some heterogeneity between the logic of succession among the empty places and the interior excess of the multiple.

Similarly, the trade unionists who defend the idea of 'supporting' the social force of immigrants, in order somehow to regularize the latter's status within imperialist society, want history to impose their solution as the only political solution imaginable. For them what is at stake is the simple, metaphysical, and atemporal nature of class, whose status defines their ideology of belonging.

One therefore searches for a way to curb the continuum hypothesis by reshuffling the axioms. For example, by formulating hypotheses regarding the plausible existence of gigantic cardinalities. It is a question of somehow bringing the excess in line, no longer from below, through inferior strata as in the constructible universe, but from above, by admitting straightaway certain pre-eminent multiplicities that are expected to order everything that precedes them.

Along this path, comparable to the nationalist, war-mongering, imperialist 'grand designs' by which the bourgeoisies seek to light the backfire of crises and popular upsurges, nothing worthwhile has been found.

Rather, it became possible to measure in what sense the control 'from below', the Gödelian constructibility, supported none of the vast existential hypotheses, due to the intrinsic poverty of its resources in terms of multiplicities.

If there exist 'very large' cardinalities (the technical definition of which I cannot get into here), there necessarily exist innumerable sets that are not constructible.

The pressure from above and that from below are incompatible. You cannot both and at the same time show off the syndicalist euphoria for negotiating the imperialist expansion in times of peace and indoctrinate the people in the risk of war and the shady appeal of conquests.

Rowbottom demonstrates that if there exists a certain species of cardinality—a 'very large' type of multiplicity—then there are, among the parts of the modest set of whole numbers (the smallest infinite set) many more that are nonconstructible than constructible.[10]

This goes to show the extent to which to posit any set as constructible, which is Gödel's path to establish the consistency of the continuum hypothesis, means to castrate the immanent power of the multiple and to strike those multiplicities that are too ambitious with the stamp of interdiction.

3

In 1963, Cohen demonstrates that the negation of the continuum hypothesis is as consistent with the axioms of set theory as its affirmation.

The 'disorder on earth' installs itself by way of demonstration.

Most amazingly, in order to build his model in which the algebraic regulation of excess comes to falter, Cohen uses a technique to which he gives the name of 'forcing': blind intuition of the fact that, at the point where the rule of succession no longer applies, what is at issue is the subjectivizing force.

Cohen's model is built along paths that are diametrically opposed to those of Gödel. We can hardly provide an idea of it, if for no other reason than that no intuition matches this model. This is a symptom of the fact that it bespeaks the excess.

In order to explore its detours, the reader will refer to the chapter by J. P. Burgess on *forcing* in *Handbook of Mathematical Logic* (404–52).

It is by the 'imaginary' extension of a stable primitive model (*ground model*) that we obtain the wherewithal to unlimit the partitive resources of the multiple.

The function of the excess of this added 'imaginary' set as an inductor can be glanced from its name: generic set.

And, certainly, any subject brings about the divided unity of the generic and the constructible.

The generic supplement is only *minimally* described. This is key: the weakest possible mastery of the language of the whole over that which is expected to make it proliferate. As Cohen himself says: 'In the present case we are starting with a single symbol for the set a and wish, in some sense, to give the least possible information about it.'[11]

Gödel, by contrast, requires at each stage the *maximum* descriptive capacity, since he retains only those parts of which an explicit formula provides a singular property.

In order to keep the information as scarce as possible, Cohen replaces the properties of implication (if p, then q) with the more evasive property of *forcing*: if there is such or such a condition, then the statement q is 'forced' to be the case.

A condition is in fact only an element of the generic set. The information that allows us to situate the extension as the theory's model can be summed up by saying that the belonging of an element to the added 'imaginary' set forces such or such a property of this extension.

A typical example of this evasive logic, or of the systematic under-information sought after by Cohen, can be found in the preferential treatment given to the universal quantifier over the existential one.

Why? Because if I have a statement of the type $(\exists x) (P(x))$, its truth according to the model requires that I designate a precise element a of this model such that P(a) is satisfied in it. This precision runs counter to the generic inspiration, which aims to distinguish as little as possible within the resources of the excess.

In this regard the generic essentially resembles the topological, which, as we established, disidentifies the element in favour of its neighbourhoods.

It follows that 'when faced with $\exists x B(x)$, we should choose to have it false, unless we have already a symbol x for which we have strong reason to insist that B(x) be true'.[12]

Sartre has many times over asserted that the relation of the intellectual to the revolution lies in his or her universalizing function. He is right about this. The excess, which is the topological law of subjectivization, induces a primacy of the universal over that which, from the existential, produced whatever was distinguishable in the old world.

Political force, once it is let loose, no longer distinguishes *as before*. Therein lies its communitarian virtue—its generic virtue.

Likewise, it no longer prescribes the same negative space. It transmutes the old law of oppositions (parliamentary ones, for example). It teaches us to say 'no' differently.

At this point we still have to break with the deterministic effects of implication.

That p implies non-q means purely and simply, in the classical logic of propositions, that p and q cannot be true at the same time. If p is true, then q must be false. The implication of a negation denotes the incompatibility of two statements. In this sense, the truth of p strictly determines that q not be true.

By contrast, in the logic of forcing, that p forces non-q means that there exists no condition that is stronger than p and that forces q. It is from the point of an inexistent relative to the statement p that the forcing of non-q is determined.

What is a 'stronger' condition? Even if Cohen defines it strictly in terms of a relation of order, we can interpret it as a condition that gives 'more information' than the initial one, or again, a condition that is more restrictive as to the characteristics of the generic model.

We will thus hold that p forces the negation of q if there is no condition, known to contain more information than p, which forces q itself. The statement q finds itself, so to speak, freed with regard to the conditions that are stronger than p.

Thus, the forcing of the negative—of non-q—as opposed to the incompatibility induced by its implication, is the result of the fact that nothing in that which locates and encompasses the condition p forces the truth of q.

Conceived of as a break, subjectivization certainly operates within a logic of forcing. The 'No!' of the revolt is not implied by the local conditions. It is forced by the inexistence of an absolute constraint that would force submission to the immediate conditions in a transcendent way.

Between formal implication and forcing there lies all the ambivalence that the dialectic introduces in the old problem of determinism.

The subject's surrection is the effect of force within the place. *This does not mean that the place implies it.*

The generic extension obtained by way of forcing, to which the added imaginary set subjects everything that can be stated about it, allows the production of an impressive quantity of new sets.

In fact, we can produce as many sets as we like. The resources of the topological turn out to be unlimited.

We thus demonstrate that the cardinality of the set of parts of a set is literally free-floating. It surpasses the cardinality of the initial set with an arbitrary quantity. It can be the successor (as Gödel shows), the successor of the successor, or it can find itself further down still in the series of cardinalities, and finally (this is the theorem of Easton), more or less as far down as one wants.

Thus, the inner resource of a set, taken in its parts, is not regulated by any numerical legitimacy. It can go past everything that one purports to assign to it as its boundary. The logic of the excess is *real*, insofar as it is impossible to limit it.

This is the reason why a minor nation, provided it counts on its own forces, can vanquish a great power (Mao). Except that it still needs the political concentration of its social parts, that is, a party.

Of such a party, the cardinality—the force: mathematicians have had the foresight to name 'power' the cardinality of a set—surpasses everything that one thinks might be expected from it.

Notice that Cohen, breaking with the old ordinal chain of the mathematician's desire, ends up converting to the superpower of immanent excess:

> A point of view which the author feels may eventually come to be accepted is that CH [the continuum hypothesis] is *obviously* false. [. . .] Now $\aleph_1$ is the set of countable ordinals and this is merely a special and the simplest way of generating a higher cardinal. The set C [the continuum] is, in contrast, generated by a totally new and more powerful principle, namely the Power Set Axiom. [. . .] This point of view regards C [the continuum] as an incredibly rich set given to us by one bold new axiom, which can never be approached by any piecemeal process of construction.[13]

What Cohen here recognizes is that between the logic of places and that of excess, there is a dialectical break.

Thus, the excess finds itself removed from any numeral allegiance. The subject, in its double register of algorithm and neighbourhood, effectuates an irreconcilable scission of its own process. We welcome those 'vicinities of the vague' in which the partitive multiplicity is dissolved, considering them to be the proof, administered by those who would desire the exact opposite, that there is a wager on the real. If, in this wager, the number inscribed on the dice is the result of a consecution, it cannot link up into a chain that which, in the thrower's gesture, produces the incalculability of its reach.[14]

Part VI

Topics of Ethics

Where?

Ten theses on the subject—Donation and limitation—Hysteria, riot—
Where is the proletariat?—Where is the unconscious?—Mathemes of
Marxism—Toward the topics

1

If I concentrate the present stage of our trajectory in ten theses on my
subject—the subject—I must enumerate them as follows:

1. The subject-effect is the split articulation of a structural vacillation
   around an empty place and a forced excess over this place.
2. From a materialist point of view, the subject-effect offers up to knowledge both the algebra of its placement and the topology of its forcing.
   It insists on being caused by that which disappears from its place and
   consists in the neighbourhoods of its cause.
3. I call subjectivization the interruption of the vacillation by the excess.
   It is a destruction.
4. I call subjective process the putting back into place of the excess into
   a splace centred on the excess itself. It is a recomposition.
5. The subject-effect is only the divisible unity of subjectivization and the
   subjective process. Each of these moments is abstract. It is not acceptable to speak of the subject except in light of a process of destruction-
   recomposition, which in turn is referred, in a second articulation, to
   the dialectic of lack and excess.

6. From the crossing of the two divided articulations it follows that subjectivization is split into anxiety and courage.

7. From the same principle it follows that the subjective process owes its unity to the twoness of justice and the superego.

8. The subject-effect is integrally designated in the topology of the four concepts: anxiety, courage, justice, and superego.

9. The topology makes a knot out of two pairs: anxiety-superego designates the effect-ψ; courage-justice, the effect-α. It is inappropriate to speak of the subject except in light of a process whose division produces the oneness of ψ and α.

10. A subject is nowhere given (to knowledge). It must be found.

2

I would like to draw attention to the tenth thesis, which concentrates the post-Cartesian nature of our endeavour.

Throughout the great classical tradition of idealism, the subject designates that transparent point of being, in a position of immediate self-donation, through which all access to existence as such must pass. All evidence, even if turns out to be void, is determined based upon the subject. Here you will recognize the formal function of the cogito. In Kant's optic, in which the subject constitutes the condition of possibility of experience without itself being experienced, there remains the evidence of morality, where we find the significance of the subject's ontological transparency.

The classical subject is thus an operator endowed with a double function. On one hand, it assignates an irreducible being of the existent; on the other, it limits that which, from the 'remainder' of being, is accessible to knowledge. It partitions that which is *immediately* given and that which is *mediately* refused to experience.

Brought to their peak, these two functions appear to be inverted. The being of the subjective existent proves to be a being of nonbeing. This is Sartre's thesis. The limit of knowledge proves to be an unlimitation. This is Hegel's thesis.

This inversion, however, is not real. The nonbeing of Sartre's free consciousness is in reality the name of its transparency. We would still be saying too much if we posited that what gives itself in transparency *is*. Consciousness is transparency of its transparency, consciousness (of) self, 'nonpositional in itself'. That such a being is nothing indicates from whence an ontology is possible, namely, from the cogito alone, which gives us *the nothing*, that is, existence in its essence.

The unlimitation of Hegelian knowledge (absolute knowledge) must include a principle of totality, the 'circle of circles' of its exhaustion, by which it limits the unlimited, conferring upon it that encyclopaedic form that one book can write in its entirety. Now, for us Cantorians, the notion that there is a whole of knowledge falls short of true unlimitation, which is the immanent movement of the excess over all conceivable totality.

The double—existential and limiting—function thus marks the classical concept of the subject throughout. It is the ground on which such a subject can be the point of *departure*.

I hold that in reality we can only *arrive* at the subject. This is what marks the time of Marx and of Freud, namely, that the subject is not given but must be found.

The importance of the configuration sketched out by Marxism in politics and by Freudianism in philosophy nevertheless consists in not giving up on the subjective element. Even though the subject is neither a transparency, nor a centre, nor finally a substance, and even though nothing attests to its necessity for the organization of experience, it nevertheless remains the case that it is the key concept from which it turns out that we can think the decision, ethics, and politics.

For each stage of Marxism (there are three) and of Freudianism (there are two), we have to solve the specific problem of the investigative operators that put into effect the discovery and grasping of the subject.

When Marx takes it upon himself to listen to the revolutionary activity of his time, to the popular historical disorder, it is a matter of pinpointing in the latter, pursuant to harsh theoretical and practical work, the dialectical form of the political subject as such. The *deduction* of its general activity presupposes only the riots of the nineteenth century. From here, it will then be necessary to unfold the complete topology of an order (the capitalist order), to develop the logic of its gaps, and to take the heterogeneous all the way to the end, in order to *name* 'proletariat' that subject which is almost not to be found on the anarchic surface of the events.

Freud listens to the hysterics' prose and body language, from which it emerges that in the end what is at issue is the subject of neurosis as such, and not who is subject to neurosis. 'Unconscious' is the name of such a subject, here too trapped in a topology, namely, that of psychic life.

Even though psychoanalysis and Marxism have nothing to do with one another—the totality they would form is inconsistent—it is beyond doubt that Freud's unconscious and Marx's proletariat have the same episte-mological status with regard to the break they introduce in the dominant conception of the subject.

'Where' is the unconscious? 'Where' is the proletariat? These questions have no chance of being solved either by an empirical designation or by the transparency of a reflection. They require the dry and enlightened labour of analysis and of politics.

Enlightened and also organized, into concepts as much as into institutions.

The only surface effect that begins to put us on the tracks of the subject (one sees this clearly in political riots as much in the hysteric's theatre) is the existence, already under the presupposition of a clarified materialism, of one *true statement* whose disposition perturbs the algebra of truth.

The subject is neither cause nor ground. It holds out in what it polarizes, and supports the effect of preceding itself in the splace: always invisible in the excess of its visibility.

3

We can never repeat enough that the texts of Marxism are first and fore-most those of militant politics. The sign of this essentiality is an urgent, phosphorescent writing, at the juncture of inscription and subjective haste. It is there, upon exiting the allegory of the prisoners, that one thinks on the go. I am of the same opinion as Julien Gracq (in parenthesis, together with Samuel Beckett, the extreme end-point of contemporary prose, if it is not the case that the former brings Chateaubriand to a close, and the latter, Pascal):

> I reread *The Class Struggles in France* and *The Eighteenth Brumaire* with an admiration and even a joy without any admixtures. Nothing comes close to the high tone and the sharpness of the trait—that from beginning to end and almost effortlessly traverses these texts—to the ferocious and buoyant cheerfulness of Marx the journalist [. . .] this revolutionary jubilation that has exclusively befallen only the very greatest—a kind of state of grace, a *gaya scienza* of the apocalypse [. . .].[1]

And the rest? The elephant that is capital? This is the hard surface of concrete on which the real match is played. Do not mistake the asphalt for Borg's game. That the same man, Marx, can be the engineer of asphalt and the champion at the net heralds the times that are to come for the polyvalent worker.

It is with great swiftness that you can find the decipherment of the political subject when Marx, Lenin or Mao, exposing themselves to the destructive real of the symptoms of history, follow a chain until they obtain the in-between of two links.

By the first, read *The Class Struggles in France*; by the second, 'The Crisis Has Matured'; and by the third, *Report on an Investigation of the Peasant Movement in Hunan*, or the strange directives during the Cultural Revolution. Typical example: 'According to my own observation I would say that, not in all factories, nor in an overwhelming majority of factories, but in quite a large majority of cases the leadership is not in the hands of true Marxists, nor yet in the hands of the masses of the workers', so that 'it seems essential that the Great Proletarian Cultural Revolution should still be carried out' (April 1969).[2] Or again, enigmatic and essential, in the year of his death (1976): 'You make the socialist revolution, and yet you do not know where the bourgeoisie is. It sits at the heart of the Communist Party.'[3]

A question of topology: Where is the bourgeoisie? But, more decisively: Where is the proletariat? Where is it, since in the place where it is algebraically prescribed (the party-State), it is the (new) bourgeoisie that is making itself comfortable?

There is not a single major text of Marxism that does not find its mainspring in the question: Where is the proletariat? It follows that politics is the unity of opposites of a topics (the current situation) and an ethics (our tasks).

In *The Class Struggles in France*, the movement to discover the subject works wonders as it is caught between the ferociousness of the polemic and the urgency of the intervention. Read, for example:

. . . while the struggle of the different socialist leaders among themselves sets forth each of the so-called systems as a pretentious adherence to one of the transit points of the social revolution as against another—the *proletariat* rallies more and more round *revolutionary Socialism*, round *Communism*, for which the bourgeoisie has itself invented the name of *Blanqui*. This Socialism is the *declaration of the permanence of the revolution*, the *class dictatorship* of the proletariat as the necessary transit point to the *abolition of class distinctions generally*, to the abolition of all the relations of production on which they rest, to the abolition of all the social relations that correspond to these relations of production, to the revolutionising of all the ideas that result from these social relations. (SW I, 282)

Here the positional extraction of the four fundamental concepts of Marxism is combined with the labour of their historical topology.

The four concepts are:

- the party (rallying of the proletariat) as advent of the historical One-One;
- the class struggle (permanent declaration of the revolution) as place of the subjective;
- the dictatorship of the proletariat as exercise focused on destruction;
- communism, not as a closed utopia but as the threefold process of economical, social, and cultural destruction-recomposition.

Naturally, if you consider that the (proletarian) subject is specified by its registering of communism under the law of its dictatorship and in the guise of the class struggle, you obtain this Z that we anticipated two years ago:

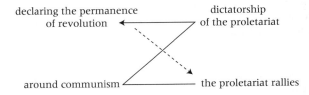

You have to admit that, put at the cross in this way, the sentence begins to 'fess up.

We are in a position to make it say even more, if we understand that the dictatorship of class is the superego modality of the subjective process, whose face of justice is communism. The word 'transition' has only an indicative value. As Mao repeats, without communist processus, there is no communism. And where is this processus concentrated if not in the 'transition' supposed to lead to it, and whose dictatorial terror supports the obverse of the restorationist law? Dictatorship of the proletariat and communism are *the same thing* (the subject-process of class politics) grasped in the scission of its identity into the superego and justice.

As for the 'permanent declaration of the revolution', it is not difficult to see how, to the uprising (June 1848: silent anxiety of the cornered workers), it adds the permanent courage of the revolution. The latter means subjectivization in the place of the class struggle. Whoever retains of it only courage forgets that it is situated at the same point as historical anxiety.

At least, that is, if there is a revolution, which is what any popular festival—of the surging, elegant, spring-like kind—is not, far from it.

Let us say that, in defiance of history, to declare the permanence of the revolution means to tear oneself away, at the heart of the real, from the mere provocation of its too-fullness.

It is when the bewildering riot lifts the ban of the law that to trace the direction of a commitment in the midst of its obtuse violence makes for the courage of a completed subjectivization.

It follows that the four apparent concepts (party, class struggle, dictatorship of the proletariat, communism) are organized into four different ones, *plus one*, the party, the subjective grouping, which is only the generic name for whatever the knot of the other four gives us to think:

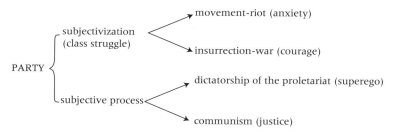

You can also classify the four concepts in the following manner:

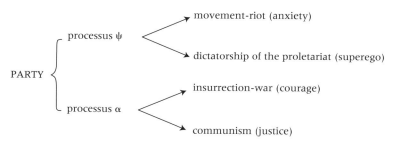

The passage from one of these diagrams to the other defines the whole question of the *discovery* of the subject.

This requires the superposition of two grids—the first one attentive to the dialectic of subjectivization/subjective process, which somehow follows the law of emergence of the subject-effect; the second, to the qualitative asymmetry within the subject, which enlaces the pulsional algebra of ψ—vanishing eclipse of the Same—and the recomposing topology of α—destruction-recomposition.

In the actual investigation, all of this derives from a movement among topologies.

We know that Freud accepts its rule. When he moves from the system unconscious-preconscious-conscious to the topography id-ego-superego, we ignore *where* to find the object that is identical to the two tables. This is because it is a matter of inducing, from one to the other, the correct position of the plus-one—the correct way of asking the question 'Where is the subject?'

Likewise, for Marx, when we move from party-class struggle-dictatorship of the proletariat-communism to things such as mode of production-relations of production-ideologies.

Where is the proletariat?

The secret of the subject is not contained *first* in one topology and *then* in another. It lies in the movement by which one blurs the other—thus re-producing the fact that a subject is the disturbance of an algebra.

The subjective twist: ψ and α

May 4, 1979

On the subject as undecidable—Hölderlin, half-way and setting
the second half on fire—Static of the *topos*—The body, the party—
Phenomenology of the four concepts

1

The subject-effect, in its formal principle, can in no way be reduced to a simple contradiction. Besides, this is the hidden reason behind the need for a topology in order to push for its theory. You must have at your disposal a network of concepts, of which 'subject' always designates the articulation, without being able to situate *within* this network the point subsumed under this term.

Whether it is a matter of the subject in the field of politics or of the subject of psychoanalysis, for these two orders—are there any others?—are those in which the question is the most developed, and despite the fact that apparently they put at our disposal two specified terms for the subjective—class in one case, the unconscious in the other—we always proceed in a way that is askew, by a theory of the splace (capital, the symbolic) in which we investigate, in a retroactive interference, the symptoms (revolt, neurosis) to which no justice can be done without situating the outplace.

We must therefore redouble the logic of the place with a logic of its interruption, a dialectic of failure, by leaning on the two slopes of materialism and having the wherewithal to think the divided regime of the occupation of places.

This is the main reason why Lacan, in a first moment, had to pin down the subject under the triple instance of the symbolic (law of the place), the imaginary (self-identity of the place) and the real (dispersion). Then, in a second moment, he had to saturate this order with a topological approximation, in certain regards without escape since the cutting (of the knot) failed really to dialecticize the lack (of the object).

Marxism approaches the subject-support of all politics (the party) on the basis of its three major concepts (class struggle, dictatorship of the proletariat, communism) whose intricate articulation defines, in Marx's own opinion (see his famous letter to Weydemeyer of March 1852), the very originality of his contribution.

As far as I am concerned, worried about ensuring the link of cause and consistency beyond the Lacanian setup, I posit that the subject-process is a contradiction of contradictions, the twisting of two processes of which one (ψ) subordinates the excess to the placement, and the other (α) inverts this order.

The impossibility to *decide* the dominant term, since the double domination imbricates two processes, is key to the theory of the subject.

The classical political debate comes down to asking the question: is it the *line* that is fundamental or the organization? This debate is in essence infinite, placing the 'correct line' in the mirror of the idea that 'the party is always right'. The core of the Maoist conception of politics posits that the construction of the party requires the mass line in matters of organization, that is: beyond the mass line *of* the party, it posits the mass line *over* the party. In doing so, it declares explicitly that the old debate is undecidable. In this regard, it puts into work the theory of the subject.

Without giving in anything at all to indeterminacy, we posit that the subject-process is resolved in the undecidable. The undecidable is the concept of its constitution.

We know since Gödel's famous theorem that to posit 'There is some undecidable' can be the result of a demonstration. This goes to show that there is a concept of the undecidable, and thus that we firmly tie the doctrine of the subject to the possibility of a calculation. We demonstrate the subject. The undecidable does not mean freedom. It is the immanent point of flight of any order whose necessity we determine at the crossover between two processes, ψ and α.

If liberty is foundational, the undecidable by contrast is inferred.

It is equally forbidden to think that between the two processes ψ

and α there exists an objective hierarchy. Neither excess nor lack has any intrinsic privilege, any more than subjectivization or the subjective process. I have polemicized against the reduction of the real to the sole figure of the causal object because it seemed to me that this Mallarméan acquisition, and the magnificent construction he drains around the vanishing term, took too much precedence over the dialectic of consistency. From this we should not draw the conclusion that the theory of the subject is thus re-centred (on the excess). There is no centre in the subjective twist. Without the anchorage of lack, the excess would be nothing but a leftist chimera, quickly reversed into its opposite: a philosophy of nature, as we see in the case of Deleuze.

Ethics, I will argue, is certainly not indifferent to the contrarian structure of the twist. It distinguishes between the strands. But it authorizes to decide only the following: there is some undecidable.

Ethics amounts to the maxim: 'Decide consequently form the point of the undecidable.'

We would be talking without saying anything, if the undecidable did not figure in a topology.

2

Hölderlin is the second great figure of the German dialectician. There where Hegel makes a circle, he produces a torsion.

Hegel deduces Prussia as a conceptual term from the State. It could be Napoleon, and Hegel toys with its equine idea (the man with the two-horned hat was passing underneath his windows).

For Hölderlin, Germany stands opposed to Greece. Its all-Kantian modernity consists in making something informal out of the formal, whereas the original Dionysians turned their 'Asiatic' fury into the unsurpassed form of the Temple. Germany is a nostalgia divisible into Greece and itself, rather than a single concept.

Hölderlin knows the topology of the subject:

The boldest moment in a day's course or in a work of art is when the spirit of time and nature, when the heavenly which takes hold of man and the object in which he is interested, oppose one another most ferociously, because the sensuous object extends only half of the way while the spirit awakens most powerfully where the second half flares up. At this moment, man has to *sustain himself the most*; hence, he also is the most exposed in his character. (ELT 110)

This admirable text is the metaphorical condensation of the four concepts.

Hölderlin is commenting upon a question that Creon asks of Antigone: whence derives her energy, her audacity, to sustain herself in the division of the law? How can she bear the assumption of justice at the precise point where, in the guise of Creon—I mean in the guise of that which, in Antigone, is the obligatory existence of the Creon-effect—the violence of the superego demands repetition?

In order to elucidate this problem, Hölderlin goes straight to the dialectical essence of subjectivization. The whole text bears its unbearable torsion.

What is the contradiction given in the risk, in the 'boldest moment'? On one hand, the 'spirit of time', that which 'takes hold of man'; on the other, 'the object in which he is interested'.

It is patent that here lies the ontological discord between the consistency that 'takes hold' and the cause (the object). Hölderlin posits on one hand the excess, and, on the other, the place. That which 'takes holds'—and whose site, because it is out of place, is called 'heavenly'—is the same thing from which follows the need to tear oneself away from the place prescribed by the lack, in the guise of the object of one's interest. It is not a source, a focus, or a cause. It is the very process of force as dis-placing. Hölderlin says so himself later on: the spirit of time 'awakens most *power*fully'.

The placed definition of the human being, tied to the sensuous causal object, goes only 'half of the way'. What a remarkable expression! *The algebra is only half-of-the-way of the subject.* The overcoming of this halfway draws a topological picture that does not come up by accident. If the contradiction appears 'most ferociously', it is because the place must be overcome so that 'the other half flares up'. Astonishing metaphorical concision! The 'other half' is the other dimension, the topological correlate of any placement. The algebra is literally set on fire by the excess.

What appears next? One must 'sustain oneself', wherein you will immediately read the constituent requisite of courage, against the background of a 'ferocious' anxiety. Courage is the name of the topological burning up of places and of interests, inasmuch as it is subordinated to the gesture of opening oneself up to becoming 'the most exposed', which is what allows one to 'sustain oneself'. To sustain oneself, therefore, in the opening of the new, the apparent unlimitation whose dialectical identity is the limitation, the character. This is because courage, the burnt precipitation (one has 'fired one's last rounds') in the excess over the place, promptly recomposes—beyond the destruction that it is—the subjective process of justice. The strand α of the subjective torsion explains why to be 'the most exposed' and to 'sustain' oneself are one and the same thing.

And it is also one and the same thing to follow 'the object in which one is interested'—which it appears should fulfil the desire—and the fact that this object is always half-way.

For this second identity is the strand ψ, whose interlacing with the other explains why, from the point of the subject, you have the risk and the day, the ferocious and the exposed, the half-way and the character, that is, anxiety, the superego, courage, and justice.

There is no 'virtue' in this. These words from Hölderlin do not designate any ability and, in a certain sense, Creon will obtain no answer to his question. It is a question of a passing moment, of a pass, in which half-way and fire forever poeticize the subject-effect.

3

The topic is in turn divided into a static and a dynamic.

The basic square only tends to combine the two divisions of the subject-process:

- according to the pair subjectivization/subjective process, which refers us on, by way of the cause and consistency, to the logic of destruction and of recomposition;
- according to the pair ψ/α, which refers to the alternating primacy of lack and excess.

The four concepts become the peaks of a network of which 'subject' names the double articulation, or to be more precise, the double trajectory.

If you think of subjectivization/subjective process, which is the *analytical* view of the subject, you obtain the two pairs anxiety/courage and superego/justice.

If you think of ψ/α, which is the *synthetic* understanding, you obtain the two pairs anxiety/superego and courage/justice.

To know the subject requires the unfolding of two trajectories. Any analysis of neurosis or of a mass revolt, operated from the point of theory-practice, clearly shows this.

In all cases, the support of the crossing is a nameable term of materiality. This term is the One of the double processus.

For psychoanalysis, it is the sexuated body.

For Marxism, it is the party. Conceived of in the spirit of Marx, as the 'rallying' of the proletariat. It is the party in its physics.

The party is the body of politics, in the strict sense. The fact that there is a body by no means guarantees that there is a subject, neither in the case of the animal body nor in that of the institutional body. But for there to be a subject, for a subject to be *found*, there must be the support of a body.

The static of the subject—the result of a chain of concepts as complex as are all those of the structural dialectic (splace, outplace, vanishing term, causality of lack, lack of lack . . .) and all those of the logic of excess (forcing, destruction, division of the law . . .); and the reprise of the whole set through the fundamental categories of materialism (algebra and topology), and so forth—gives us the following:

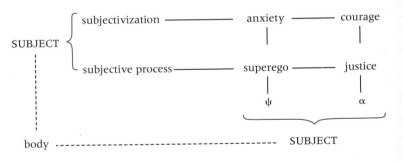

The elementary Marxist translation of this formal arrangement is constructible. This requires a whole repertoire of mediating concepts (history and politics; revolution, programme, division of the bourgeoisies, the people, alliances, modes of production, dominance, State, masses, and so on). See the diagram below.

In these schemas, the obligatory usage of lines should not hide the fact that anxiety and courage operate from the same point, as do justice and the superego. This point is that of the destruction and the recomposition.

Here the static inverts itself into the dynamic.

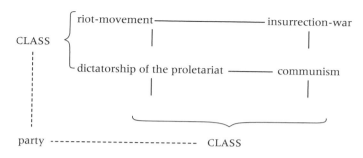

The unschematizable aspect of the subject consists in making a point out of a line.

4

I said that the four concepts are neither virtues nor abilities. Better yet: they are not even experiences. Two years ago, I proposed their abstract formulas. There you can see clearly that they are only names for certain processes, and nothing else.

Neither anxiety nor the superego nor courage nor justice are states of consciousness. They are categories of the subject-effect. What these categories give us to think is a specific material zone, which is the opening principle for any destruction of that which supports it.

1. Anxiety is that form of the interruption that, invaded by the real as too-muchness, lets this order be as dead order. Here the too-much-of-the-real interrupts the vacillation around the empty place by way of an obstruction, whereas courage, for its part, operates by way of deregulation.

We might say that anxiety designates the moment when the real *kills* the symbolical, rather than splitting it.

Hence, subjectivization blocks the rule without annulling its space. This paralysed space turns the disorder into the death of order, under the concept of this order itself.

Historically, anxiety exists as the nomination of the 'power void', that obsession which haunts the politicians. Of course, that which governs the position of this void—as if suddenly the unoccupyable place were everywhere—is the intolerance toward disorder, because the latter is retained, under the formal maintenance of the law, in the (dead) figure of order.

When toward the end of May '68, the newspaper *Le Monde* made a complete turnaround that threw it back to the side of the counterrevolution ('Enough!' Beuve-Méry put in the headline), it argued from the point of chaos and transmitted anxiety as the violent appeal to the Gaullist superego.

Anxiety effectuates the destruction of meaning as chaos in such a way that the law, always undivided, shines in the distance insofar as it no longer rules. Anxiety maintains the excess within topological adherence. Of this paralysed order, the law commands that I carry the whole corpse. The interruption is *stuck* onto the splace with the emblems of a funeral. At the origin of anxiety there lies the production, by way of the excess, of a question without an answer (courage, for its part, is an answer without a question): 'What does one want from me?' But, though fatally hit, the place in which this question is sounded remains the old order of the place.

Anxiety, as we see in the mute and suicidal riots (June 1848, for example), implies in its effect the death of destruction itself, the destruction of destruction. It is the most reflexive of the subject's concepts. It involves that form of the excess by which the place *implodes*.

2. Hence anxiety calls upon the *superego*. Anxiety is that inevitable side of subjectivization which, caught in the web of the dead order, makes an appeal to the reinforced sustenance of the law. Here the Freudians will mention the anxious practice of self-punishment. The excess is that which anxiety *is* in the intolerance of its being. It is the excess hindered by its very own principle: topological adherence. The sacrifice of the excess to the restoration of the place is what subordinates subjectivization to the conservative subjective process: the superego. This correlation defines the strand ψ of the subjective torsion.

What is the process of the superego type? As a figure of consistency, it puts the excess back into place *by distributing it everywhere according to the available places*. The superego is the structural aspect of the excess. Through it the algebraicization of the topological occurs, as if, full of subjectivizing anxiety, the place recomposed itself on its own in the terrorizing prescription of the placement.

In fact, the superego is the subjective process of terror. Hegel's description, referring implicitly to the terror under Robespierre, may here suffice. This description brings together:

– the 'destruction of the actual organization';
– the indifferent order of death;

– the universality of the excess, which makes everyone, in his or her place, suspicious.

Here we see how in the superego effect, the ferocious figure of the law, its essence of nonlaw, is set free and becomes omnipresent:

> Now that [universality] has completed the destruction of the actual organization of the world, and exists now just for itself, this is its sole object, an object that no longer has any content, possession, existence, or outer extension, but is merely this knowledge itself as an absolutely pure and free individual self. [. . .]
>
> The sole work and deed of universal freedom is therefore *death*, a death too which has no inner significance or filling, for what is negated is the empty point of the absolutely free self. It is thus the coldest and meanest of all deaths, with no more significance than cutting off a head of cabbage or swallowing a mouthful of water.
>
> In this flat, commonplace monosyllable is contained the wisdom of the government, the abstract intelligence of the universal will, in the fulfilling of itself. [. . .]
>
> When the universal will maintains that what the government has actually done is a crime committed against it, the government, for its part, has nothing specific and outwardly apparent by which the guilt of the will opposed to it could be demonstrated; for what stands opposed to it as the *actual* universal will is only an unreal pure will, *intention. Being suspected*, therefore, takes the place, or has the significance and effect, of *being guilty*; and the external reaction against this reality that lies in the simple inwardness of intention, consists in the cold, matter-of-fact annihilation of this existent self, from which nothing else can be taken away but its mere being. (Ph 359–60)

The *placed* ferociousness exterminates the intentions without regard for the facts. It suffices to be in order to be judged superfluous. Hence it is futile to study terror based on the divisible objectivity of acts. To the contrary, we must start from anxiety's incapacity to effectuate the division.

From Hegel's impeccable text (which, moreover, refuses to judge: terror is an obligatory moment in the becoming of self-consciousness), let us retain that terror is a phenomenon that belongs to the subject, and not to the State. The 'government' is only the mode of being of the universal (that is, for us, of the universality of the excess distributed throughout the entire dead empire of places). This means that terror is a modality of politics, and not the mechanical result of the modern State. If you seek to understand and forbid the Gulag, take as your target Stalin's politics in its rational subjective determination. The opposite idea, which seeks to determine Stalin's politics, or even Marxist politics in general, on the basis of the Gulag, leads only to vulgar moralism.

Now the fundamental inconvenience of vulgar moralism lies in its impotence. Whoever seeks to put an end to terror and to the Gulag must follow the Marxist road of the political subject, of which terror is a dialectical condition, a properly restorationist figure. Moral protest in reality prepares the way for the *repetition* of terror.

The essence of terror is political. We must understand the terrorist State on the basis of the subjective consistency of a mode of politics, referred back to its root: the subjectivization, the Soviet anxiety, the anxiety of civil war and of the NEP. We must think the State on the basis of terror, and not terror on the basis of the State.

The denunciation of the repressive and bloody character of a mode of politics does *not* amount to the real criticism of this politics, nor does it ever enable one to be done with it.

We Marxists are the only consistent and effective anti-Stalinists, because we are the only ones who fully grasp—in order to recast—Stalin's politics. We dread the vulgar 'anti-Stalinists' not because they scream against the camps and against torture—they are right to do so—but because, through the inoperative themes of the state's objectivity or of 'totalitarian ideology', they organize the present weakness in the face of the subjective logic of terror. Yes, we dread their political weakness, their involuntary acquiescence, even when inverted into restorationist anxiety, to the correlation ψ, without designating the latter in its subjective inherence, its profound political force.

3. *Courage* is situated at the same point as anxiety. It is that which tilts over into the excess. But it finds support in the division of the law, in a wager on the real, in such a way that it effectuates the disorder as the order of meaning. The empire of courage is the life of excess. Its reactive correlate is the dead order of which anxiety takes charge.

Courage effectuates the interruption of the dead law in favour of the excess, thus dividing the prescription of the place by *completely* investing its neighbourhoods. All courage amounts to passing through there where previously it was not visible that anyone could find a passage.

To go past the threat of death, which only ever means 'that which no longer is in its place', becomes the new law, which makes life out of death itself.

Anxiety is de-sense, based upon the subsisting splace for a blocked law.[4]

Courage is in-de-sense, based upon the excess under a split law.[5]

Do you want a simple rule for when anxiety is eating away at you? Look for the courageous act before which you show reluctance, the real that you believe to be impossible, and which is real for this very reason. Look for your current indecency. Its precision will surprise you, and anxiety is here that which guides you toward the truth.

All this is superbly put in Stephen Crane's novel *The Red Badge of Courage*. A true manual of anonymous subjectivization in which the unity of opposites between anxiety and courage literally produces the subject, in the double sense of the book's hero and its subject matter:

> He found that he could look back upon the brass and bombast of his earlier gospels and see them truly. He was gleeful when he discovered that he now despised them.
>
> With this conviction came a store of assurance. He felt a quiet manhood, nonassertive but of sturdy and strong blood. He knew that he would no more quail before his guides wherever they should point. He had been to touch the great death, and found that, after all, it was but the great death. He was a man. [. . .]
>
> Yet the youth smiled, for he saw that the world was a world for him, though many discovered it to be made of oaths and walking sticks. He had rid himself of the red sickness of battle. The sultry nightmare was in the past. He had been an animal blistered and sweating in the heat and pain of war. He turned now with a lover's thirst to images of tranquil skies, fresh meadows, cool brooks—an existence of soft and eternal peace.
>
> Over the river a golden ray of sun came through the hosts of leaden rain clouds.[6]

Impossible to give a better expression to the way in which, coupled onto anxiety, courage—a practical breach in whatever is unapparent—opens out to the serene dissipation of the law into justice.

Courage names the absent cause, obstructed by the real, by enabling a division of the place. This division puts the law to the test, instead of calling for its restoration.

4. *Justice*, the consistency for the haste of the cause, amounts to relativizing the law, whereas the superego makes it absolute. This time the effect of recomposition obeys the maxim: 'Always more of the real, and less of the law.' If, in the superego, the nonlaw is only the universal barbarism of the law, then in justice it is the corrosion of the law itself. It is the subjective principle of the withering away of right.

The active source of justice, inversely to that of the superego, is the topologization of algebra. Here the neighbourhood subordinates the elementary to itself. Justice is the *blurring of the places*, the opposite, therefore, of the right place.

Justice is retroactive—correlation α—by way of the *approximative* legitimization of courage, whereas the superego—correlation ψ—designates the *rigours* of anxiety.

The division of the subjective process happens according to the distribution of the excess, either on the side of order within each place or on the side of its withering away as an ongoing process.

The undecidable lies in the fact that this 'either . . . or . . .' forms an interlacing, and not an alternation or a simple coexistence.

The superego is the restorationist face of recomposition (which does not mean repetitive: Stalin is not the Tsar, nor is Robespierre Louis XI). Justice is its instituting face.

But every institution restores.

Admit that here you have a pleasing phenomenological digression. Combine it, I beg you, with the cold mathemes that give you its theory.

Though always blind, a decision always allows one after the fact or *après coup* to state the essence of its undecidability.

Diagonals of the imaginary

May 11, 1979

Horizontals, verticals: diagonals?—The imaginary as saturation of
the static of the subject—Examples of diagonals—Dogmatism and
scepticism—Meagreness of the imaginary—Recollection, recollection!
What do you want from me?

1

Let us spend some more time going over the static of the subject.

We have established the *horizontal* correlations: anxiety-courage is the
subjectivizing scission; and superego-justice, the contradiction of the subjective process.

We have also established the *vertical* correlations: anxiety-superego
defines the strand-ψ of the torsion; courage-justice, its strand-α.

We have posited the blocking-interruption of these two links: the body,
general *hypokeimenon* of the subject-effect and bearer of the undecidable.

Are there *diagonal* correlations? What is the meaning of the pairs
courage-superego and anxiety-justice?

A static comprised of all the systems of linkage will be called saturated.
Is this the case of the schema of the subject?

I immediately answer: Yes. *What saturates the static of the subject is nothing
but the imaginary.*

The diagonals give shape to the two great imaginary functions—which
also constitute the formal concepts of ideology: the dogmatic and the
sceptic.

The idea that the diagonal saturation is the very definition of the imaginary is fully in keeping with Lacan's teaching, just as it is part of the legitimate line of descent from the Marxist theory of ideology.

When Thomas Müntzer fires up the German countryside with a communist egalitarian discourse, he courageously subjectivizes, against the backdrop of death, and appeals to justice.

When he names his courage based on the absolute conviction that Christ seeks the fulfilment of this design, he proposes the imaginary articulation of the bravery of revolt based on the superego whose allegory is 'the Kingdom of God'.

When the Red Guards in Beijing attack the new bureaucratic bourgeoisie in order to put into effect a communist programme, they are constituted by the strand-α, except that by invoking the guarantee of the 'absolute authority of Mao Zedong thought', they become ideologically sutured to ψ.

When the institution of mass democracy, as the immediate actuality of political communism, is accompanied by terrorist prosopopeias against the 'spies' and 'traitors', this is because the law's precariousness, such as the process of the justice-type institutes it, immediately entails the exposure of anxiety, the remedy for which is an imaginary inflation of risk, as the fixation of a real whose blurred places provoke the experience of too-plenty.

When the utopian communists, ideal figures of the nonlaw, are accompanied, as we see in the case of Fourier, by an infinite detail of prescriptions and duties, setting up a combinatory of rules for the totality of the passions and in fact leaving no room or leisure for any neighbourhood, this is because it is convenient to stop the breach, supposed to be generalized, of the rule via the strict deduction of *all of the real*.

The imaginary is thus what provides the connection *between* the strands α and ψ, naming as it does, in the register of the ideal, the endless practical inversion of their respective dominance. The imaginary is what produces similitude and semblance between the lack and the excess.

By way of the imaginary, courage *evokes* the superego while at the same time *convoking* justice. The imaginary wards off anxiety from the point from which justice can be inferred and courage is induced.

Because it enables the diagonal suturing of the two strands of the subject, the imaginary reckons with the inexistent that is the identicalness to oneself. Go back to my examples, and in each case you will see that the stronghold of the imaginary lies in giving comfort to courage (by way of the superego) or to justice (by way of anxiety) through a fixed principle of identity—whether it is a question of God's law, the cult of Mao, or utopian mania.

The diagonals produce the function of the 'ego'; they produce the similar, the fertile fiction of a union of ψ and α, by which the subject shrinks from the division that brings it into being.

Lacan rightly congratulates himself for 'the wedge that I drive in here by putting back in its place the deceptive truism that identicalness to oneself, which is presumed to exist in the ego's usual sense [of itself], has something to do with a supposed instance of reality [*réel*]' (E 69/54).

This 'wedge' is nothing else than the static distinction between the horizontal (conceptual) connection and the vertical (real) connection, on one hand, and the diagonal (imaginary) connection, on the other.

The imaginary, induced by the switching of the dominant between lack and excess in the subjective twist, fallaciously represents the undecidable as always already having been decided.

Either (dogmatism) because there is an unbreached legal control over courage, or (scepticism) because the nonlaw of justice represents only the eternal undecidability of the law.

The imaginary comprises two maxims: 'Guaranteed by the other, I can and I must everything' and 'Since there is no other, I can and I must nothing.'

In every case, this means the reign of morality, which is the exact opposite of ethics.

Alas, we are all extremely moral. Nobody can escape saturation.

2

Courage in the register of the imaginary supports itself with a fixed point by which the recomposition (into justice) jumps ahead to its opposite in the superego. The assembly of the insurrection realizes an evasive scission of the law, but immediately there are only traitors to be executed.

Sartre has seen this very well in his *Critique of Dialectical Reason*, when on the basis of the group in fusion (a notion which moreover would rather have to be registered on the side of the anxious subjectivization in ψ) he generates the pledged group, where fraternity-terror reigns supreme.[7] His drawback lies in having presented as two successive figures of the same phenomenon what in fact is the coexistence of its vertical and diagonal linkages and thus in having missed the point where the imaginary is disjoined from the real. This is because Sartre holds on to a *simple* conception of the subject. He enumerates its strands, without being able to think their interlacing.

Actually, the phenomenal role of terror at work in mass democracy is what allows the imaginary absoluteness of conviction to algebraicize courage, whose essence is topological. Even though you dramatically changed according to objective but unknown neighbourhoods and followed the immanent resources of excess, you posit, in China, that everything results from 'chairman Mao's latest directive', to which obedience is immediately due; or, you, in Iran, that God proceeds by way of your modest intervention to expel Satan the Shah.

This inevitable diagonal dogmatizes courage. The correlate of anxiety thereby finds itself mediated by the showy display of a superegoic anticipation, which in any case is what it always calls upon. Anxiety requires the excess *in the same place* of terror, and this requirement is the point of the real in the correlation ψ. Courage argues from an ideal dogmaticity, the imaginary diagonal which, at the same point, guarantees that courage exposes itself to the real without destroying the destruction.

Symmetrically, the process of justice, which means the weakening of the law to the benefit of the real, generates an essential uncertainty with regard to the subjective placement. Precarious fidelity to courageous subjectivization, justice is properly that which provokes anxiety as to the rule's strength to ward off the real. Justice by no means is the procedure of serenity. Rather, it induces Ecclesiastes' notion that 'all the rivers run into the sea',[8] the chaotic imaginary of de-sense.

Justice is escorted by a vacillation of certainties, in which the blurring of the places is buttressed in the imaginary by its own eternity. 'There has never been any rule': such is the antagonizing diagonal fiction by which justice wards off the restorationist drives that are polarized by anxiety.

Everyone agrees to overcode justice with ideals, to subject the future nonlaw to some rule, to name indefinitely, from times immemorial, what will be the case when all the known places of nomination will have been ruined one after another. This is because everyone *essentially* doubts the real autonomy of justice. Everyone combines the dogmatic diagonal of the fixed point, guarantee to come from the future, with the sceptical diagonal of disorder, guarantee handed down from the past.

We need all the consistent bravery of a Marx and a Mao in order to refuse to legislate communism otherwise than from the real point of political subjectivity. We need all the rigour of Lacan in order never to argue on the basis of a case of healing

3

Arrived at this point, I confess to having little or no desire to continue. In spite of its legend, there is nothing more structural and, in the last instance, nothing more impoverished than the imaginary. It is true, there is also nothing more obviously necessary. I understand the temptation to exhaust the complete trajectory of its archetypes, which are those of good and bad fortune, adorned with the metaphors of nature. On the one hand, the register of its immanent splendour, which serves to confirm that there is (but there isn't) some Almighty. On the other, that of its anarchic indifference, in order to establish that we are put on earth without a home and without a hearth (but there is always a Place, and, Hölderlin says, a Fire).

Pascal has exhausted this question, with its misery and its grandeur. Good dialectician that he is, he looks for the divisible point from where this alternating representation disappears in favour of the pure real of the subject (Christian is the name of such a subject). This point turns out to *inexist in God* (for to be content, like Descartes, with God's existence is only idolatry) and *to exceed itself in the Text* (for it is only through a topological reading of the Testaments, dissolving the letter of the text into the figures that overflow it, that one can discover that these Scriptures are an exception to the world).

The Holy Bible is the excessive trace for the God who is lacking.

It is particularly easy to establish, for Pascal's Christian, the knot of anxiety (think of *The Mystery of Jesus*: 'He suffers this affliction and this abandonment in the horror of the night'[9]), of the superego (God unquestionably is terror), of justice (the duty of Love dissolves into grace all the worldly rules of the place) and of courage (we must wager, against mere diversion).

Misery and grandeur are the diagonals in which Pascal recognizes precisely the sceptical imaginary and the stoic inflation. Hence, it is fitting to converse with Monsieur de Saci about Epictetus and Montaigne. To dissipate the imaginary one-sidedness of morality is the negative introduction to the dialectic of the subject.

The Marxist theory of ideology suffers from the unstoppable meagreness of the diagonals. What more is there to add, except the evident viscosity of their entwining, to the separate formulations of the 'human condition', dogmatically exalted in its power as absolute (art and religion) or sceptically reduced to its deficiency and to the inexorability of death? To show that all this sticks to our skin in the form of a transcendent denial of the class struggle goes no further than the certified report of some materialist bailiff.

The world 'turned upside down' only feeds into my passion for setting it straight.

At the same time, I confess that the pressure of the imaginary, once we recognize its principle, by no means demands that we become scandalized. Even the famous 'cult of personality', in its manifest correlation to the oblique anxieties of just bravery, seems to me to stem from the inevitable presumption of the One much more so than from the dictatorial infamies which pass for real and which if needed are compatible with the most mediocre of images. Nobody has ever needed the cult of Guy Mollet's personality in order to give their massive consent, during the Algerian war, to the massacre of a million Algerians, including torture and the camps. As opposed to the Stalinist endeavour, from which at least a gigantic Russia emerged, these horrors are all the more transparent insofar as they only served to delay the inevitable independence by six or seven years and, thus, people were massacred, rigorously speaking, for nothing.

I certainly participated in the 'cult of Mao', by means of which I, like millions more, figured the fixed point with which to gauge the radical turnabout of courage and the complete transformation of both my practical existence and my convictions during the second half of the 1960s and the early 70s—years of grandeur if ever there were any. In retrospect, I have come to know its ridiculous aspects, the unrealities of the subjective trajectory by which this cult traced an imaginary diagonal and which, exposed to the real, I can now designate with clarity. But I confess that I feel no remorse whatsoever for having traversed this experience, not even for nourishing an uncontrollable nostalgia when I remember those years. After all, so-called leftist intellectuals were otherwise vigorous and innovative under Stalin than they are today in the provincial debasement of their petty sentiments and their banal habits. I buy neither the posthumous revenge of Camus over Sartre nor the excessive praise for Raymond Aron, because he would have been 'less mistaken', which is easy enough to accomplish when one does not take any risks other than to follow the pedagogy of the world as it is. As for the leftists of the post-'68 era, I consider them less the victims of a devastating illusion, as they pretend today, than carried away beyond themselves by history, from whence they drew certain images, unifying consequences and not only the illusory cause of their determination. The imaginary thus comes in to consolidate the real and not in order to install the semblant.[10]

Is this to say that we should sing the praise of the poetry of the imaginary? Of course not. It is easy to see that I honour it, as the senseless diagonal of de-sense or as the dereliction of ab-sense in the place of in-desense, only on the grounds of what supports it in the subject as effective process.

Even poetry, contrary to whatever academic explanations trail behind it, feeds on the topological dimension of language, and not on the imaginary. This is one of Mallarmé's directives:

We dwell in those true groves, where, having marked our way,
With large and humble gesture the pure poet must
Stand guard against the dream as enemy to his trust.[11]

Let us not stand guard or prohibit but sum up:

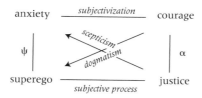

Now that it is saturated, the subject's static awaits only its momentum.

This is God's famous finger flick to put the mechanism in motion. God, that's me. As modern as anyone can ever be, I will content myself with the word of an engineer.

Schema

May 18, 1979

Unfeasible—The formal subjective—Punctuality—Axis of abolition—
Trajectories—Action, reaction, stabilization—The escargot

1

Any attempt to figure the subject as undecidable must face the impossibility of its schema. The task before us is therefore impossible. The drawing that I am about to sketch out must be interpreted in light of its projections and its limit points. It structures a few symptoms for the unschematizable.

Neither the qualitative break, whose operation is entirely practical, nor the contradiction, whose terms do not share a unified plane, can be put into an image.

There exists no geometry of the dialectic.

Lacan finishes his discourse as the draftsman of an impossible schema. He shows, without speaking, the point where the real cannot make a point.

2

First, then, the splace, as the place of the subject's becoming out-of-place. The limit of the distribution of places is fixed therein by the empty place, the unoccupyable place, which is the structural anchorage of the outplace.

How should we figure the unoccupyable place? We will show it in an oblique way by a hole.

We thus take as our point of departure a plane shot through with a hole, whereby at once we miss out on the essential fact that the hole is a place, an empty place, and thus a point like the others, disappeared among the others, if it is not lacking-in-its-place.

But how should we represent the fact that the subject, in a position of internal exclusion, vacillates 'around' the empty place that it un-occupies? This will only give us a vulgar approximation. In order to indicate that the occupation of the empty place is a structural movement, namely, the vacillating or the eclipsing, we need to have a way to schematize that 'something' of the splace occupies and does not occupy, fills and does not fill, the hole in the plane.

I decide on the solution of a vector, without origin, oriented toward the empty place. This polarization of the vector, taken at its extreme limit, makes the occupation (it is the hole that controls the orientation) and the inoccupation (the vector does not fill the void) into one.

Our second task consists in entering the topology by schematizing the excess, by visualizing the outplace. Here we need something that neither purely belongs to the splace nor simply occupies the void but that brings out the vicinity between the two and thus fastens itself onto the subject's structural aspect.

I secure this with an angular representation that, by introducing not only the plane but also the space, symbolizes whatever the excess holds in terms of a destructive tearing-away from the unity of the plane while at the same time, standing as it does directly above the vector, it remains structured by the oscillation whose vacillating flatness it interrupts.

This framing device deserves the name of *formal subjective*:

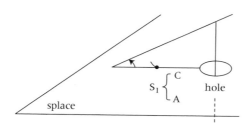

The formal subjective combines into a unique process both the vector's polarized movement toward the void and the angular representation that subtracts it from the splace.

A *subjective position* is a point S_1, which in equal measure is caught in the vectorialization (placed, consequently, at the same time as it is excluded, due to the fact that it is with regard to the empty place that it moves) and supports a differential gap in angle, in spatial vicinity to S_1 (and thus, standing in the excess of interruption over the oscillation that carries it toward the inoccupation of the hole).

This point S_1 is subjectivizing in nature, being the minimal unity of the oscillation and the interruption, of algebraic belonging and the gap of topological adherence.

The fact of its structural attraction is designated as anxiety, A, whereby that which in the excess risks *depriving it of its lack* explains why it appeals to the splace. The fact that in effect it is both excessive repulsion and privation of the polarity of lack is inscribed as courage, C.

S_1, considered in the double constraint of the vector and the angle, at one and the same point is split into A and C, one somehow 'toward the bottom', and the other 'toward the top'.

3

How should we figure the subjective process? The idea is simply to produce the trajectory of an integral, for example, by pushing from S_1 all the way up to the angular line that is supposed to mark the boundary of the formal subjective (in terms of the excess). Let us call this point S'_1. The subjective process would be the journey from S_1 to S'_1.

The gross simplification of this necessary hypothesis consists in the fact that neither the destruction nor, above all, the recomposition appears clearly.

How should we make up for this dialectical shortcoming? Recomposition means a new splace. To make an image out of the fact that the recomposition proceeds from the subjective process, we will position an axis of recomposition, complete with its own empty place directly above the previous one, as the trajectory's formal future and, thus, based on the cycle's completion. The axis of the first angle, held to mark the maximum excess, will then be presented as the axis of destruction. The duality of these axes, unified by their common anchorage in the first vectorialization, symbolizes at the level of formal framing that the subject is a process of destruction-recomposition.

In order to place the superego and justice, we give ourselves a vertical axis as a reference point to mark the limit of all conceivable destruction. This axis, aptly named axis of abolition, includes the infinite pushing back of the empty place. It is the axis according to which there would be no more law and only the real would exist; the axis of superhuman courage, of intolerable anxiety, of integral justice, and of the dead superego:

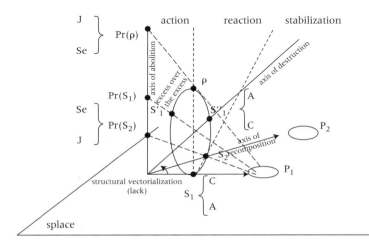

The conceptual mapping of the subjective process, beginning from the empty place, will proceed by way of projecting a subjective position onto the axis of abolition. The point of projection somehow gives us a measure relative to the trajectory. Here, again, it is doubly defined: by the splaced origin of the projection, which is its superegoic dimension; and by the axis of abolition itself, which supports its dimension of justice.

4

What is a subject-process? Let us follow its sections.

The destructive impulse given in the differential A/C carries the excess of S_1 all the way to S'_1, and actually beyond, in the fragment of the curve that we will call *the excess over the excess*, between S'_1 and S''_1. The latter in some way is the inevitable leftist instance of any subjective interlacing, the moment when destruction raises the bid and goes beyond its own structural form, beyond its angular assignation to the splace, as if caught in a vertigo of abolition—whose anxious thematic demands that one throw oneself head first into the world's inferno.

At the point ρ, which is the extreme limit of what courage is able to bear of the exposure to the real, and the maximum height for the projection J/Se, there begins a 'descent' that can be mapped in S''_1, based on the fact that anxiety here gains precedence over courage, attraction over repulsion. This is what we can call the moment of regressive subjectivization. In strict correlation, the projections provide us with a measure of the fact that the superegoic instance gains precedence over the 'rise' of justice to right the wrongs.

In S_2, finally, there is a stopping point on a recomposing vectorialization, determined by lack.

If from S_1 we trace that which connects it to ρ, the point of maximal excess, and to S_2, the stopping point in which the real dissolves itself in the immanence of parts, then we can carve out three zones in the right angle of abolition and conservation. On the left, the zone of *action*, governed by the primacy of courage and the growing vectorialization of the projection J/Se. In the middle, correlated to the regressive subjectivization, there is *reaction*, in which A gains the upper hand over C, and where the point J/Se declines once again. On the right, *stabilization*. You will understand that these are three simultaneous moments given in any subject-process. Space, in its superiority over time, is telling with regard to this coexistence.

We could obviously continue:

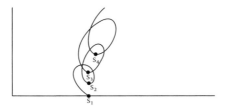

There you have, ready for disassembly, the complete escargot of periodization.

Ethics as the dissipation of the paradoxes of partisanship

May 25, 1979

Antigone once more—Ethics is the remainder of politics—Logic of the incalculable decision—To give in or to be—The Moscow trials—The partisan mindset

1

From Hegel to Lacan, the reference point for ethics is Sophoclean. Who is Antigone? That is the question.

You can imagine that I am not going to tell you that for us Marxists, Antigone is the expression of archaic social relations. Against the right of the city whose despotism is secular, these forces call upon the old unwritten right of blood and family. Now that would do you a lot of good! You would obtain the kind of Marxists truths—because it *is* true—thanks to which we have fallen behind the historical intelligence of the bourgeoisie, without moving an inch toward an energetic break.

Another way to formulate this same point is the following: there exists no Marxist ethics. At best there is an ethics *of* Marxism, which we can designate retroactively as the practical principle behind the rational calculations of politics.

Ethics falls on the side of that which, in the primacy of practice, functions as a remainder for the impossible exhaustion of theory. Take the advances and shortcomings of the protagonists of the Commune or of the Red Guards: once they have passed through theoretical reflection in view of the next stage, what remains is the fact that they incarnate the unconditional virtue of any historical account, that is, the unforgettable decision.

We can find support for this in two axioms from Hegel:

– '[. . .] the ethical order essentially consists in this immediate firmness of decision' (Ph 280)
– 'Consequently, the absolute right of the ethical consciousness is that the deed, the *shape* in which it *actualizes* itself, shall be nothing else but what it *knows*' (Ph 281)

Ethics concerns the decision in its practical absoluteness, which cannot be inferred from anything else but from its contemporaneity to the knowledge available at the time. Ethics makes a discourse out of that which can neither wait nor be postponed. It makes do with what is given.

Here, we re-encounter the subjective function of haste as formatted in Hegel's text.

Ethics essentially touches upon the undecidability of the subject. This is true even when, as all forms of wisdom aim to do, it argues from the point of view that this undecidability comes down to a pure acceptance of fact.

The notion that ethics (*Sittlichkeit*) is the logic of the incalculable decision explains why for Hegel it is inferior to morality (*Moralität*), whose realm belongs to reflection.

In this regard, we will reverse Hegel. Morality is indeed calculable, since it is caught in that which, from the splace, governs the disappearing of the subjective process, its reduction to the state of a trace. Without arguing for a superiority, our interest will be in ethics. For we know the cost of what brings Villiers de l'Isle-Adam and Rimbaud, though they are profoundly apolitical, to be on the side of the Commune, or what brings this or that reactionary peasant from Bourgogne to set up an underground resistance movement, purely on the grounds that, as he says, 'we must do something'.

Without such decisions, there would not even be any matter for politics.

Those who in these circumstances wait for the 'absolute reflection' have all the time in the world, be they Flaubert or Gide, to give a serene evaluation of the wrongs committed by both parties and to tell themselves that Mister Thiers or Pétain, though in disputable ways, objectively protect certain needs, whereas the others, dreamers no doubt, really exaggerate when they execute a nice bishop or when they shamelessly slaughter an officer of the occupying forces protected by ancient conventions and recent capitulations.

Ethics is on the agenda whenever the subjective tension obtains universality only in the particular forsaking of any will slowly to investigate the complete state of affairs.

Lacan is certainly right in reducing ethics to the question: 'Has the subject given in?' Why the verb 'to give in'? Because what is at stake in a decision is not the quality of the subject but purely and simply its being.

To give in means to disappear. Nothing will then have taken place but the place.

The whole question of contemporary politics comes down to this: is the international proletariat of France going to exist? A rational politics has no other goal but to use the existing subjectivizations in order to sustain in a topology the communist process of this existence—the consistency of that which ex-sists.

If we make ethics into the remainder of politics, we can also formulate the problem as follows: is it necessary to continue giving in to the undeniable advantages of the unionist-parliamentary splacing?

The existence of the subject gets dissipated into the nonsense of the law as soon as the maxim is to give in. Lacan says this forcefully: 'Desire, what is called desire, suffices to make life meaningless if it turns someone into a coward' (E 782/660).

By inversion, this amounts to defining courage as the core of the question.

One always gives in for the sake of some good, one's own or that of others. Lacan calls this 'the service of goods'. Notice that to give in for the sake of others is not worth much more than to give in for one's own sake. The opposite of the ethical decision is not the selfish decision, far from it. The proper opposite of ethics is betrayal, the essence of which consists in betraying oneself, in inexisting in the service of goods.

I propose four theorems:

1. One gives up on subjectivization in the name of the old subjective process.
2. The ground for the conceptual framework of ethics is the subjective interlacing of ψ and α.
3. It is necessary to give in, for any subject includes the process-ψ. Ethics is possible, for any subject includes the process-α.
4. The fundamental concept of the ethics of Marxism is confidence.

2

If the political subject is what the party as body is able to bear in terms of the undecidable, and if betrayal is the proper opposite of ethics, can we not equate ethics and partisanship? The recognizable figure of the one who gives in would then be the *renegade*. This is something that, since Judas, is an old temptation of any apparatus in which political subjects find their *hypokeimenon*.

In this logic, in which the State latently defines the adequate form of that which no longer exists as party-subject except as its semblance, it is absolutely necessary that the political enemy, or even just the universal suspect, be violently kept in the unnameable and null place of the traitor and the spy.

We can find testimony of the fact that this place is unnameable in the incredible mix of metaphors by which the 'socialist' prosecutor Vyshinsky wants to pass it off as a pure nothingness:

> Our whole country, from young to old, is awaiting and demanding one thing: the traitors and spies who were selling our country to the enemy must be shot like dirty dogs!
>
> Our people are demanding one thing: crush the accursed reptile!
>
> Time will pass. The graves of the hateful traitors will grow over with weeds and thistle, they will be covered with the eternal contempt of honest Soviet citizens, of the entire Soviet people. But over us, over our happy country, our sun will shine with its luminous rays as bright and as joyous as before. Over the road cleared of the last scum and filth of the past, we, our people, with our beloved leader and teacher, the great Stalin, at our head, will march as before onwards and onwards, towards Communism![12]

In the Moscow trials, which are the theatrical staging of the party as the continuous process of purging and bloody self-devouring, the State is the Law fearing neither God nor man that proclaims to be the solar and integral realization of communist justice and, casting the traitor out of place into the anonymity of a vanished tomb, dissolves ethics purely and simply into terror.

When one of the designated renegades, Bukharin, tries to stop the worst by straying from his obligatory script, look how he replaces the ethical principle, which alone is capable of justifying the terrorist superego, with the splaced principle of calculation, error, and, thus, politics.

Vyshinsky wants absolutely that Bukharin declare himself a British or German spy, for that would exclude the accused from any place what-soever in the space of the State, which is the only thing that is intoler-able from the point of view of ethics and legitimizes the death penalty. Bukharin, subject to all kinds of violence and deprived of an affirmative subjectivity as political resistant, defends himself on this precise point with a rare stubbornness, going so far so as to treat his denouncers as provocateurs:

> Vyshinsky: I am asking you about connections with some police authority.
> Bukharin: I had no connections with any police authorities whatsoever.
> Vyshinsky: Then why was it so easy for you to join a bloc which was engaged in espionage work?
> Bukharin: Concerning espionage I know absolutely nothing.
> Vyshinsky: What do you mean, you don't know?
> Bukharin: Just that.
> Vyshinsky: And what was the bloc engaged in?
> Bukharin: Two people testified here about espionage, Sharangovich and Ivanov, that is to say, two agents-provocateurs. (383)

When a declaration extorted from Khodjayev mentions a conversa-tion about acts of espionage, Bukharin seeks support in his identity as an intellectual in order not to give in—just as he in a way will do in his final declaration with the famous theory of double consciousness, which allows him to surrender politically without annulling himself *qua* subject:

> Vyshinsky: Did you carry on a conversation [with Khodjayev at his country place]?
> Bukharin: I carried on a conversation and kept my head on my shoulders all the time, but it does not follow from this that I dealt with the things of which Khodjayev just spoke; this was the first conversation. . . .
> Vyshinsky: It is of no consequence whether it was the first or not the first. Do you confirm that there was such a conversation?
> Bukharin: Not such a conversation, but a different one, and also secret.
> Vyshinsky: I am not asking you about conversations in general, but about this conversation.

> Bukharin: In Hegel's 'Logic' the word 'this' is considered to be the most difficult word. . . .
>
> Vyshinsky: I ask the Court to explain to the accused Bukharin that he is here not in the capacity of a philosopher but a criminal, and he would do better to refrain from talking here about Hegel's philosophy, it would be better first of all for Hegel's philosophy. . . .
>
> Bukharin: A philosopher may be a criminal.
>
> Vyshinsky: Yes, that is to say, those who imagine themselves to be philosophers turn out to be spies. Philosophy is out of place here. I am asking you about that conversation of which Khodjayev just spoke; do you confirm it or do you deny it?
>
> Bukharin: I do not understand the word 'that'. We had a conversation at the country house. (421)

The symptomatic importance of this point, where ethics and politics in their contradictory articulation determine the abject status of the subject, is such that Vyshinsky ends up explicitly opposing the two terms:

> Vyshinsky: I will be compelled to cut the interrogation short because you apparently are following definite tactics and do not want to tell the truth, hiding behind a flood of words, pettifogging, making digressions into the sphere of politics, of philosophy, theory and so forth—which you might as well forget about once and for all, because you are charged with espionage and, according to all the material of the investigation, you are obviously a spy of an intelligence service. (423)

Thus, in order to disqualify Bukharin in his capacity as subject, it is absolutely key to make him *forget politics*.

The prioritizing of official adjectives attached to Liu Shaoqi's name as the emblematic target during the storm of the Cultural revolution, according to which he, 'the No. 1 Party person in power taking the capitalist road, is a renegade, hidden traitor and scab who has concealed himself in the Party and is a crime-steeped lackey of imperialism, modern revisionism and the Kuomintang reactionaries' (GPCR 183–184), weaves together with precision that which pertains to politics in the thinkable frame of the struggle between two paths (modern revisionism, the capitalist road, ultimately betrayal of the working class) and that which draws vigour from the purely ethical remainder (secret agent, imperialism, spy for Formosa, criminal).

In all these cases, it does not suffice to overpower the adversary on the sole ground that he was the object to be combated. But underneath the division of the party, betrayal of that which stands for its soul, it is also necessary to evoke the unnameable ethical failure. And if it does not exist, then there is cause to invent it.

What these flat and—as their future has shown—entirely empty horrors warn us about is that the formal recognition of ethics as the only possible principle of self-condemnation (hence the sinister theatre in Moscow requires the confession and the abjection) changes into its opposite if the political content, of which ethics is supposed to be the remainder, happens to be reduced to the objectivity of the party-State.

In order truly to arrive at ethics, we must at least not give up on politics as a subjective process, on communist politics. This is impossible if one chooses *the wrong party*, in all the senses of the expression.[13]

The partisan mindset can certainly involve abnegation and obedience or, as Stalin says, 'conscious submission' and 'unity of will'.[14] Ethical courage amounts to the force to traverse anxiety, since this means nothing else but the capacity to consider oneself null. Who will say whether we can continuously do without this kind of annulling subjectivization?

But the partisan spirit is also the reverse. When it is subordinated to politics, and not to organization, it demands absolute participation in the movement of the real, the detection of the breach from where to tip over into avant-gardistic destruction. Look at the directives of the Cultural Revolution with regard to the cadres:

It is therefore imperative to persevere in the line of 'from the masses, to the masses'. Be pupils of the masses before becoming their teachers. Dare to make revolution and be good at making revolution. Don't be afraid of disturbances. Oppose the taking of the bourgeois stand, the shielding of Rightists, attacks on the Left and repression of the great Proletarian Cultural Revolution. Oppose the creation of a lot of restrictions to tie the hands of the masses. Don't be overlords or stand above the masses, blindly ordering them about.[15]

In such circumstances, no corporeal hierarchy can exempt you from the test of courage. If the party pretends to protect you from it, you should become the party all by yourself. You must in turn know how to consider the party as null, solely so that it continues to exist as the body of a subject. This captures the complete meaning of the maxim: 'Dare to go against the tide', about which Wang Hongwen (today in prison . . .) at the 10th

Congress of the Chinese Communist Party, in the purest style of Antigone, indicates to what extent we must see in it the complete opposite of the 'service of goods':

> When confronted with issues that concern the correct political line and the overall situation, a true Communist must act without any selfish considerations and dare to go against the tide, without fear of being removed from his post, excluded from the Party, thrown in jail, forced to divorce, or put in front of the firing squad.[16]

It is clear that here it is the very existence of the party itself that is at issue, since by giving in, one would gain only its statist desubjectivization, its counterrevolutionary termination.

The ethics of Marxism consists in resolving the paradoxes of partisanship on the solid terrain of the theory of the subject.

This solution is accomplished in the division of one concept, confidence, which depending on its point of application, contains the need for discipline and the inevitability of rebellion.

Classical detour

June 2, 1979

Neither the sun nor death—Apogees and decadences—The four kinds
of ethics—What happened not so long ago—Discourses—Confident or
believing?

1

You can neatly distinguish, since always, two genres of ethics. Either you
infer an ethics from the order of the world, to which the subject must
correspond, without excluding the need for the contortions of the converted; or you infer it from the subject's will, by no means dependent on
the world's possibilities, without excluding that the world may order the
repetition of this willing.

This says as much as that the question is broached according to the
splace or according to the outplace; according to subjectivization or
according to the subjective process; according to the possible or according
to the impossible.

Let me add in passing that a maxim that is very much in vogue among
parliamentary politicians, especially 'from the left', is the one that declares:
'Politics is the art of the possible.' Nowhere does the class nature of truth
appear with such nakedness. This maxim for sure is true, and it may even
be excellent, *for them*. As far as I am concerned, I posit explicitly that *politics
is the art of the impossible*.

The outer border of the first ethical tendency affirms that an integral
mastery of the knowledge of the world is accessible so that the right

place of the subject is representable therein as its Good. From an absolute knowledge follows a complete reconciliation. Once past the cognitive conversion, the subjective process of wisdom is eternal. Herein we can recognize the seriousness of the axis of verticalization, in which the real and the law are reciprocatable without remainder.

Certain variants of the communist idea resemble this theme of harmony, by which justice, unmoored from the subject, becomes a category of being.

If any reserve of the excess dries up, it is actually its structural anchoring that is struck by annulment. For the essence of all forms of wisdom lies in positing that one can eliminate the lack. Their doctrine is one of a full space.

At the other extreme of the ethical field, we find the thesis that nothing is to be expected from being in terms of the subject's will. The world only ever offers you the temptation to give in. This is the story told in all the nineteenth-century novels of formation: the infinite, ethical or amorous subjectivity of the young man must learn its radical inadaptation to all objectivity. In order to become a well-placed and respectable character, he must take it down a notch. The novelist is the ironic historiographer of the betrayal of oneself.

This figure can thus uphold the ethical process only in the tragedy of renouncing the world, in the unaltered process of pure subjectivization. This time we can recognize the intrinsic valorization of the excess over the excess, wherein it is a matter of maintaining oneself (most often in death) without ever letting oneself slide back into regressive subjectivization and recomposition.

Typically, the metaphors of the first kind of ethics are diurnal and solar, as we see in Plato. Upon exiting the cave of shadows, one is blinded, the day appears in excess over its own light. The metaphors of the second kind are nocturnal and lunar. Consider Wagner, the second act of *Tristan*, where one is conversing on the bench of desire about the metaphysical advantages of death and the night, at least, that is, as long as the noble cuckold does not come and interrupt this obscene philosophical reunion by introducing the symbolic principle of the embarrassing third, to which in the opera, between the guilty tenor and soprano, so many excellent basses devote themselves.

The fact that in this night all cows are black, as Hegel objected against Schelling, is precisely a virtue for those who, in transgressing the prescribed place and in deferring only to its local differential, want to have nothing to do with an exact discrimination of bovines.

'Neither the sun nor death can be looked at steadily,' La Rochefoucauld observed, thereby dismissing both extreme forms of ethics.[17] This is because he opted for the nihilist version, from whose vantage point the other three can be observed with a particular sharpness.

Besides, La Rochefoucauld is right in short-circuiting the two metaphors. Day and night belong to the same eras. All forms of wisdom, just as all existential dissidences, refer to times of height and to times of crisis. For if a vigorous ascending class is able to model history and the concepts of its speculation upon its force, this obviously is due to the fact that it hypostatizes its will into the integral affirmation of the wisdom of the world, and to dissenters it leaves only the place of the general denial, of radical discordance. And if, inversely, we are in a ruinous and thoughtless epoch, in the putrefaction of the selfsame place where we remain and from which no new political subject is the internal excluded or the placed excess, then the opposite temptations—resigning oneself to the course of the world, supposed to be necessary, or withdrawing from it completely—begin to communicate from all sides. When the Greek city fell in ruins, to the sole benefit of the military, first the Macedonians and then the Romans, this is what the opposite and yet similar schools of Epicurus and the Stoics busied themselves with.

There remains the case when, essentially neither good nor bad, the world is what the subject recomposes from a point where the subjective undecidable does not demand that one give up. The fact of discordance then is recognized as the out-of-place condition of subjectivization; that discordance is also taken up in a process of appropriation designates the subjective process of recomposition; and that there is discordance in this process connotes the regressive subjectivization insofar and whatever it induces in terms of repetition in the subjective process.

Between day and night, the metaphor would be that of *the carrier of fire*, which Mallarmé's star fixes without excess. Aeschylus made a tragedy out of it: *Prometheus*.

2

There are four kinds of ethics:

1. The ethics of praise, where one has a place of one's own within a world open to evaluation.

2. The ethics of resignation, where one keeps to one's place in a devaluated world.
3. The ethics of discordance, where one stands in the outplace of a place that is intrinsically devaluated.
4. The Promethean ethics, where one posits that the place is yet to come in a world open to re-evaluation, which the fire of just excess recomposes.

The first two kinds of ethics refer to the whole; the last two, to the not-all. This is a dialectical division of the rectangle.

Another one immediately jumps off the page: the ethics of praise is optimistic (according to being), as is the Promethean (according to the process). Resignation and discordance are pessimistic.

It is clear that these two attitudes refer to the primitive articulations of the subject, within a historical setting that puts them to the test.

You will have no difficulty arguing the following:

— praise connotes justice, insofar as it follows the axis of the law's real dissipation, but its imaginary limit is the theme of an absolute place, of a real splace, a limit which moreover is saturated with anxiety—look at the diagonals.
— resignation singles out the superego, the terrorizing order that has no need for disguising itself as value in order to ascribe the subject to the law *qua* nonlaw.
— discordance touches upon anxiety, which knows that it touches upon the real only through the inconsolable loss of the dead world.
— Prometheus is the character who, in defiance of the gods, keeps the becoming of courage running on empty.

On this basis we will posit that the first two kinds suture ethics to the subjective process, and the other two, to subjectivization; and that the distinction between optimism and pessimism goes no further than to repeat the intertwining of the strand-α and the strand-ψ.

The only interest of this approach would be to confirm that ethics gives us a name for the subject as historically realized in the form of discourse.

It would be a fallacy to conclude that there exists an ethics of courage, another of the superego, and so on. It is misleading to follow the slope of the structure.

A subject exists only through a historicized linkage of the four concepts. Ethics is a position in the complete field of its four poles (praise, discordance, resignation, Prometheus), whereby one of them is never anything else than the way to gain access to the other three.

Thus, the Giscardian conjuncture—let this be the name for the political disarray that followed the disarray of the intellectuals after 1976 at the latest—witnesses how the ethical debate of times of crisis makes a comeback. Does this mean that resignation suddenly imposes itself all by itself? No. First we must realize that, as the result of the years 1966–73, there remains a Promethean reference whose denial is constitutive of the conjuncture in question. The 'critique of militantism', the refutations of Marxism, and the attack against the 'master discourses', are the necessary passageways, and often the only substance, for the re-establishing of morals and rights. Secondly, we observe that the philosophies of desire, by relying on the cheap cuts of the previous upheaval—that is, the bourgeois liberation of mores—have spread a discordant nihilism that its corrosive power designated as the inevitable critical ally of resignations on the rise. Finally, it appears that the intellectuals' consent for French imperialist society (parliamentary 'liberties', human rights, unionism, contempt for the Third World, and so on), even though it is limited at first to an ethics of personal behaviour, cannot do without the collective praise that is latent in this kind of world order, praise that will have exploded (this future anterior is added in July 1981) during the festivities in honour of the rose, where the intellectual plebs rallied *en masse* to the State, as soon as it received the decoration of the provincial emblems of calm force.

An ethical framework thus always arises within a complex saturated totality. The ethical debate subsumes any particular ethics. For, if ethics is that which a subject makes into the rule in terms of its consistency, it can obtain this synthetic position only by the necessary nomination of the other possibilities.

Beyond the descriptive categories that I have used, therefore, we must indicate the *subjective formations* of ethics, which do not coincide with the subject's concepts.

These formations constitute discourses. Therein lies their difference from the subject's processes. An ethics designates explicitly a general articulation of the subject, which enters into its consistency and functions according to the regime of the aftermath or *après-coup*.

It is not part of the order of the imaginary either, since it traces no diagonal between the strands of α and ψ. Still, it is of course true that dogmatism and scepticism *infect* ethics as much as they saturate the subject.

An ethics is the surname of an existing subject-effect.

To lure you, I give you two of its surnames.

Belief is the discourse of the ethics of praise; *confidence*, that of Prometheans.

But the affair becomes more complicated when any idiot can realize that belief means confidence in the splace, whereas confidence is belief in the outplace.

Between Prometheus and praise, it seems the difference is only that of the direction of a vector.

If it is from the point of confidence that Marxism touches upon ethics, as I . . . believe is the case, then it should not surprise us that it turns back into belief. Confidence is this prepolitical arrangement, this remainder of calculable action, without which Marxism has never begun or rebegun.

To fail means nothing, and it always happens. To fail is a category of politics. It is only to give in that belongs to ethics. Certainly those who give in argue on the basis of failures. But those are only discourses. The truth is that what constitutes failure as cause is the fact of having given in.

In politics, it is to consistency that the failure incorporates itself.

If after 1973 one witnessed the 'failure' of the rebellious mass movement of May–June 1968, it was only from the point of a political process—the party to come as consistency of the class subject—that it became possible to measure the extent to which the mass movement, required for any subjectivization, is a cause only insofar as it disappears.

To argue based on this disappearance in order to settle down for a life of order actually means to abdicate the subject itself. Far from being able to evoke the 'movement's failure' as the cause for this abdication, we must be honest and rigorous enough to admit that one has failed *oneself* to hold steady in α and that, thus unhinged, the torsion—purely by means of isolating ψ—no longer has a subjective valence and puts you purely and simply *back into your place*.

In matters of Marxist politics and the subject of class, there is only one way of giving in, which is by losing confidence.

From 1976 onward, our intellectuals have lost confidence *en masse*, arguing instead—without being totally wrong about this—that they had never been more than believers. Does one always have to believe in order to have confidence? As far as I am concerned, I have confidence in the people and in the working class in direct proportion to my lack of belief in them. Insofar as I believe in them, which always induces the *expectation* of a sizeable popular movement, my confidence begins to vacillate. I nevertheless do not cease to believe in them, knowing full well that to vacillate defines the structure of the subject. This leaves us its history, which corresponds to what I have confidence in.

Love what you will never believe twice

June 9, 1979

Belief and confidence—How Yukong moved the mountains—From yesterday to today—Nihilism and fatalism—The division of confidence—'And yet, this is the eve'

1

If belief is what enables the possibility of salvation, and consequently the subject's potential eternity in a splacement which is finally real, confidence is concentrated in the fidelity to courage, conceived as the differential of a recomposition which is more porous to the real, less exposed to the law.

At the two extremities of Marxism, you will find the following theses:

'It is not the consciousness of men that determines their being, but, on the contrary, their social being that determines their consciousness' (Marx, Preface to *Contribution to the Critique of Political Economy*).

'Marxism implies manifold principles, but, in the final analysis, they can all be reduced to a single sentence: "It is right to revolt against the reactionaries"' (Mao, ubiquitous quotation during the Cultural Revolution).[18]

The first thesis may sustain you in the belief that communist consciousness will necessarily emerge since the succession regulated by the contradictory becoming of a mode of production makes it so that, beyond capitalism, there is only the association of free workers and the reign of the principle 'to each according to their needs'. Stripped to its bare bones, this certainty entails that at the end of the development of productive forces we encounter the withering away of the State. And such a certainty is all the more acceptable when one considers that an entire scientific apparatus confers upon it the dignity of a modern belief.

But the laws of algebra are imprescriptible, and it is indeed a Marxist algebra that is at work in political economy. From the standpoint of the subject, if it exists, the scientific serenity of economism necessarily issues into the following kind of lyrical declarations:

Oh our fatherland! You are our powerful anchor.
In order to defend your dignity, we fast.
When we are gripped by hunger,
We think of you
And all our pain vanishes.
Oh President Mao! You are the red sun that lights up our hearts.
Following your teachings, we fight a frontal battle against the enemy.

When we suffer terrible torture,
We think of you
And our body stops aching![19]

Why? Because to confide the becoming of justice to being means in turn that the Just is *one* man. Only the superegoic humbling of oneself can put a stop to the imminent certitude of the objective end of the law.

The belief in productive fatalism and the cult of personality are two sides of the same historical ethics. Stalin gives us its fusional version: five-year plans and the Little Father of the people make the same fixed point of belief and organize the one and only planetary praise. The Cultural Revolution is this ethics in its disjoined state. In the name of Mao, one thunders against Liu Shaoqi's 'theory of productive forces'. Yet, nothing less than the absoluteness of a thought was needed in order to fight the absoluteness of productive capitals. Belief against belief. It was even required to seek out the adversary on his own terrain, by showing how a complete submission to Mao's thought multiplied the production of tomatos, as in a materialist renewal of the miraculous catch of fish, or made it possible to build a ten thousand ton freighter, barehanded, in a shipyard hardly equipped for the assembling of simple boats. See for instance *Selected Philosophical Essays by Workers, Farmers and Soldiers* (Beijing, 1972).

Above all, do not believe there is any hint of irony in what I am saying. Caught in the real movement whereby the communist recomposition furiously gropes its way, these texts carry a dialectical and moral grandeur against which the contentment of our miseries cannot raise any objection. The fact is that subjectivization follows the dictates of the discourse of belief in order to shatter the obstacle.

The relation to the obstacle is the criterion of delimitation between confidence and belief, Promethean ethics and the ethics of praise. 'How Yukong Moved the Mountains', a fable Mao often made use of, focuses precisely on this delimitation. By attempting to move the mountain with a pickaxe, old Yukong turns it into the pretext for an impossible confidence. He courageously subjectivizes in discourse some point of the real—conceived as impossibility with respect to the rule—and takes it upon himself to divide this rule, that is, to *attack* the real, at the price of countless jibes. If the good genie then moves the mountain—the relay of belief, now subordinated to confidence—one should not at all see in it the multinational wisdom whereby 'Heaven helps those who help themselves', but the conviction that having confidence in oneself, in the mode of the destructive scission of local constraints, generalizes the process of the subject. The genie is what everyone will do, thousands of men armed with pickaxes, as long as, against their resignation, you have been the Prometheus of a particular destruction.

There is nothing here that is redolent of a logic of examples. The important thing is to touch upon the real. No one will imitate you. You will simply have destroyed the belief in the obstacle, you will have displaced the place of the impossible.

The essence of confidence lies in having confidence in confidence. This is why it is right to revolt. In other words, there is no useless courage. The idea of useless courage, like its anxious reverse, the Francoists' *Viva la muerte*, is nothing but the reactionary parody of ethics.

Belief denies the obstacle precisely because it believes in it. If the good genie does not remove the mountain, it is because there is a reason for the mountain to be where it is. Clearly, I can circle around it to the sound of trumpets. Trumpet or pickaxe, that is the whole question. Belief adorns the obstacle with its allegoric discourse. Confidence, situated at the same point, digs deeper without waiting, and pays attention to the *holes* of which the rule prescribes the inoccupation without controlling all their neighbourhoods.

Those who gave up on revolution, whether they talk about the Gulag or the retreat of the masses, show that, if they were part of the movement, of '68 and its consequences, they never seriously partook in the subject whose evanescent cause they beheld in those occurrences. These people belong to the structure. They lived under the regime of self-identity, all the way to attaining the most complete disidentification. They only benefited from an ornamental belief. Now they tell us that they had taken 'the masses' as a master-signifier. That is correct. But they should acknowledge that the event did not call for this. To tell the truth, there was nothing but a minor crack in the imperialist splace, of which the movement, which always comes to a close, was the algebraic cause. Those who, like we did, saw in the first place a lack (the subjective and political precariousness, the absence of a party) and not a fullness (revolt, the masses in the streets, the liberation of speech) had something on which to nourish their confidence, while the others had nothing left but the possibility of betraying their belief.

2

Those ethics that lie between confidence and belief—neither Prometheus nor the sage—have something in common: they all claim that no path is ever opened to fill the gap between subjective evaluation and the norm of the world. These are ethics of the impasse. They exist necessarily, since it is true that every rule is an im-passe of the real.

The difference between them lies in the fact that resignation takes the issue in terms of the whole—the kingdom of necessity—while discordance, being reflexive, maintains evaluation to the point of risking death—the nocturnal kingdom of freedom.

The discourse of resignation is *fatalism*. The discourse of discordance is *nihilism*.

You should arrange the four discourses of ethics, enclosed in the subjective crossing, as in the diagram below.

Let us explain the arrows.

Fatalism pleads from the point of the superego (law = nonlaw) in order to hold that the opposition between good and evil is inessential with regard to necessity. Like all discourses of transition, it is unstable. In the midst of a great storm, inflexibility might lead the fatalist, who confides in everything rather than in himself, to side with the subject of courage. During a period of glamour and order, he leans towards belief, since he

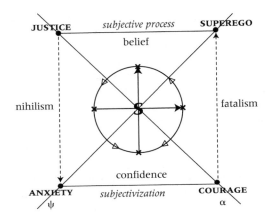

has no firm mooring for the impasse and maceration. This time belongs to the beauties of the superego and, seen from afar and with the eyes of the fatalist, it vaguely resembles justice. It is not right to despair of the fatalist discourse. It is necessary to fight against it, targeting its weak point: the oscillation between belief and confidence.

In the factories, the fatalistic discourse is very well implanted. 'Workers will be workers', 'We will always be fucked over', 'Here nobody wants to do anything', and so on. Defeatism is the spontaneous philosophy of proletarians. Although the coarseness and stupidity of this discourse are dis-couraging, for those who are enlightened by the theory of the subject it is nevertheless a divisible and precarious historical production. An organized micro-confidence (a communist workers' group) locally disrupts its rule.

The question that we must be able to anticipate concerns rather the sudden temptation of belief. It is less important to mistrust the gloomy discourse of resignation than its immoderate future of praise. The party, that which is called the party, cannot rest content with the fact it is believed in. We do not promise anything, hence there is no reason to follow us. We demand and organize the partitioning of a confidence. The fatalist is thus an acceptable and risky interlocutor.

As for nihilism, it knows two modes of emergence.

As a figure of crisis and critical dissolution, it is passive if it does nothing but arrange into a discourse the call of anxiety to the superego. We all know these introverted and ravaged stances that immediately give in and yield the way to the fascination of terror. The transitive action of passive nihilism results from the fact that it is always a defeated belief, a belief that has come undone. Alas, the trajectory which, beginning with belief, leads to fatalism by way of passive nihilism has been the trajectory of a considerable part of my generation. The final maxim of this process is 'We are right to be satisfied with little'—for instance, with François Mitterrand. This means that, initially, the 'It is right to revolt' was upheld exclusively through the fiction of a praise. The passive nihilist is more alien to us than the fatalist, since he has fatalism *ahead of him*.

Conversely, active nihilism is, at the most obscure point of its argumentation, polarized by an inapplicable confidence. One will say that this is a crisis of confidence that precedes its object, while the crisis of belief within passive nihilism follows it.

Today, the young are gladly nihilist. But passive nihilists can enlist them only by means of a temporary misunderstanding. In vain, they wish to convey to the young the idea that the essence of discordance consists in the defeat of beliefs, the crisis of ideologies, the crash of Marxism. For vigorous active nihilism is in search of a form of confidence and, if we are no more able to convey one to it directly than the passive nihilists, we can wait with . . . confidence.

Active nihilism valorizes only itself. This is always better than to end up tolerating the world. The passive nihilist is already a realist, packing his bags for the posts and places of social fate. The active nihilist inherits nothing. *He never believed*, and therein lies all his strength. Unless he joins religious sects, through which he will leap to the most rancid products of belief, he is a traveller without luggage, whose only future is courage, and it is toward this courage that his anxiety guides him by the sureness of the real.

The active nihilist is particularly odious and particularly promising. Every day, he squanders the existential capacity of which he loudly declares himself the bearer. Talking to him has too many consequences for him to assent to it easily. He is indifferent to the recomposition of the world, as long as it has not been seized by a collective reckoning or touched by the restricted action of the avant-garde.

The palindrome that serves as a title in Guy Debord's situationist film— a cinematic balance-sheet of the achievements of twenty years (1955–75) of active nihilism— speaks about the active nihilist: '*In girum imus nocte et consumimur igni*', 'Whirling we walk at night and we are consumed by fire.'

We place all our hopes in the fact that this fire may consume the world, having once again become Prometheus' fire through the mediation offered by political confidence.

Are we not in a condition—and here lies the place of the structure of the subject—to say with Samuel Beckett: 'In any case we have our being in justice, I have never heard anything to the contrary'?[20]

3

Let us situate confidence within the ethical debate. Itself oriented towards belief, it opens a way out for active nihilism, while fatalism is its halting point.

Confidence organizes the entire ethical field. Like the other three discourses, it prescribes some functions to its poles.

Mao divides confidence, he divides the ethics of Marxist politics:

> We must have confidence in the masses and we must have confidence in the Party. These are two cardinal principles. If we doubt these principles, we shall accomplish nothing.[21]

The 'cardinal' character of these two principles is bound to their ethical signification. Without them, Marxist politics has not even begun. We can do precisely nothing, since the subject of the verb 'doing' remains inconsistent. Confidence is that from which class politics draws its cause (as remainder) and its consistency (as discourse of the subject).

Confidence is twofold. What does 'confidence in the masses' mean? It means that the vanishing of the masses causes the Cause of communism; that the political subject weaves itself from ψ but also from α; that the imaginary superegoic diagonal may be short-circuited.

Confidence in the masses comes down to the fact that it is possible, and hence required, to disconnect courage, in flashes, from the imaginary diagonal that appeals to the superego, by gaining a foothold in the anticipation of justice. Such an anticipated effectuation confides the task of the subject to the active masses—the real cut within history's rule.

Conversely, confidence in the party comes down to particularizing the superego-effect (special discipline, internal rules, sacrifices . . .). It means recognizing that recomposition is not the advent of an absolute splace. It means fending off the anxiety induced by justice, and to do so through the precision of the subjective process, the recomposing exactitude of the dictatorship of the proletariat. It means seeing that the subject is also woven from ψ. Confidence in the party sustains justice with regard to anxiety through the delimitation of the superego. In this way, it disconnects the imaginary diagonal that refers justice directly to anxiety.

Anticipation (of justice) and delimitation (of the superego) compose the divisible movement of the discourse of confidence.

The anticipatory side—that of the masses—welcomes active nihilism. It is always utopian-democratic, a gesture of abandonment, and its histori-cal vulnerability easily fuses it to that aspect of nihilism which carries the bitter sovereignty of the subject. A confidence that is soaked in this bitter-ness for too long is a drunken confidence. By short-circuiting belief, it risks turning into passive nihilism.

The delimiting side—that of the party—is oriented towards belief. It is gladly military and absolutist, exalting and glorifying its leaders. It is the bearer of the maintenance and tenacity of the political subject. The importance of its function—being the guardian of the distance from the vanishing of the masses, an effect of keeping on the edge within its own law—should not make one forget that, when confidence is closed off from active nihilism, it mutates and ossifies. An undivided confidence in the party only gives birth to a mediocre belief. If history, in its harsh passes, demands of us some excess of idolatry, some substantial love of our apparatus—a body fallen prey to the four concepts of the subject—we should nonetheless remain alert and return from it by way of the tonic frequentation of nihilism and the sour taste of uprising.

Love what you will never believe twice.

All confidence is abandonment and discipline. This is what sets it out in the circuit that goes from nihilism to belief. The fourth figure always plays the dummy. Fatalism is the dummy for the circuits of confidence.

Confidence dispels the paradoxes of partisanship, since it is only from communism, as an immanent resource of the excess registered in the his-toric cut of popular storms, that stem—*in the second place*—confidence in the party and the acceptance of its harsh rule.

We have confidence in dictatorship in proportion to our concrete con-fidence, which can be measured in step with politics, in the existence among the people of this subject through the effect of which the State shall be foreclosed.

Each and every day, in the ordered labour that wagers on its effec-tuation, warding off the joint chimeras of dogmatism and scepticism, the discourse of confidence whispers to us: 'Yet this is the eve. Let us all accept new strength, and real tenderness. And at dawn, armed with glowing patience, we will enter the cities of glory.'[22]

If the splendour of cities is often nothing but the effect of an indispensable and dreamy belief, it is nonetheless sufficient for us always to be able to say, in confidence as in truth: 'This is the eve.'

Translator's Endnotes and References

Translator's Introduction

1   Alain Badiou, *Saint Paul: The Foundation of Universalism*, trans. Ray Brassier (Stanford: Stanford University Press, 2003), 26.

2   Peter Hallward, *Badiou: A Subject to Truth* (Minneapolis: University of Minnesota Press, 2003), 30.

3   Aside from the obligatory but generally short chapters devoted to *Théorie du sujet* in the available introductions to Badiou's philosophy, two early discussions in particular stand out for their depth and detail: Natacha Michel's interview, in two parts, with Badiou on the occasion of the book's original publication in French, 'Re-naissance de la philosophie: *Théorie du sujet*. Entretien avec Alain Badiou', *Le Perroquet: Quinzomadaire d'opinion* 6 (1982): 1, 9–11; and '*Théorie du sujet*: Entretien avec Alain Badiou, 2,' *Le Perroquet* 13–14 (1982): 1, 10–13; and Claudine Haroche and Isabelle Michot-Vodoz, 'Autour de *Théorie du sujet* d'Alain Badiou', *La ronde des sujets*, special issue of *DRLAV: Revue de Linguistique* 30 (1984): 27–44. At the time, there were also four short book reviews published by Jacques Rancière (in *Bulletin des Révoltes Logiques*), Catherine Clément (in *Le Matin*), Gilles Anquetil (in *Les Nouvelles Littéraires*), and François Regnault, 'Le Mathème émigré—Un sujet politique,' *L'Ane* 7 (1982): 33–4. In English, see Bruno Bosteels, 'Alain Badiou's Theory of the Subject: Part I. The Recommencement of Dialectical Materialism?' *PLI: The Warwick Journal of Philosophy* 12 (2001): 200–229; and 'Alain Badiou's Theory of the Subject: The Recommencement of Dialectical Materialism? Part II', *PLI: The Warwick Journal of Philosophy* 13 (2002): 173–208. Among the general introductions in English, see the sections devoted to *Theory of the Subject* in Jason Baker, *Alain Badiou: A Critical Introduction* (London: Pluto Press, 2002), 40–43; Hallward, *Badiou*,

333

31–41; and Oliver Feltham, *Alain Badiou: Live Theory* (London-New York: Continuum, 2008), 32–83. More recently, the book has attracted the attention of those whom I am tempted to call Young Lacanians, in analogy with the Young Hegelians in nineteenth-century Germany. See, in particular, Ed Pluth and Dominiek Hoens, 'What if the Other is Stupid? Badiou and Lacan on "Logical Time"', *Think Again: Alain Badiou and the Future of Philosophy*, ed. Peter Hallward (London–New York: Continuum, 2004), 182–90; Ed Pluth, 'Badiou and Žižek on Acts and Subjects', *Signifiers and Acts: Freedom in Lacan's Theory of the Subject* (Albany: State University of New York Press, 2007), 115–37; and Adrian Johnston, *Badiou, Žižek, and Political Transformations: The Cadence of Change* (Evanston: Northwestern University Press, 2009). By contrast, despite the book's obvious interest for Lacanians, *Theory of the Subject* receives no mention whatsoever in Slavoj Žižek's own well-known analysis of Badiou in *The Ticklish Subject: The Absent Centre of Political Ontology* (London–New York: Verso, 1999), 127–70; nor in Yannis Stavrakakis, 'Excursus on Badiou', *The Lacanian Left: Psychoanalysis, Theory, Politics* (Albany: State University of New York Press, 2007), 150–60. Žižek does respond to (my summary of) the book, in the Preface to the new edition of *For They Know Not What They Do: Enjoyment as a Political Factor* (London–New York: Verso, 2002), lxxxi–lxxxviii. Back in France, on the other hand, a group of self-declared 'antiphilosophers' or 'antischolastics' on the fringes of academia takes *Théorie du sujet* at least as seriously as Badiou's later works following *L'Être et l'événement*. See Méhdi Belaj Kacem, *Événement et répétition* (Auch: Tristram, 2004); Fabien Tarby, *La philosophie d'Alain Badiou* (Paris: L'Harmattan, 2005); and Rémy Bac, *Le soustraction de l'être: La question ontologique de la vérité de Heidegger à Badiou* (Paris: Le Grand Souffle, 2008).

4   Alain Badiou, *Being and Event*, trans. Oliver Feltham (London: Continuum, 2005), 4 (translation slightly modified).

5   Alain Badiou, *Théorie du sujet* (Paris: Éditions du Seuil, 1982), 46/28 (all subsequent references will include the page number of the French original followed by the page number in the present English translation, separated by a slash). Later in the book, Badiou suggests that perhaps there would be no more than two forms of the subject, one political and the other psychoanalytical, whose topology we owe to Marx and Freud. See *Théorie du sujet*, 301/285.

6   Alain Badiou, *Conditions* (Paris: Éditions du Seuil, 1992), 234 n. 41. The notion of 'suture', which is the process whereby philosophy abdicates its autonomous task and delegates the pursuit of truth to a single one of the four truth procedures that serve as its conditions (e.g., to politics in the Marxist suture of philosophy, to science in positivism, to poetry after Nietzsche and Heidegger, and perhaps to love after Levinas) is discussed in

Alain Badiou, *Manifesto for Philosophy*, trans. Norman Madarasz (Albany: State University of New York Press, 1999), 61–7.

7   Badiou, *Manifesto for Philosophy*, 108 (translation modified).

8   *Theory of the Subject*, in this sense, stands as a grand philosophical summa and the most systematic conceptual formalization of Badiou's activism in the small Maoist organization (Groupe pour la fondation de) l'Union des Communistes de France marxiste-léniniste (UCFML), founded between the fall of 1969 and early 1970, and integrating ex-members split off from the Unified Socialist Party (PSU) in which Badiou had been active, and the ex-Gauche Prolétarienne, with which Sylvain Lazarus and Natacha Michel were affiliated. Right before the formation of the UCFML, Badiou had tried in vain to give shape to a 'party of a new type' from within the ranks of the PSU. See Alain Badiou, *et al.*, *Contribution au problème de la construction d'un part marxiste-léniniste de type nouveau* (Paris: Maspero, 1969). For an overview of the role of Maoism in Badiou's philosophy, see Bruno Bosteels, 'Post-Maoism: Badiou and Politics', *Alain Badiou and Cultural Revolution*, a special issue of *positions: east asia cultures critique* 13.3 (2005): 575–634. The same special issue also contains several translations and a complete bibliography of documents pertaining to the period of Badiou's militantism in the UCFML. A wealth of information can also be found in the footnotes to the translation of Badiou's 'The Flux and the Party: In the Margins of *Anti-Oedipus*', trans. Laura Balladur and Simon Krysl, *Polygraph* 15–16 (2004): 75–92.

9   Unsigned, 'Sur le XXe siècle et la politique', *La Distance Politique* 35 (2001): 3–4. The critique of the party-form was partly responsible for the formation of Organisation Politique (OP), founded in 1985 as a scission from the UCFML. For more information about the OP, see the theses of the group in the brochure *Qu'est ce que l'Organisation politique?* (Paris: Le Perroquet, 2001). The best overview is still Hallward, 'Politics: Equality and Justice', *Badiou: A Subject to Truth*, 223–42. Badiou also discusses some of the activities of this group in his interview with Hallward, reprinted as an 'Appendix: Politics and Philosophy', in Alain Badiou, *Ethics: An Essay on the Understanding of Evil*, trans. Peter Hallward (London–New York: Verso, 2001), 95–144.

10 Badiou, *Saint Paul*, 2.

11 Badiou, *Théorie du sujet*, 143–4/126. See also Alain Badiou, *Peut-on penser la politique?* (Paris: Éditions du Seuil, 1985), 112: 'Political organization is required for the intervention by way of the wager to make a process out of the gap between an interruption and a fidelity. In this sense, organization is nothing other than the consistency of politics.'

12 Badiou, *Being and Event*, 407.

13 Badiou, *Ethics*, 80–87; and Alain Badiou, *The Century*, trans. Alberto Toscano (Cambridge: Polity Press, 2007), 65: 'The other path that the century

335

sketched out—the one that attempts to hold onto the passion for the real without falling for the paroxysmal charms of terror—is what I call the subtractive path: to exhibit as a real point, not the destruction of reality, but minimal difference. To purify reality, not in order to annihilate it at its surface, but to subtract it from its apparent unity so as to detect within it the minuscule difference, the vanishing term that constitutes it.' As an alternative to the path of destruction, Badiou thus returns to a concept—the vanishing term—whose structural overtones he had criticized strongly in his earlier work. The reader should keep in mind, though, that these two paths—like all other major alternatives in *The Century*—are presented without any intrinsic hierarchical qualification or judgement.

14 Badiou, *Logics of Worlds: Being and Event, 2*, trans. Alberto Toscano (London–New York: Continuum, 2009), 396. This line obviously echoes one of Mao Zedong's famous directives from the period of the Cultural Revolution: 'Without destruction there can be no construction' (June 8, 1966). In an interview with Peter Hallward and myself, Badiou also points out this reprise: 'I am obliged here to reintroduce the theme of destruction, whereas in *Being and Event* I thought I could make do with supplementation alone. In order for that which does not appear in a world suddenly to appear within it (and appear, most often, with the maximal value of appearance), there is a price to pay. Something else must disappear. In other words, something must die, or at least must die to the world in question', in Alain Badiou, 'Beyond Formalisation: An Interview', trans. Alberto Toscano and Bruno Bosteels, *The One or the Other: French Philosophy Today*, ed. Peter Hallward, special issue of *Angelaki* 8.2 (2003): 131. See also Badiou's text, 'Destruction, négation, soustraction' (unpublished).

15 Vladimir I. Lenin, 'The Three Sources and Component Parts of Marxism (1913)', *Collected Works* (Moscow: Progress Publishers, 1977), vol. 19, 21–8 (trans. modified).

16 Badiou, *Théorie du sujet*, 198/182.

17 See also 'Hegel en France', in Alain Badiou, Joël Bellassen, and Louis Mossot, *Le noyau rationnel de la dialectique hégélienne* (Paris: François Maspero, 1978), 11–17. The thirteen footnotes in this pamphlet (published in the Yenan 'Synthèses' series edited by Badiou and Lazarus for the UCFML), which for the most part consists of the translation of the Chinese philosopher Zhang Shiying's text of the same title, serve as an excellent summary of Badiou's overall argument for a materialist dialectic in *Theory of the Subject*.

18 Badiou, *Théorie du sujet*, 36/18.

19 See, especially, Louis Althusser, 'Contradiction and Overdetermination' and 'On the Materialist Dialectic', *For Marx*, trans. Ben Brewster (London–New York: Verso, 2005), 87–128 and 161–218. Incidentally, Althusser's attempt

to circumvent what he considers the ironclad determinism of his own earlier, dialectical-materialist understanding of structural causality in *For Marx* and *Reading Capital*, an attempt which heavily relies on ancient atomism in his posthumous writings on the aleatory materialism of the encounter, can be said to have been pre-empted by his former student Alain Badiou in *Theory of the Subject*. See Louis Althusser, *Philosophy of the Encounter: Later Writings, 1978–1987*, trans. G. M. Goshgarian (London–New York: Verso, 2006). Of course, in his discussion of ancient atomism and the clinamen, Badiou also has in mind, albeit without mentioning them, Marx's doctoral dissertation, *Difference between the Democritean and Epicurean Philosophy of Nature* (1841), and Gilles Deleuze's important appendix, 'Lucretius and the Simulacrum', *The Logic of Sense*, trans. Mark Lester with Charles Stivale, ed. Constantin V. Boundas (New York: Columbia University Press, 1990), 266–79.

20 Badiou, *Théorie du sujet*, 128/110. Mallarmé's writing, needless to say, constitutes a major touchstone for almost every thinker in the tradition of so-called 'French theory'. This can be appreciated in the special section on 'The Central Case of Mallarmé', with excerpts from Jean-Paul Sartre, Maurice Blanchot, Jacques Derrida and others, in *Literary Debate: Texts and Contexts: Postwar French Thought*, vol. II, ed. Denis Hollier and Jeffrey Mehlman (New York: The New Press, 2001), 189–255. Badiou's reading in *Theory of the Subject* in particular owes much to the older work of Gardner Davies in *Vers une explication rationnelle du 'Coup de dés': Essai d'exégèse mallarméenne* (Paris: José Corti, 1953) and *Mallarmé et le drame solaire: Essai d'exégèse raisonnée* (Paris: José Corti, 1959). Its findings are summarized and then expanded in Badiou, 'La méthode de Mallarmé: soustraction et isolement,' *Conditions*, 108–29. A complete overview of Badiou's Mallarmé would also have to take into account Meditation 19 in *Being and Event*; 'A Poetic Dialectic: Labîd ben Rabi'a and Mallarmé' and 'Philosophy of the Faun', both in *Handbook of Inaesthetics*, trans. Alberto Toscano (Stanford: Stanford University Press, 2005), 46–56 and 122–41; 'Rhapsody for the Theatre: A Short Philosophical Treatise', trans. Bruno Bosteels, *Theatre Survey* 49.2 (2008): 187–238; and 'First Provisional Theses on Logic', in *Briefings on Existence: A Short Treatise on Transitory Ontology*, trans. Norman Madarasz (Albany: SUNY Press, 2006), 119–24. Pierre Macherey discusses some of the peculiarities of Badiou's interpretation in 'The Mallarmé of Alain Badiou', trans. Marilyn Gaddis Rose and Gabriel Riera, *Alain Badiou: Philosophy and Its Conditions*, ed. Gabriel Riera (Albany: State University of New York Press, 2005), 109–15. See also Jean-Jacques Lecercle's discussion of the paradoxes of Badiou's approach to poetry in general, in 'Badiou's Poetics', *Think Again: Alain Badiou and the Future of Philosophy*, ed. Peter Hallward (London: Continuum, 2004), 208–17. Another useful point of comparison is Jacques Rancière's brilliant but as yet untranslated *Mallarmé: La politique de la sirène* (Paris: Hachette,

1996). See Badiou's comments on Rancière's Mallarmé, in *Logics of Worlds*, 562–4.

21 Badiou, *Théorie du sujet*, 151/133 and 154/136.

22 *Ibid.*, 149/131.

23 *Ibid.*, 156/138.

24 *Ibid.*, 178/161. See also Judith Butler, *Antigone's Claim: Kinship between Life and Death* (New York: Columbia University Press, 2000), 57: 'In George Steiner's study of the historical appropriations of *Antigone*, he poses a controversial question he does not pursue: What would happen if psychoanalysis were to have taken Antigone rather than Oedipus as its point of departure?'

25 Badiou, *Théorie du sujet*, 182/165.

26 See Jacques Derrida. 'Force of Law: The "Mystical Foundation of Authority"', trans. Mary Quaintance, *Acts of Religion*, ed. Gil Anidjar (New York: Routledge, 2002), 230–98. Both Badiou and Derrida use the expression 'force of law' and relate it to an element of inherent 'nonlaw' (respectively *non-loi* and *non-droit* in French). Derrida does so in a close reading of Walter Benjamin's 'Critique of Violence', *Reflections: Essays, Aphorisms, Autobiographical Writings*, ed. Peter Demetz (New York: Schocken, 1978), 277–300. Žižek contributes to this debate in terms of the Benjaminian distinction between mythic and divine violence, among other places, in *Violence* (New York: Picador, 2008), but the reference to some form of nonlaw as the obscene supplement of enjoyment behind all public law is a constant in all of Žižek's work. For a more detailed discussion of this striking theoretical conjuncture, anticipated in *Theory of the Subject*, see Bruno Bosteels, 'Force of Nonlaw: Alain Badiou's Theory of Justice', *Cardozo Law Review* 29.5 (2008): 1905–26.

27 Badiou, *Théorie du sujet*, 204/187–8.

28 *Ibid.*, 209/193.

29 *Ibid.*, 210/194–5.

30 With his commentary on Hölderlin, Badiou is clearly answering, if not mimicking, Heidegger, whose poetic 'suturing' of philosophy can be said to originate in the German poet. Cf. Martin Heidegger, *Elucidations of Hölderlin's Poetry*, trans. Keith Hoeller (Amherst: Humanity Books, 2000). See Badiou's own, partly apologetic explanation in *Being and Event*: 'We know what role the poets play, from Parmenides to René Char, passing by Hölderlin and Trakl, in the Heideggerean exegesis. I attempted to follow in his footsteps—with entirely different stakes—in *Théorie du sujet*, when I convoked Aeschylus and Sophocles, Mallarmé, Hölderlin and Rimbaud to the intricacy of the analysis' (10). In the context of French philosophy, on the other hand, Badiou's reading of Hölderlin offers an intriguing counterpoint to that of the late Philippe Lacoue-Labarthe. To appreciate this polemic, the reader may want to compare Badiou's meditation on Hölderlin in *Being and*

Event, 255–61, with Lacoue-Labarthe's answers to the notion of the 'age of the poets' that Badiou proposes in 'L'âge des poètes', part of a seminar edited by Jacques Rancière, *La politique des poètes: Pourquoi des poètes en temps de détresse* (Paris: Albin Michel, 1992), 21–63. Several texts in this polemic are now compiled and translated in Lacoue-Labarthe, *Heidegger and the Politics of Poetry*, trans. Jeff Port (Urbana: University of Illinois Press, 2007); see also the Translator's Introduction, titled 'The Courage of Thought', ix–xviii. For Lacoue-Labarthe's own independent approach to Hölderlin's theatre in general and Antigone in particular, see 'De l'éthique: à propos d'*Antigone*', *Lacan avec les philosophes* (Paris: Albin Michel, 1991), 19–36; and *Métaphrase, suivi de Le théâtre de Hölderlin* (Paris: PUF, 1998). Given the importance for Badiou of Hölderlin's notion of 'reversal' (*Umkehr* in German, *retournement* in French), the reader may also want to contrast Badiou's commentary with Catherine Clément, 'The Owl and the Nightingale: Hegel and Hölderlin', *Syncope: The Philosophy of Rapture*, trans. Sally O'Driscoll and Deirdre M. Mahoney (Minneapolis: University of Minnesota Press, 1994), 62–72; and Françoise Dastur's *Hölderlin: Le retournement natal* (La Versanne: Encre marine, 1997).

31 Badiou, *Théorie du sujet*, 296/280.

32 *Ibid.*, 62/44. The notion of 'referentiality', which Badiou adopts in *Peut-on penser la politique?* in order to explain the role of Marxism as an active political referent, successively, in the workers' movement, the construction of socialist States, and the national wars of liberation, is borrowed from his friend and fellow-militant Sylvain Lazarus, writing under the pseudonym Paul Sandevince, in 'La fin des références', *Le Perroquet* 42 (1984): 10. Marxism is in crisis, Badiou will argue similarly in *Peut-on penser la politique?*, because this system of referentiality has been exhausted.

33 Badiou, *Théorie du sujet*, 146/128. Alberto Toscano has done much to retrieve this aspect of historical and political periodization in Badiou's work. See, for instance, 'Marxism Expatriated', *Prelom: Journal for Images and Politics* 8 (2006): 154–69.

34 Badiou, *ibid.*, 198/182.

35 *Ibid.*

36 Badiou, *Being and Event*, 1 (translation modified). The extent to which this post-Cartesian doctrine of the subject may involve a philosophical anthropology, not of finitude but of the infinite and the generic in the tradition of Ludwig Feuerbach, is discussed in Nina Power, 'Towards an Anthropology of Infinitude: Badiou and the Political Subject', *The Praxis of Alain Badiou*, ed. Paul Ashton, A.J. Bartlett and Justin Clemens (Melbourne: re.press, 2006), 309–38.

37 Badiou, *Théorie du sujet*, 145/127.

38 Badiou, *Théorie du sujet*, 198/182. In *Peut-on penser la politique?*, Badiou

will similarly affirm: 'If Marxism is indefensible, this is because it must be started' (56); and later: 'We must redo *The Communist Manifesto*' (60).

39   Jacques-Alain Miller, 'Action de la structure', *Cahiers pour l'analyse* 9 (1968): 93–105; 'Matrix', trans. Daniel G. Collins, *lacanian ink* 12 (1997): 44–51; 'Suture (Elements of the Logic of the Signifier)', trans. Jacqueline Rose *Screen* 18.4 (1977–8): 24–34. In French, Miller's early texts have been collected and reissued in *Un début dans la vie* (Paris: Gallimard, 2002).

40   Badiou, *Peut-on penser la politique?*, 14. The UCFML, Badiou's Maoist organization at the time of *Théorie du sujet*, did devote two important studies to the political economy of so-called 'crisis capitalism' and 'state monopoly capitalism'. See *Marxisme-léninisme et révisionnisme face à la crise économique* (Paris: Maspero, 1976) and *Transformations du capitalisme* (Paris: Maspero, 1976).

41   Badiou, *Logics of Worlds*, 71.

42   See Étienne Balibar, 'The Basic Concepts of Historical Materialism', *Reading Capital*, trans. Ben Brewster (London: NLB, 1970), 199–308; and Michel Foucault, *The History of Sexuality*, trans. Robert Hurley (New York: Pantheon Books, 1978–85); and *The Hermeneutics of the Subject: Lectures at the Collège de France, 1981–1982*, ed. Frédéric Gros, trans. by Graham Burchell (New York: Palgrave-Macmillan, 2005). A useful, Althusserian-inspired intervention in this debate can be found in Peter Haidu, *The Subject Medieval/Modern* (Stanford: Stanford University Press, 2004). The work of the Argentine philosopher León Rozitchner, who does for Freudo-Marxism what Badiou does for Lacano-Althusserianism, goes to great lengths in order to bring out the necessarily religious, Christian matrix of capitalist subjectivity. See especially his book on Saint Augustine, which offers a useful counterpoint to Badiou's book on Saint Paul and to his reading of Christianity in *Theory of the Subject*: León Rozitchner, *La Cosa y la Cruz: Cristianismo y capitalismo (En torno a las* Confesiones *de san Agustín)* (Buenos Aires: Losada, 1997). Parts of this work have been translated into English in *Polygraph: An International Journal of Culture & Politics* 19/20 (2008): 33–53.

43   Badiou, *Logics of Worlds*, 4 (trans. modified).

44   Badiou, *Logics of Worlds*, 86. Alberto Toscano discusses the continuity between *Theory of the Subject* and *Logics of Worlds* in terms of this complex subjective space as opposed to the rather more monolithic subject of fidelity that can be found in *Being and Event*, in 'The Bourgeois and the Islamist, or, The Other Subjects of Politics', *The Praxis of Alain Badiou*, 339–66.

45   *Logics of Worlds*, 391.

46   *Ibid.*, 375 (trans. modified).

47   *Ibid.*, 83 (trans. modified to restore the italicized stress of the original).

48   Badiou, 'Philosophy and the "death of communism"', in *Infinite Thought: Truth and the Return of Philosophy*, trans. and ed. Oliver Feltham and Justin Clemens (London: Continuum, 2003), 126–7.

Preface

1 'To introduce myself into your tale' (*M'introduire dans ton histoire*) is the title of a poem by Stéphane Mallarmé, which in turn is comparable to Horace's *De te fabula narratur* ('It is a tale told for you' or 'The joke is on you')—also one of Marx's many favourite references from the classics and, more generally, a common phrase used in prefatory remarks.

2 See, for example, Auguste Comte, *Discours sur l'ensemble du positivisme* (Paris: L. Mathias, 1848), 126. For Comte, each proletarian is a spontaneous philosopher and each philosopher is a systematic proletarian—with 'proletarian' carrying above all a moral or spiritual sense as opposed to the political and economical uses of the term in Marx.

3 A reference to François Mitterrand's election to the Presidency in France, in May 1981, and the resulting celebrations in favour of the 'rose' of French socialism.

4 An obvious pun on 'index' as a list of prohibited works.

5 Julien Gracq, *Lettrines* (Paris: José Corti, 1967), 138–40. Badiou uses a shorter quotation from the same fragment in his conference 'The Paris Commune: A Political Declaration on Politics', included in *Polemics*, trans. Steve Corcoran (London–New York: Verso, 2006), 281–2.

Part I. The Place of the Subjective

1 On September 14, 1967, Mao is reported to have stated: 'Within the working class, there is no basic clash of interests. Under the proletarian dictatorship, the working class has absolutely no reason to split into two hostile factional organizations' ('Directives Regarding Cultural Revolution', *Selected Works*, vol. 9). Available online at http://www.marxists.org.

2 In French, this sentence combines an almost gnomic appeal with an everyday, colloquial simplicity: *Tout ça qui est se rapporte à ça dans une distance de ça qui tient au lieu où ça est.* An alternative translation would be: 'Every it that is relates to it in a distance to it that stems from the place where it is.' The reader should also keep in mind that *ça* in French serves as the official translation of Freud's *id* (German *es*, as in the famous dictum *Wo es war, soll Ich werden*).

3 This sentence, both in its style and in its content, echoes the one annotated in the previous note. In French: *Tout ce qui est d'un lieu revient sur la part de lui-même qui en est déterminée pour déplacer la place, déterminer la détermination, franchir la limite. Etre d'un lieu* could also be translated in set-theoretical terms as 'to belong to a place', especially since a few lines down Badiou himself will introduce for the first time the opposition between belonging and inclusion, borrowed from set theory.

4 In French: *Tout ce qui est d'un tout lui fait obstacle en tant qu'il s'y inclut.* Based on

the opposition between belonging and inclusion, I have translated *être d'un tout* as 'belonging to a whole'. Another translation for *un tout* could be 'a totality', and the reflexive *s'y inclut* could also be rendered as 'includes itself in it'.

5   The French expression *peu de réalité* ('scant reality') is often invoked by Badiou in ways similar to Lacan's usage. As Bruce Fink annotates in his Translator's Endnotes to Lacan's *Ecrits*, it was André Breton who introduced the expression in his 1924 'Introduction au discours sur le peu de réalité', *Point du jour* (Paris: Gallimard, 1970).

6   In French: *Il faut tenir hors lieu*. Other translations could be 'We must stay out of place' or 'It is necessary to hold off place'.

7   Spinoza, *Ethics*, ed. and trans. G. H. R. Parkinson (Oxford: Oxford University Press, 2000), Part I, Prop. 10, Schol.

8   In French, *passe en force* is a strict homonym for *pas sans force*, 'not without force'. *Passer en force* refers to the violent movement of 'pushing through' a law or a decision, of 'opening a passage' or 'imposing one's way' by force. *Ce qui passe en force* could thus be translated as 'what pushes through by force' but this would have meant losing out on the wordplay between *impasse* and *passe* that Badiou is developing here as part of his attempt to go a step beyond Lacan.

9   Lenin's phrase in actual fact states that 'politics is a concentrated expression of the economy', as Badiou correctly quotes below. The suggestion of expressivism, no doubt, makes this less palatable to the Althusserian in Badiou, insofar as Althusser in his canonical work adamantly opposes all such expressive links between the different instances of a social totality and this totality itself. See Vladimir I. Lenin, 'Once Again on the Trade Unions, the Current Situation, and the Mistakes of Trotsky and Bukharin', *Collected Works* (Moscow: Progress Publishers, 1965), vol. 32, 70–107: 'I said again in my speech that politics is a concentrated expression of economics, because I had earlier heard my "political" approach rebuked in a manner which is inconsistent and inadmissible for a Marxist. Politics must take precedence over economics. To argue otherwise is to forget the ABC of Marxism. Am I wrong in my political appraisal? If you think so, say it and prove it. But you forget the ABC of Marxism when you say (or imply) that the political approach is equivalent to the "economic", and that you can take "the one and the other".'

10   Lacan introduced this expression in his 1971–2 Seminar XIX: . . . *ou pire*. See *Autres écrits* (Paris: Éditions du Seuil, 2001), 547–52. Literally, the expression means 'There's one' or 'There's some one'. Bruce Fink, in his translation of Lacan's Seminar XX: *Encore* from the following year proposes 'There's such a thing as One' (S XX, 128).

11   Hegel's *Tätigkeit*, translated as 'act' in English, is rendered as *le faire* in the French translation used by Badiou. For this reason, I have kept both expressions, 'act' and 'making', in translating Badiou's paraphrase of Hegel. *Faire* is

an enormously flexible verb in French, and, as I will indicate for a number of instances below, this is all the more true in *Theory of the Subject*.

12 For Faust's different readings of the line from the Gospel according to John, 'In the beginning was the Word', all the way to the conclusion 'In the beginning was the Deed', see Goethe, *Faust, Part One*, trans. David Luke (Oxford: Oxford University Press, 1998), verses 1224–1237. In German, *Im Anfang war der Tat* echoes the lines from Hegel's *Science of Logic* about *Tat* and *Tätigkeit* just quoted by Badiou.

13 In French, the expression *passe en force*, commented upon above, is here applied to *sa place*, the place of the subject. Alternative translations might be 'pushes through (past) its place', 'passes its place as force' or even 'makes its place pass into force'.

14 See Joseph Stalin, 'Foundations of Leninism (1924)', *Leninism*, trans. Eden & Cedar Paul (London: George Allen & Unwin, 1928), 173.

15 In this paragraph and the previous one, Badiou is playing on *justesse*, 'rightness' or 'correctness', and *justice*, 'justice'. In English, 'right' or 'just' ideas translates *des idées justes*.

16 In French, *fait parti* literally means 'makes (up) a party' or 'makes for a party', 'constitutes a party', but also 'plays or performs the role of party'.

17 In French, *ça fasse je* picks up on the sentence commented upon above (note 2), with *ça* again having both a common meaning, as in any 'it' or 'something' whatsoever, and a technical meaning as the equivalent of the Freudian id. *Faire*, too, is notoriously flexible and involves both an active 'making' or 'doing' (as in the act or deed from Goethe's *Faust*) and an intransitive 'becoming' or 'coming into being' (as in Freud's dictum *Wo es war, soll Ich werden*, 'Where it was I shall come into being').

18 The term translated as 'protesting' is *revendicatives* in French. This refers to the trade unionist figure of politics, based on 'demands', 'claims' or 'vindications' as protestations against injustice and exploitation, usually aimed at the State. For Badiou, the term for this reason is mostly pejorative.

19 In this sentence and the previous one, the verb used in French is once again *faire*, 'making', 'practising', 'forming', 'constituting' and so on: *la bourgeoisie fait de la politique* and *la bourgeoisie fait sujet*.

20 'Where there is oppression, there is resistance' is a phrase commonly attributed to Mao Zedong. Laura Balladur and Simon Krysl, in their careful translation of Badiou's 'The Party and the Flux', annotate this phrase as follows: 'For all its future resonance, the "origin" of the phrase is elusive: some Chinese sources suggest its source may not be in Mao's writings at all. Mao used the phrase in his interview with Edgar Snow (1/9, 1965): it continued to recur during the Cultural Revolution and was forced—of all places—into the Joint Communiqué from Richard Nixon's 1972 visit to China.'

21 *Practise Marxist politics* translates the French *faire de la politique marxiste*.

Other possible translations include 'make' or 'do' or 'put into practice' Marxist politics. The emphasis of *faire* is on the active, militant, organized nature of Marxism *qua* politics.

Part II. The Subject under the Signifiers of the Exception

1   In French, *la destruction d'une qualité de force* can be read as both an objective and a subjective genitive, that is, as 'the destruction of or by a certain quality of force'.

2   Another half-colloquial, half-gnomic sentence: *Du réel, à force de le tordre, ils nous donnent le jus*, in which 'force' by 'torsion' extracts all the 'juice' from the real.

3   The sentence plays on *pluie des astres*, 'rain of falling stars', and *désastre*, 'disaster'.

4   Mallarmé, 'Igitur', *Œuvres complètes* (Paris: Gallimard, 1951), 441.

5   In French, *le passeur sur places de la force* evokes the figure of the *passeur* or 'passer' within the Lacanian procedure of *la passe*. For Badiou, the emphasis is on the act of passing an element of force onto a system of places in such a way that this element not only remains in the same spot but also makes the original force disappear.

6   Here, in a nutshell, we are given a logic of the mark, which will be more familiar to readers of Derrida. *Dé-marqué*, 'de-marcated', can also mean 'marked down' or 'discounted', as with merchandise on sale.

7   The sentence is structured around the pun on the homonymous *point réel*, 'real point' or 'point of the real', and *point réelle*, 'not at all real.'

8   In French, the sentence plays on the internal rhyme between *font l'histoire*, 'make history', and *sont l'histoire*, 'are history'.

9   In French, this one-liner brings together the word play on *font/sont* and *disparaître/pour être*: *Elles font ce qu'elles sont, mais en disparaissant pour être.*

10 Badiou is alluding to Mallarmé's sonnets 'Victorieusement fui le suicide beau' ('The fine suicide fled victoriously' CP 69) and 'Tout Orgueil fume-t-il du soir' ('Does every Pride in the evening smoke' CP 73).

11 The expression 'produces movement' translates the French *fait mouvement*.

12 In French, *en personne* can also mean 'in no one' or 'in nobody', which is consistent with Mallarmé's idea (mentioned below) of logic as impersonified reason.

13 The reader may wish to turn to Mallarmé's poem in French, quoted from his *Œuvres complètes*:

A la nue accablante tu
Basse de basalte et de laves
A même les échos esclaves
Par une trompe sans vertu

Quel sépulcral naufrage (tu
Le sais, écume, mais y baves)
Suprême une entre les épaves
Abolit le mât dévêtu

Ou cela que furibond faute
De quelque perdition haute
Tout l'abîme vain éployé

Dans le si blanc cheveu qui traîne
Avarement aura noyé
Le flanc enfant d'une sirène

To avoid imprecision in the translation, a good strategy is to compare and combine the available English renderings. Thus, in what follows, I selectively rely on translations and paraphrases of Mallarmé's poetry from both Oxford University Press and the University of California Press. One error common to both editions is the failure to understand *à même* as meaning 'flush with' or 'right up to', referring to the proximity of the *basse de basalte et de laves* to *les échos esclaves*.

14 The expression 'the lack of being' in this case is a translation of *le défaut de l'être*, following the model of *le manque à être*. *Défaut* can also mean 'defect', 'shortcoming', 'failing' or 'fault'.

15 The expression 'to put at fault' here translates *mettre en défaut*. Another translation could be 'to cause to default', which in the present context would mean to reveal the place where society is shown to be wanting or lacking.

16 Mallarmé, *Selected Letters of Stéphane Mallarmé*, ed. and trans. Rosemary Lloyd (Chicago: The University of Chicago Press, 1988), 77.

17 In addition to 'meaning', *sens* could also be translated as 'sense' or 'direction', which would be consistent with the leap provoked by the poetic operation of annulment in Mallarmé's case.

18 A play on *coup de force* and *coup de la force*.

19 Mallarmé, *Œuvres complètes*, 428.

20 Another translation for *fait théorie du sujet* would be 'makes a theory out of the subject'.

21 Badiou here is entertaining the option of adding another tercet (entirely of his own invention) to Mallarmé's poem:

Morte à l'excès qui fut son chant
Sinon qu'annule de sa haine
Le mât d'écume naufrageant

22 On the notion of the party as 'advanced detachment of the working people' (actually a quote from Lenin), see Joseph Stalin, 'Concerning Questions

of Leninism (January 25, 1926)', *Works* (Moscow: Foreign Languages Publishing House, 1954), vol. 8, 13–96.

23   On the party as 'leadership nucleus' and as 'powerful nucleus for the whole people', see among other places Mao Zedong, 'Preliminary Conclusions of the Land Investigation Campaign (August 29, 1933)', *Selected Works*, vol. 6; and 'The Role of the Chinese Communist Party in the National War (October 1938)', *Selected Works*, vol. 2. All quotations available online at http://www.marxists.org.

24   On the notion of 'open wide', see Mao Zedong, 'Speech at the Chinese Communist Party's National Conference on Propaganda Work (March 12, 1957)', *Selected Works*, vol. 5. This notion is also discussed at some length in the Circular from May 16, 1966 that heralds the beginning of the Cultural Revolution in China.

25   A reference to the song 'The Internationale': 'C'est la lutte finale/ Groupons-nous, et demain/ L'Internationale/ Sera le genre humain' ('This is the final struggle/ Let us gather together, and tomorrow/ The Internationale/ Will be the human race').

26   Mao, 'Talk On Questions Of Philosophy (1964)', *Selected Works*, vol. 9.

27   Mallarmé, *Œuvres complètes*, 433. English translation by Mary Ann Caws available online at http://www.studiocleo.com/librarie/mallarme/prose.html.

28   Mallarmé, *Œuvres complètes*, 441.

29   Here Badiou, in an astounding if not scandalous feat, quotes a series of consecutive lines from *A Dice Throw*, all the while erasing the typographical differences and similarities between them in terms of font type and size. In French, this 'flat' rendition reads as follows: 'Rien de la mémorable crise où se fût l'événement accompli en vu de tout résultat nul humain n'aura eu lieu (une élévation ordinaire verse l'absence) que le lieu, inférieur clapotis quelconque comme pour disperser l'acte vide abruptement qui sinon par son mensonge eût fondé la perdition, dans ces parages, du vague en quoi toute réalité se dissout' (*Théorie du sujet*, 112; cf. *Œuvres complètes*, 474–5).

30   References, respectively, to 'Another Fan (Belonging to Mlle Mallarmé)' and 'Herodias (Scene)'.

31   This is from the sonnet 'Tout Orgueil fume-t-il du soir' ('Does every Pride in the evening smoke').

32   These three terms are taken from the consecutive sonnets 'Does every Pride . . .', 'Surgi de la croupe et du bond . . .' ('Arisen from the rump . . .'), and 'Une dentelle abolit . . .' ('A lace vanishes . . .').

33   In French, the sentence is somewhat ambiguous: *C'est manière de force que de jouer pour finir avec la fascinante et impersonelle séduction des signifiants séparables.*

34   In French, *conscience* means both 'conscience' and 'consciousness'. Badiou

is exploiting this double meaning, as the subsequent allusion to class-consciousness makes abundantly clear.

35 In French, Mallarmé's sonnet reads as follows:

> Ses purs ongles très haut dédiant leur onyx
> L'Angoisse, ce minuit, soutient, lampadophore,
> Maint rêve vespéral brûlé par le Phénix
> Que ne recueille pas de cinéraire amphore
>
> Sur les crédences, au salon vide: nul ptyx,
> Abolit bibelot d'inanité sonore,
> (Car le Maître est allé puiser des pleurs au Styx
> Avec ce seul objet dont le Néant s'honore).
>
> Mais proche la croisée au nord vacante, un or
> Agonise selon peut-être le décor
> Des licornes ruant du feu contre une nixe,
>
> Elle, défunte nue en le miroir, encor
> Que, dans l'oubli fermé par le cadre, se fixe
> De scintillations sitôt le septuor.

For the English version, I have used Weinheim's translation from the University of California Press, all the while replacing 'Anguish' with 'Anxiety'.

36 See Mallarmé, *Œuvres complètes*, 1490.
37 See *Selected Letters of Stéphane Mallarmé*, 87.
38 Another translation for *ce qui fait ici sujet de l'angoisse* could be 'whatever turns anxiety here into a subject'.

Part III. Lack and Destruction

1 See Hegel's famous line in *The Phenomenology of Spirit*: 'Time is the Notion itself that *is there* and which presents itself to consciousness as empty intuition' (Ph 487). Badiou misquotes the original German, as if Hegel had written '*die Zeit ist der Begriff da*', whereas the actual line from the original reads: '*Die Zeit ist der daseiende Begriff selbst*'. Alexandre Kojève also comments on this passage in 'A Note on Eternity, Time, and the Concept', *Introduction to the Reading of Hegel*, ed. Allan Bloom, trans. James H. Nichols Jr. (New York: Basic Books, 1969), 101. Finally, Badiou introduces a pun on *là*, 'there', which translates the German *da*, and *le la du diapason*, the 'la' of the tuning fork. I have tried to retain something of this pun by using the expression 'that sets the tone'.

2 The French here uses *se clive*, 'splits', and *clivage*, 'splitting'. Another translation could be 'cleaves off' and 'cleavage' or even 'scission'. Badiou clearly has in mind the Maoist connotations of the logic of splitting or scission, as

in the slogan 'One divides into two', suggested by the Lacanian *quand un fait deux*.

3 The French here is quite convoluted: *la théorie analytique tient cette équivoque dans l'instruction du désir d'où s'appréhende le sujet*, which could also be translated as 'the theory of psychoanalysis holds this equivocation to be instructive about the way the subject can be apprehended on the basis of desire'.

4 The reader should keep in mind that this simplification of the world also refers to Mallarmé's definition of the act, alluded to above: 'The one available act, forever and alone, is to understand the relations, in the meantime, few or many; according to some interior state that one wishes to extend, in order to simplify the world' ('Music and Letters', D 187).

5 An allusion to Mallarmé's 'Prose (for des Esseintes)'.

6 Lenin, *Materialism and Empirio-Criticism*, in vol. 14 of his *Collected Works*, trans. Abraham Fineberg: 'Frankly and bluntly did Bishop Berkeley argue! In our time these very same thoughts on the "economical" elimination of "matter" from philosophy are enveloped in a much more artful form, and confused by the use of a "new" terminology, so that these thoughts may be taken by naïve people for "recent" philosophy!' (28).

7 A reference to Xavier (brother of Joseph) de Maistre's *Voyage autour de ma chambre* (1790), translated as *A Journey around my Room*, foreword Alain de Botton, trans. Andrew Brown (London: Hesperus Press, 2004).

8 'Half-saying' here translates Lacan's *mi-dire*, that is, the notion that truth can only be 'half-said' or 'half-spoken', whereby *mi-dit* is an obvious, Mallarméan-sounding homonym for *midi*, 'noon' or 'midday'. In his unpublished seminar on Lacan's antiphilosophy, Badiou discusses at length the differences and similarities between Lacan's 'half-said' and Mallarmé's 'midday', compared to Nietzsche's 'noon' as the time of the 'shortest shadow'.

9 The French here, *mi-di(t)*, combines into a single word the otherwise homonymous *mi-dit* ('half-said') and *midi* ('noonday' or 'midday').

10 Badiou may be thinking of Louis Althusser's discussion of the universal and the specific, in *For Marx*, trans. Ben Brewster (London–New York: Verso, 2005), 183.

11 'Discrepancy' here translates *décalage*, a term especially dear to Badiou's former teacher Althusser (notably in his early reading of Jean-Jacques Rousseau), which can also mean 'interval', 'lag', or 'gap'. See Althusser, 'Rousseau: The Social Contract (The Discrepancies)', *Politics and History*, trans. Ben Brewster (London: New Left Books, 1972), 113–60.

12 The French *une mise en biais* ('slanting') could also be translated as 'a putting askew', 'a sideways glance', or a 'looking awry', as in the eponymous book by Slavoj Žižek. 'Twisted' here translates *tordu*, as in that which underwent a torsion, not straight.

13 Before quoting Lacan, Badiou uses the following expressions: *l'être-à-côté* ('being-to-the-side'), *l'être-para* ('para-being'), *du par-être* ('par-appearing'). Bruce Fink's explanation is useful in this context: 'The neologism Lacan creates here, *par-être*, is pronounced exactly like *par-aître*, which means 'to appear' or 'appearing'. Two sentences further on, Lacan intends both meanings when he says that 'being presents itself, always presents itself, by *par-être*', i.e., by appearing and being beside (or alongside)' (S XX, 44–5 n. 19).

14 In French, *paravent* ('smokescreen' or 'screen') adds a further pun to the Lacanian neologisms based on *par-être*.

15 In French: *'Nous ne sommes rien, par-soyons le Tout'*, which is a clear allusion to another famous line from 'The Internationale': *'Nous ne sommes rien, soyons tout'*. The effect of introducing Lacan's neologism of *par-être* into this line consists in slanting the view away from the dogmatic totality toward what lies beside or alongside the whole.

16 The French *sceau* ('seal') could also be translated as 'mark', 'stamp' or 'stamping'. In the discussion of Mallarmé above, I used 'seal' to translate *frappe* and 'stampings' for *timbrages*.

17 See Lenin, 'Once Again on the Trade Unions, the Current Situation, and the Mistakes of Trotsky and Bukharin', *Collected Works*, vol. 32, 70–107.

18 For Lacan, the best that this *bien-dire* or 'well-saying' can amount to is a *mi-dire*, 'half-saying' or 'half-stating'.

19 See Lenin, 'Marxism and Insurrection', *Collected Works*, vol. 26, 22–7: 'Of course, this is all by way of example, only to illustrate the fact that at the present moment it is impossible to remain loyal to Marxism, to remain loyal to the revolution unless insurrection is treated as an art'.

20 The suggestion is that Lacan, the Lenin of psychoanalysis, can also be its Mao, insofar as Lacan I and Lacan II would be like a king succeeding himself. Also implied is the notion that Jacques-Alain Miller, though a Maoist around 1968, is *not* the Mao of psychoanalysis.

21 The French here, referring to Lacan's *droiture à tenir sur la torsion* ('his steady uprightness about torsion'), continues the series of puns on straightness, rightness, steadiness, and torsion.

22 In French, the word translated as 'practice' in English is not *pratique* but *expérience*, just as in the previous sentence Marxism is defined as *le propos expérimenté de soutenir l'advenue subjective d'une politique. Expérience* and *expérimenté*, in this context, should not be read with the existential pathos of experience but in the sense of a formal and practical experiment, similar to what happens in inventive science or in artistic innovation.

23 An allusion, with inverted gender, to *Détruire, dit-elle*, the title of a famous novel and film by Marguerite Duras (1969), ostensibly inspired by May '68. Beyond this reference, the expression, even in the masculine form *Détruire*,

dit-il as used by Badiou, has taken on a life of its own and is frequently invoked in literary and artistic circles.

24 An allusion to Friedrich Nietzsche's well-known remark, in a letter to Brandes from December 1888: 'I prepare an event that, in all likelihood, will break history in two, to the point where a new calendar will be needed, and in which 1888 will be the Year 1.' In rejecting this view, *Théorie du sujet* clearly anticipates Badiou's conclusion, in a conference from 1992 on Nietzsche, about the 'antiphilosophical' nature of this 'break' *qua* archipolitical 'act' of grand politics. See Badiou, *Casser en deux l'histoire du monde?* (Paris: Les Conférences du Perroquet, 1992).

25 The French, *sceau*, was previously translated as 'seal' but here as 'stamp' so as to retain echoes of the pun on the homonymous *saut*, 'jump'.

26 Jacques-Alain Miller, 'Matrix', trans. Daniel G. Collins, *lacanian ink* 12 (1997): 48–9 (trans. modified).

27 The French here, *De là qu'il fait sujet*, could also be translated as 'Whence its quality as subject', 'From this it follows that it makes (for) a subject', or 'This explains why it constitutes a subject'. The use of an indefinite article in English, however, might wrongly suggest that there are several—or at least two—subjects (the proletariat and the bourgeoisie), whereas Badiou is correcting himself precisely on this point so as to affirm, as he did in the previous session of his seminar: 'There is only one political subject, for any given historicization.'

28 In French, the expletive *ne* that usually accompanies negation is absent: *le sujet aboutit à rien* (which I have rendered as 'the subject leads to nothing'), as opposed to *le sujet n'aboutit à rien* (which could be translated as 'the subject does not lead to anything').

29 In French, *se fait* and *s'effet*, with the latter being a neologism on Badiou's part, are homonymous. The whole sentence, though, is quite obscure: *la politique prolétarienne . . . est ce qu'elle se fait (s'effet) ne pas être (s'effet qui a nom 'communisme')*. The basic underlying idea is that the proletariat, like the unconscious, brings into being some element of nonbeing. Or, rather, through the unconscious and the proletariat, the ontological opposition of being and nonbeing itself is subverted.

30 The French, *la botte* in *c'est la botte!*, refers to a special coup, for example in fencing, or a secret weapon, unrecognized by the adversary. *Porter une botte à quelqu'un* thus can mean to attack or interpellate someone in an unforeseen way.

31 The French expression, *s'adosse au* (here translated as 'leans up against') beautifully conveys an image of truth with its *dos* ('back') up against the real.

32 In French, *une plaie* ('a sore') here also means 'a pain (in the neck)' or 'nuisance'.

33 Badiou, in personal conversations with the translator, suggests that *'mes tortillons'* could refer to the twisted elucubrations in Lacan's brain, but I have the impression that Lacan is rather referring to his students and disciples and *their* mental elucubrations. My translation tries to keep the ambiguity alive.

34 'Jams up' here translates the French *coince*, a notion Badiou will discuss below in the context of Lacan's topologies. Other translations could be 'wedges' or 'traps'.

35 'Blocks' here translates the French *fait coincement*.

36 The French here, *changer l'homme dans ce qu'il a de plus profond*, corresponds to the first sentence of the famous 'Sixteen Points' decision, adopted by the Central Committee of the Chinese Communist Party on August 8, 1966, marking the beginning of the Chinese Cultural Revolution. In English, the full line reads as follows: 'The great Proletarian Cultural Revolution now unfolding is a great revolution that touches people to their very souls', in *The Chinese Cultural Revolution: Selected Documents*, ed. and with notes by K. H. Fan (New York–London: Monthly Review Press, 1968), 162. See also Badiou's comments in 'The Cultural Revolution: The Last Revolution?', trans. Bruno Bosteels, *positions: east asia cultures critique* 13 (2005): 489–90.

37 In French, this whole sentence is a bit convoluted: *Tenons la prise, plutôt, d'un biface subjectif, dont l'articulation nous donnera de la peine, pour y jointer la destruction fécondante et le bonheur d'y manquer*. The reference to *le bonheur d'y manquer* counters Lacan's mention of the happiness to be alive, quoted above.

38 In French, *morgue* can mean both 'morgue' or 'mortuary' and 'arrogance', 'smugness', 'superciliousness'. I have tried to keep hints of both meanings by using 'deadly arrogance' as a translation.

39 In French, *au-delà ou en deça* ('beyond or shy of') is also used by Lacan, S XX, 44.

40 The French here, *mise en défaillance*, is translated as 'the active failure'. Another possible rendering would be 'the putting into failure'.

41 In French, *droits*. This extends the pun, used earlier, on 'right' ideas and 'twisted' paths to truth. Here, in addition, the opposition is between 'straight' and 'contorted'.

42 'Lapses back' here translates *retombe*, which previously, in Part I, served as the French translation of Hegel's *Rückfall*, 'relapse', in the dialectical process.

43 In the notation of the 'mathemes' of anxiety, the superego, courage, and justice, I have used 'locus' for *lieu*, whereas elsewhere 'place' serves to translate both *lieu* and *place*. The mathemes are one of the few instances in *Théorie du sujet* where these two French terms are kept separate.

44 This is an allusion to a famous saying which the old Mao frequently used to

refer to the international situation during the Cultural Revolution. It was published in *Renmin Ribao (People's Daily)* on November 9, 1967: 'There is great disorder under heaven and the situation is excellent' (*Tianxia da luan, xinghsi da hao*). The Chinese notion for 'disorder', *luan*, which can also be translated as 'disturbances,' 'upheaval' or 'chaos', is typically rendered as *troubles* in French. Whence the most common, slightly abridged version used by Badiou: *Les troubles sont une excellente chose*. This rendering, which I have respected and kept as literal as possible in my own translation, furthermore enables Badiou to play on the opposition between *voyer clair*, 'to see clearly,' and *trouble*, 'opaque,' 'cloudy,' 'confused' or 'shady.'

45   A pun on *mi-dit*, 'half-said' or 'half-stated', and *mau-dite*, 'ill-said' or 'cursed'.

46   Joseph Conrad, *The Nigger of the 'Narcissus'* (New York: Norton, 1979), 145.

47   Spinoza, *Ethics*, 221 (Part III, Prop. 59, Schol.).

48   *Ibid.*, 211.

49   In French, *s'implace* is a neologism on Badiou's part. The reflexive use of the verb could also be translated as 'unplaces itself'.

50   Aeschylus, *Eumenides*, trans. Christopher Collard (Oxford: Oxford University Press, 2002), 98–100. Badiou's French translation has 'anxiety' (*angoisse*) for what is translated as 'trouble' in this English version.

51   Aeschylus, *ibid.*, 103–105.

52   In French, the expression in this case is *un sujet de droit*, whereas for the most part Badiou talks about law (*loi*) rather than right (*droit*).

53   This is from the last page of 'A Season in Hell', just after the famous line '*Il faut être absolument moderne*', in Arthur Rimbaud, *Complete Works*, trans. Paul Schmidt (New York: Harper & Row, 1967), 213: 'Never mind hymns of thanksgiving: hold on to a step once taken', in French: '*Point de cantiques: tenir le pas gagné*'.

54   The original sentence in French, *Quoi qu'il faille revenir—et que ce retour soit sujet—peut sourdre et s'éclairer le franchissement de ce qui ne comporte plus aucun retour*, defies all quick and easy translations.

55   In French, a pun on *démission missionaire*.

56   See the letter 'Marx to K. Kugelmann in Hanover (London, April 12, 1871)', SW II, 420. The French translation of this letter has *détruire* for 'smash'.

Part IV. A Materialist Reversal of Materialism

1   In French, '*Qu'est-ce qui fait sujet?*' once again relies on the malleability of the verb *faire*. Alternative translations could be 'What constitutes a subject?' or 'What makes for a subject?'

2   A reference to Alain [Émile-Auguste Chartier], *Le Citoyen contre les pouvoirs* (Paris: Éditions du Saggitaire, 1926).

3   In French: *Il faut* faire *le marxisme*.

4   'Found anew' here translates *refondre*, which aside from 'founding' or 'grounding anew' also carries connotations of 'recasting' or 'resourcing oneself'. Further down, 'overhaul' will translate *refonte*.

5   'Un-establishment' and 'un-established' here translate the French *désétablissement* and *désétablie*, the opposite of *rétablir l'ordre*, 'to restore order' or 'to re-establish order'.

6   The allusion is to the French revolutionary Jacques Hébert, who was guillotined on March 24, 1794, after having become an opponent of Maximilien Robespierre himself for his excessive secularism and worship of Reason.

7   Lacan, *Télévision* (Paris: Éditions du Seuil, 1974), 19; *Television*, trans. Denis Hollier, Rosalind Krauss and Annette Michelson, ed. Joan Copjec (New York: W. W. Norton, 1990), 8.

8   *Ibid.*, 16/5 (trans. modified).

9   In French, the sentence plays on *faire nœud* ('to operate as a nodal point') and *faire centre* ('becoming a centre'). *Nœud* also means 'knot' or 'node'.

10 Lacan, 'Le sinthome', *Ornicar?* 7 (1977): 12 ('Séminaire du 13 janvier 1976').

11 'Absent-mindedly' here translates the French *avec étourderie*, which could be an allusion to Lacan's text *L'étourdit* (1973), itself a pun on Molière's play *L'étourdi* (*The Blunderer* or *The Scatterbrain*).

12 The French, *être des lisières* ('a being of the thresholds'), could also be translated as 'a being of limits' or a 'border-entity'. See also Badiou, 'The Flux and the Party: In the Margins of *Anti-Oedipus*', trans. Laura Balladur and Simon Krysl, *Polygraph* 15–16 (2004): 75–92.

13 See Marx, 'Private Property and Communism', *Economic and Philosophical Manuscripts of 1844*, in Marx and Engels, *Collected Works*, vol. 3, 297.

14 See 'Engels to Conrad Schmidt', in Marx and Engels, *Collected Works*, vol. 50, 462.

15 *Ibid.*, 466: 'Or are the concepts which prevail in the natural sciences fictions because they by no means always coincide with reality? From the moment we accept the theory of evolution all our concepts of organic life correspond only approximately to reality. Otherwise there would be no change: on the day when concepts and reality completely coincide in the organic world development comes to an end. The concept fish includes a life in water and breathing through gills: how are you going to get from fish to amphibian without breaking through this concept? And it has been broken through and we know a whole series of fish which have developed their air bladders further into lungs and can breathe air. How, without bringing one or both concepts into conflict with reality are you going to get from the egg-laying reptile to the mammal, which gives birth to living young? And in reality we have in the monotremata a whole sub-class of egg-laying mammals—in

1843, I saw the eggs of the duck-bill in Manchester and with arrogant nar-row-mindedness mocked at such stupidity—as if a mammal could lay eggs—and now it has been proved! So do not behave to the conceptions of value in the way I had later to beg the duck-bill's pardon for!' (trans. modified)

16 In French: *Qui trop au miroir se fie, l'ornithorynque le défie.*

17 The French here, *Je sois(t) perdu*, plays on the distance between the first (*sois*) and the third person (*soit*), introduced into the subject, not unlike Rimbaud's famous *Je est un autre.*

18 The French here is slightly more cryptic: *La problématisation est trouée du réel pour la vérité.* Alternative translations include 'Problematization means the breakthrough of the real toward the truth' or 'Problematization is how the real pierces through for the truth'.

19 Friedrich Engels, *Anti-Dühring, ibid.*

20 Lacan, 'Séminaire R. S. I.', *Ornicar?* 3 (1975): 105. English translation: 'Seminar of 21 January 1975', *Feminine Sexuality: Jacques Lacan and the école freudienne*, ed. Juliet Mitchell and Jacqueline Rose, trans. Jacqueline Rose (New York: W. W. Norton, 1983), 164.

21 Littré indicates that *sphinx* at one time was a feminine noun in French, in conformity with Greek, where the sphinx is feminine. This is what seems to be implied in the use of *sphinge.*

22 In French: *D'ignorer le reste le fait, lui, rester.*

23 In French: *D'ignorer le miroir le met, lui, en miroir du monde.*

24 The French here, *Ce qui est du tout exige la position de l'autre, qui n'est pas du tout*, is quite ambiguous in that *n'est pas du tout* can be understood both as 'which is not of the whole' or 'which does not not belong to the whole' and 'which is not at all'.

25 The French, *en effet de bord sur elle-même*, could also be translated as 'with an effect of being its own border' or 'to the effect of constituting its own border'.

26 Lacan, 'R. S. I., année 1974–75', *Ornicar?* 3 (1975): 97–8 ('Séminaire du 14 janvier 1975').

27 In French: *Ce dont une coupure historique fait rencontre.* This is one instance where *coupure*, aside from 'cut' (as in Lacan's topologies), could also be translated as 'break' (as in a Bachelardian 'epistemological break').

28 The French here, *ce qui s'évanouit en réel*, could also be translated as 'that which vanishes in the real' or 'that which really vanishes'.

29 On August 10, 1966, Mao addresses the crowd in a statement on meeting the masses: 'Concern yourself with affairs of the state', his directive is reported to have been, sometimes translated as 'You should pay attention to state affairs and carry the Great Proletarian Cultural Revolution through to the end!' See 'Directives Regarding Cultural Revolution', *Selected Works*, vol. 9.

30   In the original French, as Badiou confirmed in personal correspondence with the translator, *La perte et perdue* contains a typo for *La perte est perdue*.

31   This quote is from the famous circular of 'Sixteen Points' that marked the onset of the Great Proletarian Cultural Revolution. In English, see 'The Party Decision', *The Chinese Cultural Revolution*, point 9 (titled 'Cultural Revolutionary Groups, Committees, and Congresses').

Part V. Subjectivization and Subjective Process

1   Lacan, 'R. S. I., année 1974–75', *Ornicar?* 4 (1975) 97–8 ('Séminaire du 11 février 1975').

2   *Ibid.*

3   In French: *J'aime l'idée du parti politique, comme on aime ce qui consiste en sujet, d'avoir été, parce qu'une fois perdu, le dirigeant à venir de sa résilitation.*

4   This heading is a quote from Saint-John Perse's poem *Vents* (Paris: Flammarion, 1968), second song. In French: *'Se hâter! Se hâter! Parole de vivant!'*

5   For further information about this famous quotation attributed to Mao, see the Translator's endnote 44 to Part III above.

6   This is most likely a reference to Lenin's 1920 pamphlet, *Left-Wing Communism: An Infantile Disorder*, in vol. 31 of his *Collected Works*: 'The fundamental law of revolution, which has been confirmed by all revolutions and especially by all three Russian revolutions in the twentieth century, is as follows: for a revolution to take place it is not enough for the exploited and oppressed masses to realise the impossibility of living in the old way, and demand changes; for a revolution to take place it is essential that the exploiters should not be able to live and rule in the old way. It is only when the "lower classes" do not want to live in the old way and the "upper classes" cannot carry on in the old way that the revolution can triumph' (71).

7   This quotation (*Tianxia da luan, da dao tianxia da zhi*), in which Mao once again relies on the classical Chinese notions of 'all-under-heaven' (*tianxia*) and 'disorder' (*luan*) but this time to achieve 'great order under heaven,' is most famously found in a letter to his wife Jiang Qing from July 8, 1966. An English translation of this letter appeared as 'Mao Tse-tung's Private Letter to Chiang Ch'ing,' *Issues and Studies* 9.4 (June 1973): 94–6. Unfortunately, in this translation, the saying in question is glossed over and combined with the following sentence into 'The situation changes from a great upheaval to a great peace once every seven or eight years' (94). It is not an existing proverb, as Badiou suggests, so much as an original creation based on an ancient expression which Mao's flair for quotable one-liners, not unlike Badiou's own taste for such gnomic formulations, turned into a popular quasi-aphoristic sentence.

8   In French, the expression *non-lieu* has the juridical sense of 'no ground for trial'. In the present context, aside from evoking the topology of place and outplace, not to mention the etymology of the Greek *utopia* as 'nonplace', the term could also be translated as 'nonevent'.

9   In French, '*la' femme* evokes a quasi-archetypal understanding of Woman or universal womanhood, which is precisely what is put under erasure or barred in Lacan's formulas of sexuation: '*la' femme, en effet, inexiste au tout*. Despite the awkwardness of the translation, I have rendered this in English as '"the" woman'. In the next sentence, a paraphrase of Hegel's famous reading of Antigone in the *Phenomenology of Spirit*, I use 'Woman' with a large capital to translate *la femme*.

10 See Thomas Jech, *Set Theory* (New York: Academic Press, 1978), 331.

11 Paul J. Cohen, *Set Theory and the Continuum Hypothesis* (New York–Amsterdam: W. A. Benjamin, 1966), 112.

12 *Ibid.*

13 *Ibid.*, 151 (I have modified the English in accordance with the changes that Badiou introduced in his French translation—all changes meant to make the text more accessible).

14 In these final lines, Badiou is quoting from Mallarmé's 'Un coup de dés': '*dans ces parages / du vague / en quoi toute réalité se dissout*' all the way to the image of the *lanceur* or 'dice thrower'.

Part VI. Topics of Ethics

1   Julien Gracq, *Lettrines* (Paris: José Corti, 1967), 67–70.

2   See Mao, 'Talk at the First Plenum of the Ninth Central Committee of the Chinese Communist Party (April 28, 1969)', *Selected Works*, vol. 9, available online at http://www.marxists.org.

3   Mao as reported in 'The Great Cultural Revolution Will Shine For Ever', *Peking Review* 19 (May 21, 1976): 6–10.

4   In French, the neologism *dé-sens*, which evokes 'un-sense' or 'dis-sense', is homonymous with *décence*, 'decency'. Another, more cumbersome, translation to keep the neologism could be 'dis-sense-y'.

5   In French, *in-dé-sens*, a homonym for *indécence*, 'indecency', further extends the neologistic pun on that which runs counter to common sense and decency.

6   Stephen Crane, *The Red Badge of Courage*, ed. Sculley Bradley, Richmond Croom Beatty, E. Hudson Long, revised by Donald Pizer (New York: W. W. Norton, 1976), 109.

7   On the fused group and the pledged group, see Jean-Paul Sartre, *Critique of Dialectical Reason*, trans. Alan Sheridan-Smith, foreword Fredric Jameson (New York–London: Verso, 2004), 343–404 and 433–9.

8   Ecclesiastes 1:7.

9   See Blaise Pascal, *Pensées*, ed. and trans. Roger Ariew (Indianapolis: Hackett, 2005), 273 (S749/L919).

10 In the French original, the last lines of this sentence are missing. In personal correspondence with the translator, Badiou proposes to make up for this gap as follows: *et non cause illusoire de leur détermination. L'imaginaire vient ainsi consolider le réel et non installer le semblant.*

11 This is from the last stanza of Mallarmé's 'Toast funèbre' ('Funereal Toast'). In French, the lines read:

> C'est de nos vrais bouquets déjà tout le séjour
> Où le poète pur a pour geste humble et large
> De l'interdire au rêve, ennemi de sa charge.

12 A. Y. Vyshinsky, Procurator of the USSR/State Prosecutor, in *Report of the Court Proceedings in the Case of the Anti-Soviet 'Bloc of Rights and Trotskyites' heard before the Military Collegium of the Supreme Court of the USSR* (Moscow: People's Commissariat of Justice of the USSR, 1938), 697. Subsequent page numbers in the body of the text refer to this same edition.

13 The French here, *parti*, has both a strictly political meaning ('party') and a more general sense ('decision', 'stance', 'position', 'standpoint'). The sentence thus talks about the risk of taking the wrong decision as much as of choosing the wrong party.

14 Stalin, *Leninism*, 171.

15 See 'The Party Decision', in *The Chinese Cultural Revolution*, 176–7.

16 See Wang Hongwen, 'Report on the Revision of the Party Constitution (Delivered at the Tenth National Congress of the Communist Party of China on August 24 and Adopted on August 28, 1973', *The Tenth National Congress of the Communist Party of China (Documents)* (Beijing: Foreign Languages Press, 1973), 48.

17 See François Duc de La Rochefoucauld, *Maxims*, trans. Leonard Tancock (New York: Penguin, 1959), 23 (maxim 26).

18 'One has reason to revolt against the reactionaries' or 'It is justified to rebel against the reactionaries' is a phrase coined in a speech by Mao, made in 1939 to celebrate Stalin's 60th birthday: 'There are innumerable principles of Marxism, but in the last analysis they can all be summed up in one sentence: "To rebel is justified." For thousands of years everyone said: "Oppression is justified, exploitation is justified, rebellion is not justified." From the time when Marxism appeared on the scene, this old judgment was turned upside down, and this is a great contribution', in Stuart R. Schram, *The Political Thought of Mao Tse-Tung* (New York: Praeger, 1969), 427–8. For a detailed analysis of the different meanings of this phrase, see Chapter 1 from Badiou's *Théorie de la contradiction* (Paris: François Maspero, 1975),

translated as 'An Essential Philosophical Thesis: "It is Right to Rebel against the Reactionaries"', trans. Alberto Toscano, *positions: east asia cultures critique* 13 (2005): 669–77.

19 See *Forty-One Red Hearts are with Chairman Mao Forever* (Beijing: Foreign Languages Press, 1967), 18–19.

20 Samuel Beckett, *How it Is* (New York: Grove Press, 1988), 124.

21 See *On the Question of Agricultural Co-operation* (July 31, 1955), in *Quotations from Mao Tse Tung* (Beijing: Foreign Languages Press, 1972), 3 (trans. modified to render Badiou's insistence on 'confidence').

22 This quote is from the end of Rimbaud's 'A Season in Hell', *Complete Works*, 213 (trans. modified).

Thematic Repertoire

This repertoire is obviously incomplete and, furthermore, it contains several bizarre entries.

It deals only laterally with what is essential. Thus, the word 'Maoism' is not pronounced in it and the concepts of the subject are almost absent from it. It arranges for a few *service entrances*.

I. ART AND LITERATURE

Art and the crowd: 65–8.

Poetry as the annulment of exchange: 73.

Explanation of the sonnet 'A la nue accablante tu': 74–83.

Style as philosophical requirement: 75.

Theatre, of superior essence: 84–7; operator of Sophocleism: 161–2.

Brief explanation of *A Dice Throw . . .* : 92–4.

The forced function of perorations: 95–7.

Explanation of the sonnet 'Ses purs ongles très haut' ('Her nails on high . . .'): 100–10.

Poetry as topology of language: 159, 303.

Explanation of the ending of Aeschylus' *Eumenides*: 164–5.

Ethical meaning of the novel of formation: 333.

The second act of Wagner's *Tristan*: 318, 333.

See also: S. Beckett, J. Conrad, S. Crane, J. Gracq, La Rochefoucauld, Pascal, Rimbaud, Sophocles, Aeschylus.

II. HISTORICAL CIRCUMSTANCES

a. The Effective Universals

June 1848: 172, 204, 283; anxiety: 292.

The Paris Commune: xl, 20; inexhaustible analyser: xli; its double assessment: 45–6; the people and destruction: 172–3; wedging of a double mode of being: 230–1; anticipation and retroaction: 251.

October 1917: 20; as assessment of the Commune: 47–9; the insurrection as violation of politics: 170; as periodization of Marxism: 204.

The Cultural Revolution: 11, 42; identity of position with the Commune: 47; Mallarméan artistic function: 67; as signifier of exception: 88; first communist revolution: 185; forcing the empty place of Leninism: 205; repeating the Commune so as to make it into the real: 231; its dogmatic diagonal: 314–15; and ethics: 315–16; and the superego: 325–6.

b. National Data

The Revolution of 1789–93: 38; nature of its materialism: 185; the Terror: 293–4.

World War I: xl.

World War II: xl.

Resistance: xl.

Colonial wars: xl, 260.

May–June 1968: xl, 11, 292; objective and subjective: 41–2; the great sixties: 302; movement, or subject (?): 322.

c. Scattered References

Peasant wars in Germany: 298.

The Third International: 20, 126; as domain of the possible: 204; masculine: 262.

The Portuguese Revolution of 1974–5: 71.

d. Others

Council of Nicea: 15.
Renaissance: 38.

III. God

Aporias of the Creation: 4–5.
Theory of Incarnation: 15–16.
Logic of heresies: 16–17.
Theatre's essential catholicity: 84–5.
Saint Paul and the second foundation of Christianity: 125.
The stakes for the first materialism: 186.
The Christian Two: 190–1.
In the imaginary diagonal courage-superego: 298.
Islamic: 300.
That He inexists in the world and exceeds the Text: 301.

See also: Malebranche, Pascal, Saint Paul

IV. LOGIC AND MATHEMATICS

a. *Modus Operandi:* the transmission of mathematics: 39–40; of their dialectical usage: 148–9; science of the real: 154; in the razorblade of the Marxist barber: 210; quick glance at the golden ages: 216.

b. *Logic and Set Theory:* extraordinary sets and the axiom of regularity (or of foundation): 90–1; Cantor's theorem: 215–17; quantifiers: 272; arithmetics of cardinals: 266–7; the continuum hypothesis: 266; consistency of the continuum hypothesis with constructible sets: 267–70; Rowbottom's theorem, large cardinals: 269–71.

c. *Algebra and Number Theory:* 219–20; torsion groups: 149–54; the extension of the countable or denumerable: 202–5; definition of algebra: 210; definition of belonging: 211; axioms of Peano: 226.

d. *Topology:* 219–20; Möbius strip: 35; global and local: 120–1; definition of topology: 210–11; commentary on the axioms of neighbourhoods: 221–3; Borromean knot: 226–8.

V. TRADITIONAL PHILOSOPHY

Ancient atomism: 53–61.
Classification of philosophies: 116–21.
History of materialisms: 187–9.
Structural trajectory of idealisms: 190–2.
An old theme: 234–6.
Classical theories of the subject: 278–80.

Ethical discourses: 321–9.

See also: Aristotle, Descartes, Heidegger, Plato, Kant

VI. PSYCHOANALYSIS STRICTO SENSU

American psychoanalysis: 30, 144, 198.
École freudienne de Paris: 40–1.
The transmission of psychoanalysis: 40.
Its shipwreck for the benefit of ethics: 136.
The psychoanalytical cure and political re-education: 142–4.
In an inconsistent totality with Marxism: 280.
Does not argue from a case of healing: 301

See also: Freud

VII. POLITICAL THEORY

a. Politics and History

History: it does not exist: 92; who are its actors?: 180–1; the four fundamental contradictions of the contemporary world: 217.

Politics: as structure of fiction: 85–6; in retreat: 85–6; lamp-bearing: 108; iterative and break-up of the One: 114–15; in internal exclusion to its object: 130; its ef-fact of not being: 134; opposed to trade unionism: 141; equivocity of the concept of relation of force: 170; from the One to the One One: 213–14; without proper name: 219; the point of view of class on the State in the masses: 229; the inexistent proper to the State: 262; line and organization: 286; and ethics: 309–16; to fail and to give in: 322.

b. The Four Fundamental Concepts of Marxism

Class struggle, contradiction bourgeoisie/proletariat: structure: 7; struggle ≠ contradiction: 24; schema: 43; seen by Mallarmé: 98–100; the relation of class as impossible: 126–7; class point of view and truth: 173; one of the four concepts: 282–4.

Revolution: false time to conclude: 96; proper name of the impossible of Marxism: 128; other of the Other: 156; anxiety and courage: 172; ≠ communism: 205–6; algebraic: 229; the class seizes the mass: 246; interruption: 256–7.

Dictatorship of the proletariat: reciprocatable with communism: 188; one of the four concepts: 282–4.

Communism: 78, 96; as annulment of the State: 88–92; fallacious halting point: 108; definition: 134; justice: 159; concrete: 184; and the dictatorship of the proletariat: 188; revolution: 205–6; topological: 235; the revolution is its abstract moment: 244; one of the four concepts: 282–4; utopian: 298; is not legislatable except diagonally: 300.

c. Mass and Class

Masses, mass movement: clinamen: 58–9; vanishing term of history: 63–4; it is right to rebel: 106, 234; name of the real: 136; is not implied but forced: 273; confidence in the masses: 330.

Working class: procedure of its scission: 9; it makes a nodal point of the two definitions of capitalism: 26; as social class and as political class: 188; its three levels of consistency: 236–8; spontaneous fatalism: 328.

Proletariat: torsion: 129–30; what a revolution presents to another revolution: 134; name of the truth as not-all: 173; makes the working class disappear: 238; where is it?: 280–4; political existence, ethical existence: 330–1.

d. The New Bourgeoisie

Modern revisionism, PCF: determines the class: 9; two bourgeoisies, two revolutions: 82–3; superficial critique of 1968: 196–7; statist knot of the party: 229–30; USSR: 74, 83; it exists: 83; demonstrating the contradiction Leninist party/communism: 206; its novelty: 246; Sino-Soviet split: 225.

Gulag, totalitarianism: totalitarianism does not exist: 12; falseness of the thesis 'A camp is a camp': 142; the politics of Terror: 293–4; Moscow trials: 312–15.

Socialism: it does not exist: 7–8; immobile mover: 235.

The State: reversal of the statist lack: 82; and revolt: 106; it never proves the existence of the proletariat: 134; superego: 146, 159; and the indivision of the law: 184; object of Leninism: 205–6; in a Borromean knot with the masses and the classes: 228–30; never a guarantee of communism: 235.

e. Conjuncture

Imperialist society: 7, 141, 262–3.

Multinational people: xl; the immigrant proletarian as empty place (equality of rights) and excess (international proletariat of France): 262–4.

Trade unionism, unionist worldview: 9, 26–7; abstract element of the subjective: 237; makes consistency out of the capitalist cause: 238; and the nation-State: 266–70.

Youth: active nihilism: 329.

The intellectuals: xl; greater during the Stalin era: 302; and the ethical debate after 1976: 321–2.

f. The Subject, the Party

One does not love one another in them: 40; Leninism for the university: 46; relation to the masses: 91; subjective point of politics: 115; as communist: 182–3; as schematism: 191–2; asymptotic: 198; in the contradiction revolution/communism: 205; as One One: 213; tying together the knot: 229; third level of consistency: 237–8; supports the four discourses in the Lacanian sense: 246–7; body of politics: 290; ethical meaning of the partisan mindset: 312–16; confidence in the party: 330–1.

Index of Proper Names

I recall that absent from the enumeration below are: Engels, Hegel, Hölderlin, Lacan, Lenin, Mallarmé, Mao Zedong, Marx.

When it is a question of a simple mention by way of illustration, the page number is italicized.

Aeschylus *84*, 156, 158, 161–3, 166–8, 319

Alain 181

Althusser, L. *23*, 187, 224

Aristotle *49*, *122*, 191, 235

Aron, R. 302

Beckett, S. 280, 330

Berkeley, G. 117–18

Bernstein, E. *208*

Beuve-Méry, H. 292

Brecht, B. *84*

Brezhnev, L. I. 97

Bukharin, N. 312–14

Camus, A. *302*

Cantor, G. *216*, 217, 261, 266

Chateaubriand, F.-R. *280*

Cohen, P.-J. 271–4

Comte, A. xxxvii, *49*

Conrad, J. 159

Crane, S. 295

De Saci, I. 301

Debord, G. 329

Deleuze, G. *22*, 207, 287

Democritus 59–60, *69*

Descartes, R. *40*, 187, 301

Devlin, K. J. 267–8

Duras, M. *131*

Epictetus 301

Epicurus 319

Eudoxus 203, *205*

Euripides *165–6*

Fermat, P. *40*

Flaubert, G. *310*

Foucault, M. 187, 188

Fourier, Ch. 298
Freud, A. 209
Freud, S. *115*, 124, 125–8, *132*,
    135, *161*, 166, 174, 197, *225*,
    279–80, 284

Galois, E. 216
Gauss, C. F. *216*
Gide, A. *310*
Glucksmann, A. 182
Gödel, K. 267, 268–9, 270–1, *273*,
    286
Goethe, J. W. von 35
Gracq, J. xli, 280

Hébert, J. 186
Heidegger, M. 7, *69*, 234–5
Hilbert, D. 216
Hugo, V. *95*

Jech, T. 365
Jones, E. *209*
Jung, C. G. *208*

Kant, I. *95*, 117–19, *186*, 191, 194,
    201, 278, *287*
Kautsky, K. 191
Khrushchev, N. 180, *208*

La Mettrie, J. 121
La Rochefoucauld, F.
    319
Lassalle, F. 209
Leibniz, G. W. *24*, 69
Lévi-Strauss, C. 207
Lin Biao *17*, 180
Liu Shaoqi *17*, 314, *325*
Louis XI *296*
Lucretius *121*

Malebranche, N. 37
Marchais, G. *97*
Mersenne, M. *40*
Miller, J.-A. 132–5
Milner, J.-C. 262–3
Mitterrand, F. *45*, *329*, 351
Mollet, G. 302
Montaigne 301
Müntzer, T. 298
Newton, I. *186*

Pascal, B. *40–1*, *280*, 301
Pétain, Ph. xl, *310*
Plato 184, 191, 193, 318
Pol Pot 181
Politzer, G. 179
Pompidou, G. 42
Pythagoras 202–5

Reich, W. 208
Rimbaud, A. *116*, 168, 216, *310*, *332*
Robespierre, M. *292*, *296*
Rousseau, J.-J. 41
Rowbottom, F. 269–70

Saint Luke *23*
Saint Paul 125, 191
Saint Peter *125*
Saint Thomas *122*
Saint-John Perse *254*
Sandevince, P. xxxix, xliv
Sartre, J.-P. 272, 278, 299, 300, *302*
Schelling, F. W. J. 318
Séguy, G. *42*
Shafarevitch, I. 154
Sophocles 155–6, 158, 161–6, 168,
    309, *315*
Spinoza, B. 22, 37, 160

Stalin, J. *xl*, 20, 38, 81, 91, *117*, *180*, *193*, 205, *209*, 225–6, 232, 294–6, 302, *312*, 315, 325

Thiers, A. 310

Viélé-Griffin, F. 97
Villiers de l'Isle Adam, A. *310*

Voltaire 186
Vyshinsky, A. I. 312–14

Wagner, R. *65*, *89*, 107, *236*, 318, 333
Wang Hongwen 315–16

Zola, E. *98*

The explicit nominations are unfair. Here I must speak of Gardner Davies, luminous analyst of Mallarmé, and of François Regnault, who teaches me the theatre.